THIS BOOK BELONGS TO

..............................................................................

# MARTHA STEWART'S

## HORS D'OEUVRES

# HAND BOOK

# MARTHA STEWART'S
## HORS D'OEUVRES
# HAND BOOK

BY *MARTHA STEWART*
WITH *SUSAN SPUNGEN*

PHOTOGRAPHS BY *DANA GALLAGHER*

CLARKSON POTTER | PUBLISHERS | NEW YORK

TO THE FOOD DEPARTMENT OF MARTHA STEWART LIVING
*So many delicious, well-designed recipes and meals have emerged from our kitchens. Thanks so much.*

Published by Clarkson N. Potter, Inc., 201 East 50th Street, New York, New York 10022.
Member of the Crown Publishing Group.
Random House, Inc.
New York, Toronto, London, Sydney, Auckland
www.randomhouse.com

Clarkson N. Potter, Potter, and colophon are trademarks of Random House, Inc. Printed in Japan

Design by Scot Schy

Library of Congress Cataloging-in-Publication Data
Martha Stewart
[Hors d'oeuvres handbook]
Martha Stewart's hors d'oeuvres handbook / by Martha Stewart;
photographs by Dana Gallagher. —1st ed.
Includes index.
1. Appetizers. I Title.
TX740.S743 1999         98-39161
641.8′12—dc21
ISBN 0-609-60310-8
10 9 8 7 6 5 4

# acknowledgments

A book project as large as this one requires the collaborative efforts of many people. I would like to thank everyone who devoted so much time, energy, and talent to the making of this book. Special thanks to Susan Spungen, my food editor, who has developed a distinctive voice in the food pages of MARTHA STEWART LIVING and most importantly contributed it to this book. Scot Schy created a timeless yet modern design and shaped the visual personality of the book. Thank you to Kathleen Hackett, my editor, for her tireless, heroic efforts to ensure that this book is as informative, well-organized, and useful as it can be. Dana Gallagher captured all of the recipes and ideas in beautiful, clear photographs without ever repeating herself. Ayesha Patel-Rogers used her sense of elegance and refinement and her exquisite taste to choose all the beautiful things that enhance the food. Claire Perez contributed her creativity, common sense, and highly evolved palate and kept the photo shoots superbly organized. Stephana Bottom patiently supervised the testing and writing of every recipe in the book, contributed the instructive notes, sidebars, and menus, and kept the manuscript in shape through every stage. Kate Edelbaum-Heddings shared excellent ideas and her simple, straightforward approach to food. John Willoughby did a wonderful job writing the lucid and instructive text.

Thank you to the talented women in the MARTHA STEWART LIVING test kitchens, especially Judy Lockhart, who tested every single recipe, and Wendy Sidewater, Liza Jernow, Amy Gropp-Forbes, Lorrie Hulston, Liv Grey, and Lena Dushaj. Connie Pikulas sourced some of the more unusual ingredients and tools in the book and kept everyone organized. Christina Hockley and Christine Osmond inspired us with their ideas in the early stages.

Many thanks to Gael Towey and Eric A. Pike at Martha Stewart Living Omnimedia, and to my longtime friends at Crown and Clarkson Potter, Alberto Vitale, Chip Gibson, Lauren Shakely, Laurie Stark, Mark McCauslin, Jane Treuhaft, Teresa Nicholas, and Merri Ann Morrell.

Finally, thanks to the many food purveyors, friends, chefs, restaurateurs, and caterers who have inspired me over the years.

# contents

# introduction

I have a little book that was written in 1940 called HORS D'OEUVRE AND CANAPÉS. The author was a young man named James Beard and the publisher, M. Barrows and Company, New York. Mr. Beard translates the French phrase hors d'oeuvre as "outside the meal" and discusses the widespread belief that hors d'oeuvres were indeed tempting tidbits served before a meal, little snacks that were designed and intended to stimulate the appetite, never to satisfy it.

In another, much earlier volume, written in the nineteenth century by Mrs. Beeton, hors d'oeuvres are described as small side dishes that are generally served cold but could include the following: oysters, anchovies, sardines, herring, prawns, olives, crisp toasts, croustades, fleurettes, cheese biscuits, tartlets, vols au vent, croquettes, fritters, open-faced sandwiches, canapés, and rissoles.

For me, hors d'oeuvres are a chance for the host or hostess to show off skills in the creation of flavorful bite-sized jewels or other imaginative concoctions that can be served as simple accompaniments for a pre-dinner drink or as elaborately displayed and garnished "cocktail" food. Hors d'oeuvres must be two things at once: delicious and attractive!

In compiling the recipes for this comprehensive book, Susan Spungen, my food editor, my staff, and I carefully considered each and every suggestion and tried to make sure each hors d'oeuvre was both lovely to look at—if it was fancy and complex or simple and homey—and delicious to eat. The book is meant to be a handbook with some chapters devoted to instructive "how to" and others more conceptual for different classifications of hors d'oeuvres, such as layered and stacked or skewered and threaded. There are clear photographs to guide you step by step and others to inspire you in the presentation and serving of the food. I think you will find our chapter on drinks an excellent guide to some of the best drinks you have ever sipped while eating some of the tastiest hors d'oeuvres you have ever put in your mouth.

The service of these appetite "enhancers," as Mrs. Beeton called them, has changed dramatically since the turn of the century. Many times "heavy" hors d'oeuvres can fill in for an actual meal—an Italian antipasto or a selection of Asian dumplings can easily replace dinner. Sometimes I will cook two or three kinds of blini and serve a large portion of caviar to my guests and we will consider it much more than a stimulant to our appetites. In China, Spain, and Russia, finger foods have a savory quality and a salty tang and they go well with beer, vodka, or red wine. We give recipes not only for my favorite "jewels," but also for these heartier alternatives.

*Martha Stewart*

# BUILDING BLOCKS FOR
# THE BEST HORS D'OEUVRES

*Recipes appear on pages 227–249*

OPPOSITE The produce section in the grocery store is an excellent source for cups and wrappers. Look for leaves that are sturdy and of the right shape to act as a cup, or flexible enough to use as a wrap.

TREVISO RADICCHIO
SPEARS

BIBB LETTUCE

BELGIAN ENDIVE

ARTICHOKE
LEAVES

RED ENDIVE

GRAPE LEAF

CUCUMBER CUPS TECHNIQUE | RECIPE ON PAGE 229

PATTYPAN SQUASH CUP

CHERRY TOMATO
CUPS

MUSHROOM CAPS

LADY APPLE CUP

Vegetables and fruits that have been
carefully hollowed out can be used
to hold a wide variety of sweet and
savory fillings. For the best effect
and easiest eating or sipping, use
very small versions. OPPOSITE Two
simple, inexpensive tools—a melon
baller and a vegetable peeler—are
all you need to make charming
"bowls" for a single sip of soup.

CUCUMBER CUP

GLOBE GRAPE CUPS

GRILLED STARS

TOASTED BREADBOX

TOASTED BRIOCHE ROUNDS

SIMPLE CROSTINI

CLASSIC TOAST POINTS

SEASONED PÂTE À CHOUX PUFFS

PITA CUPS

GOLDEN CROUSTADES

HOMEMADE POTATO CHIP

SWEET POTATO GAUFRETTES

Bread can be shaped in all kinds of ways to use as hors d'oeuvre bases, from simple slices to tiny boxes. Be sure to choose the appropriate starch base to complement the filling or topping. A fragile potato chip, for example, requires a delicate topping, while toasted crostini are excellent for very moist or heavy mixtures.

MINIATURE FLOUR TORTILLAS | RECIPE ON PAGE 235

Making tortillas by hand allows you to form just the right size to hold one or two bites of topping. OPPOSITE Alternatively, packaged tortillas can be cut with a 2-inch biscuit cutter to make them fit in the palm of your hand.

CUSTOM-CUT STORE-BOUGHT TORTILLAS | TECHNIQUE ON PAGE 235

Cut into simple circles with a biscuit cutter, brushed with olive oil, and tucked into mini muffin tins and baked, store-bought corn tortillas become crispy cups for filling. OPPOSITE Make an impact with color by seasoning traditional crepes with ingredients such as green tea or turmeric; stack them in neat piles with the fillings served alongside, or fill and arrange them in alternating colors on a serving tray.

GREEN TEA CREPES

CURRY CREPES

BLUE CORN CREPES

CREPES | RECIPES ON PAGES 236–237

These crisp dipping triangles require nothing more than cutting pitas into wedges, seasoning them with anise seed, black onion seed, and kosher salt, and toasting for several minutes. OPPOSITE For variety, buy tartlet molds in several different shapes.

INDIAN-SPICED PITA TOASTS | RECIPE ON PAGE 242

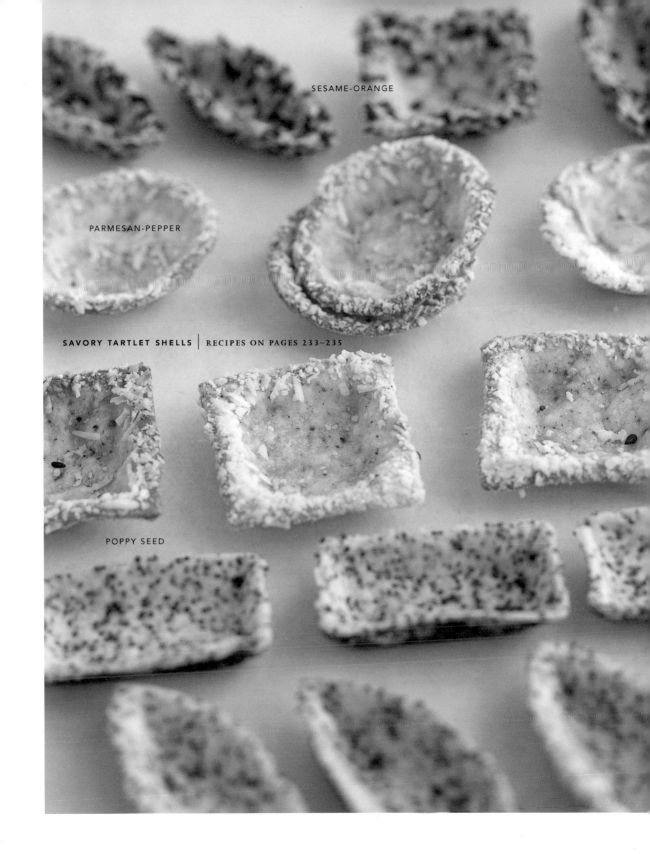

SESAME-ORANGE

PARMESAN-PEPPER

**SAVORY TARTLET SHELLS** | RECIPES ON PAGES 233–235

POPPY SEED

# 2

## LAYERED AND
## STACKED

*Recipes appear on pages 251–277*

OPPOSITE Toasted Brioche Rounds topped with successive layers of wasabi mayonnaise, fresh mango, and crabmeat salad exemplify the layered-and-stacked approach to hors d'oeuvres.

MANGO CRAB STACK | RECIPE ON PAGE 273

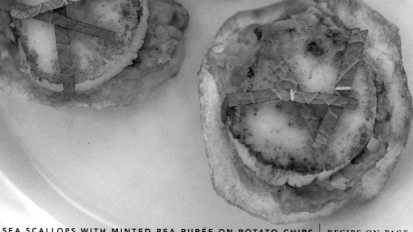

SEA SCALLOPS WITH MINTED PEA PURÉE ON POTATO CHIPS | RECIPE ON PAGE 271

Artichoke leaves cradle shrimp stacked on top of marinated fennel and garnished with crumbled feta cheese. OPPOSITE Create layers of flavor and texture, beginning with a crispy potato chip swabbed with a creamy pea purée, topped with a succulent scallop, and ending with a burst of mint flavor.

ROASTED SHRIMP WITH ARTICHOKES AND FENNEL │ RECIPE ON PAGE 263

The template for these potato wafers can be cut into any shape you desire, using an X-Acto knife and plastic container lid. Spreading the batter directly on a Silpat baking mat makes for easy cleanup. OPPOSITE Elegantly layered and stacked to form a deluxe hors d'oeuvre: whisper-thin potato wafers, crème fraîche, and gravlax garnished with caviar touched with dill.

POTATO WAFER TECHNIQUE | RECIPE ON PAGE 246

GRAVLAX, CRÈME FRAÎCHE, AND CAVIAR NAPOLEON | RECIPE ON PAGE 272

*CLOCKWISE FROM BOTTOM RIGHT*
Nori sheets, thin slices of smoked
salmon, sushi rice, and wasabi paste
are layered three times to create the
stacked look. A very sharp knife is
essential for cutting squares cleanly.
*OPPOSITE* For visual impact, arrange
these bite-size squares on a spacious
platter. Serve them with small
glasses of cold sake garnished with
reed-thin slices of cucumber.

NORI STACKS WITH SMOKED SALMON | RECIPE ON PAGE 270

29

POTATO BACON PIZZA

THREE OVEN-READY PIZZAS | RECIPES ON PAGES 253–254

PIZZA WITH WILD MUSHROOMS AND
FONTINA CHEESE

GREEK PIZZA

PIZZA WITH WILD MUSHROOMS AND FONTINA CHEESE | RECIPE ON PAGE 254

Japanese eggplant is very straight and narrow, the perfect shape for making these tiny rounds topped with mozzarella, oven-dried tomatoes, and fresh oregano. OPPOSITE Give the illusion that these succulent slices were cut from a pizza pie; simple crosswise cuts, made at alternating angles, produce tiny versions of traditional wedges.

EGGPLANT CRISPS | RECIPE ON PAGE 255

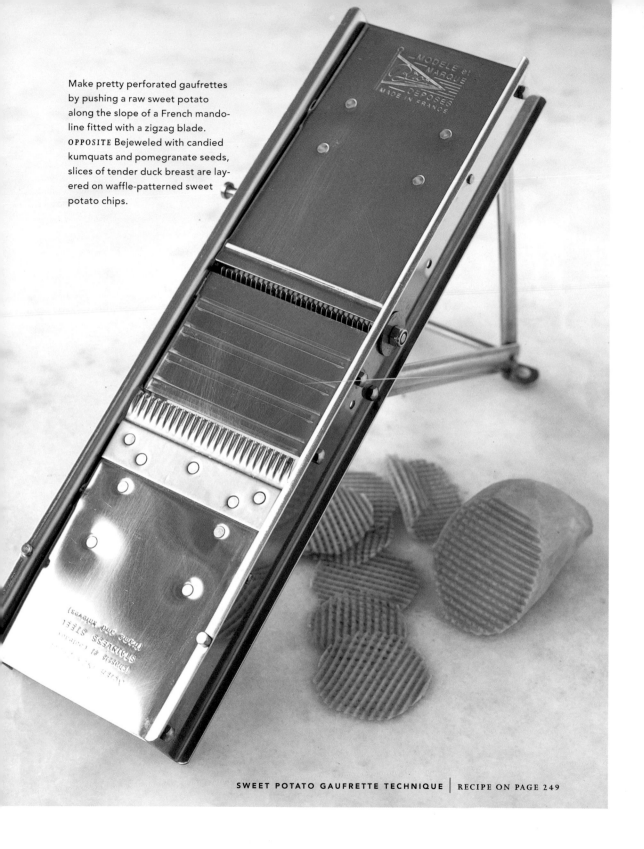

Make pretty perforated gaufrettes by pushing a raw sweet potato along the slope of a French mandoline fitted with a zigzag blade. OPPOSITE Bejeweled with candied kumquats and pomegranate seeds, slices of tender duck breast are layered on waffle-patterned sweet potato chips.

**SWEET POTATO GAUFRETTE TECHNIQUE** | RECIPE ON PAGE 249

MAPLE-GLAZED DUCK BREAST ON SWEET POTATO GAUFRETTES | RECIPE ON PAGE 275

POMMES ANNETTE TECHNIQUE | RECIPE ON PAGE 272

Although composed of many layers, Pommes Annette hold together well enough to be arranged casually, as they are here in a pewter candy compote lined with crisp parchment paper. *OPPOSITE* A total of ten layers of fresh thyme leaves, fingerling potato rounds, and tangy goat cheese are arranged in each opening of a mini muffin tin, which is then topped with a second tin to compress the layers.

GRILLED CHICKEN AND
ROASTED RED PEPPER QUESADILLA

ASSORTED QUESADILLAS | RECIPES ON PAGES 258–261

When preparing the toppings for
these sand-dollar-size quesadillas,
cut the ingredients into bite-size
pieces for an uncluttered look and
effortless eating.

LOBSTER AND
MUSHROOM QUESADILLA

CHORIZO AND
MANCHEGO CHEESE QUESADILLA

ROASTED SWEET POTATO AND
TOMATILLO QUESADILLA

ROASTED SWEET POTATO AND TOMATILLO QUESADILLAS | RECIPE ON PAGE 258

SAVORY FRENCH TOAST │ RECIPE ON PAGE 262

Egg-drenched brioche slices topped
with tomato and basil are baked
casserole-style, then cut into coin-
shaped pieces. They can be cut into
small squares or rectangles as well
as circles. OPPOSITE Small enough to
serve in stacks of three, mini quesadillas taste especially good with
glasses of ice-cold Mexican beer.

TOSTONE TECHNIQUE | RECIPE ON PAGE 249

Succulent jerk chicken is bundled between crispy tostones and tied with a blanched chive. The spicy "sandwiches" hold together beautifully with or without the chive tie. Here they are served scattered along a tropical leaf. OPPOSITE Twice-fried plantain slices are flattened with a meat pounder after the first fry to achieve a super-crisp chip.

Flavored with fresh ginger and jalapeños and bound together with flour and egg, the rice mixture for the rice cakes is pressed into a rimmed baking sheet, refrigerated, then broken into small pieces and fried. OPPOSITE Torn cilantro leaves and very thin slices of jalapeño pepper lend a cool, almost serene appearance to this Asian-flavored hors d'oeuvre.

GRILLED SWORDFISH ON GINGER-JALAPEÑO RICE CAKES | RECIPE ON PAGE 274

When serving an hors d'oeuvre that consists of only two layers, the most attractive appearance is achieved by mounding the top layer in the center of the base, pyramid-style. OPPOSITE Terrines can be cut into half-inch slices and served on simple crostini, or they can be arranged on a platter along with knives for guests to cut their own. Always cut the first few slices as an example of the preferred size.

**CELERIAC POTATO PANCAKES WITH APPLE-ONION COMPOTE** | RECIPE ON PAGE 262

SEARED SALMON AND
POTATO TERRINE

ROASTED VEGETABLE
TERRINE

ASPARAGUS AND SHIITAKE
MUSHROOM TERRINE

**THREE TERRINES** | RECIPES ON PAGES 264–269

PETIT CROQUE MONSIEUR | RECIPE ON PAGE 274

48

After adding the toppings to the Pissaladière, I cut it into bite-size pieces, leave them all in the pan, and serve it as if the tart were still whole. OPPOSITE Hearty traditional dishes look most appetizing when served in a manner that conveys informality, like these tiny sandwich wedges of ham, gruyère, and whole-grain mustard garnished with caramelized pears, presented on the cutting board where they were sliced.

PISSALADIÈRE | RECIPE ON PAGE 256

# 3

# WRAPPED, ROLLED, FILLED, FOLDED, AND STUFFED

*Recipes appear on pages 279–309*

OPPOSITE Wrapped hors d'oeuvres should never be limited to variations on bread; cucumbers sliced paper thin lengthwise are a striking wrap for bite-size pieces of sushi-quality tuna seasoned with chili mayonnaise and black sesame seeds.

SPICY TUNA ROLLS | RECIPE ON PAGE 285

BLACK SESAME SEEDS

SUSHI-QUALITY TUNA
WITH CHIVES

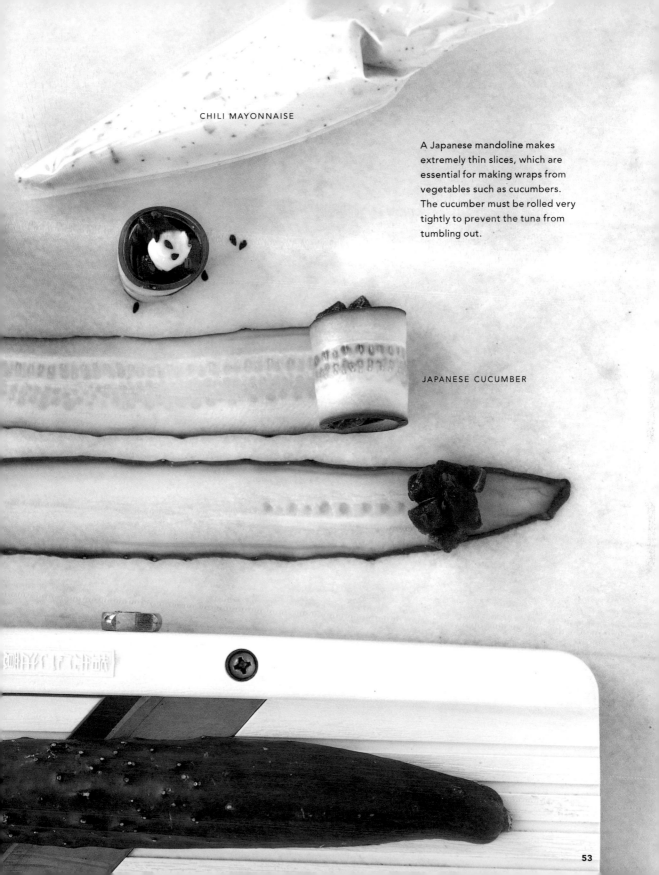

CHILI MAYONNAISE

A Japanese mandoline makes extremely thin slices, which are essential for making wraps from vegetables such as cucumbers. The cucumber must be rolled very tightly to prevent the tuna from tumbling out.

JAPANESE CUCUMBER

POLENTA

PORCINI WITH CAMEMBERT

With the merest amount of effort, the cap of a white mushroom becomes a sturdy carrier, its mild, earthy flavor the quintessential base for all manner of assertively flavored fillings. OPPOSITE Heated rock salt, loosely packed into a rimmed platter, provides a sturdy bed for and keeps warm tiny potatoes garnished with fresh, thinly shaved white truffles.

BROCCOLI RABE AND PANCETTA

LEEK, FENNEL, AND GOAT CHEESE

TWICE-BAKED TRUFFLED POTATOES | RECIPE ON PAGE 308

CASSOULET CROUSTADES | RECIPE ON PAGE 288

Crispy basil leaves are strewn about a platter full of cheese-filled ravioli and fiery tomato dipping sauce. Serve hors d'oeuvres on several different small tables and include wine at each one to encourage party guests to circulate. OPPOSITE Bread squares are tucked into mini muffin tins to create a crunchy cup for cassoulet. When arranging an hors d'oeuvre table, use a cakestand, such as this Italian ceramic fluted version, for added height and visual diversity.

GOLDEN RAVIOLI WITH ARRABBIATA SAUCE | RECIPE ON PAGE 307

WELSH RAREBIT IN TOASTED BREADBOXES TECHNIQUE | RECIPE ON PAGE 293

58

No bigger than a jewel box, this breadbox is filled with a classic rarebit cheese mixture and garnished with a slice of cherry tomato. OPPOSITE To make the breadboxes, all you need is a good serrated knife for slicing the bread and a sharp paring knife for carving out the inside.

**WELSH RAREBIT IN TOASTED BREADBOXES** | RECIPE ON PAGE 293

SCALLOP CEVICHE WITH AVOCADO PURÉE IN TOASTED CORN CUPS | RECIPE ON PAGE 287

Bibb lettuce, with its natural cup shape, is an ideal wrap for free-form hors d'oeuvres and a sauce. OPPO-SITE Pleated cups made from corn tortillas, cut to fit into mini muffin tins, are sturdy enough to hold juicy fillings such as ceviche.

LIMA BEAN FALAFEL FRITTERS IN LETTUCE CUPS WITH TAHINI-YOGURT SAUCE │ RECIPE ON PAGE 299

DUMPLING WRAPPERS | NOTE ON PAGE 283

These rolls, wrapped in gossamer rice paper, are cut on an angle on one end and flat on the other so that they stand upright on a platter. OPPOSITE A wide variety of good-quality dumpling skins can be found in any Asian market.

DUMPLING INGREDIENTS | RECIPES ON PAGES 281–284

RICE NOODLES

CHIVES
SHALLOTS
SHRIMP

CILANTRO

SCALLOPS

ARUGULA

EGG

BEAN SPROUTS

GARLIC

LEMONGRASS

CELLOPHANE
NOODLES

DUMPLING WRAPPERS

GRATED GINGER

Dumpling wrappers can enclose fillings in several ways: a pleated seam is rather elegant, a chive-cinched center creates a charming purse, and a flat seam gives the dumplings a modern, streamlined look. Whatever style you choose, it is important to brush the edges with water before sealing so they stay together. OPPOSITE Impeccably fresh, flavorful ingredients, prepared with care just before filling the wrappers, make the most delicious dumplings.

POTSTICKER

SHRIMP AND
BEAN SPROUT SHAO MAI

SCALLOP, ARUGULA, AND
LEMONGRASS DUMPLINGS

**DUMPLING ASSEMBLY** | RECIPES ON PAGES 281–284

Dumplings look lovely served on plain metal trays or platters, but they can also be set out right in their bamboo steaming baskets lined with soft lettuce leaves or other greens. Accompany them with small bowls of dipping sauces.

SHRIMP AND
BEAN SPROUT SHAO MAI

HOT CHILI OIL

SCALLOP, ARUGULA, AND
LEMONGRASS DUMPLINGS

POTSTICKERS

SCALLION-SOY
DIPPING SAUCE

CRABMEAT SOUP DUMPLING ASSEMBLY | RECIPE ON PAGE 283

Asian soup spoons are both beautiful and practical for individual servings of these cunning crabmeat dumplings, which release a bit of delightful hot soup when you bite into them. Serve them with sips of tea in sake cups. OPPOSITE The secret to these dumplings is to encase a cube of chicken stock in the wrappers along with the crabmeat filling; when the dumplings are cooked, the chilled stock becomes hot chicken broth.

CRABMEAT SOUP DUMPLINGS | RECIPE ON PAGE 283

Endive spears are shaped perfectly for arranging individual ingredients along their length. Begin by placing the heaviest items at the base and progress to the lightest at the tip, as I do with a goat cheese quenelle, a fresh fig, a glazed pecan, and a feathery sprig of frisée. OPPOSITE To form the quenelles, all you need are two small teaspoons and a bowl of water for rinsing the spoons after shaping each.

ENDIVE WITH GOAT CHEESE, FIG, AND HONEY-GLAZED PECANS | RECIPE ON PAGE 307

CRISPY ASPARAGUS STRAWS | RECIPE ON PAGE 286

FRICO TACOS WITH MÂCHE | RECIPE ON PAGE 293

Frico, the Italian cheese crisps, are
shaped into tacos using the palm of
your hand. Lacy and delicate, frico
tacos are best suited for holding
mâche or other feather-light fillings.
OPPOSITE A crisp, white wine
served in small tumblers complements perfectly the earthy flavor of
asparagus wrapped first in prosciutto, then in phyllo, and then
sprinkled with Parmesan.

WHITE BEAN PURÉE
AND FRIED SAGE

MIXED OLIVE
SALAD

ROQUEFORT
WATERCRESS
CUCUMBER

PANZANELLA
FILLING

GRILLED SHRIMP AND
CORN SALAD

**CHERRY TOMATO FILLINGS** | RECIPES ON PAGES 304–306

From the bottom of the cherry tomatoes, a tiny piece is sliced away to create a flat surface so that they won't roll around on the platter. Though the tomatoes give the illusion of being overstuffed, the fillings are loosely spooned into them —just enough for the ingredients to peek out of the top. OPPOSITE Smooth purées make excellent fillings for cherry tomatoes or other hollowed-out fruit and vegetables because they can be piped in. But chunky fillings also work well, as long as all of the ingredients are diced quite small.

HARICOTS VERTS

WHITE BEAN PURÉE

PANZANELLA

GRILLED SHRIMP AND
CORN SALAD

ROQUEFORT AND WATERCRESS

MIXED OLIVE SALAD

CHÈVRE GRAPES | RECIPE ON PAGE 302

CALAMARI SALAD IN PITA CUPS | RECIPE ON PAGE 292

A salad in an edible bowl: calamari, chickpeas, tomatoes, cucumbers, and olive tapenade are served on a mini toasted pita half. OPPOSITE Juicy hollowed Globe grapes are rimmed with crushed pistachios, then filled with goat cheese shaped into smaller globes using cheesecloth, which leaves a beautiful imprint on them.

ASSORTED EMPANADITA FILLINGS | RECIPE ON PAGES 294–295

ESCAROLE AND
FONTINA

Place your choice of fillings on the
empanada dough, fold it in half, and
crimp the edges with a fork. Brush
the tops with egg wash, a mixture of
egg and milk, to achieve the shiny,
golden finish of authentic
empanadas (OPPOSITE).

CHICKEN, APPLE,
AND CHEDDAR

BEEF

ASSORTED EMPANADITAS | RECIPES ON PAGES 294–295

TOMATO, BASIL, AND OLIVE

SWISS CHARD, SHALLOT,
AND PARMESAN

BASIC PASTRY
DOUGH TARTLETS

OPPOSITE Partially baked tartlet shells are filled first with the solid ingredients, then the egg mixture is poured over; make sure that you do not fill them to the rim, since the filling tends to rise during baking.

SWISS CHARD, SHALLOT, AND PARMESAN TARTLET

TOMATO, BASIL, AND OLIVE TARTLET

**PASTRY DOUGH TARTLETS** | RECIPES ON PAGES 291–292

Phyllo should be covered with a damp kitchen towel as you cut individual sheets to layer into the lightly buttered muffin tins. OPPOSITE Filled with a savory mix of chicken, ground almonds, and spices, these bite-size versions of the savory Moroccan pie get a dusting of powdered sugar once they are cool.

WORKING WITH PHYLLO | TECHNIQUE ON PAGE 297

BISTEEYA | RECIPE ON PAGE 296

If you are serving crepes for an informal gathering, provide shallow bowls rather than plates so that the fillings don't tumble out of the wrap. OPPOSITE If guests are to assemble the crepes themselves, serve the fillings in a deep bowl; they will stay hotter.

PLUM WINE FLANK STEAK IN GREEN TEA CREPES WITH PLUM WINE SAUCE | RECIPE ON PAGE 298

CURRIED VEGETABLES IN CURRY CREPES | RECIPE ON PAGE 298

SEARED TUNA IN SESAME-ORANGE TARTLETS

SAVORY TARTLETS | RECIPES ON PAGES 289–290

WILD MUSHROOMS IN PARMESAN-PEPPER TARTLETS

LEMON CHICKEN SALAD IN POPPY SEED TARTLETS

As if in a bread basket, filled pizzas are cut into small wedges and served hot on folded tea towels. OPPOSITE Small plates of various filled tartlets can be arranged on a tea sandwich stand or even on a stand designed to hold several potted plants.

ROBIOLA PIZZA WITH WHITE TRUFFLE OIL | RECIPE ON PAGE 309

For visual drama, crisp garnishes such as apple chips can be slipped between the filling and the container so they peek above the hors d'oeuvres. OPPOSITE Fill several small bowls or platters with these popular risotto balls.

LADY APPLES WITH CELERIAC SLAW | RECIPE ON PAGE 306

FONTINA RISOTTO BALLS | RECIPE ON PAGE 303

# 4

## TEA SANDWICHES, CLASSIC CANAPÉS, AND SIMPLE CROSTINI

*Recipes appear on pages 311–333*

OPPOSITE I find something innately appealing about a selection of tea sandwiches set out for guests to choose as the fancy takes them. It's also a great way for your guests to sample wonderful flavor combinations.

CURRIED EGG SALAD

SMOKED SALMON

**ASSORTED TEA SANDWICHES** | RECIPES ON PAGES 314–320

PROSCIUTTO AND
PORT-FIG BUTTER

GOAT CHEESE AND CHIVE

TARRAGON SHRIMP SALAD

B-L-TEA SANDWICHES

SERRANO HAM

LEMON CRAB SALAD

SERRANO HAM TEA SANDWICH ASSEMBLY | RECIPE ON PAGE 316

PAIN DE MIE | RECIPE ON PAGE 238

A pullman loaf pan is shaped like a tall rectangle with a lid that slides shut so the bread conforms to the pan when it rises during baking. OPPOSITE With just white and whole-wheat bread and two differently shaped cutters, you can create whimsical tea sandwiches and canapés. Here, the pullman loaf is sliced horizontally, which makes for very efficient preparation.

**TUNA NIÇOISE FICELLES** | RECIPE ON PAGE 321

Layering the ingredients so each item is distinct gives these sandwiches a bountiful appearance. OPPOSITE Vary the presentation of tea sandwiches and canapés: some look best well-spaced on large plates while others, such as these sesame seed–encrusted chicken sandwiches, make a more compelling appearance when grouped together.

SESAME-CRUSTED CHICKEN SALAD TEA SANDWICHES | RECIPE ON PAGE 320

CURRY

DILL

LEMON-CHIVE

GINGER-CILANTRO LIME

PORT-FIG

ORANGE-TARRAGON

WATERCRESS

SHALLOT-PARSLEY

ANCHOVY

SUN-DRIED TOMATO
ROSEMARY

ASSORTED COMPOUND BUTTERS | RECIPES ON PAGES 391–394

HOTHOUSE CUCUMBER

COOKED SHRIMP

SHALLOT-PARSLEY
BUTTER

SHRIMP, CUCUMBER, AND DILL BUTTER CANAPÉS | RECIPE ON PAGE 329

DILL

For a dramatic appearance, slice cucumbers lengthwise into paper-thin ribbons using a mandoline, then cut crosswise to form squares for a canapé layer. OPPOSITE Compound butters keep longer if frozen and are always ready to use, since they thaw quickly. Shape them into logs, wrap tightly in plastic, and freeze. Simply slice off and thaw as needed.

**OPPOSITE: SEVEN NEW CANAPÉS** | RECIPES ON PAGES 322–328

1  CHOPPED EGG AND ASPARAGUS

2  BEEF CARPACCIO

3  LENTIL AND FETA CHEESE

4  TARAMASALATA AND CAVIAR

5  SMOKED SALMON CREAM CHEESE AND CUCUMBER

6  WESTPHALIAN HAM AND CELERIAC RÉMOULADE

7  CARROT CUMIN

For a small gathering, two or three different canapés can be set out on strongly contrasting platters. *OPPO-SITE* For larger parties, lay out rows of canapés of assorted shapes and colors to create a geometric impact on an hors d'oeuvres table.

**GRILLED ZUCCHINI CANAPÉS** | RECIPE ON PAGE 325

**CLAM AND CURRY BUTTER CANAPÉS** | RECIPE ON PAGE 329

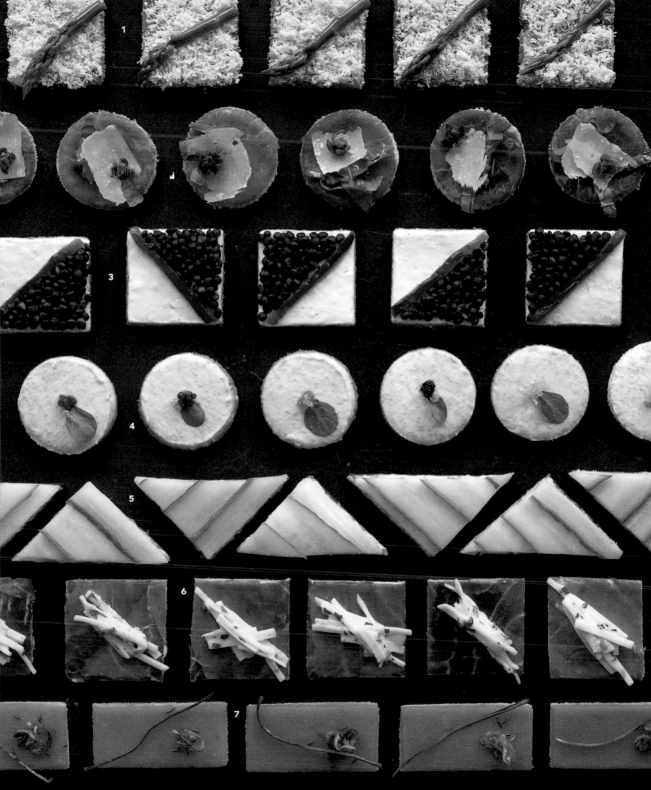

99

ROASTED RED PEPPER HUMMUS

TAPENADE AND GOAT CHEESE

Canapés can be any shape you
like, as long as they are bite-size.
Triangles are created by quartering
sliced bread squares on the diagonal; cookie cutters can be used to
make circles and flowers. OPPOSITE
Slices of translucent daikon are a
beautiful contrast to the half-circles
of bright green wasabi caviar.

SMOKED SALMON FLOWER

WASABI CAVIAR AND DAIKON CANAPÉS │ RECIPE ON PAGE 326

Many wonderful breads in various shapes and sizes are readily available in bakeries across the country. Not only do thay make clever containers, but they keep tea sandwiches fresh during a party.

BREADBOX TECHNIQUE | NOTE ON PAGE 318

SERRANO HAM TEA SANDWICHES | RECIPE ON PAGE 316

Tuck triangular sandwiches at right angles into a pullman loaf so that the sharpest edges peek over the top of the breadbox. OPPOSITE An electric knife makes quick work of crafting breadboxes. Be sure to cut the pullman loaf as straight as possible so the bread you remove can be sliced for tea sandwiches.

**STEAK AU POIVRE CROSTINI** | RECIPE ON PAGE 332

**FAVA BEAN AND PECORINO CROSTINI** | RECIPE ON PAGE 333

When sliced paper-thin, pecorino and other hard cheeses become a delicate, lacy topping for crostini. *OPPOSITE* When making crostini or other hors d'oeuvres that are topped with a sauce, proportion is important; use just enough sauce to moisten the hors d'oeuvre but not so much that it drips onto the serving platter.

CAPRESE

TOASTED GOAT CHEESE
AND SHREDDED BEET

PÂTÉ DE FOIE GRAS WITH
CARAMELIZED PLUM

Choose serving surfaces that are
suited to the particular hors
d'oeuvre. Rustic crostini, for example, look wonderful on wood surfaces strewn with a few branches of
herbs. OPPOSITE For a more formal
gathering, serve individual crostini
on small unpatterned plates.

MOREL AND ROASTED
GARLIC POTATO

SAUTÉED
CHICKEN LIVER

**TWO RUSTIC CROSTINI** | RECIPES ON PAGES 330–331

# 5

## SKEWERED AND THREADED

*Recipes appear on pages 335–345*

OPPOSITE Beef wrapped around crisp bell peppers then skewered with a patterned toothpick exemplifies the playful approach that skewering inspires. Like many such hors d'oeuvres, this one is served with a dipping sauce.

Tiny skewered squares of parsnips, turnips, carrots, beets, and white and sweet potatoes tucked into a café au lait bowl are delicious paired with the classic Italian dipping sauce of warm olive oil seasoned with slow-baked garlic and anchovies. OPPOSITE Sprigs of woody herbs such as rosemary make excellent skewers, particularly if you keep the leaves attached to one end.

ROASTED ROOT VEGETABLE SKEWERS WITH BAGNA CAUDA | RECIPES ON PAGES 338 AND 390

GRILLED SHIITAKE MUSHROOMS ON ROSEMARY SKEWERS | RECIPE ON PAGE 337

MOROCCAN SALMON SKEWERS WITH CITRUS DIPPING SAUCE | RECIPE ON PAGE 339

Light hors d'oeuvres such as these squares of salmon look beautiful on Asian toothpicks with jaunty bamboo handles. For variety, skewer some bites with the fennel crust facing up, others down.

**PROSCIUTTO-WRAPPED SHRIMP** | RECIPE ON PAGE 341

Fresh sugarcane is cut into thin skewers, one end whittled to a sharp point to pierce the chicken and fruit. Leave plenty of room on the skewers so that guests can easily pick them up. OPPOSITE Thread skewers through the tail and head of shrimp to make a compact package.

**TROPICAL CHICKEN ON SUGARCANE SKEWERS WITH PEANUT-PLANTAIN DIPPING SAUCE** | RECIPE ON PAGE 338

Couscous filling is spooned into a grape leaf, rolled into a log, then wrapped in lamb and secured with decorative skewers. OPPOSITE Fill a small bowl with dip, then set it inside a much larger complementary bowl. If using extra-long skewers like this pistol-handled bamboo version, thread the food close to the tip so guests can eat the hors d'oeuvre right off the skewer.

**DOLMADES TECHNIQUE** | RECIPE ON PAGE 343

LAMB AND COUSCOUS DOLMADES WITH MINTED YOGURT SAUCE | RECIPE ON PAGE 343

SKEWERED BOCCONCINI SANDWICHES TECHNIQUE | RECIPE ON PAGE 337

OPPOSITE Make mini cheese sandwiches by stringing bay leaves,
bread slices, and tiny mozzarella
balls onto long wooden skewers.
Warm anchovy dressing flavored
with strands of lemon zest, parsley,
and capers is drizzled over the skewered sandwiches, served family style;
each skewer holds four sandwiches.
Offer these hors d'oeuvres with
small plates for individual servings.

SKEWERED BOCCONCINI SANDWICHES | RECIPE ON PAGE 337

FIGS IN A BLANKET | RECIPE ON PAGE 345

Bathed in a rich balsamic glaze, pork-wrapped figs are a bit messy to pick up with your fingers, making them ideal for skewering. OPPOSITE Wide ribbons of beef and vegetables cradled in lettuce leaves are taken in hand. The skewered meat is dipped into the sauce, the lettuce leaf is bundled around it, and the whole package is pulled off the skewer. The tiered service is created with three pieces—a pewter tazza on the bottom, a pewter compote in the middle, and a transferware handleless teacup on top for the soy-ginger dipping sauce.

BEEF BULGOGI IN LETTUCE LEAVES WITH SOY-GINGER DIPPING SAUCE | RECIPE ON PAGE 342

Inspired by the traditional stew of Louisiana, these skewers feature okra and shrimp, classic gumbo ingredients. OPPOSITE Fresh snow peas are folded onto bamboo picks, their sharp points making it easy for guests to help themselves to the meatballs.

**SHRIMP GUMBO SKEWERS WITH CREOLE DIPPING SAUCE** | RECIPES ON PAGES 341 AND 388

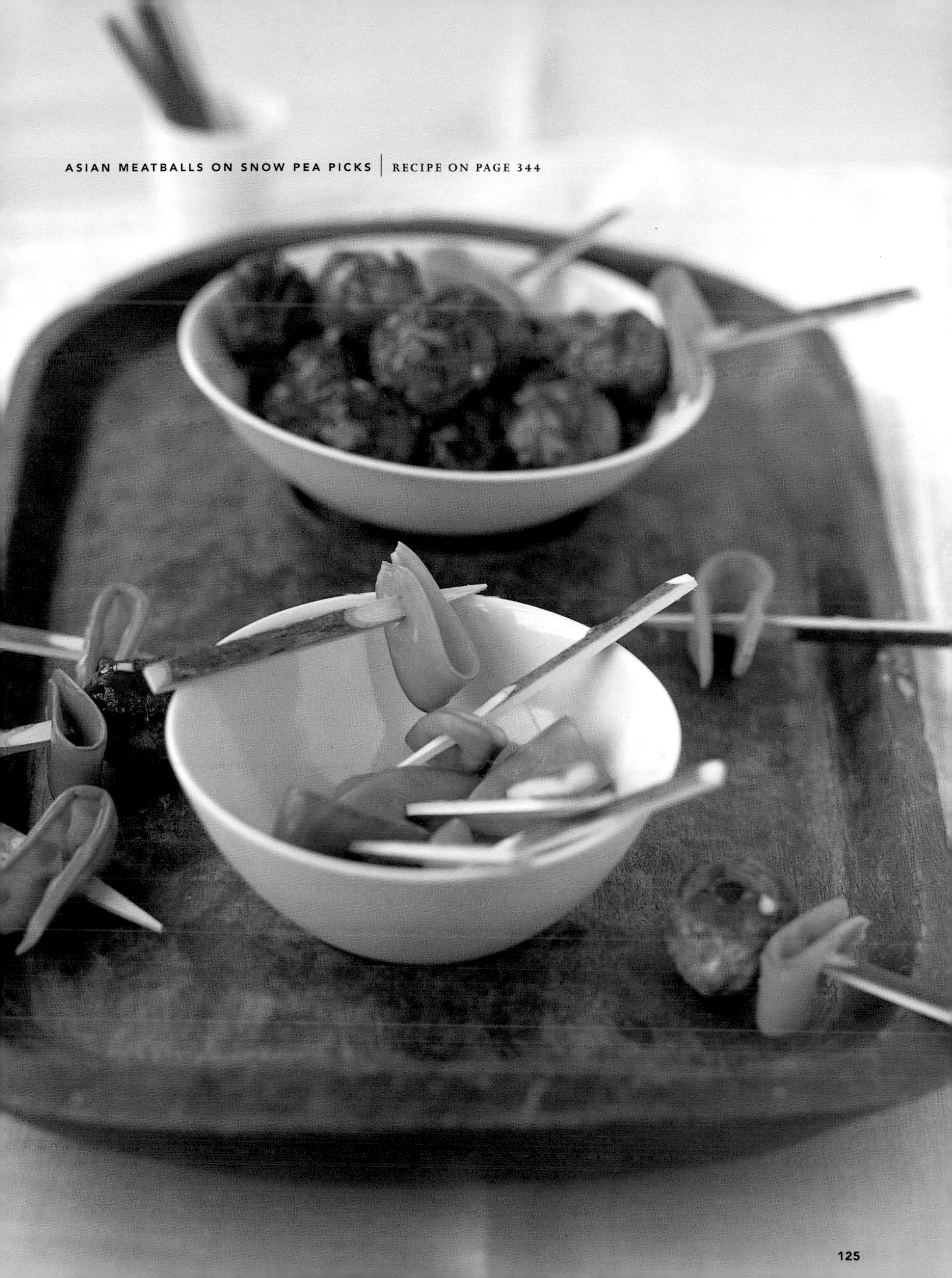

ASIAN MEATBALLS ON SNOW PEA PICKS | RECIPE ON PAGE 344

# 6

## BITES AND PIECES

*Recipes appear on pages 347–381*

OPPOSITE Deviled quail eggs are a perfect example of the visual drama
that can be achieved by re-creating a traditional hors d'oeuvre in miniature.
For an elegant presentation, set them on baby spinach leaves.

FINES HERBES

CURRY-CUMIN

TARRAGON
MAYONNAISE

ANCHOVY

KALAMATA OLIVES

CAVIAR AND
CRÈME FRAÎCHE

PICKLED GINGER AND
WASABI CAVIAR

HARD-BOILED AND DEVILED QUAIL EGGS | RECIPE ON PAGE 358

BACON AND THYME

NUTMEG AND
SEA SALT

The bright colors and varied shapes of vegetables combined in a briny marinade, as they are here, are shown to best advantage in a 4-gallon glass jar. Provide a long-handled slotted spoon for serving. OPPOSITE Baked hors d'oeuvres such as miniature popovers are best served warm, right out of the muffin tin.

BLUE CHEESE POPOVERS | RECIPE ON PAGE 371

MARINATED OLIVES | RECIPES ON PAGES 356–357

FRENCH OIL-CURED OLIVES WITH
LAVENDER AND HERBES DE PROVENCE

MIXED PROVENÇAL OLIVES WITH
PRESERVED LEMON AND OREGANO

PICKLED BELLA DI CERIGNOLA
OLIVES WITH FENNEL AND ORANGE

WARM SPICY KALAMATA OLIVES

PICHOLINE OLIVES WITH ROASTED
GARLIC AND RED ONION

Few bites or pieces are easier to prepare yet more flavorful and satisfying than marinated olives. They evoke the pleasures of the Mediterranean, and can be prepared days or even weeks ahead of time. Serve a variety in a single large bowl, or put out several smaller bowls with one type of marinated olive in each (OPPOSITE).

**MIXED OLIVES WITH CAPER BERRIES** | RECIPE ON PAGE 358

For baked mussels, use the half shells of the mollusk as a natural serving cup. OPPOSITE Savory crackers are guaranteed to be fresh when you make them yourself. Ideal to have on hand, the flavored doughs can be kept in the freezer and sliced and baked as needed.

BAKED MUSSELS | RECIPE ON PAGE 353

CHEDDAR-CORNMEAL

PARMESAN-ROSEMARY

BLUE CHEESE–PECAN

ICEBOX CRACKER DOUGHS | RECIPES ON PAGES 364–366

GRUYÈRE-THYME

ICEBOX CRACKERS | RECIPES ON PAGES 364–366

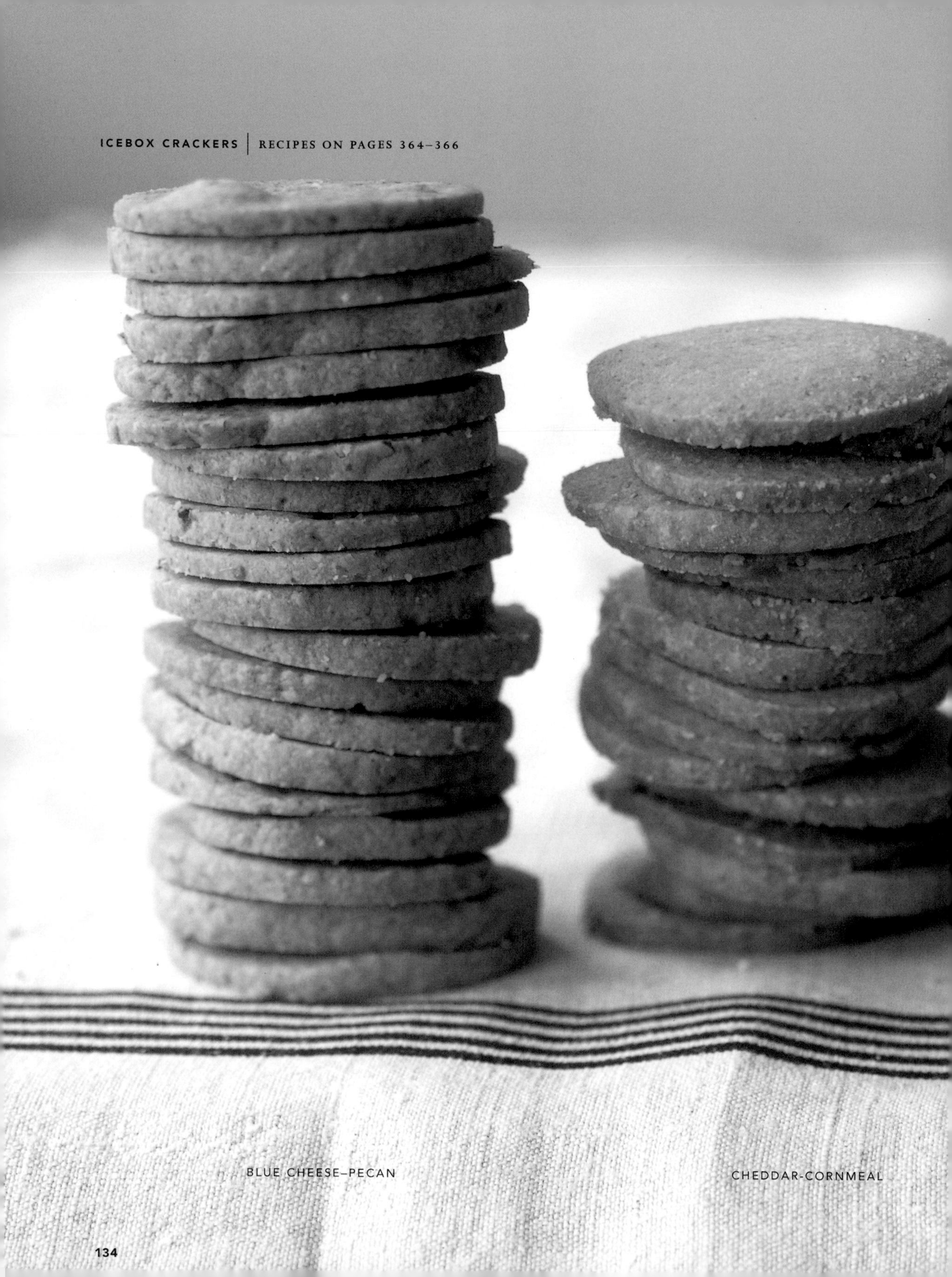

BLUE CHEESE–PECAN

CHEDDAR-CORNMEAL

Rather than laying crackers or other similarly shaped hors d'oeuvres out flat, try stacking them for a more striking appearance on an hors d'oeuvre table. A sprig of the appropriate herb, placed on the top of each cracker before baking, not only looks pretty but also indicates the flavor of the herbed crackers.

GRUYÈRE-THYME                    PARMESAN-ROSEMARY

**MOLASSES-GLAZED COCKTAIL RIBS** | RECIPE ON PAGE 349

The ideal food to eat with your fingers, the meat on baby back ribs shrinks away from the bone during cooking, creating a convenient handle for picking them up. OPPOSITE A large cutting board makes an excellent surface on which to place several individual components of an hors d'oeuvre.

CRISPY CHORIZO WITH CABRALES AND APPLES | RECIPE ON PAGE 352

This scaled-down but hearty version of charcuterie is perfect for a gathering at which the hors d'oeuvres make the meal. Setting out four or five types of prepared mustard takes only a moment, yet it creates a feeling of bounty.

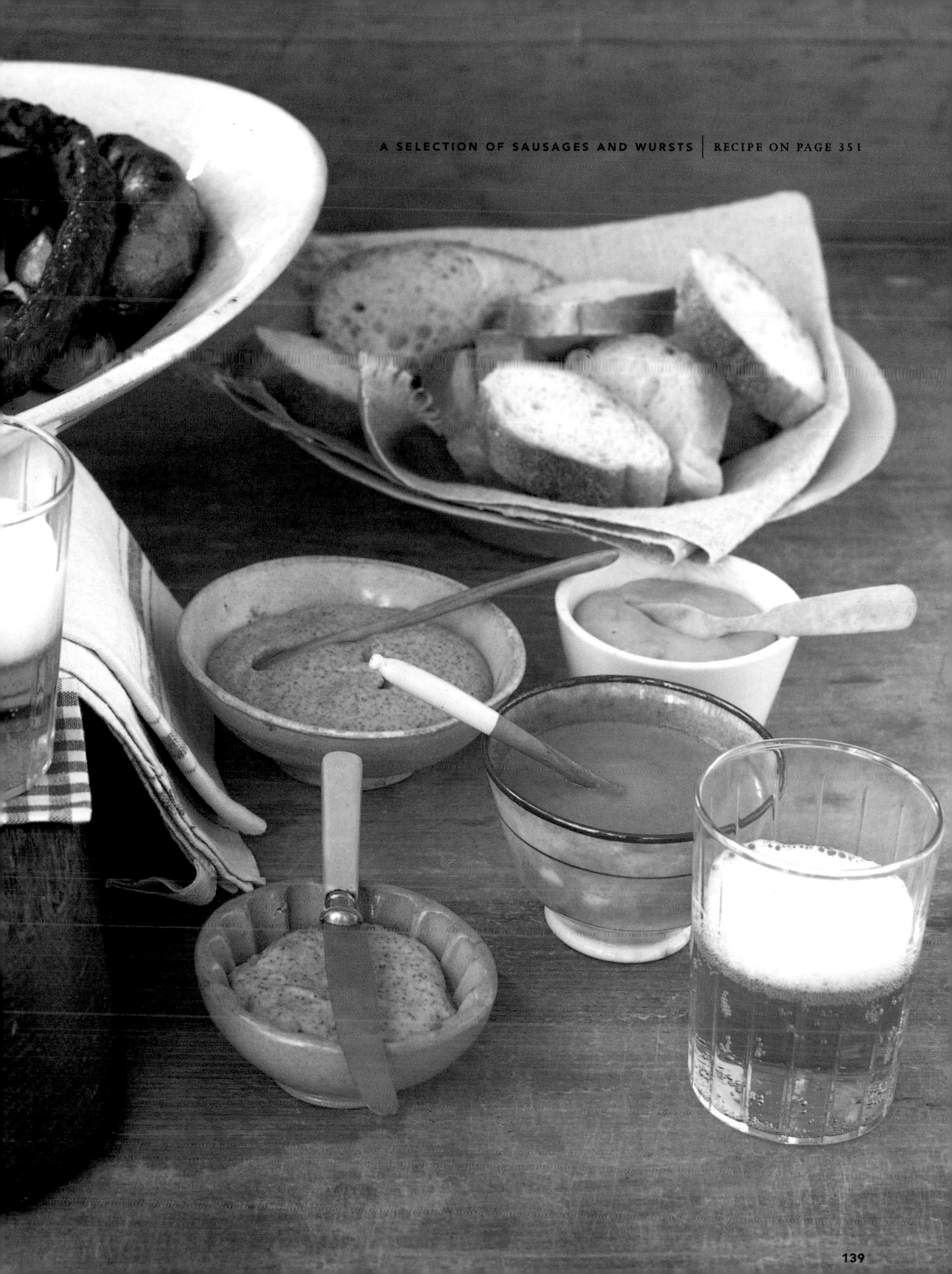

A SELECTION OF SAUSAGES AND WURSTS | RECIPE ON PAGE 351

Sweet and smoky, a bite or two of these bacon squares is just enough to satisfy. *OPPOSITE* Sherry is a delicious alternative to wine when serving spiced nuts.

SWEET PEPPERED BACON BITES | RECIPE ON PAGE 349

COCONUT CURRY MACADAMIA NUTS

HONEY-ROASTED
ALMONDS

GINGER-SCENTED
PECANS

TOASTED PEANUTS WITH
INDIAN SPICES

WARM MIXED NUTS WITH
ROSEMARY AND SHALLOTS

SPICY PAPRIKA CASHEWS

HONEY-ROASTED SEED AND
NUT CLUSTERS

A large bowl filled to the brim always looks inviting. When serving nuts in shells, such as pistachios, set out a smaller dish for the discarded shells. OPPOSITE The cocktail-size version of the warm, soft, giant pretzels sold on every street corner in New York City, these pretzel pieces are seasoned with coarse salt, sesame seeds, poppy seeds, and Parmesan cheese.

PRETZEL BITES | RECIPE ON PAGE 370

CUMIN-PARMESAN QUICK STICK

SAFFRON BREAD STICK

CURRY-TURMERIC QUICK STICK

PARMESAN-POPPY SEED PUFF PASTRY STRAW

CILANTRO, CHILI, AND LIME BREAD STICK

PARMESAN-PARSLEY PUFF PASTRY STRAW

YEAST BREAD STICK

CURRY, TURMERIC, AND BLACK ONION SEED BREAD STICK

CUMIN-PARMESAN QUICK STICK

LEMON-DILL BREAD STICK

For variety, arrange a selection of twisted and straight, fat and thin bread sticks, quick sticks, and puff pastry straws together. I like to place them vertically in glasses or vases, but they can also be set in baskets lined with linen towels.

ASSORTED COCKTAIL STICKS | RECIPES ON PAGES 366–370

PARMESAN-PARSLEY PUFF PASTRY STRAW

PAPRIKA-CAYENNE BREAD STICK

LEMON-DILL BREAD STICK

To make puff pastry straws, brush the puff pastry with egg wash, sprinkle with poppy seeds and grated Parmesan, then cut into strips, twist, and bake. A dough scraper is a particularly useful tool for this process. OPPOSITE Seeded yeast bread sticks are cut and shaped, then brushed with olive oil and sprinkled with coarse salt before baking.

PARMESAN-POPPY PUFF PASTRY STRAW TECHNIQUE | RECIPE ON PAGE 370

ASSORTED VEGETABLE QUICK STICKS | RECIPE ON PAGE 369

Plain bread sticks can be wrapped with prosciutto di Parma, then served with fresh figs and balls of delicious cavaillon melon or cantaloupe. OPPOSITE Bread sticks made without yeast get their distinctive colors from fresh vegetables and herbs such as carrots, beets, and parsley.

PROSCIUTTO-WRAPPED BREAD STICKS WITH CAVAILLON MELON AND FIGS | RECIPE ON PAGE 367

VEGETABLE CRUDITÉS | RECIPE ON PAGE 374

Crudités need not be boring or staid. Long, thin shapes bursting out of a collection of clear glasses provide plenty of visual impact. For contrast, include round cherry tomatoes and circular rolls of vegetables such as cucumber, yellow squash, and daikon sliced super-thin on a mandoline.

BUTTERMILK PEPPERCORN DIP

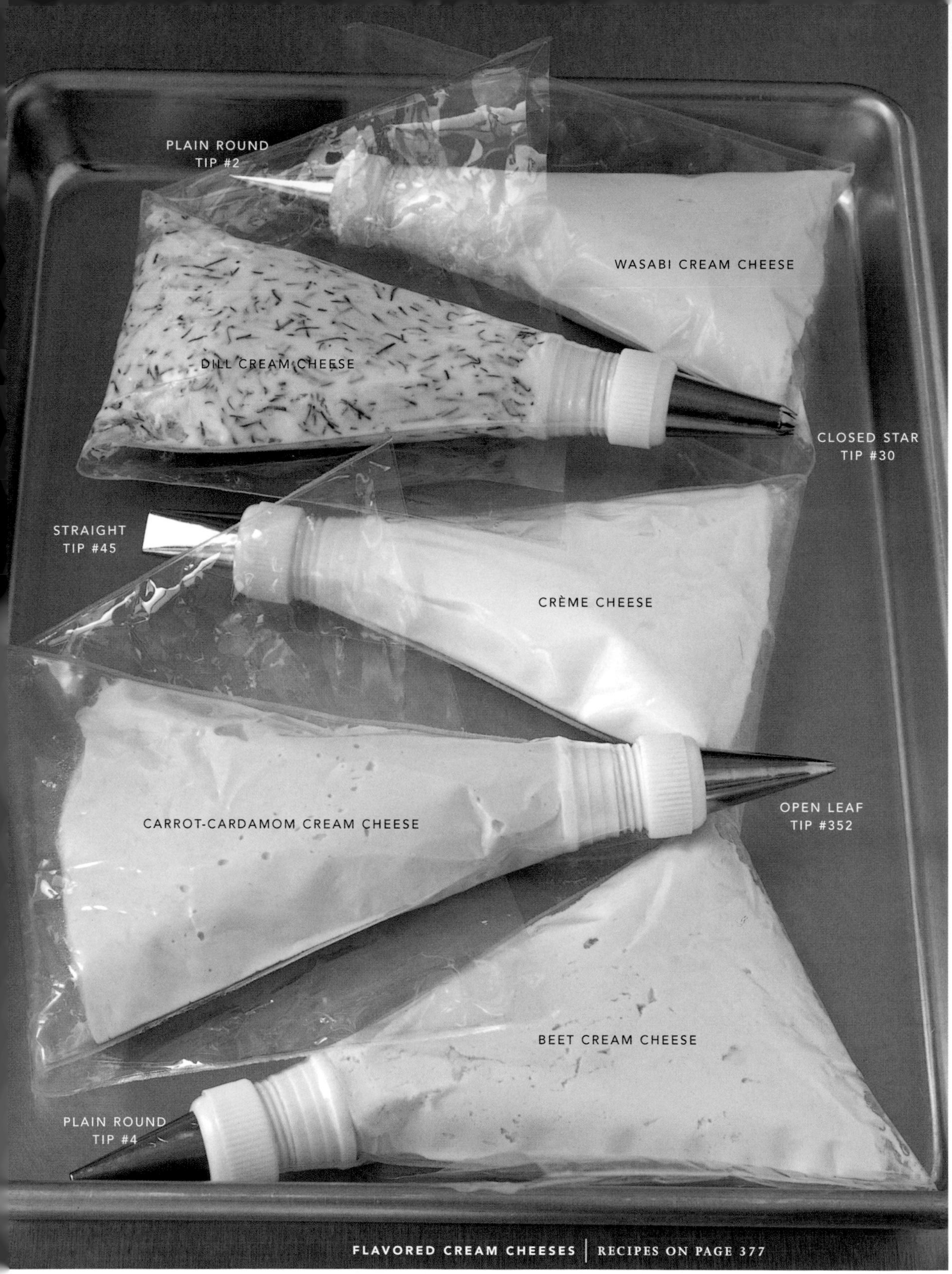

PLAIN ROUND
TIP #2

WASABI CREAM CHEESE

DILL CREAM CHEESE

CLOSED STAR
TIP #30

STRAIGHT
TIP #45

CRÈME CHEESE

CARROT-CARDAMOM CREAM CHEESE

OPEN LEAF
TIP #352

BEET CREAM CHEESE

PLAIN ROUND
TIP #4

**FLAVORED CREAM CHEESES** | RECIPES ON PAGE 377

Vegetables with flavored cream cheese piped on top are a more elegant take on crudités. Use slices of round vegetables, baby carrots halved lengthwise, or vegetables like celery and endive that naturally hold the filling. OPPOSITE Freezer bags work just as well as traditional pastry bags for piping: Snip one of the corners and fasten the pastry tip as you would on a vinyl bag.

153

GLOSSARY OF OYSTERS | NOTE ON PAGES 354–355

BLUE POINT

SNOW CREEK

MALPEQUE

CAPE NEDICK

BELON

MARTHA'S
VINEYARD

Coarse sea salt mixed with a little water becomes a pretty and practical bed for shucked oysters. Unlike the traditional bed of ice, which melts quickly and is not easily manipulated, coarse salt can be shaped to create the perfect supportive perch, so every bit of the delicious oyster liquor stays in the shell. OPPOSITE Sauces as colorful as those served with oysters look best in clear glass bowls. Use various shapes and sizes, and arrange them on a cakestand for easy access.

CLASSIC MIGNONETTE

FOUR SAUCES FOR OYSTERS | RECIPES ON PAGE 396

LEMON-TABASCO SAUCE

SAKE-LIME SAUCE

HOT SESAME AND CHILI SAUCE

SAVORY BISCOTTI | RECIPES ON PAGES 372–373

BROWNED-BUTTER, LEMON, AND CAPER BISCOTTI

Nestled in a linen-lined wire basket, assorted savory biscotti are wonderful for dunking into medium-bodied red wine.

ORANGE, PISTACHIO, AND
BLACK OLIVE BISCOTTI

FENNEL AND GOLDEN RAISIN BISCOTTI

A SELECTION OF CAVIARS | NOTE ON PAGE 380

SEVRUGA

SALMON ROE

OSETRA

BELUGA

WHITEFISH ROE

Spoon caviar onto toast points
spread with crème fraîche for a luxurious hors d'oeuvre. To serve the
caviar with a spoon, use specially
designed mother-of-pearl, bone,
glass, or other nonmetal spoons.

BLINI WITH CAVIAR AND CRÈME FRAÎCHE | RECIPE ON PAGE 381

Caviar with the classic accompaniments: white onion, chopped egg white and egg yolk, crème fraîche, and buckwheat blini. Serve the caviar on ice so it stays cold.

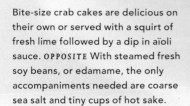

Bite-size crab cakes are delicious on their own or served with a squirt of fresh lime followed by a dip in aïoli sauce. OPPOSITE With steamed fresh soy beans, or edamame, the only accompaniments needed are coarse sea salt and tiny cups of hot sake.

**CLASSIC CRAB CAKES WITH CHILI-LIME AÏOLI** | RECIPE ON PAGE 352

EDAMAME WITH SEA SALT | RECIPE ON PAGE 379

SEAFOOD CRUDITÉS WITH CHILI-LIME AÏOLI | RECIPE ON PAGE 378

Serve an assortment of chilled shellfish and fresh vegetables adorned with flowering chives, broccoli rabe, and rosemary in bowls of different sizes or graduated compotes. Use the smallest vessel for the aïoli dipping sauce.

Small, simple glasses of chilled white wine go perfectly with bowls of toasted and seasoned legumes. OPPOSITE The ideal size for a small gathering, this ham makes at least twenty-four tiny sandwiches.

SPICED CHICKPEAS AND CRUNCHY SPLIT PEA BITES │ RECIPES ON PAGE 363

ORANGE-HONEY GLAZED BLACK FOREST HAM AND BISCUITS | RECIPES ON PAGES 350–351

# 7

## DIPS, SPREADS, SAUCES, RELISHES, AND SALSAS

*Recipes appear on pages 383–401*

OPPOSITE Richly flavored dips are best served in small dishes accompanied by big stacks of dippers, like the crostini used here.

BRANDADE WITH GARLIC CONFIT | RECIPE ON PAGE 387

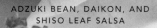

FRUIT AND VEGETABLE SALSAS | RECIPES ON PAGES 400–401

APPLE, GINGER, AND BEET SALSA

GRILLED VEGETABLE SALSA

TROPICAL FRUIT SALSA

MIXED TOMATO SALSA

ADZUKI BEAN, DAIKON, AND
SHISO LEAF SALSA

Salsas are quick to make and keep well when covered
and refrigerated, so it's easy to make several varieties in
advance, then provide your guests with different choices.
OPPOSITE Triangles of pita toasts, crostini, and corn chips
are traditional dippers, but adding some more unusual
ones such as apple chips, crispy wontons, or taro chips
gives the display more variety.

172

WHOLE-WHEAT TORTILLA CHIPS

PITA TOASTS

APPLE CHIPS

TOMATO TORTILLA CHIPS

FRIED LOTUS CHIPS

SOURDOUGH TOASTS

SPINACH TORTILLA CHIPS

TARO CHIPS

CRISPY WONTONS

FLOUR TORTILLA CHIPS

THREE DELICIOUS DIPS | RECIPES ON PAGES 388–390

ROASTED RED PEPPER AND
EGGPLANT DIP

WHITE BEAN AND
MUSTARD GREENS D

TOASTED PEPITA DIP

Use spoon-like dippers such as
sourdough toasts and flatbreads for
relatively loose dips, and stick-like
dippers such as sesame bread sticks
for thicker ones.

RIPE
TOMATOES

JALAPEÑO
PEPPERS

MEDIUM-SIZE
ONION

RIPE AVOCADO

CILANTRO

KOSHER SALT

**INGREDIENTS FOR CLASSIC GUACAMOLE** | RECIPE ON PAGE 399

Guacamole is made in three simple steps. *ABOVE LEFT* Mash the onions, cilantro, chilies, and salt in a molcajete with a tejolote, or use a heavy kitchen bowl and the back of a wooden spoon. *ABOVE RIGHT* Add the diced avocado and mash. *RIGHT* Mix in the diced tomatoes.

FRESH COCKTAIL SAUCE

TARRAGON MUSTARD SAUCE

CHILI-LIME AÏOLI

CILANTRO-ALMOND RELISH

HOT CRAB DIP | RECIPE ON PAGE 385

Sturdy breads and crackers such as sourdough crisps or bread sticks are best suited to dips with chunky ingredients like the crabmeat in Hot Crab Dip. OPPOSITE Sea beans are a unique and appropriate garnish for a platter of steamed shrimp and accompanying sauces.

BLACK BEAN DIP | RECIPE ON PAGE 386

Warm dips can be served straight from the oven in dishes such as this ovenproof bowl. OPPOSITE Always include one or two vegetarian hors d'oeuvres on your party menu, such as this delicious lentil dip.

SPICY YELLOW DHAL DIP | RECIPE ON PAGE 385

# 8

# FONDUE, FRICO, AND
# A SELECTION OF FINE CHEESES

*Recipes appear on pages 403–419*

OPPOSITE A classic European dessert, cheese accompanied by fruit is also a
wonderful hors d'oeuvre. Offer a variety of cheeses, including some firm and some soft,
some very intense, and some milder for guests who may not have bold taste buds.

French cheeses go perfectly with a selection of fruits and sherry for sipping. Supply several knives—table knives for slicing the soft cheeses, a sharper knife for the harder ones.

BUCHERON

MORBIER

REBLOCHON

PRINCE DE CLAVEROLLE

AGED MIMOLETTE

EDEL DE CLÉRON

PAVÉ D'AFFINOIS

MONTBRIAC

L'AMI DU CHAMBERTIN

A PRESENTATION OF FRENCH CHEESES | GLOSSARY ON PAGES 414–415

EMMENTALER
GRUYÈRE
VACHERIN FRIBOURGEOIS

WHITE WINE

KIRSCH

FRESHLY
GROUND
BLACK
PEPPER

GARLIC CLOVES

GRATED NUTMEG

**INGREDIENTS FOR CLASSIC SWISS FONDUE** | RECIPE ON PAGE 405

A VARIETY OF FONDUE DIPPERS | NOTE ON PAGE 406

DRIED FIGS

PEAR AND APPLE WEDGES

CUBED BREADS

TOASTED MUSTARD SEEDS

WALNUTS AND
GRAPES

TOASTED CARAWAY SEEDS

NUTMEG-DIPPED POTATOES

POPPY SEEDS

APPLE AND PROSCIUTTO

ASPARAGUS AND
CAULIFLOWER

TOASTED FENNEL SEEDS

A very simple but wonderfully delicious hors d'oeuvre, Camembert baked in its box can be served with nothing more than chunks of crusty French bread for dipping. OPPOSITE Artichoke hearts, mushroom halves, and bread cubes are excellent dippers for rich fondues like this one with shaved black truffles.

**BAKED CAMEMBERT** | RECIPE ON PAGE 410

FONTINA FONDUE WITH BLACK TRUFFLES | RECIPE ON PAGE 405

Tangy goat cheese comes in a wide variety of styles, wrappings, and shapes, as well as flavors. I like to set out a selection of these cheeses accompanied by nothing more than a few perfect pieces of fruit and antique silver knives for slicing.

CAPRIOLE CROCODILE TEAR

SAINTE-MAURE DE TOURAINE

CAPRIOLE BANON

EGG FARM DAIRY FRESH CHÈVRE

CROTTIN DE CHAVIGNOL

**ASSORTED GOAT CHEESES** | GLOSSARY ON PAGES 411–413

CABÉCOU

VALENÇAY

LE CHEVROT

SELLES-SUR-CHER

PICO PICANDINE

191

To make frico tacos, place small handfuls of the grated cheese and flour mixture on a nonstick pan and cook until melted and browned. Place the cooked cheese pancake on a paper towel and form it in your hand with an offset spatula. OPPOSITE Assorted frico—shaped over rolling pins, on small bowls, or simply free form—look gorgeous in a Venetian glass compote or other footed glass container.

ASSORTED FRICO | RECIPE ON PAGES 408–409

With Spanish cheeses, I like to serve traditional Spanish tapas such as serrano ham, blood oranges, almonds, roasted peppers, black olive bread, marinated olives, and radishes. Fino sherry is an appropriate drink to accompany these cheeses.

QUESO DE MURCIA AL VINO (DRUNKEN GOAT)

ARTISANAL
AGED MANCHEGO

MAHÓN
ARTISANO

SUSPIRO DE CABRA

CABRALES

TETILLA

Mozzarella melts from the warmth of the tomato sauce that surrounds it as it bakes, giving it the perfect consistency for scooping onto sturdy crusted Pugliese bread. OPPOSITE Manchego and Monterey Jack cheeses are flavored with roasted jalapeño and poblano peppers to create this Mexican-style fondue.

POACHED MOZZARELLA | RECIPE ON PAGE 407

CHILE CON QUESO WITH ROASTED POBLANO PEPPERS | RECIPE ON PAGE 407

A SELECTION OF AMERICAN CHEESES | GLOSSARY ON PAGES 413–414

VELLA DRY JACK

WABASH CANNONBALL

SALLY JACKSON
AGED SHEEP'S-MILK
CHEESE

Sweet dried fruits such as figs and dates, nuts like whole almonds and walnut halves, and thin slices of country bread are good accompaniments for American cheeses.

MAYTAG BLUE

GRAFTON VILLAGE CHEDDAR

EGG FARM DAIRY
WILD RIPENED CHEDDAR

OLD CHATHAM CAMEMBERT

HERBED AND SPICED GOAT CHEESE BALLS | RECIPE ON PAGE 410

Parmigiano-Reggiano can be broken into large pieces and served with truffle oil for drizzling. OPPOSITE Goat cheese balls rolled in paprika, cracked black pepper, thyme, curry powder, or toasted pecans look very festive on a plate drizzled with spicy olive oil.

# 9

## SIPS AND DRINKS

*Recipes appear on pages 421–441*

OPPOSITE There's nothing quite so elegant as a classic cocktail, and none is more classic than a martini. But that doesn't mean it has to be staid; try using a caper berry and a brine-cured olive in place of the usual olive or onion.

CLASSIC MARTINI | RECIPE ON PAGE 432

COSMOPOLITAN

CAIPIRINHA

PEAR MARTINI

BLOODY MARY

SAZERAC

Drinks become cocktails only when properly garnished, as they are here with, from left to right, lime zest, lime wedges, lemon zest, skewered cucumber tiles, sugared pear slices, colored sanding sugar, mint leaves, cherries, orange wedges, kumquat slices, and sugared rose petals.

PLANTER'S PUNCH

POMEGRANATE MARGARITA

FRESH LIME DAIQUIRI

LIMÓN

MAI TAI

MANGO COCKTAIL

KUMQUAT COCKTAIL

PUB DRINKS | RECIPES ON PAGE 437

Mixers such as black currant juice, hard cider, or champagne transform a simple beer into an especially delicious drink. Serve pub drinks in traditional pilsner glasses, water goblets, or highball glasses, or make up a batch in a pitcher.

SNAKEBITE

BLACK CURRANT JUICE

SNAKEBITE AND BLACK

STOUT

PANACHE

BLACK VELVET

FIVE RETRO DRINKS | RECIPES ON PAGES 429–433

SUMMERTIME CHARTREUSE

REVERSE MARTINI

It's fun to serve tried-and-true cocktails, but with a new twist on the old garnish. Put slices of three different olives in a Reverse Martini, add kumquat and lemon to a Tom Collins, float star fruit in a Blue Margarita, and hang a candied ginger slice on a glass of Ginger Fever.

BLUE MARGARITA

TOM COLLINS

GINGER FEVER

ROSÉ SANGRIA

WHITE WINE PUNCH

Sangrias and punches are colorful as well as refreshing, so serve them in glass pitchers. Provide tall glasses for guests as well as ice-tea spoons for dipping out the fruit.

RED SANGRIA

PIMM'S CUP

ORANGE-ROSEMARY CORDIAL

STRAWBERRY CORD

VANILLA RUM CORDIAL

I serve these jewel-toned homemade cordials in a variety of decanters along with soda water for diluting and cordial glasses for those guests who want to drink them straight. Top each decanter with an appropriate fruit stopper.

PASSION FRUIT CORDIAL

RASPBERRY-THYME CORDIAL

SODA WATER

BEEF CONSOMMÉ SIP | RECIPE ON PAGE 423

Sake cups are the perfect size for serving a sip or two of hearty soups. OPPOSITE Sips can be served in a variety of sake cups, tea cups, demitasse cups, and little bowls.

**BUTTERNUT SQUASH SIP WITH SEASONED PEPITAS** | RECIPE ON PAGE 424

Even wonton soup can be served as an hors d'oeuvre when a single dumpling is spooned into a cup that is just the right size. OPPOSITE Some cups are meant to be eaten; carved from cucumbers, they are just tall enough to hold a sip of soup, but not too tall to bite into.

MUSHROOM SIP WITH BARLEY WONTONS │ RECIPE ON PAGE 425

**GAZPACHO IN CUCUMBER CUPS** | RECIPE ON PAGE 426

# CLASSICS

*Recipes appear on pages 443–465*

OPPOSITE One of the most popular hors d'oeuvres during my catering
days was a perfectly ripe wheel of Brie, glazed with caramel brittle and garnished
with pecans. It remains a favorite.

RUTH LESERMAN'S CARAMEL BRIE | RECIPE ON PAGE 458

SMOKED TROUT MOUSSE ON
CUCUMBER SLICES | RECIPE ON PAGE 464

ROQUEFORT GRAPES | RECIPE ON PAGE 451

SPICY ALMONDS | RECIPE ON PAGE 464

PÂTE A CHOUX WITH
ONION JAM | RECIPE ON PAGE 453

SHRIMP TOAST | RECIPE ON PAGE 461

SKEWERED TORTELLINI | RECIPE ON PAGE 457

RED POTATOES WITH SOUR CREAM
AND CAVIAR | RECIPE ON PAGE 462

**PHYLLO TRIANGLES WITH ASSORTED FILLINGS** | RECIPES ON PAGES 448–450

**TARTLETS WITH LEEK CHIFFONADE** | RECIPE ON PAGE 455

**MARINATED SHRIMP WRAPPED IN SNOW PEAS** | RECIPE ON PAGE 456

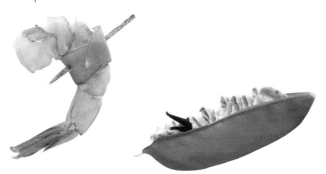

**CHINESE PEARL BALLS** | RECIPE ON PAGE 450

**SNOW PEAS WITH CRABMEAT FILLING** | RECIPE ON PAGE 452

**GRAVLAX ON BLACK BREAD WITH MUSTARD-FENNEL SAUCE** | RECIPE ON PAGE 447

**PÂTÉ ON PEAR SLICES** | RECIPE ON PAGE 462

**GAYLA'S ORANGE-RAISIN MUFFINS WITH SMOKED TURKEY AND QUINCE JELLY** | RECIPES ON PAGES 445–446

**SAVORY PALMIERS** | RECIPE ON PAGE 463

**STEAMED MUSSELS AND TOMATO–RED ONION SAUCE** | RECIPE ON PAGE 458

**MOCK DRUMSTICKS** | RECIPES ON PAGES 461–462

**EGGPLANT CAVIAR ON FRENCH BREAD TOAST** | RECIPES ON PAGES 446–447

**PATTYPAN SQUASH FILLED WITH RED PEPPER CHEESE** | RECIPE ON PAGE 456

**FOUR CLASSIC DRINKS** | RECIPES ON PAGE 465

I always have the ingredients on hand to make classic fruit drinks. The eggnog, which I created for one of the first parties I hosted, remains the highlight of my holiday gatherings.

OCEAN SUNRISE

PIÑA COLADA

THE ORIGINAL EGGNOG

CAMPARI AND FRESH ORANGE JUICE

the
# RECIPES

# BUILDING BLOCKS
## FOR THE
## BEST HORS D'OEUVRES

*Photographs for these recipes appear on
pages 10–21*

WHETHER IT'S THE STOCK FOR A SOUP OR THE GREENS FOR A COMPOSED SALAD, EVERY GOOD DISH BEGINS WITH A GOOD BASE. FOR HORS D'OEUVRES, THE BASES ARE JUST THAT: THE ITEMS THAT YOU PUT OTHER INGREDIENTS INTO OR ON TOP OF.

The most interesting hors d'oeuvres are constructed on bases that are somewhat surprising and a bit unusual. This doesn't mean you should search for bizarre edible bases, but you should use your imagination. Not everything has to be placed on a cracker or a square of bread, although there is certainly nothing wrong with either of those when used with a bit of originality.

I use a range of bases that fall into several categories. Among my favorites are small cups made from hollowed-out fruits and vegetables. These always have a special appeal to guests because they are both whimsical and delicious. For small hors d'oeuvres, I fill grapes as well as red and yellow cherry tomatoes. Somewhat more substantial fillings can be nestled in cups made of cucumbers, lady apples, mushrooms, and even pattypan squash. In this same way, I use cups and wrappers provided by the natural shape of greens such as endive leaves, artichoke petals, and romaine lettuce.

Another group of bases that are easy to build upon are flatbreads. Most international cuisines include some variation on this theme, and each is easily adapted to create hors d'oeuvres you can eat out of hand. From the buckwheat pancakes known as blini to Italian crostini slices, these breads are very versatile. Then, of course, there are the tortillas of Mexico. I use the flour variety in a miniaturized version, which takes on the shape of a bite-size bowl and is perfect for serving a salad as an hors d'oeuvre. Corn tortillas, on the other hand, can be tucked into mini muffin tins to form sturdy, delicious toasted cups for looser fillings.

Chips are another source of wonderful bases upon which to spoon, spread, and layer all manner of toppings. I expand the category beyond potato chips with crisp chips made from taro, apples, lotus, wonton wrappers, and flour tortillas. The latticed French wafers known as gaufrettes add a note of delicate sophistication to the group. And, although they are not chips in the truest sense, deep-fried tostones made from green plantains and rice cakes flavored with ginger and jalapeño can be used in very much the same way.

Marvelous bases can also be fashioned from bread. Pain de Mie, the French bread baked in a rectangular pan with a lid, is ideal for creating star-shaped toasts, tiny breadboxes, and perhaps the most versatile and simple to make base of all, the croustade, a square bread slice toasted in a muffin tin to create an edible cup that holds just about anything. If the shape and size of a base doesn't come naturally, you can always mold basic pastry dough, as well as herb- and spice-infused short doughs, into boat-shaped, square, round, and rectangular, and fluted tartlet molds. These shells are perfect for making ahead, since they keep well and are versatile enough to hold everything from chicken salad to tuna tartare.

All of the bases in this chapter are used in the chapters of recipes that follow. While these recipes are the ones I have found to be successful at my own parties, the bases are designed to work with other flavoring combinations as well, and I encourage you to experiment and use them in ways that suit your own entertaining style.

## CUPS AND WRAPPERS

When selecting fruit or vegetables to be used as cups, look for small varieties that can be eaten in one bite. Otherwise, they can become messy and awkward to eat. For wrappers, choose greens that are sturdy and supple. In some cases, the outer leaves may be good for wrapping, the inner for cupping. The members of the radicchio and endive families fit into this group, as do Bibb, Boston, romaine, and iceburg lettuces. Escarole and red and green leaf lettuces make excellent wrappers, as do kale and red cabbage, if blanched.

In addition to the recipes for which specific cups and wrappers are called for, the following are also delicious spooned into them: Guacamole (page 399), Crumbled Parmesan Cheese with Truffle Oil (page 410), Curried Egg Salad (page 319), Tarragon Shrimp Salad (page 314), Roasted Red Pepper and Eggplant Dip (page 390), Toasted Pepita Dip (page 388), and White Bean and Mustard Greens Dip (page 389).

## CUCUMBER CUPS

**MAKES ABOUT 2 DOZEN** | photograph on page 13

*Look for cucumbers that are narrow, such as Kirbys, seedless hothouse, and Japanese cucumbers, so that the cups will be only 1 or 2 bites.*

5 seedless cucumbers, each about 10 ounces and 11 inches long, ends trimmed

If the cucumbers are waxed, peel them. Cut each crosswise into five 1¾-inch pieces. With a small melon baller, carefully scoop out the insides of each piece, leaving a ¼-inch border around the edge and a ½-inch border on the bottom. The cucumber cups may be prepared up to 4 hours in advance, arranged on damp paper towels, tightly covered, and refrigerated.

## CHERRY TOMATO CUPS

**MAKES 2 DOZEN** | photograph on page 13

*Use a serrated knife to slice these bite-size tomatoes; the blade will cut through the skin much easier and more cleanly than a standard blade.*

24 cherry tomatoes, washed and dried

Using a serrated knife, slice about ⅛ inch from the top of each tomato. If the tomatoes do not sit upright, trim a tiny piece from the uncut side to create a flat bottom. (Do not cut off too much or the filling will leak out.) With the tip of a knife, gently loosen the flesh around the inside of each tomato. Scoop out the seeds with a small melon baller The tomatoes can be prepared 1 hour in advance and kept at room temperature.

## LADY APPLE CUPS

**MAKES 2 DOZEN** | photograph on page 13

*These bite-size apples make the perfect edible container for a variety of fillings, including Celeriac Salad (page 306) and Chicken Salad (page 320). Don't confuse lady apples, which are delicious raw, with crab apples, which must be cooked with sugar to tame their tartness.*

24 lady apples (about 3½ pounds)
2 tablespoons fresh lemon juice

Slice ¼ inch off the top of each lady apple. Reserve the tops for garnish. Using a melon baller, scoop out the flesh and seeds, taking care to keep the apple skin intact. With the tip of a small knife, remove the tough core from the outside bottom of the apple, taking care not to puncture the skin. Lightly coat the inside of each apple with the lemon juice. Cover the apples with plastic wrap and refrigerate for up to 1 hour before using.

## PATTYPAN SQUASH CUPS

**MAKES 2 DOZEN** | photograph on page 13

Fill the hot pattypan squash with White Beans and Mustard Greens Dip (page 389), Leek, Fennel, and Goat Cheese filling (page 300), or Polenta filling (page 301). Alternatively, let the squash come to room temperature and spoon any of the cherry tomato fillings (pages 304–306) into them.

2 dozen miniature pattypan squash, washed and patted dry

**1** Slice ¼ inch off the top of each squash. Using a melon baller, scoop out the flesh and seeds.

**2** Place 12 squash into a steamer basket over 1 inch of boiling water, and cover tightly. Steam until the squash are bright yellow and tender when pierced with the tip of a knife, about 3 minutes. Remove and set on a rack to drain. Repeat with the remaining squash. The steamed squash can be stored in an airtight container in the refrigerator for 3 to 4 hours. Bring to room temperature before using.

## GOLDEN MUSHROOM CAPS

**MAKES 2 DOZEN** | photograph on page 13

Roasting mushroom caps at high heat brings out their inherent deep flavor, so they taste much better when stuffed. Buy mushrooms with caps small enough to eat in one bite, about 1¼ inches in diameter. If you use larger mushroom caps, buy fewer, or there will not be enough filling to stuff them. Reserve the stems if you are making the Broccoli Rabe and Pancetta Stuffed Mushrooms (page 300) or the Porcini Stuffed Mushrooms with Camembert (page 301).

24 small button mushrooms
2 tablespoons extra-virgin olive oil
Kosher salt and freshly ground black pepper

**1** Preheat the oven to 400° F. Remove the stems from the mushrooms and reserve if they are used in the filling. Use a damp cloth or mushroom brush to clean the mushrooms. Brush each mushroom with the olive oil. Add salt and pepper to taste.

**2** Place the mushrooms, cap-side up, on a baking sheet. Roast until the mushrooms are golden and their liquid begins to seep from the cavity, 6 to 7 minutes. Place cap-side up on paper towels to drain. The mushroom caps can be stored in an airtight container for up to 4 hours.

## GRAPE CUPS

**MAKES 2 DOZEN** | photograph on page 13

Grapes about the size of large marbles are easiest to fill. Red Globe grapes are perfect; they're large enough and the seeds are simple to scoop out. Red Globes are available from August through early January. If you prefer green grapes, the Perlette variety is available in the spring through most of the summer.

12 red or green round grapes, washed and dried

**1** Using a sharp knife, slice the grapes in half crosswise. Trim the uncut sides of each half just enough to achieve a flat bottom so that the grapes do not roll around.

**2** Using a small melon baller, gently scoop out the flesh and the seeds of the grape, leaving enough flesh to keep the grape stable and firm. Repeat with the remaining grapes and store cut-side down in single layers on damp paper towels, tightly covered, in the refrigerator until ready to use. Grape cups may be made 4 to 6 hours before filling.

## ARTICHOKE LEAVES

**MAKES ABOUT 2 DOZEN** | photograph on page 11

*The larger the artichoke, the more leaves it will have that are sturdy enough for serving. Adding olive oil to the cooking water prevents the artichoke from absorbing too much water and keeps the leaves firm and supple. The leaves are meant to be scraped clean between the teeth, the rough petals discarded. Artichoke leaves are used in Roasted Shrimp with Artichokes and Shaved Fennel (page 263) and can also be used as a dipper for the Hot Crab Dip (page 385), Black Bean Dip (page 386), or any of the salsas (pages 400–401).*

1 large (8-ounce) artichoke

1 lemon, halved

1 tablespoon kosher salt

3 tablespoons extra-virgin olive oil

**1** Rinse the artichoke with cool water and peel away any discolored or broken leaves. Trim the stem to 1 inch. Bring a medium pot of water to a boil over high heat. Squeeze the juice from both lemon halves into the water, then add the halves to the water along with the salt and the olive oil. Add the artichoke and simmer over low heat until tender, 20 to 30 minutes. (You should be able to pierce the stem end with the tip of a knife and pull the leaves off easily.) Drain and cool.

**2** Peel away the leaves, reserving all the firm leaves for serving. Using a spoon, carefully trim the hairy choke until the heart is neat and clean. Reserve the heart for Roasted Shrimp with Artichokes and Shaved Fennel (page 263). The leaves may be prepared a day ahead and kept in an airtight container in the refrigerator.

---

**NOTE** | Working with Grape Leaves

Used predominantly in Greek and Middle Eastern cooking to wrap foods such as seasoned rice, chicken, and meat (see Lamb and Couscous Dolmades, page 343), grape leaves are available packed in brine in the international section of the grocery store. You will rarely if ever find fresh grape leaves commercially available. To prepare packaged grape leaves for eating, rinse them well to remove any traces of salt. Spread them out onto a work surface and pat dry. Using a paring knife, cut out the tough center stem. Cover the grape leaves with a damp kitchen towel to keep them from drying out and becoming brittle as you prepare them. If you happen to come across fresh grape leaves, simmer them in water for 10 minutes to soften them before using.

---

## ENDIVE PETALS

**MAKES ABOUT 3 DOZEN** | photograph on page 11

*It is important to choose the very freshest endive, with firm, crisp leaves, so that the leaves hold up well when filled. Avoid endive with brown spots, wrinkled or wilted leaf tips, bright green leaves, and any soft spots.*

4 firm, fresh heads of Belgian endive

Cut ½ inch off the bottom (root end) of each head of endive. Separate the leaves. Trim the leaves to measure about 4 inches in length. The leaves may be kept, in a single layer under a damp paper towel, in the refrigerator for up to 4 hours.

## BASIC PASTRY DOUGH TARTLET SHELLS

**MAKES 2½ DOZEN 2¾ x ⅜-INCH OR 2¼ x ¾-INCH TARTLETS** | photograph on page 80

*This easy, versatile dough may be stored, wrapped tightly, in the refrigerator for 24 hours. Freeze the dough, double-wrapped in plastic wrap, for up to 3 weeks. Be certain that you add only enough water for the dough just to come together; too much may cause the dough to become tough.*

2 cups all-purpose flour

½ teaspoon kosher salt

12 tablespoons (1½ sticks) unsalted butter, chilled, cut into small pieces

⅓ cup ice water

**1** Place the flour and the salt in the bowl of a food processor. Pulse to combine. Add the cold butter and pulse until the mixture resembles coarse meal. Slowly add the ice water, pulsing to combine, until the dough comes together. Transfer the dough to a sheet of plastic wrap and form into a flat disk. Chill in the refrigerator for 1 hour or overnight.

**2** Preheat the oven to 400° F. with 2 racks. Transfer the dough to a lightly floured surface. Cut the dough into 2 equal pieces. Wrap 1 piece in plastic wrap and return to the refrigerator. Roll out the other half to a ⅛-inch thickness. Use a 3-inch round cookie cutter to cut out 15 rounds. Press each round into a tartlet mold and trim away any excess. Repeat with the remaining dough. Arrange the molds on 2 baking sheets. Prick the bottom of each tartlet shell with a fork. Cover the sheet pans with plastic wrap and chill the dough in the pans until firm, about 15 minutes.

**3** Bake the tartlets until set and dry, 12 to 14 minutes, rotating the pans halfway through for even cooking. Do not brown. Transfer the tartlets to a wire rack to cool.

---

**TECHNIQUE** | Blind Baking Tartlet Shells

Tartlet molds are available in a variety of shapes and sizes. My favorite sizes for flavored tartlet shells are the 2¾-inch boat-shaped mold, the 1¾-inch brioche mold, the 1½-inch square mold, and the 1¾-inch round mold. I find that these hold just the right portion of prepared filling for a satisfying hors d'oeuvre. The nature of the fillings for the pastry dough tartlets—they're baked in the shell—is such that the tartlet molds must be slightly larger; use 2¾ x ⅜-inch and 2¼ x ¾-inch fluted tartlet molds.

Because the fillings for the tartlets are either cold or require different cooking times than the pastry, you should blind bake the shells, which simply means baking them unfilled. To do this, place a second mold on top of the chilled dough-lined mold. If you use this method, work in batches depending on the number of molds you have. Alternatively, place parchment paper cut out approximately 1 inch larger than the shape of the mold on top of the chilled unbaked dough, fill with dried beans or rice, and bake as directed. The unfilled tartlets can be stored, arranged in a single layer separated by parchment, in a rigid container for up to 1 week or in the freezer for up to 1 month.

## SESAME-ORANGE TARTLET SHELLS

**MAKES 3 DOZEN** | photograph on page 21

2 tablespoons unsalted butter, chilled, cut into
    small pieces, plus 2 tablespoons melted
    butter for buttering the molds
¼ cup black sesame seeds
¼ cup sesame seeds
1 cup all-purpose flour
½ teaspoon kosher salt
⅛ teaspoon freshly ground black pepper
1 teaspoon grated orange zest, finely chopped
Pinch of cayenne pepper
¼ cup ice water
1 large egg white, lightly beaten

**1** Brush 36 tartlet molds with the melted butter.
Sprinkle each with ¼ teaspoon of the black or the
plain sesame seeds (or a mixture of both), to
lightly coat the bottom and sides. Set aside.

**2** Place the flour, salt, pepper, orange zest,
cayenne, 2 tablespoons each black and plain sesame
seeds in the bowl of a food processor. Process for 5
seconds to combine. Add 2 tablespoons chilled butter. Process until the mixture resembles coarse meal,
about 10 seconds. With the machine running, add
the ice water through the feed tube and process just
until the dough is well combined, about 5 seconds;
the dough will not form a ball. (Add more ice
water, 1 teaspoon at a time, if the dough seems dry.)
Turn the dough out onto a lightly floured work surface. Using your hands, shape it into a 6-inch-wide
disk. Wrap in plastic wrap, and refrigerate for at
least 1 hour, or overnight.

**3** Preheat the oven to 350° F. with the rack in the
center. Transfer the dough to a lightly floured surface. Roll out the dough into a circle about ¹⁄₁₆ inch
thick and 13 inches in diameter. Sprinkle the
remaining sesame seeds onto the surface of the

dough. Roll over the dough once or twice with a
rolling pin to press the seeds into the dough. (If
the dough becomes hard to work with or sticky,
scoop it up with an offset spatula and transfer to a
parchment-lined baking sheet and refrigerate until
firm.) Turn 1 tartlet mold upside down near the
edge of the dough. Use a sharp knife to cut an outline around the mold. Press dough into the mold
and pinch off any excess dough. Brush the edges
of the dough with the egg white. Repeat with the
remaining molds. Use a fork to prick the bottom
and sides of the dough. Chill in the refrigerator.
Place a second mold on top of each dough-lined
mold and transfer to a rimmed baking sheet.

**4** Bake for 4 minutes, remove the top molds, and
continue baking until the dough is cooked through
but still white, 5 to 8 minutes. Cool the tartlets in
the molds on a wire rack for about 10 minutes.

## POPPY SEED TARTLET SHELLS

**MAKES 3 DOZEN** | photograph on page 21

*Lining the mold with poppy seeds gives these a wonderfully
coarse texture. For a smooth tartlet, skip this step and add all
of the poppy seeds in step 2.*

2 tablespoons unsalted butter, chilled, cut into
    small pieces, plus 2 tablespoons melted
    butter for buttering the molds
¼ cup poppy seeds
1 cup all-purpose flour
½ teaspoon kosher salt
⅛ teaspoon freshly ground black pepper
¼ cup ice water

**1** Brush 36 tartlet molds with the melted butter.
Lightly coat the bottom and sides of each mold
with ¼ teaspoon of the poppy seeds. Set aside.

CONTINUED ON FOLLOWING PAGE

**2** Place the flour, salt, pepper, and remaining 1 tablespoon of poppy seeds in the bowl of a food processor. Process for 5 seconds to combine. Add the 2 tablespoons chilled butter. Process until the mixture resembles coarse meal, about 10 seconds. With the machine running, add the ice water through the feed tube and process just until the dough is well combined, about 5 seconds; the dough will not form a ball. (Add more ice water, 1 teaspoon at a time, if the dough seems dry.) Turn the dough out onto a lightly floured work surface. Using your hands, shape the dough into a 6-inch-wide disk. Wrap the disk in plastic wrap and refrigerate for at least 1 hour, or overnight, to chill.

**3** Preheat the oven to 350°F. with the rack in the center. Transfer the dough to a lightly floured surface. Roll out the dough into a circle about ¹⁄₁₆ inch thick and 13 inches in diameter. (If the dough becomes hard to work with or sticky, scoop it up with an offset spatula and transfer to a parchment-lined baking sheet and refrigerate until firm.) Turn 1 tartlet mold upside down near the edge of the dough. Use a sharp knife to cut an outline around the mold. Use your fingers to press the dough into the mold, pressing firmly to adhere the poppy seeds onto the bottom. Pinch off any excess dough. Continue until all the molds are filled. Use a fork to lightly prick the bottom and sides of the dough. Chill in the refrigerator. Place a second mold on top of each dough-lined mold to maintain the shape while blind baking (see page 232). Transfer the molds to a rimmed baking sheet.

**4** Bake for 4 minutes, remove the top molds, and continue baking until the dough is cooked through but still white, 5 to 8 minutes. Remove the tartlets from the oven and cool them in the molds on a wire rack for about 10 minutes.

# PARMESAN-PEPPER TARTLET SHELLS

**MAKES 3 DOZEN** | photograph on page 21

*Fill these with Wild Mushroom filling (page 254) or the Beef Carpaccio (page 327) drizzled with a little herbed vinaigrette.*

> 2 tablespoons unsalted butter, chilled, cut into small pieces, plus 2 tablespoons melted butter for buttering the molds
> 1 cup all-purpose flour
> ½ teaspoon kosher salt
> 2 teaspoons freshly ground black pepper
> 1 ounce Parmesan cheese, grated on the small round holes of a box grater to yield ¼ cup
> ¼ cup ice water
> 1 large egg white, lightly beaten

**1** Brush 36 tartlet molds with the melted butter. Set aside.

**2** Place the flour, salt, pepper, and half of the Parmesan in the bowl of a food processor. Process for 5 seconds to combine. Add the 2 tablespoons chilled butter. Process until the mixture resembles coarse meal, about 10 seconds. With the machine running, add the ice water through the feed tube and process just until the dough is well combined, about 5 seconds; the dough will not form a ball. (Add more ice water, 1 teaspoon at a time, if the dough seems dry.) Turn the dough out onto a lightly floured work surface. Using your hands, shape the dough into a 6-inch-wide disk. Wrap the disk in plastic wrap and refrigerate for at least 1 hour, or overnight, to chill.

**3** Preheat the oven to 350°F. with the rack in the center. Transfer the dough to a lightly floured surface. Roll out the dough into a circle about ¹⁄₁₆ inch thick and 13 inches in diameter. (If the dough becomes hard to work with or sticky, scoop it up with an offset spatula and transfer to a parchment-lined baking sheet and refrigerate until firm.) Turn 1 tartlet mold upside down near the edge of the dough. Use a sharp knife to cut an outline around the mold. Use your fingers to press the dough into the mold. Pinch off any excess dough. Continue until all the molds are filled.

**4** Place the remaining Parmesan in a small bowl. Brush the edges of the dough with the egg white. Turn the mold with the dough upside down and dredge the edges in the cheese. Repeat for all the molds. Use a fork to lightly prick the bottom and sides of the dough. Chill in the refrigerator. Place a second mold on top of each dough-lined mold to maintain the shape while blind baking (see page 232). Transfer the molds to a rimmed baking sheet.

**5** Bake for 4 minutes, remove the top molds, and continue baking until the dough is cooked through but still white, 5 to 8 minutes. Remove the tartlets from the oven and cool them in the molds on a wire rack for about 10 minutes.

---

**TECHNIQUE** | Making Tortillas Soft

Tortillas that are slightly brittle can be softened by steaming; if they are so brittle that they border on crisp, they are past softening. To soften slightly brittle tortillas, wrap in a heavy kitchen towel, place in a steamer basket, and set in a large pan filled with 1 inch of water. Cover and steam over medium-high heat until warm throughout, 5 to 8 minutes.

---

# MINIATURE FLOUR TORTILLAS

**MAKES ABOUT 7 DOZEN** | photograph on page 16

*These are the perfect base to make ahead, since they are reheated when the fillings are added. For a quick version, large store-bought flour tortillas may also be cut into bite-size rounds with a 2-inch cookie cutter. The tortillas may be frozen in an airtight container up to 1 week. To warm, wrap the tortillas in aluminum foil and heat in a 250° F. oven for 25 to 30 minutes.*

3 cups all-purpose flour
1 teaspoon kosher salt
⅓ cup vegetable shortening
1 cup warm water (105° to 110° F.)

**1** In the bowl of a food processor, combine the flour and the salt. Pulse to combine. Add the shortening and pulse until the mixture resembles coarse meal. With the machine running, slowly add the warm water through the feed tube, and mix until the dough forms a ball, about 30 seconds. Transfer the dough to a lightly floured surface and knead until soft and not sticky. To form the tortillas, divide the dough into ¾-inch balls, about 84 pieces. Cover the pieces with a damp cloth.

**2** On a lightly floured surface, press the balls with the back of a spatula into flat circles, about 2½ inches in diameter. Keep all of the dough covered with a damp kitchen towel while working.

**3** Heat a cast-iron skillet over medium-high heat until very hot, 4 to 8 minutes. Do not add any oil. Working in batches, place the tortillas in the skillet and cook until the top buckles and becomes speckled with brown spots, about 30 seconds. Flip the tortillas and continue cooking until brown spots begin to appear, about 30 more seconds. Transfer the completed tortillas to a clean kitchen towel to keep warm. The tortillas may be used immediately or cooled and stored in an airtight container, refrigerated, for 2 days.

===

## CURRY CREPES

**MAKES 2 DOZEN 4-INCH CREPES** | photograph on page 19

*Serve these golden crepes with the Curried Vegetable Filling (page 298).*

2 large eggs

1 cup milk

2 tablespoons unsalted butter, melted

½ teaspoon ground turmeric

¼ teaspoon curry powder

1 cup all-purpose flour

¼ teaspoon kosher salt

**1** In a large bowl, whisk together the eggs, milk, ⅓ cup of water, and the butter. Whisk in the turmeric and the curry. Then whisk in the flour and the salt, whisking until all of the lumps have

disappeared. Transfer the batter to an airtight container and refrigerate for at least 30 minutes or up to 1 day.

**2** Heat a small nonstick crepe pan or skillet over medium-low heat. If the batter has begun to separate, gently stir it to bring it together again. Once the pan is thoroughly heated, place a scant 2 tablespoons of the crepe batter into the skillet and swirl the pan to evenly coat the bottom with the batter. (If the batter does not swirl easily, add 1 to 2 tablespoons of water to the batter to thin it slightly.) Cook the crepe until the top appears dry, about 1 minute. Using a small spatula, gently flip the crepe and cook until the bottom appears lightly browned and the crepe slides easily in the pan, about 1 minute more. Transfer the crepe to a paper towel and cover with another paper towel, continue with the remaining batter, and serve. The crepes may be made in advance and refrigerated or frozen (see Note, below).

---

**NOTE** | Preparing and Storing Crepes

===

Despite their wonderfully thin, delicate, and elegant appearance, the classic French pancakes known as crepes are deceptively simple to make. I make a savory crepe batter for hors d'oeuvres and a sweet one for dessert crepes. By adding ingredients such as turmeric and powdered green tea to the savory batter, you can easily make crepes with very pretty colors and intriguing flavors. To achieve whisper-thin crepes, use a very well seasoned cast-iron skillet or nonstick skillet.

Fresh-made crepes may be wrapped in aluminum foil and kept warm in the oven for 2 hours. Unlike blini (page 245), crepes contain no yeast, so they store well. You may make them 1 day in advance; stack the completely cooled crepes directly on top of each other, wrap the stack in plastic wrap, and refrigerate until the following day. To freeze crepes for up to 2 weeks, double-wrap them in plastic wrap.

Remove plastic wrap and warm refrigerated crepes for about 20 minutes in a 250° F. oven before serving. To reheat frozen crepes, remove the plastic wrap, wrap in aluminum foil, and place in a 250° F. oven for 30 minutes, or until warm throughout.

## GREEN TEA CREPES

**MAKES 2 DOZEN 4-INCH CREPES** | photograph on page 19

*Lightly scented and imbued with the color of green tea powder (see Sources, page 487), these crepes are delicious with Plum Wine Flank Steak (page 298).*

2 large eggs

1 cup milk

2 tablespoons unsalted butter, melted

½ teaspoon powdered green tea

1 cup all-purpose flour

½ teaspoon kosher salt

**1** In a large bowl, whisk together the eggs, milk, ⅓ cup of water, and the butter. Whisk in the green tea powder, flour, and salt, whisking until all of the lumps have disappeared. Transfer the batter to an airtight container and refrigerate for at least 30 minutes or up to 1 day.

**2** Heat a small nonstick crepe pan or skillet over medium-low heat. If the batter has begun to separate, gently stir it to bring it together again. Once the pan is thoroughly heated, place a scant 2 tablespoons of the batter into the skillet and swirl the pan to evenly coat the bottom. (If the batter does not swirl easily, add 1 to 2 tablespoons of water to the batter to thin it slightly.) Cook the crepe until the top appears dry, about 1 minute. Using a small spatula, gently flip the crepe and cook until the bottom appears lightly browned and the crepe slides easily in the pan, about 1 minute more. Transfer the crepe to a paper towel and cover with another paper towel, continue with the remaining batter, and serve. The crepes may be made in advance and refrigerated or frozen (see page 236).

## BLUE CORN CREPES

**MAKES 2 DOZEN 4-INCH CREPES** | photograph on page 19

*These are delicious wrapped around Black Bean Dip (page 386), Tropical Fruit Salsa (page 400), Mixed Tomato Salsa (page 400), Guacamole (page 399), or Scallop Ceviche with Avocado Puree (page 414).*

2 large eggs

1 cup milk

2 tablespoons unsalted butter, melted

⅔ cup blue cornmeal

⅔ cup all-purpose flour

½ teaspoon kosher salt

**1** In a large bowl, whisk together the eggs, milk, ⅓ cup of water, and the butter. Whisk in the cornmeal, flour, and salt, whisking until all of the lumps have disappeared. Transfer the batter to an airtight container and refrigerate for at least 30 minutes or up to 1 day.

**2** Heat a small nonstick crepe pan or skillet over medium-low heat. If the batter has begun to separate, gently stir it to bring it together again. Once the pan is thoroughly heated, place a scant 2 tablespoons of the batter into the skillet and swirl the pan to evenly coat the bottom. (If the batter does not swirl easily, add 1 to 2 tablespoons of water to the batter to thin it slightly.) Cook the crepe until the top appears dry, about 1 minute. Using a small spatula, gently flip the crepe and cook until the bottom appears lightly browned and the crepe slides easily in the pan, about 1 minute more. Transfer the crepe to a paper towel and cover with another paper towel, continue with the remaining batter, and serve. The crepes may be made in advance and refrigerated or frozen (see page 236).

## PAIN DE MIE

**MAKES 2 LOAVES** | photograph on page 93

12 tablespoons (1½ sticks) unsalted butter, room
  temperature, cut into small pieces, plus
  more for preparing the pans
3 ¼-ounce packages active dry yeast
  (2 tablespoons)
½ cup warm water (110° F.)
5 teaspoons kosher salt
4 cups warm milk
10 cups all-purpose flour

**1** Prepare 2 pullman pans, 16 × 3½ × 3½ inches,
by buttering the underside of the lid as well as the
bottom and the sides, and set aside. In 2 separate
medium bowls, dissolve the yeast in the warm
water and dissolve the salt in the warm milk.

**2** Place the yeast mixture and the milk into a
large dough bowl, or the bowl of an electric mixer
with a dough hook. Add the flour, 2 to 3 cups at a
time, mixing with a wooden spoon or dough hook
at low speed until a sticky dough is formed, about
8 cups of flour total. Turn the dough out onto a
floured board and knead as you add the remaining
2 cups of flour. Continue kneading until all of the
flour has been incorporated and the dough is
somewhat smooth. Add the butter, 1 tablespoon at
a time, kneading until the dough is smooth, 10 to
15 minutes. The dough will go through a very
sticky stage, and after kneading it will remain
slightly sticky.

**3** Place the dough in a large bowl, cover with
plastic wrap or a dampened towel, and let it rise
until almost tripled in bulk, 2 to 3 hours. Punch it
down, knead for several minutes, and let rise a second time until doubled in bulk, about 1 more hour.
Punch the dough down again and turn it out on a
floured board. Divide the dough in half. Flatten the
dough into 2 rectangles the length of the pans, and

**NOTE** | Pain de Mie

Pain de Mie, also referred to as a pullman
loaf, is a classic French white bread with a
fine yet compact texture. It is an indispensable base for making perfectly shaped,
uniform hors d'oeuvres since it is easy to
slice evenly. Pain de mie is baked in a rectangular pan, often referred to as a pullman pan, with a sliding lid that is closed
while the bread bakes, compressing the
dough into a perfect rectangle and making the texture of the bread very dense.
The pan measures 16 × 3½ × 3½ inches. If
you can't find this pan, use a loaf pan that
has approximately the same dimensions.
Improvise for the lid by placing a baking
sheet over the dough, and place at least 6
pounds of ovenproof weight, such as a
cast-iron skillet, on top. Pain de mie
freezes beautifully, double-wrapped in
plastic wrap, for 3 weeks.

a few inches wider. Fold the dough into thirds,
lengthwise, so that the dough remains the length
of the pan. Place the dough in the prepared pans,
seam-side down. Press the dough carefully into the
corners of the pans, breaking all air bubbles. Cover
the pans with the sliding tops, if you are using the
traditional pullman pans, or with buttered baking
sheets and a heavy weight, and let rise until the
dough fills two-thirds of the pan, about 30 minutes.

**4** After 15 minutes, heat the oven to 450° F.
Bake the loaves for 30 to 40 minutes. Reduce the
temperature to 375° F. and continue baking 15 to
20 minutes more, or until the bread has risen to

the top of the pan, the crust is golden brown, and the sides have shrunk away from the pan. Turn the bread out onto a cooling rack. The loaf should sound hollow when tapped on the bottom. If it makes a dull thud when tapped, return the pans to the oven and bake for 5 to 10 minutes more. Turn the bread out onto racks to cool completely, and wrap very well when cool. The bread slices best one day after baking.

## PIZZA DOUGH

**MAKES ENOUGH FOR THREE 10-INCH ROBIOLA PIZZAS OR FOUR 14-INCH OVAL PIZZAS** | photographs on pages 31 and 32

1 cup warm water (110° F.)

¼ teaspoon sugar

1 ¼-ounce package active dry yeast
(2 teaspoons)

2¾ to 3¼ cups all-purpose flour

1½ teaspoons kosher salt

1½ tablespoons extra-virgin olive oil, plus more for oiling the bowl

**1** Pour the warm water into a small bowl. Add the sugar and sprinkle in the yeast. Using a fork, stir the mixture until the yeast has dissolved and the water has turned putty colored. Let the yeast stand until it becomes creamy and foamy, about 5 minutes.

**2** In the bowl of a food processor, combine 2¾ cups flour and the salt, pulsing 3 to 4 times. Add the yeast mixture and 1½ tablespoons of olive oil. Pulse until the dough comes together, adding more flour as needed until the dough is smooth, not tacky, when pinched between two fingers. Transfer to a clean surface. Knead the dough 4 or 5 turns and shape it into a ball.

**3** Brush the inside of a medium bowl with olive oil, and place the dough in the bowl, smooth-side

**NOTE** | Pizza Dough

The pizza dough used to make Robiola Pizza (page 309) and the pizzas on pages 253, 254 can be made in advance and refrigerated for up to 12 hours or frozen for up to 3 weeks. It is a good idea to divide the dough into 3 or 4 sections, depending on how you plan to use it later.

To prepare the dough in advance, follow the recipe through step 3, tightly cover with plastic wrap, and refrigerate. When ready to use, remove the plastic wrap, punch the dough down with your fists, and let it sit at room temperature until soft and pliable, about 30 minutes.

To freeze the dough, punch it down after the first rise in step 3. Fold it back onto itself 4 or 5 times as instructed. Divide the dough and roll it out to the desired-size rounds. Stack the rounds, separated by parchment paper, then double-wrap the stack tightly in plastic wrap and freeze. To use, unwrap the frozen dough and thaw slightly until the rounds are easily separated. Place each round in a lightly oiled bowl and thaw at room temperature for 3 to 3½ hours, until each is completely thawed and the dough has doubled in size. Proceed as in step 4 of the recipe.

up. Cover tightly with plastic wrap, and place in a warm spot until doubled in size, about 40 minutes. Remove the plastic wrap, and push your fist into the center of the dough to punch it down. Working

CONTINUED ON FOLLOWING PAGE

in the bowl, fold the dough back onto itself 4 or 5 times. Turn the dough over, folded-side down, cover with plastic wrap, and return to the warm spot to rise again until the dough has doubled in size, about 30 minutes.

**4** Punch down the dough again, and transfer it to a clean surface. Using a bench scraper or a sharp knife, divide the dough evenly into the number of pieces specified in the recipe, kneading each piece 4 or 5 times. Use the dough as directed.

## EMPANADA DOUGH

**MAKES ENOUGH FOR 4 DOZEN** | photograph on page 79

*The pastry packages known as empanadas (Spanish for "baked in pastry") are the classic snacks of South America. The dough may be kept for 1 day in the refrigerator, tightly wrapped in plastic wrap. For longer storage, double-wrap the dough and freeze it for 4 weeks. To thaw, leave it at room temperature until soft enough to roll out, about 1 ½ hours.*

3 ¾ cups all-purpose flour

¾ teaspoon kosher salt

1 tablespoon sugar

6 tablespoons vegetable shortening

12 tablespoons (1 ½ sticks) unsalted butter, chilled, cut into small pieces

½ cup plus 2 tablespoons ice water

In the bowl of a food processor, combine the flour, salt, and sugar. Add the vegetable shortening and the butter, and pulse until the mixture resembles coarse meal. With the machine running, slowly add the water through the feed tube, and pulse until a ball of dough forms. Transfer the dough to a piece of plastic wrap. Use your hands to pat the dough into a 4-inch disk. Wrap the dough with plastic wrap and refrigerate for 1 hour, or overnight, until completely chilled.

## PUFF PASTRY

**MAKES 2 POUNDS, 11 OUNCES OF DOUGH, ENOUGH FOR 40 BREADSTICKS** | photograph on page 147

*Although it is much quicker to make than classic puff pastry, this version still creates many delicate, flaky layers of pastry.*

3 ¾ cups all-purpose flour

1 ½ teaspoons kosher salt

1 pound (4 sticks) unsalted butter, chilled

1 cup ice water

**1** Combine the flour and the salt in a large, chilled stainless-steel bowl. Slice the butter into paper-thin pieces. Using a pastry blender, or working with your fingertips, cut the butter into the flour until the butter is the size of peas, about ½ inch in diameter. (Do not use a food processor.)

**2** Using a fork, stir in the water gradually, pressing the dough together with your hands as it becomes damp. Turn the dough out onto a well-floured board and roll it into a rough rectangle with a short side facing you. The dough will be very crumbly. Fold the dough into thirds, and turn it a quarter turn to the right. Roll the folded dough into a large rectangle, 9 × 16 inches, and fold into thirds again. This completes the first double turn. Brush away any excess flour. Wrap the dough in plastic wrap and chill for 30 minutes.

**3** Repeat rolling and folding 2 more times, chilling for 30 minutes after each double turn. With each turn the dough will become smoother and easier to handle. Roll out and bake as instructed in the recipe. The dough can be stored, wrapped well in plastic wrap, in the refrigerator for up to 2 days, or frozen for up to 3 months. To thaw, place in the refrigerator for 24 hours.

Making good choux pastry is easy once you become familiar with the way that the dough should look and feel. Properly prepared pastry is slightly shiny and is somewhat sticky to the touch. On humid days, you may need to reduce the number of eggs in order to achieve the right consistency. To test the pastry, run a wooden spoon down the middle of the dough; it should form a trough that quickly closes in on itself. The pastry should also form a "hook" when lifted with a wooden spoon.

## SEASONED PÂTE À CHOUX PUFFS

**MAKES 6½ TO 7 DOZEN** | photograph on page 15

*Also known as choux pastry, this classic pastry from the French repertoire is unlike other pastry doughs. Eggs are beaten into a flour and butter mixture until a thick, slightly sticky paste is formed. The dough is piped out into little mounds that puff up into beautiful, domed pastries when baked.*

8 tablespoons (1 stick) unsalted butter, cut into small pieces

½ teaspoon kosher salt

1 cup all-purpose flour

5 large eggs

1 teaspoon poppy seeds

1 teaspoon sesame seeds

1 teaspoon roughly chopped fresh rosemary

**1** Preheat the oven to 425°F. with 2 racks. Line 2 12 × 17-inch baking sheets with parchment paper. Set aside. Place 1 cup of water, the butter, and the salt in a small heavy-based saucepan. Bring to a boil over medium-high heat. When the mixture boils,

immediately remove the saucepan from the heat. Using a wooden spoon, add the flour all at once and stir until smooth. Return the saucepan to the burner over high heat and stir the mixture until it becomes a smooth mass and a thin film forms on the bottom of the pan, 1 to 1½ minutes. (This indicates that the flour is cooked.) Transfer the mixture to a bowl and allow to cool slightly, about 5 minutes.

**2** Add 4 of the eggs one at a time, beating well after each addition, until the batter becomes smooth again. (Once the eggs have been added, the batter can remain covered at room temperature for up to 2 hours.)

**3** In a small bowl, whisk the remaining egg with 1 teaspoon water and set aside. Transfer the batter to a pastry bag fitted only with a coupler (no tip or coupler is needed as long as the opening of the pastry bag is only ½ inch). Holding the tip of the bag about 1 inch above the baking sheet, pipe the dough onto the prepared pans, forming mounds 1 inch in diameter and ½ inch high, placing each mound about 1 inch apart. (About 40 should fit on each baking sheet.) Use water-dampened fingers to round off the top of each puff. Using a pastry brush, lightly brush the choux mounds with the egg wash. Sprinkle the choux alternately with the poppy seeds, sesame seeds, and rosemary.

**4** Bake the choux for 12 minutes. Reduce the heat to 375°F. Remove one baking sheet at a time from the oven and carefully pierce the side of each puff with a wooden or metal skewer to let any steam and moisture escape. Return quickly to the oven, rotating the direction of the baking sheet, and repeat with the second baking sheet. Bake until the puffs are golden and just beginning to brown, 10 to 15 minutes more. The puffs should be firm on the outside and not sticky or doughy on the inside. Cool the puffs on a wire rack. The puffs can be frozen in a rigid airtight container for up to 3 weeks.

## TOASTED BRIOCHE ROUNDS

**MAKES 3 DOZEN** | photograph on page 14

*Brioche is available in several different sizes, from small buns to large round and rectangular loaves. While a 1-pound loaf is the easiest to work with in this recipe, it doesn't matter what shape or size you purchase, so long as the total weight is 1 pound. Challah bread is a good substitute if brioche is unavailable.*

1 1-pound loaf of brioche, cut into ¾-inch-thick slices

2 tablespoons unsalted butter

Using a 1½-inch round cookie cutter, cut out 36 rounds of brioche from the slices. Place 1 tablespoon of the butter in a 12-inch skillet. Melt the butter over medium heat. Add half of the rounds and cook until golden, turning once, 1 to 2 minutes per side. Repeat with the remaining butter and rounds. Let them cool on a wire rack or paper towel. The brioche rounds may be stored in an airtight container at room temperature for up to 2 days.

## PITA CUPS

**MAKES 4 DOZEN** | photograph on page 15

*Miniature pita breads are generally available in packages of 24. Look for them in the deli section of your grocery store.*

24 miniature pita breads

1 tablespoon olive oil

Slice the pitas in half horizontally along their natural seam. Heat 1½ teaspoons of the oil in a medium skillet over medium heat until warm. Working in batches of 10 to 12, place the pita halves, cut-side down, in the pan. Cook, turning once, until golden and crisp, 5 to 7 minutes. Transfer the halves to a paper towel to cool. Repeat with the remaining pita halves, adding 1½ teaspoons oil to the pan. The pita halves may be stored in an airtight container at room temperature for up to 2 days. To recrisp, warm the pitas in a 300° F. oven for 5 minutes.

## INDIAN-SPICED PITA TOASTS

**MAKES 5 DOZEN** | photograph on page 20

*Use either whole-wheat or white pita bread to make these spicy triangles. Although it resembles the seeds of onions, the spice called black onion seed (see Sources, page 487) actually comes from the nigella plant. To make plain pita toasts, simply omit the spices.*

10 pieces (1 1½-pound package) pita bread

3 tablespoons extra-virgin olive oil

1 tablespoon whole anise seed, toasted and ground (see page 386)

2½ teaspoons black onion seed

Kosher salt

**1** Heat the oven to 400° F. Place 2 wire cooling racks on 2 baking sheets. Liberally brush the top of each pita bread with olive oil, then sprinkle each with ¼ teaspoon each of the anise seed, the black onion seed, and the salt. Place 5 pitas on each rack. Bake until softened and just starting to color, 4 to 6 minutes. (Do not allow the pitas to turn golden brown or they will be too crispy to cut.)

**2** Transfer immediately to a cutting board and cut each pita, while warm, into 6 even wedges. The pita toasts may be kept in an airtight container at room temperature for up to 2 days.

## GOLDEN CROUSTADES

**MAKES 2 DOZEN** | photograph on page 15

*There is virtually no limit to the uses for these golden containers. Use the trimmed crusts to make fresh bread crumbs (see page 321). Croustades may be made 1 day in advance and kept in an airtight container at room temperature, or kept in the freezer for up to 3 weeks.*

1 1-pound loaf of very thinly sliced white
      sandwich bread, crusts trimmed to make
      2½-inch squares
3 tablespoons unsalted butter, melted

Preheat the oven to 375° F. with the rack in the center. Using a pastry brush, lightly coat both sides of the bread squares with the melted butter. Using your fingers, press 1 bread square into each opening of a 24-hole miniature muffin tin, one with openings measuring 2 inches across the top and 1 inch deep. Bake until the edges of the bread are golden brown, 5 to 8 minutes.

## TOASTED CORN CUPS

**MAKES 2 DOZEN** | photograph on page 18

*White corn tortillas, which are the softest variety, are the easiest to work into muffin tins. If you use tortillas made from yellow corn, be sure that the ones you choose are very soft and pliable. Slightly brittle tortillas may be steamed to soften them (see page 235). The corn cups may be made several days ahead and kept in an airtight container at room temperature, or frozen for up to 3 weeks. Frozen corn cups thaw very quickly. To crisp thawed cups, arrange them in a single layer on a baking sheet and warm in a 250° F. oven for 3 to 5 minutes.*

12 6-inch (1 9½-ounce package) white corn
      tortillas
3 tablespoons canola or corn oil

**1** Preheat the oven to 350° F.

**2** Heat a large cast-iron skillet over medium-high heat. Place a tortilla in the skillet and cook for 20 seconds. Flip the tortilla and warm the other side, until warm to the touch, about 15 seconds.

**3** Transfer the tortilla to a work surface and brush both sides of the tortilla with the canola oil. Use a 2½-inch round cookie cutter to cut out 2 circles from each tortilla. Press each round into an opening of a 24-hole mini muffin tin. Repeat until all of the openings are filled. Bake until the cups are crisp and just beginning to color, 5 to 10 minutes. Remove the cups from the tin and transfer to a wire rack to cool.

## SIMPLE CROSTINI

**MAKES 5 DOZEN** | photograph on page 14

*The broiling time for these varies from oven to oven; watch them carefully as they darken. The crostini can also be placed directly on an outdoor grill or a grill pan. Brush lightly with olive oil rather than butter. Grill them on both sides until light grill marks appear, 1 to 3 minutes.*

1 large (8-ounce) baguette, about 26 inches
      long, sliced on the diagonal in ¼- to ⅓-
      inch-thick slices
4 to 6 tablespoons unsalted butter, at room
      temperature

**1** Place the rack in the upper third of the oven and turn on the broiler. Spread both sides of each slice of bread lightly with the butter.

**2** Arrange the slices on 2 baking sheets. Broil, 1 baking sheet at time, for 1½ to 2 minutes; turn the slices over and toast until golden, about 1 minute more. Transfer to a rack to cool. The crostini may be made up to 2 days ahead and kept in an airtight container at room temperature.

## CLASSIC TOAST POINTS

**MAKES 2 DOZEN** | photograph on page 14

*Far superior to packaged toasts of any kind, this very versatile base is wonderful for topping with caviar and crème fraîche (page 381) or spread with any of the compound butters (pages 391–394) for the simplest hors d'oeuvres. For more assertive accompaniments, such as the Fruit and Vegetable Salsas (pages 400–401), Toasted Pepita Dip (page 388), White Bean and Mustard Greens Dip (page 389), and Roasted Red Pepper and Eggplant Dip (page 390), grill the bread.*

12 thin slices Pain de Mie (page 238) or thin white sandwich bread, crusts removed

**1** Cut each bread slice in half on the diagonal.

**2** To toast: Heat the oven to 300°F. Arrange the triangles on a baking sheet. Bake, turning once, until the triangles are dry and slightly toasted, 5 to 7 minutes per side. Transfer to a wire rack to cool.

**3** To grill: Heat a grill pan or outdoor grill over medium-high heat until hot. Working in batches, grill the triangles until golden and slight grill marks show, 3 to 5 minutes per side. Transfer to a wire rack to cool.

**4** The toast points can be stored in an airtight container in the refrigerator for up to 1 week or frozen for up to 6 months.

## TOASTED BREADBOXES

**MAKES 4 DOZEN** | photograph on page 14

*A firm-textured, dense loaf of bread is best to make these crisp cubes. Cooking time will vary with the type of bread used. Breadboxes taste best the day they are made.*

1 1½-pound loaf of firm white bread, unsliced
8 tablespoons (1 stick) unsalted butter, melted

**1** Preheat the oven to 375°F. Slice the bread into 1-inch-thick slices. Trim the crusts. Cut the slices into 1-inch squares. Using a small sharp paring knife, cut a ¾-inch-deep square into the top of each breadbox, leaving a ¼-inch border around the edge and the bottom.

**2** Arrange the breadboxes on a baking sheet. Brush the bread with the butter, lightly coating each side. Bake until the boxes are golden brown, 20 to 30 minutes, turning the boxes on their sides after about 15 minutes so they will bake evenly. Transfer to a paper towel to cool. Once cool, the breadboxes may be kept in an airtight container at room temperature for 1 to 2 days.

## GRILLED STARS

**MAKES 2 DOZEN** | photograph on page 14

*Thinly sliced white sandwich bread may be cut with any shape 2-inch-wide cookie cutter and grilled to create a sturdy serving base. Simple geometric shapes hold toppings best and are easiest to pick up and to eat.*

12 thin slices Pain de Mie (page 238) or thin white sandwich bread, crusts removed

Using a star-shaped cookie cutter, cut out 2 stars from each slice of bread. Heat a grill pan or outdoor grill over medium-high heat until hot. Working in batches, grill the stars until golden and slight grill marks show, 3 to 5 minutes per side depending on the heat. Transfer to a wire rack to cool. Grilled stars can be stored in an airtight container at room temperature for 2 to 3 days.

## BUCKWHEAT BLINI

**MAKES 8 DOZEN** | photograph on page 162

*Buckwheat flour is available in gourmet food stores or by mail order (see Sources, page 487). Plan to serve 3 to 4 blini to each of your guests, since the pancakes are bite-size.*

1 ¼-ounce package active dry yeast
    (2 teaspoons)
1 ½ cups warm water (110°F.)
1 ½ cups all-purpose flour
1 ½ cups buckwheat flour
3 large eggs, separated
5 tablespoons unsalted butter, melted
1 teaspoon kosher salt
1 teaspoon sugar
1 ½ cups warm milk

**1** In a large bowl, combine the yeast and the warm water. Set the bowl in a warm place for the yeast to proof until it is creamy and foamy, about 10 minutes.

**2** Slowly add the all-purpose flour to the yeast. Whisk to combine and remove any lumps. Cover the bowl with a damp towel and set it in a warm place to rise slightly and get puffy, about 1 hour.

**3** In a separate medium bowl, combine the buckwheat flour, egg yolks, 4 tablespoons of the butter, the salt, sugar, and milk. Whisk to combine and remove lumps. Use a spatula to stir the buckwheat mixture into the risen flour-yeast mixture. Combine thoroughly. Cover with the damp towel and set in a warm place to rise by about half, about 1 hour; the mixture will be bubbly.

**4** Beat the egg whites with a whisk until they are stiff but not dry. Fold the egg whites gently into the batter.

**5** Heat a heavy cast-iron skillet over medium heat. Brush the pan with the remaining butter and drop 1 tablespoon of the batter into the pan at a time. If your pan is large enough to hold more than 1 without crowding, cook several at a time. Cook until the bottom turns golden and bubbles begin to appear on the top, about 45 seconds. Flip and cook until golden and cooked through, about 30 seconds more. Repeat with the remaining batter. The blini may be stacked on a baking sheet, covered with plastic wrap, and kept at room temperature for 2 to 3 hours.

---

**NOTE** | Blini

Blini, the classic Russian buckwheat pancakes, are yeast-risen, which gives them a wonderful fluffy texture and complex flavor. Traditionally served with sour cream and caviar or smoked salmon, the silver-dollar-size pancakes make perfect bases for hors d'oeuvres. Blini may be made 1 day in advance and stored in an airtight container with each layer separated by parchment paper. They do not freeze well. To reheat, arrange blini in a single layer on a baking sheet, cover with aluminum foil, and warm them in a 300°F. oven for 5 to 7 minutes.

## POTATO WAFERS

**MAKES ABOUT 10 DOZEN** | photograph on page 26

*These wafers are very delicate—they can be shaped into any simple design using a handmade stencil. To make a stencil, cut a 3 × 2-inch rectangle from a plastic container lid or a plastic coffee can lid. Then cut out a fish, or any shape, to fit. I use a Silpat nonstick baking mat (see Sources, page 486) for ease and efficiency.*

1 8-ounce Idaho baking potato
4 tablespoons unsalted butter, cut into 6 pieces,
    at room temperature
¼ cup egg whites (about 2 large)
Kosher salt

**1** Peel the potato and cut it into 2-inch pieces. Place in a medium pot of water and bring to a boil. Cook the potatoes until fork-tender, 8 to 10 minutes. Drain thoroughly. Pass the potatoes through a food mill fitted with the medium disk. Place the warm potatoes in a medium bowl and using a rubber spatula, stir in the butter until fully incorporated. Whisk in the egg whites until a smooth batter forms. Salt to taste. Allow the batter to rest at room temperature, loosely covered, for at least 20 minutes and no more than 2 hours.

**2** Preheat the oven to 325°F. with a rack in the center. Place the stencil on a Silpat nonstick baking mat or directly on a baking sheet. Using a small offset spatula, place ½ teaspoon of the batter in the center of the stencil and gently smooth the batter into the stencil shape. Carefully lift the stencil and wipe clean. Repeat the process until the cookie sheet is full. Bake the wafers, rotating the pan during cooking for even browning, until golden, 12 to 16 minutes. Using a small spatula, transfer the wafers to a wire rack to cool. Repeat with remaining batter. The potato wafers may be kept for 24 hours in an airtight container at room temperature.

## GINGER-JALAPEÑO RICE CAKES

**MAKES 2 DOZEN** | photograph on page 44

*Make the rice mixture 1 day in advance and refrigerate it so that it is well chilled. These cakes taste delicious topped with Grilled Swordfish (page 274).*

½ cup long-grain white rice
1 small jalapeño pepper, seeds and ribs removed,
    minced
1 large egg
1 tablespoon freshly grated ginger
¼ cup all-purpose flour
½ teaspoon baking powder
1 teaspoon kosher salt
3 tablespoons olive oil

**1** Bring 1 cup of salted water to a boil in a medium saucepan. Stir in the rice, reduce to a simmer over low heat, cover, and cook until the water is absorbed, 15 to 20 minutes. Transfer the cooked rice to a large bowl and allow to cool slightly.

**2** In a small bowl, whisk together the jalapeño pepper, egg, and ginger. Set aside. In a separate bowl, combine the flour, baking powder, and salt. Add the egg mixture to the rice. Stir in the flour mixture. The mixture will be sticky.

**3** Lightly brush a 12 × 17-inch rimmed baking sheet with olive oil. Transfer the rice mixture to the baking sheet. Moisten your fingers with water and spread the mixture out evenly into a thin, compact layer, about ¼ inch thick and 10 inches square. Brush a piece of parchment or wax paper with olive oil. Cover the rice mixture with the parchment paper, oil-side down, pressing firmly to even out the layer. Cover with plastic wrap and refrigerate for at least 1 hour, or up to 24 hours, until firm.

**4** Heat 1 tablespoon of the olive oil in a large skillet over medium heat for 1 to 2 minutes. Working in batches of 10, slip a spatula under the chilled mixture and break off 1½- to 2-inch pieces of the rice mixture; the edges should be rough. Slip them one at a time into the skillet. Cook the rice cakes until golden brown, 3 to 4 minutes on each side. Transfer to paper towels. Repeat until all the rice mixture is used, adding ½ to 1 tablespoon of oil to the pan for each batch. The rice cakes may be stored in an airtight container in the refrigerator for up to 1 day. Reheat refrigerated rice cakes on a baking sheet in a 400° F. oven until warm, about 5 minutes.

## HOMEMADE POTATO CHIPS

**MAKES 14 DOZEN** | photograph on page 15

*There are several secrets to making crispy homemade chips. The first is to use plenty of oil; peanut oil works the best for these chips. The second secret is frying in small batches, which prevents the oil temperature from dropping too low, and frying at 340° F.—20 degrees lower than usually recommended— which allows the chips to cook through without burning. A third secret is to slice the potatoes on a mandoline. This wonderful tool makes it much easier to create uniform potato slices, which will fry evenly.*

   2 large (about 1¼ pounds) Idaho baking
       potatoes, peeled
   2 quarts peanut oil, for frying
   Kosher salt

**1** Slice the potatoes into ¹⁄₁₆-inch-thick slices using a mandoline. Transfer the potato slices to a bowl of cool water to prevent discoloration.

**2** Heat the oil in a shallow 10- to 12-inch skillet until a frying thermometer registers 340° F. Place about 16 potato slices on a clean kitchen towel or paper towel and thoroughly pat dry. Carefully slip the potato slices into the oil. (Fry all of the slices in these small batches to ensure the oil temperature remains close to 340° F.) Use tongs or a slotted spoon to move the slices in the oil. Fry until just

golden, 2 to 3 minutes. Transfer to paper towels to drain, and sprinkle with salt. Repeat until all the potato slices are fried. Let cool. The chips may be made in advance and kept in an airtight container at room temperature for up to 4 days. In very humid weather, the chips may absorb moisture and soften. To recrisp them, heat in a warm oven. Under these conditions, they are best made just 1 day in advance.

## APPLE CHIPS

**MAKES 3 DOZEN** | photograph on page 173

*Granny Smith and Ida Red apples are best for making chips large enough for dipping.*

   1 cup sugar
   1 Granny Smith or Ida Red apple, peel on
   1 tablespoon vegetable oil

**1** Preheat the oven to 175° F. In a medium saucepan over medium heat, bring the sugar and 1 cup of water to a simmer, stirring occasionally. Meanwhile, slice the apples ¹⁄₁₆ inch thick using a mandoline. Slice 1 side of the apple to the core, turn, and slice the other side; discard the core.

**2** When the sugar is completely dissolved, place 5 or 6 slices of the apple into the sugar syrup and simmer for 20 seconds. Remove with a slotted spoon and drain the slices on a wire rack. Continue until all the apple slices are completed.

**3** Lightly brush 2 baking sheets with the vegetable oil and arrange the apple slices in a single layer. Bake until the apples are crisp, 2 to 2½ hours. The apple chips will keep in an airtight container at room temperature for up to 2 days.

## FLOUR TORTILLA CHIPS

**MAKES 4 DOZEN** | photograph on page 173

*These are a nice low-fat alternative to corn chips. Specialty food and gourmet stores often carry flour tortillas flavored with ingredients such as spinach and tomato (see Sources, page 487).*

12 6- to 8-inch round flour tortillas

Preheat the oven to 375° F. Cut the tortillas into 1-inch-wide strips; discard the leftover rounded end pieces. Alternatively, cut the tortillas into 8 wedges as in a pizza. Place the prepared tortillas on a baking sheet and bake until crisp, 5 to 7 minutes.

## FRIED LOTUS CHIPS

**MAKES ABOUT 3 DOZEN** | photograph on page 173

*These crisp, light chips, which taste faintly of coconut, can be made only with preboiled lotus root, which is available in the refrigerated section of most Asian markets (see Sources, page 487).*

2 quarts peanut oil, for frying
1 5¼-ounce piece of packaged boiled lotus root
Kosher salt

In a narrow, deep pan or an electric fryer, heat the oil until it registers 360° F. on a frying thermometer. Drain the liquid from the lotus root package. Thinly slice the lotus root on a mandoline into ⅛-inch- to 1/16-inch-thick pieces. Place up to 6 slices of lotus root at a time into the oil and fry until light golden, about 3 minutes. Transfer the lotus root to a paper towel to drain, and lightly sprinkle with the salt. Repeat with the remaining lotus root. The chips may be stored in an airtight container at room temperature for up to 3 days. Recrisp them in a warm oven, if necessary.

## TARO CHIPS

**MAKES ABOUT 6 DOZEN** | photograph on page 173

*The starchy tuber known as taro is a staple throughout the Pacific Islands; these days it is also gaining popularity all over the Pacific rim. Here I bake it in the oven to make crisp chips.*

1 12-ounce taro root
1 tablespoon plus ½ teaspoon olive oil
Kosher salt

Preheat the oven to 350° F. Peel the taro root and thinly slice it into 1/16-inch-thick slices using a mandoline. Lightly brush two 12 × 17-inch baking sheets with olive oil and spread the chips onto the tray. Brush the tops of the chips with olive oil and bake until crisp, 14 to 16 minutes. Transfer the chips to a paper towel to cool and sprinkle with salt.

## CRISPY WONTONS

**MAKES ABOUT 7 DOZEN** | photograph on page 173

*Cut any shape you like out of the wonton wrappers. I prefer rectangles because they make dips and salsas easy to scoop up.*

2 quarts peanut oil, for frying
1 12-ounce package wonton wrappers

In a narrow, deep pan or an electric fryer, heat the oil until it registers 360° F. on a frying thermometer. Cut the wonton wrappers in half. Working in batches, carefully place 2 to 3 wontons in the heated oil; don't crowd the wontons, as they need space to expand. Fry until the wontons become large, bubbly, and golden, about 30 seconds. Transfer the wontons to a paper towel to drain. Repeat with the remaining wontons. The wontons may be stored in an airtight container at room temperature for up to 3 days. Recrisp in a warm oven, if necessary.

## SWEET POTATO GAUFRETTES

**MAKES ABOUT 4 DOZEN** | photographs on pages 15 and 34

These pretty latticed wafers make excellent bases for the Maple-Glazed Duck Breast (page 275), or they make an excellent dipper for the Buttermilk Peppercorn Dip (page 389). Because sweet potatoes have a higher sugar content than white potatoes, the temperature of the frying oil must be lower to achieve a crispy chip without burning. If the oil becomes too hot, turn off the heat, drop a cube of bread into the skillet, allow it to brown, remove, turn the heat on, and proceed with the recipe. You must use a French mandoline (see Sources, page 486) to make these.

1 quart peanut oil, for frying
1 large sweet potato, peeled
Kosher salt

Heat the oil in a medium heavy skillet until it reaches 300°F. to 320°F. on a frying thermometer. Meanwhile, using a French mandoline adjusted to the zigzag blade, cut the potato into ⅛-inch-thick slices, creating the waffle pattern by turning the potato ¼ turn after each slice. Place 6 to 8 chips at a time in the hot oil and fry until crisp, 2 to 3 minutes per side. Transfer with a slotted spoon to drain on paper towels. Sprinkle with salt. The chips may be stored in an airtight container at room temperature for up to 3 days. Recrisp them in a warm oven, if necessary.

## TOSTONES

**MAKES 4 DOZEN** | photograph on page 42

Tostones are savory chips made from plantains. Often described as cooking bananas, plantains are prepared differently in Latin American countries depending on their state of ripeness. When ripe, they are used in snacks and desserts. When green, they have a more starchy quality and are cooked much as potatoes are cooked in North America. Double-frying the plantain chips cooks them all the way through while also making them crispy.

1 quart peanut oil, for frying
1½ pounds green plantains
Kosher salt

**1** Heat the oil in a medium heavy skillet or an electric fryer until a frying thermometer registers 360°F. Meanwhile, peel and slice the plantains crosswise into ¼-inch-thick pieces. Working in batches of 8, gently slip the plantains into the hot oil. Fry until just golden, 1 to 2 minutes. Transfer the 8 plantain pieces to paper towels to drain.

**2** While the plantains are still warm, use the flat side of a meat pounder or a metal spatula to lightly press down on each plantain just until the edges split slightly; do not smash them flat.

**3** Return the 8 plantains to the hot oil and fry until golden brown and crispy, 1 to 2 minutes. Transfer to paper towels, sprinkle with salt, and let cool. Continue until all the plantain chips are completed. The plantain chips should be stored in an airtight container when cool, but they are best used within 6 hours. The tostones can be heated in a warm oven before serving.

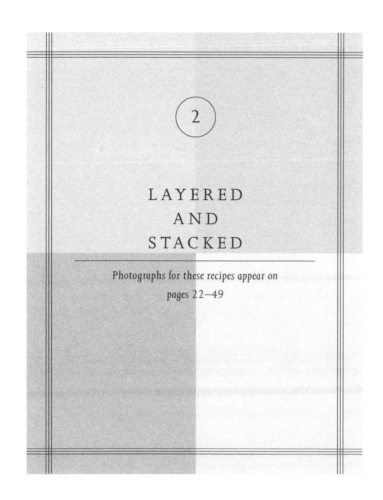

## 2

# LAYERED
# AND
# STACKED

Photographs for these recipes appear on
pages 22–49

I FIND LAYERED AND STACKED HORS D'OEUVRES PARTICULARLY APPEALING BECAUSE, BY THE SIMPLE ACT OF TOPPING ONE INGREDIENT WITH ANOTHER, YOU CAN CREATE SOMETHING THAT IS MORE THAN THE SUM OF ITS PARTS. FROM TALL TO

short, many layers or just two, here are more than two dozen hors d'oeuvres in which the ingredients are discreetly arranged so that you can taste the flavor and texture of each and experience a unique flavor combination at the same time.

Nori Stacks with Smoked Salmon provide a good example of how this technique works. By layering sake-flavored rice and thin-sliced salmon between sheets of the Japanese dried seaweed called nori, then topping it with piquant wasabi caviar, I make a striking and delicious hors d'oeuvre that is virtually guaranteed to be a visual as well as a culinary treat for my guests.

The Nori Stacks recipe demonstrates another important virtue of stacked and layered hors d'oeuvres: Multiple portions can be fashioned relatively quickly by making one large version and cutting it into unexpected shapes. Other examples of this approach include three topped pizzas, one stuffed pizza, and a pissaladière, a southern French tart that is actually a pizza at heart. I make rectangular rather than circular pizzas because this gives me the option of cutting them into squares, triangles, or rectangles for individual servings.

Terrines are another large item that work beautifully when divided into small servings. Cut into half-inch slices, these glistening rectangles layered with gorgeous vegetables and seafood make a stunning presentation. Since they can be fully assembled two days in advance and refrigerated, they are also excellent for those occasions when you are planning an hors d'oeuvres buffet and need to do much of the preparation ahead of time.

I am always looking for new and unusual bases and layerings for my stacked hors d'oeuvres. I take advantage of the firm, meaty texture of swordfish, for instance, by slicing it thin and layering it on Ginger Rice Cakes spread with a spicy mayonnaise. Large potato chips serve as a base for minted pea purée topped with seared scallops, while waffled potato chips—made here with sweet potatoes—form the base for duck breast brushed with maple glaze. Mashed potatoes spread thin and baked are transformed into wafers that comprise the delicate layers of potato-wafer Napoleons with gravlax, crème fraîche, and caviar. Savory French Toast cut into rounds becomes the foundation on which a tomato slice and a bit of basil rest. Creating new combinations like these is largely a matter of having an open mind and thinking about what flavors and textures both taste delicious and look good when layered together.

The beauty of this technique also lies in the ease with which you can reinvigorate classic combinations simply by adding one layer. For example, slices of small, sweet Forelle pears enrich the flavor of a traditional Croque Monsieur sandwich, and small potato rounds spread with herbed goat cheese and stacked on top of one another inside mini muffin tins become enticing Pommes Annette, a takeoff on the classic French dish Pommes Anna.

Like the other hors d'oeuvres in this book, the stacked and layered selections in this chapter work equally well as part of a large hors d'oeuvre buffet, as appetizers for a small group, or even as a collection of small dishes that make a meal.

## POTATO BACON PIZZA

**MAKES FOUR 14 x 4-INCH PIZZAS; 15 TO 18 ONE-INCH WEDGES PER PIZZA** | photograph on page 30

*Feel free to improvise with different potatoes and herbs. Slice the potatoes just before arranging them over the dough.*

12 ounces sliced bacon, regular or thick-cut, chilled

1 recipe Pizza Dough (page 239), divided into 4 rounds

All-purpose flour, for dusting

8 ounces small red potatoes, skin on

Cornmeal, for dusting

Olive oil

Kosher salt and freshly ground black pepper

¼ cup fresh rosemary

2 ounces Parmesan cheese, grated on the large holes of a box grater to yield ¾ cup

**1** Preheat the oven to 500° F. for at least 10 minutes with the oven rack in the lower third of the oven. If using a pizza stone, place it in the lower third of the oven and preheat the oven to 500° F. for at least 30 minutes. Remove the bacon from the package in 1 piece. Slice the bacon crosswise into ½-inch pieces. Place the bacon in a large skillet and cook over medium-low heat until most of the fat is rendered and the bacon is just beginning to brown, 4 to 6 minutes. Drain on paper towels and set aside.

**2** Place 1 round of pizza dough on a lightly floured work surface. Keep the remaining 3 rounds of dough covered with a clean towel, at room temperature. Using your hands, work the dough into an 8 × 2-inch rectangle. Continue to work the dough, using a rolling pin if necessary, until the dough makes a 14 × 4-inch rectangle.

**3** Using a mandoline, cut the potatoes into ¹⁄₁₆-inch-thick slices.

**4** Sprinkle a baking sheet or a wooden paddle with cornmeal and transfer the dough onto it.

**5** Arrange the potato slices, overlapping slightly, on the pizza. Brush with oil and season with salt and pepper. Sprinkle with one quarter of the rosemary, the bacon, and the Parmesan. Transfer the baking sheet directly onto the oven rack. If using a pizza stone, slide the pizza off of the wooden paddle directly onto the heated stone. Bake until the crust is golden, 8 to 12 minutes, rotating the pizza halfway through baking. Repeat with the remaining dough and ingredients. Slice crosswise at alternating angles, into wedges. Serve warm.

---

**VARIATIONS** | Pizza Toppings

Pizza dough is a versatile base for unlimited topping combinations. Among my favorites are:

**MEDITERRANEAN PIZZA** Grilled eggplant, ricotta salata cheese, and roasted red bell peppers (see page 266)

**PIZZA VERDE** Shredded mozzarella; while the pizza is hot and just before serving, add mâche (plus additional greens, if desired) and vinaigrette

**MIXED OLIVE PIZZA** Mixed Olives (page 358) and roasted garlic purée (page 265)

**WHITE PIZZA** Gruyère, Parmesan, and Asiago cheeses, with chopped fresh flat-leaf parsley and rosemary

**PROVENÇAL PIZZA** Sliced tomatoes with chopped fresh marjoram, basil, and a drizzle of extra-virgin olive oil

## PIZZA WITH WILD MUSHROOMS AND FONTINA CHEESE

**MAKES FOUR 14 x 4-INCH PIZZAS; 15 TO 18 ONE-INCH WEDGES PER PIZZA** | photograph on page 30

*Use as varied an assortment of fresh, wild mushrooms as you can find. Gently wipe the dirt off them with a damp cloth. To achieve the perfect sear, the mushrooms must be cooked over medium-high heat in a pan large enough to accommodate them. Resist the temptation to shake the pan too often.*

1¼ pounds assorted fresh wild mushrooms such as oyster, shiitake, and chanterelle, wiped clean, shiitake stems removed

3 tablespoons olive oil, or more as needed

Kosher salt and freshly ground black pepper

1 recipe Pizza Dough (page 239), divided into 4 rounds

All-purpose flour, for dusting

Cornmeal, for dusting

12 ounces fontina cheese, grated on the large holes of a box grater to yield 4 cups

**1** Preheat the oven to 500°F. for at least 10 minutes with the oven rack in the lower third of the oven. If using a pizza stone, place it in the lower third of the oven and preheat the oven to 500°F. for at least 30 minutes. Slice the larger mushrooms and stems into ⅛-inch pieces. (Leave the very small mushrooms whole.) Heat 3 tablespoons of the olive oil in a large skillet over medium-high heat. Working in batches, sauté about a quarter of the mushrooms at a time, without shaking the pan, 3 to 5 minutes, until they are just barely cooked. Season with salt and pepper to taste. Set aside. Continue sautéing the remaining mushrooms, adding more olive oil to the pan as needed, until completed. Set aside.

**2** Place 1 round of pizza dough on a lightly floured work surface. Keep the remaining 3 rounds of dough covered with a clean towel, at room temperature. Using your hands, work the dough into an 8 × 2-inch rectangle. Continue to work the dough, using a rolling pin if necessary, until the dough makes a 14 × 4-inch rectangle.

**3** Sprinkle a baking sheet or a wooden paddle with cornmeal and transfer the dough onto it. Sprinkle the dough with one quarter of the cheese. Top with one quarter of the mushrooms. Season with salt and pepper to taste.

**4** Transfer the baking sheet directly onto the oven rack. If using a pizza stone, slide the pizza off of the wooden paddle directly onto the heated stone. Bake until the crust is golden, 8 to 12 minutes, rotating the pizza halfway through baking. Repeat with the remaining dough and ingredients. Slice crosswise at alternating angles, into wedges. Serve warm.

## GREEK PIZZA

**MAKES FOUR 14 x 4-INCH PIZZAS; 15 TO 18 ONE-INCH WEDGES PER PIZZA** | photograph on page 30

*Drain the feta cheese well in a fine-mesh sieve or on a paper towel to prevent the dough from getting soggy. I often add roasted red peppers (page 266) to this delicious combination.*

1 recipe Pizza Dough (page 239), divided into 4 rounds

All-purpose flour, for dusting

Cornmeal, for dusting

8 ounces feta cheese

12 ounces (about 40) red and yellow cherry tomatoes, oven-dried (see page 257)

32 pitted black olives (2 ounces), such as oil-cured or kalamata, quartered

2 tablespoons fresh oregano

Kosher salt and freshly ground black pepper

**1** Preheat the oven to 500° F. for at least 10 minutes with the oven rack in the lower third of the oven. If using a pizza stone, place it in the lower third of the oven and preheat the oven to 500° F. for at least 30 minutes. Place 1 round of pizza dough on a lightly floured work surface. Keep the remaining 3 rounds of dough covered with a clean towel, at room temperature. Using your hands, work the dough into an 8 × 2-inch rectangle. Continue to work the dough, using a rolling pin if necessary, until it makes a 14 × 4-inch rectangle.

**2** Sprinkle a baking sheet or a wooden paddle with cornmeal and transfer the dough onto it. Sprinkle the top with one quarter each of the feta cheese, tomatoes, and olives. Top with one-quarter of the oregano. Add salt and pepper to taste.

**3** Transfer the baking sheet directly onto the oven rack. If using a pizza stone, slide the pizza off of the wooden paddle onto the heated stone. Bake until the crust is golden, 8 to 12 minutes, rotating the pizza halfway through baking. Repeat with the remaining dough and ingredients. Slice crosswise at alternating angles, into wedges. Serve warm.

---

**NOTE** | Japanese-Style Bread Crumbs

If you are unable to get Japanese bread crumbs, white bread, prepared properly, can be used in place of them. To make 1 cup, toast 8 slices of white bread, crusts removed, at 350° F. until they are completely dried out and very crisp, 5 to 10 minutes. Let cool. Chop the bread slices to a coarse crumb; if the crumbs are too fine, you will not achieve the light, airy texture of the Japanese version.

---

# EGGPLANT CRISPS

**MAKES 2 DOZEN** | photograph on page 33

*The secret to the light, airy crust of these delicious crisps is Japanese bread crumbs, panko. Made from wheat and honey, they are very large and flaky, unlike the traditional dense, compact bread crumbs used to make the eggplant Parmesan that inspired them. Look for Japanese bread crumbs in Asian markets, or see Sources, page 487. When dipping the eggplant, use one hand for the dry ingredients, the other for the wet.*

8 ounces mozzarella cheese

1 quart peanut oil, for frying

½ cup all-purpose flour

Kosher salt and freshly ground black pepper

2 large eggs, lightly beaten

1 cup Japanese bread crumbs (panko) or
     Japanese-style bread crumbs (see Note, left)

2 medium Japanese eggplant, cut crosswise into
     ¼-inch-thick slices

12 small cherry tomatoes, oven-dried (see
     page 257)

2 tablespoons fresh oregano

**1** Cut the mozzarella into small pieces, each about ¼ inch thick. If using fresh mozzarella, place on a paper towel to drain.

**2** Preheat the oven to 375° F. with the rack in the center. Heat the peanut oil in a small, deep saucepan, or an electric fryer, until the temperature on a frying thermometer registers 360° F. Place the flour, seasoned with salt and pepper, and eggs in 2 separate shallow bowls. Place the bread crumbs in a third shallow bowl. Dredge each eggplant slice in the flour, then dip into the beaten eggs and finally into the bread crumbs.

**3** Fry the eggplant slices in batches of 6 pieces, until golden brown, 5 to 8 minutes. Transfer to a paper towel to drain. Repeat with the remaining eggplant.

CONTINUED ON FOLLOWING PAGE

**4** Arrange the fried eggplant slices on a baking sheet. Top each eggplant slice with 1 piece of mozzarella and a slice of oven-dried tomato. (The crisps may be prepared up to this point and left at room temperature up to 3 hours.) Bake in the oven until the cheese melts, 5 to 7 minutes. Top each with oregano and serve hot.

## PISSALADIÈRE

**MAKES TWO 8 x 12-INCH TARTS; 48 PIECES TOTAL** | photograph on page 49

*New Yorkers have their pizza slice, and Provençals have their pissaladière, a savory, flaky tart. Be patient when caramelizing the onions. They must cook slowly in order to achieve a deep amber color and slightly candied flavor. The tomatoes may be made 1 day ahead and stored in an airtight container in the refrigerator. Bring them to room temperature before assembling the tarts. Pissaladière can be served at room temperature or reheated in a 350° F. oven for 10 minutes.*

3 tablespoons olive oil

6 garlic cloves, minced

5 pounds onions (about 4 large), sliced and cut into ¼-inch-thick rings

1 tablespoon fresh thyme, plus 8 sprigs for garnish

1 bay leaf

Kosher salt and freshly ground black pepper

12 flat anchovy fillets, finely chopped

All-purpose flour, for dusting

½ recipe Puff Pastry (page 240) or 1 17-ounce package frozen puff pastry (2 unbaked sheets), thawed

1 large egg, lightly beaten for egg wash

20 small cherry tomatoes, oven-dried (see page 257)

32 niçoise olives (2 ounces), pitted and left whole

**1** Heat the oil in a large skillet over medium heat. Add the garlic and cook, stirring occasionally, until lightly browned, 3 to 5 minutes. Increase the heat to medium-high and add the onions and cook, stirring every 5 minutes, until the onions are slightly golden, about 25 minutes. Reduce the heat to low, add the thyme, the bay leaf, and salt and pepper to taste. Cook, covered, stirring occasionally, until the onions are very soft and caramelized, 40 to 60 minutes. (If the bottom of the pan starts to brown and the onions stick, add a few tablespoons of water and stir.) Remove the bay leaf and stir in the anchovies. Set aside. (The mixture can be held in the refrigerator, in an airtight container, for 1 to 2 days.)

**2** Preheat the oven to 400° F. Line a baking sheet with parchment paper. On a lightly floured surface, roll out 1 sheet of the puff pastry to a 10 × 14-inch rectangle. Trim ½-inch-wide strips from each side of the puff pastry and set aside. Brush a little of the egg wash around the edges of the pastry, and place the reserved strips on the egg-washed area to make a raised border. Prick the base of the dough all over with the tines of a fork. Brush the egg wash over the raised borders and over the center of the pastry. Chill the dough in the refrigerator for 20 minutes. Bake the pastry until it is golden and puffy, 10 to 15 minutes. Remove from the oven. Repeat with the remaining sheet of puff pastry.

**3** To assemble: Scatter an equal amount of the caramelized onions on each tart. Top with the oven-dried tomatoes, olives, and the sprigs of thyme. Return to the oven and heat until the onions are warm. Using a serrated knife, cut each tart into 24 2-inch pieces.

Oven-drying tomatoes is a technique that restaurant chefs have been using for years. It is an extremely simple process, and can easily be done in a home kitchen. Oven-drying allows you to control the degree to which the tomatoes are dried. I dry them only slightly, so they are still juicy and a little plump, but their flavor and sweetness are intensified in the drying process. If you are used to the leathery texture of sun-dried tomatoes, these will be a revelation.

The basic method is the same for any size or color of tomato, but the cooking time and the amount of oil needed will vary with the size.

Heat the oven to 275° F. Toss the tomatoes with the appropriate amount of olive oil and transfer them to a parchment-lined baking sheet. If sliced, set them cut-side up. Sprinkle the tomatoes lightly with salt and pepper. (At this stage, the tomatoes may also be sprinkled with any herb you choose for added flavor.) Cook until the tomatoes begin to shrivel and shrink in size, but the centers still remain moist. The timing will vary greatly according to the ripeness of the tomatoes, particularly if using larger ones, so doneness must be judged more by sight than by time. Remove the tomatoes from the oven and let them cool. They may be made 1 day ahead and stored in an airtight container in the refrigerator. Return to room temperature before using, or warm slightly in a low oven for 5 to 10 minutes.

### CHERRY AND PEAR TOMATOES

May be dried whole or cut in half. For every 2 dozen cherry tomatoes, toss with 2 teaspoons of olive oil. Cook for 30 to 40 minutes.

### PLUM TOMATOES

May be dried cut in half, or in quarters. For every 6 plum tomatoes, toss with a scant tablespoon of olive oil. Cook for 1½ to 3 hours, depending on ripeness and size.

### ALL OTHER TOMATOES

May be dried cut into thirds or quarters, or wedges. For every 6 tomatoes, toss with a scant tablespoon of olive oil. Cook for 2 to 4 hours, depending on ripeness and size.

### FOR THE GRILLED VEGETABLE SALSA (PAGE 401)

Sprinkle the tomatoes with 1 teaspoon chopped fresh thyme after they are sprinkled with the salt and pepper. Proceed with the recipe.

## QUESADILLAS

In Mexico, small quesadillas are traditionally served before the main course. Several versions are typically passed on a tray with toasted pumpkin seeds. While palm-size quesadillas make excellent starters, they are substantial enough to be served as a meal.

The variations on the classic quesadilla fillings of beef, pork, or chicken, cheese, and peppers are limited only by your imagination. The following recipes were inspired by some of my favorite combinations of ingredients, but you can mix and match these and other ingredients (see page 260) to suit your own taste. Serve the quesadillas with chilled glasses of beer or frozen margaritas.

## ROASTED SWEET POTATO AND TOMATILLO QUESADILLAS

**MAKES 3½ DOZEN** | photograph on page 39

*Each component of this dish can be made in advance, ready for assembly and final cooking. The ancho chili paste can be prepared, the bell peppers roasted and skinned, and the sweet potato roasted and the flesh scraped out 1 day ahead. Store each in an airtight container in the refrigerator and return them to room temperature before you assemble the quesadilla.*

1 large (13-ounce) sweet potato

8 ounces fresh goat cheese

1 recipe Miniature Flour Tortillas (page 235)

1 large roasted poblano or red bell pepper (see
      page 266), cut into ⅛-inch-wide strips

8 ounces tomatillos, husks removed, sliced into
      1/16-inch pieces

¼ cup ancho chili paste (see page 259)

Kosher salt and freshly ground black pepper

**1** Preheat the oven to 400° F. with the rack in the center. Line a baking sheet with parchment paper. Use a fork to prick the sweet potato and place it on the baking sheet. Roast until very soft and the sugar begins to caramelize and the tip of a knife is easily inserted, about 1 hour. Set aside to cool.

**2** Halve the sweet potato lengthwise. Scrape out the flesh and transfer to a bowl; set aside. Discard the skin. Reduce the oven temperature to low.

**3** To assemble: Spread a thin layer of goat cheese, about ½ teaspoon, onto half of the tortillas. Spread 1 teaspoon of the roasted sweet potato over the cheese. Top with 2 pepper strips and a tomatillo slice. Drizzle ½ teaspoon ancho chili paste over each and top with a small dollop of cheese. Sprinkle with salt and pepper to taste. Cover the filling with a second tortilla. Press down gently so that the layers stick together. Repeat with the remaining tortillas. Cover the tortillas with plastic wrap or a damp towel to prevent them from drying out.

**4** Heat a dry cast-iron skillet over medium heat until very warm, 1 to 2 minutes. Working in batches, cook the quesadillas until the cheese is melted and they are warm throughout, about 1½ minutes per side. Cover with foil and keep warm in the oven. Repeat with the remaining quesadillas. Serve warm.

Lending both hot spiciness and a balance of sweetness to a dish, dried ancho chilies are the sweetest of the dried chilies, their flavor ranging from mild to pungent. They are about 3 to 4 inches long, and their color can be deep red to dark brown. Dried ancho chilies are available in many gourmet and specialty food stores. Look for soft, pliable chilies and avoid brittle or dusty ones. **DRIED ANCHO CHILI PASTE** The chilies can be made into a very versatile paste that can be used as an ingredient or a condiment. A batch can be kept, in an airtight container in the refrigerator, for 4 to 5 days. Or it can be frozen for 1 month. The paste is delicious on any of the quesadillas or empanaditas (pages 294–295). **TO MAKE THE PASTE** Place 2 ounces of dried ancho chilies (or more if you like) in a small bowl. Pour 2 cups of boiling water over the chilies, and let sit for 30 minutes. Drain the chilies, reserving the liquid. Remove and discard the seeds and stems. Place the chilies in the bowl of a food processor and blend the mixture until a thick paste forms. Add about ¼ cup of the reserved liquid to thin the paste until it is smooth. Add ½ teaspoon kosher salt and ¼ teaspoon freshly ground black pepper, and pulse to combine. Two ounces of chilies makes about ½ cup of paste.

# CHORIZO AND MANCHEGO CHEESE QUESADILLAS

**MAKES 3½ DOZEN** | photograph on page 39

*Chorizo is a highly seasoned pork sausage. It can be bought cured or raw; be sure to buy cured for this recipe. Manchego is a rich, golden sheep's milk cheese from Spain.*

1 teaspoon olive oil
1 medium red onion, cut into ⅛-inch-thick rounds
10 ounces cured chorizo links, cut crosswise into ⅛-inch slices
14 ounces Manchego cheese, sliced paper-thin
1 recipe Miniature Flour Tortillas (page 235)
2 dozen chives, cut into 2-inch lengths
Kosher salt and freshly ground black pepper

**1** Heat a grill pan or a skillet brushed with olive oil over medium-high heat until hot, 1 to 2 minutes. Cook the onion rounds until grill marks appear and the onion is soft, about 1 minute per side. Transfer to a plate and set aside.

**2** Cook the chorizo about 1 minute on each side until slight grill marks appear. Drain the sausage on paper towels and set aside.

**3** To assemble: Place a layer of cheese on half of the tortillas. Top with onion, chorizo, and chives. Add another layer of cheese. Season with salt and pepper to taste. Cover the filling with a second tortilla. Press down gently so that the layers stick together. Repeat with the remaining tortillas. Cover the tortillas with plastic wrap or a damp towel to prevent them from drying out.

**4** Heat a dry cast-iron skillet over medium heat until very warm, 1 to 2 minutes. Working in batches, cook the quesadillas until the cheese is melted and they are warm throughout, about 1½ minutes per side. Cover with foil and keep warm in the oven. Repeat with the remaining quesadillas. Serve warm.

## VARIATIONS | Quesadilla Fillings

Adjust the amount of each ingredient to suit your taste. Cut them to fit on the miniature tortillas.

Good-quality prepared pestos and tapenades, such as mushroom, green and black olive, or artichoke

Good-quality prepared salsas and fresh mozzarella

Feta cheese, fresh oregano, and tomatoes

Olive paste, fresh cilantro, and fontina cheese

Brie, prosciutto, and cumin

Thinly sliced ham, Monterey Jack cheese, and minced jalapeños

Cherry tomatoes, mozzarella, and basil

Shredded chicken, goat cheese, and radishes

Crispy bacon, shredded lettuce, scallions, and cheese

Chives, smashed avocado, and cooked shrimp

Mango or papaya, fresh cilantro, and crabmeat

Sliced red bell peppers and smashed chickpeas or cannellini beans

Smoked salmon, arugula, and cream cheese

Roast beef, prepared horseradish, and cream cheese

Scrambled eggs, ham, and cheese

Diced jicama, fresh corn, and Monterey Jack cheese

**MAKES 3½ DOZEN** | photograph on page 38

*It saves time to buy 1 cooked lobster tail for this recipe, rather than buying a small whole lobster and cooking it yourself. The price is generally about the same. Or you may substitute small cooked shrimp for the lobster.*

1 teaspoon olive oil

8 ounces white button mushrooms, wiped clean, very thinly sliced

Kosher salt and freshly ground black pepper

1 recipe Miniature Flour Tortillas (page 235)

12 ounces ricotta cheese

2½ cups baby spinach, torn spinach, or other small lettuce leaves

1 10-ounce cooked lobster tail, cut into ½-inch pieces

¼ cup fresh tarragon

**1** Heat a medium skillet brushed with olive oil over medium-high heat until warm. Cook the mushrooms, stirring, until softened and slightly colored, 3 to 5 minutes. Sprinkle with salt and pepper to taste and set aside.

**2** To assemble: Arrange half of the flour tortillas on a baking sheet. Spread 2 teaspoons of the ricotta onto each of these tortillas. Place a spinach leaf on top of the cheese. Cover with 1 slice of the reserved mushrooms, 2 pieces of lobster, and 3 tarragon leaves. Add a small dollop of cheese, and season with salt and pepper to taste. Cover the filling with a second tortilla. Press down so that the layers stick together. Repeat with the remaining tortillas. Cover the tortillas with plastic wrap or a damp towel to prevent them from drying out.

**3** Heat a dry cast-iron skillet over medium heat until very warm, 1 to 2 minutes. Working in batches, cook the quesadillas until the cheese is melted and they are warm throughout, about 1½ minutes per side. Cover with foil and keep warm in the oven. Repeat with the remaining quesadillas. Serve warm.

## GRILLED CHICKEN AND ROASTED RED PEPPER QUESADILLAS

**MAKES 3½ DOZEN** | photograph on page 38

*Roasting your own fresh red peppers is very easy, and they are so much better than those packaged in jars. The delicious smoky flavor of fresh charred peppers is the key to this simple recipe.*

14 ounces boneless, skinless chicken
    breasts
1 teaspoon olive oil
Kosher salt and freshly ground black
    pepper
¼ cup ancho chili paste (see page 259)
1 recipe Miniature Flour Tortillas
    (page 235)
2 roasted red bell peppers (see page 266),
    cut into ⅛-inch-wide strips
⅓ cup fresh cilantro
5 ounces Cheddar cheese, cut into very
    thin slices

**1** Working one at a time, place a chicken breast between 2 sheets of plastic wrap. Use a meat pounder or a rolling pin to evenly and gently pound the chicken breast to about a ¼-inch thickness. Lightly brush a grill pan with olive oil and heat over medium-high heat until hot, about 1 to 2 minutes. Season the chicken with salt and pepper to taste and grill until cooked through, 4 to 8 minutes, turning once. Transfer the chicken to a plate and set aside to cool. Repeat with the remaining chicken. Cut the chicken into ⅛-inch- to ¼-inch-thick strips.

**2** To assemble: Spread a thin layer of the chili paste onto half of the tortillas. Top with 1 to 2 pieces of the chicken, 2 strips of roasted pepper, 1 or 2 leaves of cilantro, and 3 to 4 slices of Cheddar cheese. Season with salt and pepper to taste. Cover the filling with a second tortilla. Press down gently so that the layers stick together. Repeat with the remaining tortillas. Cover the tortillas with plastic wrap or a damp towel to prevent them from drying out.

**3** Heat a dry cast-iron skillet over medium heat until very warm, 1 to 2 minutes. Working in batches, cook the quesadillas until the cheese is melted and they are warm throughout, about 1½ minutes per side. Cover with foil and keep warm in the oven. Repeat with the remaining quesadillas. Serve warm.

## SAVORY FRENCH TOAST

**MAKES 3 DOZEN** | photograph on page 41

*Brioche makes the very best French toast, but you can use any dense loaf of white bread for these savory little rounds. The toasts are best served warm, within 1 hour of baking. They may be reheated in a 250° F. oven for 10 minutes. Pack them tightly together on the baking sheet to prevent them from drying out.*

1½ tablespoons plus 2 teaspoons all-purpose
    flour

¾ teaspoon baking powder

1½ teaspoons kosher salt

3 large eggs

1⅓ cups milk

3½ ounces Parmesan cheese, grated on the
    large holes of a box grater to yield
    1¼ cups

1 tablespoon unsalted butter, for buttering
    the pan

1 12-ounce loaf of brioche, cut into 6 1-inch-
    thick slices

1 medium tomato, cut into ¼-inch dice

¼ cup plus 2 tablespoons chopped fresh
    basil, plus leaves cut into thin strips
    for garnish

**1** Preheat the oven to 350° F. with the rack in the center. In a small bowl, combine the flour, baking powder, and salt. Set aside. In a large bowl, whisk together the eggs and the milk. Whisk the flour mixture into the eggs, until the batter is smooth. Whisk in the cheese; the batter will be clumpy and look curdled.

**2** Generously butter a 13 × 9 × 2-inch pan. Set aside. Using tongs, dip the brioche slices into the batter, coating well. Arrange the slices side by side in the buttered pan. Set aside.

**3** Stir the diced tomatoes and chopped basil into the remaining batter. Pour the batter over the brioche slices.

**4** Bake the French toast until golden brown, 30 to 40 minutes. Let cool for 5 to 10 minutes before cutting with a 1½-inch cookie cutter into 36 rounds. Garnish with the remaining basil strips and serve warm.

## CELERIAC POTATO PANCAKES WITH APPLE-ONION COMPOTE

**MAKES 2 DOZEN** | photograph on page 46

*Celeriac, also known as celery root, adds the subtle green flavors of celery and parsley to these little potato pancakes. Celeriac knobs vary greatly in size; buy a small one, about 1 pound, for this recipe. The pancakes should be served within 4 to 6 hours of being made; reheat them on a baking sheet in a 350° F. oven for 7 to 10 minutes.*

¼ of a small celeriac

1 small yellow onion, grated on the fine holes
    of a box grater to yield ⅓ cup

1 medium baking potato, grated on the
    large holes of a box grater to yield
    1½ cups

3 tablespoons all-purpose flour

1 teaspoon kosher salt

¼ teaspoon white pepper

1 tablespoon unsalted butter, for buttering
    the pan

24 small sprigs fresh rosemary

1 recipe Apple-Onion Compote (page 398)

**1** Preheat the oven to 425° F. Using a box grater, grate the celeriac on the large holes to yield about 1 cup. In a medium bowl, combine the celeriac, onion, potato, flour, salt, and pepper.

**2** Butter a 12 × 17-inch baking sheet. Place a 1½-inch round cookie cutter near one corner on the baking sheet. Fill the cutter with 1 tablespoon of the potato mixture and pat down the mixture to fill the cutter evenly. Gently lift the cutter up and repeat this process on the baking sheet, using the remaining potato mixture to make a total of 24 pancakes.

**3** Transfer the pan to the oven and bake for 15 minutes to set the pancakes. Remove the pan from the oven and flip the pancakes. Return to the oven and continue to bake until the pancakes are crispy and golden on the outside, 10 to 12 minutes more. Transfer the pancakes to paper towels to drain. Garnish each warm pancake with rosemary. Serve with the Apple-Onion Compote.

## ROASTED SHRIMP WITH ARTICHOKES AND FENNEL

**MAKES 2 DOZEN** | photograph on page 25

*The artichokes may be made a day ahead and kept, refrigerated, in an airtight container. Set out an empty bowl for collecting the discarded artichoke leaves.*

2 tablespoons grated lemon zest

3 tablespoons fresh lemon juice

½ teaspoon kosher salt

¼ teaspoon freshly ground black pepper

3 tablespoons extra-virgin olive oil

1 small red onion, chopped into ¼-inch dice to yield ¼ cup

1 tablespoon chopped fresh oregano, plus leaves for garnish

¼ of a small fennel bulb (about ¼ pound), thinly shaved on a mandoline, fronds chopped and reserved

Artichoke Leaves (page 231), heart reserved and cut into ¼-inch dice

12 medium shrimp, peeled and deveined (see page 310)

2 ounces feta cheese, crumbled

**1** Preheat the oven to 425° F. with the rack in the center. In a small bowl, whisk together the lemon zest, lemon juice, salt, and pepper. Slowly whisk in the olive oil until well combined. Add the chopped red onion, chopped oregano, shaved fennel, and artichoke heart.

**2** Cut each shrimp in half lengthwise. Arrange the shrimp halves on a baking sheet. Roast in the oven until pink, 1½ to 3 minutes.

**3** Arrange the artichoke leaves on a serving platter. Place a piece of shaved fennel on each leaf, and top with a shrimp half. Spoon about ½ teaspoon of the marinade over each shrimp. Sprinkle crumbled feta, fennel fronds, and an oregano leaf over each. These will keep, covered with plastic wrap, for about 1 hour in the refrigerator. Return to room temperature before serving and drizzle with the remaining vinaigrette.

Terrines are ideal party food. They can be made 2 days ahead of time, they feed a large number of guests, and their layered look makes a dramatic visual impact on the hors d'oeuvre table. In fact, terrines are so impressive in appearance that they seem difficult to make. To the contrary, they are as easy to make as meat loaf, relying on a simple layering technique for their patterned beauty.

Traditional terrines are very often prepared with excessive gelatin—the main ingredient in aspic, the flavorless jelly that holds most molded terrines together. These recipes use very little gelatin or none at all. The two recipes that do use gelatin combine it with ingredients such as tomato juice and vegetable stock to create a flavorful aspic. The Asparagus and Shiitake Mushroom Terrine needs no aspic at all, relying instead on a goat cheese–labneh mixture to moisten and bind the layers.

## ROASTED VEGETABLE TERRINE

**MAKES 24 ½-INCH SLICES** | photograph on page 47

*If at any time the gelatin mixture thickens during preparation, simply reheat over a low flame to return it to its fluid consistency. Serve this terrine thinly sliced on Simple Crostini (page 243) or on lettuce leaves.*

½ cup olive oil

1 tablespoon kosher salt, or more to taste

1 teaspoon freshly ground black pepper, or more to taste

1 medium eggplant, about 2 pounds

1 medium zucchini, about 1 pound

1 cup tomato juice

1 tablespoon plus 1 teaspoon unflavored gelatin

1 head of roasted garlic (see page 265)

2 roasted red bell peppers (see page 266), sliced into 1-inch-wide strips

12 fresh basil leaves

2 roasted yellow bell peppers (see page 266), sliced into 1-inch-wide strips

1 recipe Simple Crostini (page 243), or 24 large lettuce leaves

1 recipe Tahini Yogurt Dipping Sauce (page 398)

**1** Preheat the oven to 400° F. Line 2 baking sheets with parchment paper. Line a 12 × 2¼ × 1¾-inch metal terrine with plastic wrap, leaving a 3-inch overhang of plastic on each side. In a small bowl, combine the olive oil, salt, and freshly ground pepper, and set aside.

**2** Using a mandoline or a very sharp knife, slice the eggplant and zucchini lengthwise, about ¼ inch thick. Arrange the eggplant and zucchini slices on the baking sheets. Brush the oil mixture over both sides of the vegetables. Bake until they are cooked through, flexible, and tender, 20 to 25 minutes. Transfer the sheets to racks to cool, about 10 minutes.

**3** Place ½ cup tomato juice in a small saucepan over medium heat. Place the remaining tomato juice in a small heatproof bowl, and sprinkle with gelatin. Let sit for 5 minutes to soften the gelatin. Hold the bowl over the warm saucepan, and stir until the gelatin is dissolved, about 2 minutes. Add the gelatin mixture to the hot juice and remove from the heat.

**4** Transfer the juice to the bowl of a food processor. Squeeze the cloves of the roasted garlic into the bowl with the juice and process until well combined, about 15 seconds. Season with salt and pepper to taste. Transfer to a medium bowl.

5 Dip the eggplant slices in the tomato juice mixture. Set aside the 2 thinnest slices. Arrange the others crosswise, slightly overlapping, so that the ends of the eggplant drape over the sides of the terrine. Arrange the 2 reserved slices lengthwise at either end of the mold, leaving about ½ inch of eggpplant hanging over either end.

6 Layer the red pepper strips lengthwise on top of the eggplant, dipping each slice into the juice mixture as you go. Repeat the process with the zucchini, basil leaves, and the yellow pepper strips. Pour the remaining juice mixture into the terrine mold.

7 Fold the overhanging eggplant on the top of the filling, pressing down gently to compress the terrine. Seal with the overhanging plastic wrap. Place on a baking sheet, top with a second baking sheet, and place a weight on top. Refrigerate overnight. The terrine may be made 2 days in advance, tightly wrapped, and refrigerated until ready to serve.

8 To unmold, unwrap the plastic from the top of the terrine, place an inverted serving platter over the terrine, and quickly turn the terrine over onto the platter. Gently remove the mold and the plastic wrap. Using a serrated knife, cut the terrine crosswise into ½-inch slices. Arrange a slice on each crostini and serve with the Tahini Yogurt Dipping Sauce.

## TECHNIQUE | Roasting Garlic

Roasting garlic turns the pungent, aromatic flesh of garlic cloves into a mildly sweet, buttery treat. Garlic heads differ in size, but an average-size head will make about 2 tablespoons of garlic purée.

TO MAKE ROASTED GARLIC Heat the oven to 400° F. Place a head of garlic in a small ovenproof baking dish, and drizzle it lightly with ½ teaspoon olive oil. Roast until soft and golden brown and the tip of a knife easily pierces the flesh, 45 minutes to 1 hour. Cut about ½ inch from the top of the garlic head, just enough to expose the cloves. Using either your hands or the dull edge of a large knife, squeeze the cloves out of their skins and into a small bowl. Discard the papery skins. Using a fork, mash the cloves together until smooth. Use the roasted garlic immediately, or store in an airtight container in the refrigerator up to 3 days.

Fresh large peppers, both hot and sweet, have a tough, transparent outer skin that should be removed unless they are served raw. The easiest way to loosen the skins is by charring them over a gas burner or under the broiler. Peppers may be roasted, peeled, seeded, and ribs removed as described below 1 or 2 days in advance of their use in a recipe. Roasted peppers may be covered with olive oil and refrigerated for 1 week. Drain the olive oil from the peppers before using. If storing roasted peppers without oil, wrap them tightly in plastic wrap in an airtight container and refrigerate for up to 1 week.

**TO ROAST FRESH PEPPERS** Place the peppers directly on the trivet of a gas-stove burner over high heat or on a grill. Just as each section turns puffy and black, turn the pepper with tongs to prevent overcooking. (If you don't have a gas stove, place the peppers on a rimmed baking sheet and broil in the oven, turning as each side becomes charred.) Transfer the peppers to a large bowl and cover immediately with plastic wrap. The juices, which can be added to the liquid component of the recipe for deeper flavor, will collect in the bowl. Let the peppers sweat until they are cool enough to handle, approximately 15 minutes. The steam will help to loosen the skins.

Transfer the peppers to a work surface. (If you have sensitive skin, wear thin plastic gloves when handling the peppers.) Peel off the blackened skin and discard. There may be bits of charred skin that are not easily peeled away; it is fine to leave them. Refrain from rinsing the peeled peppers, since it dilutes the smoky flavor of the charred peppers. Halve the peppers and open them flat out on the work surface. Use the blade of a paring knife to remove the seeds and the hard seed cluster at the top. Remove the ribs. Slice each pepper according to recipe instructions.

## ASPARAGUS AND SHIITAKE MUSHROOM TERRINE

**MAKES 24 ½-INCH SLICES** | photograph on page 47

*This terrine also makes an excellent first course served over greens and dressed with a simple vinaigrette. Use the inner leaves of the leeks first, since the darker outer leaves tend to be less tender. Labneh, a tart, creamy Middle Eastern yogurt cheese, is available in most large grocery stores and specialty food stores (see Sources, page 487). Button mushrooms may be substituted for the shiitakes.*

24 medium shiitake mushrooms, stems removed
1 tablespoon kosher salt
1 teaspoon freshly ground black pepper
¼ cup olive oil
4 medium leeks (see page 271), white parts finely chopped and greens separated into leaves, well washed
1 small bunch of thin asparagus, about 30 spears
½ cup fresh goat cheese
½ cup labneh cheese
1 recipe Simple Crostini (page 243)

**1** Preheat the oven to 400°F. Line a 12 × 2¼ × 1¾-inch metal terrine with plastic wrap, leaving a 3-inch overhang of plastic on each side.

**2** In a medium bowl, toss the mushrooms with 2 teaspoons of salt, the pepper, and 2 tablespoons of olive oil. Arrange on a baking sheet and bake until roasted and golden brown, 15 to 20 minutes. Transfer the sheet to a rack to cool completely.

**3** In a large sauté pan, add the remaining olive oil and heat over medium heat. Add the chopped leeks. Cook, stirring occasionally, until softened and translucent, about 5 minutes; do not allow the leeks to brown. Transfer the leeks to a medium bowl to cool.

**4** Bring a medium pot of heavily salted water to a boil. Add the asparagus and cook until tender, about 2 minutes. Transfer to a colander and rinse under cold running water. Drain and set aside. To the same pot, add the leek greens and cook until tender, 2 to 3 minutes. Transfer the leeks to a colander, rinse under cold running water, and drain.

**5** In a medium bowl, combine the goat cheese, labneh, and remaining salt with the sautéed leeks; using a rubber spatula, stir until smooth. Arrange the leek greens in the terrine mold crosswise and slightly overlapping, with the ends of the greens hanging over the edges. Using a small rubber spatula, spread a thin layer of the cheese mixture along the bottom of the terrine. Arrange 1 layer of asparagus over the cheese mixture; trim the asparagus to fit. Cover with another thin layer of the cheese mixture, followed by another layer of asparagus. Continue with another thin layer of the cheese mixture and a layer of mushrooms. Repeat with 2 more layers of asparagus and cheese.

**6** Fold the overhanging leeks over the top of the terrine. Seal with the overhanging plastic wrap. Place on a baking sheet, top with a second baking sheet, and place a weight on top. Refrigerate overnight. The terrine may be made 2 days in advance, tightly wrapped, and refrigerated until ready to serve.

**7** To unmold, unwrap the plastic from the top of the terrine, place an inverted serving platter over the terrine, and quickly turn the terrine over onto the platter. Gently remove the mold and the plastic wrap. Using a serrated knife, cut the terrine crosswise into ½-inch slices. Arrange a slice on each crostini and serve.

## SEARED SALMON AND POTATO TERRINE

**MAKES 24 ½-INCH SLICES** | photograph on page 47

*Use the largest flat-leaf spinach you can find to wrap this delicious terrine. Silvery green Swiss chard leaves also work well here. Avoid red chard; the color bleeds into the filling.*

2 medium Yukon Gold potatoes, about 12 ounces

2 medium carrots

2 bunches large flat-leaf spinach, rinsed well, stems removed

1 cup homemade vegetable stock or canned vegetable broth

1 teaspoon grated lemon zest

1 tablespoon plus 1 teaspoon unflavored gelatin

1 tablespoon fresh lemon juice

Kosher salt and freshly ground black pepper

1 bunch of snipped fresh chives, thinly sliced

1 tablespoon olive oil

½ pound salmon fillet, skin removed, cut lengthwise into ¾-inch-wide strips, 6 to 8 inches long

1 recipe Simple Crostini (page 243)

1 recipe Tarragon-Mustard Sauce (page 398)

**1** Line a 12 × 2¼ × 1¾-inch metal terrine with plastic wrap, leaving a 3-inch overhang of plastic on each side. Using a mandoline, slice the potatoes into a ⅛-inch julienne; transfer to a bowl of cold water. Repeat with the carrots.

**2** Bring a medium pot of salted water to a boil. Blanch the potatoes until tender, 2 to 3 minutes. Using a slotted spoon, remove the potatoes and rinse under cold running water, drain on a towel, and set aside. Using the same boiling water, repeat with the carrots, cooking for about 2 minutes. Follow with the spinach leaves, blanching for 10 to 15 seconds. Rinse under cold running water, drain on a towel, and set aside.

**3** Bring ¾ cup of the vegetable stock and the lemon zest to a simmer in a small saucepan. Place the remaining ¼ cup of stock in a small bowl and sprinkle the gelatin evenly over the surface; let sit for 2 minutes. Hold the bowl over the simmering stock and stir for 1 minute, until the gelatin is dissolved. Stir the gelatin mixture into the stock, add the lemon juice, and season with salt and pepper.

**4** In a medium bowl, combine the chives, potatoes, and carrots. Add enough vegetable aspic to moisten the ingredients, about ¼ cup. Set aside.

**5** Heat the olive oil over medium-high heat in a large skillet. Season the salmon with salt and pepper and sear the salmon strips on each side, until medium rare, about 30 seconds per side. Transfer to a plate to cool.

**6** Place the remaining aspic in a small bowl. Dip the spinach leaves into the aspic one at a time and line the bottom and sides of the terrine mold with the leaves slightly overlapping, leaving about 1 inch overhanging on all sides. Fill the mold a third of the way with the reserved potato mixture. Arrange the salmon pieces down the center of the mold. Spoon the remaining potato mixture into the mold. Spoon the remaining aspic over the filling.

**7** Fold the spinach leaves over the top of the terrine, adding more if necessary to cover the top. Seal with the overhanging plastic wrap. Place on a baking sheet, top with a second baking sheet, and place a weight on top. Refrigerate overnight. The terrine may be made 2 days in advance, tightly wrapped, and refrigerated until ready to serve.

**8** To unmold, unwrap the plastic from the top of the terrine, place an inverted serving platter over the terrine, and quickly turn the terrine over onto the platter. Gently remove the mold and the plastic wrap. Using a serrated knife, cut the terrine crosswise into ½-inch slices. Arrange a slice on each crostini and serve with the mustard sauce.

An especially appealing dish to serve, terrines please the eye as well as the palate. They can be layered with all manner of ingredients, and if you are adventurous enough to experiment with other seafood or vegetables, be sure to consider what the terrine will look like once sliced.

Terrines have a strong, geometric presence on the hors d'oeuvre table, their shape achieved by using molds designed specifically for them (see Sources, page 486). I find the miniature terrine molds to be perfect for hors d'oeuvre–size portions. The Teflon-coated, collapsible models tend to be the most user-friendly; the hinged corners are secured with pins that, once removed, allow the sides of the mold to easily fall away from the terrine.

One of the surest ways to guarantee a perfectly shaped, smooth terrine, whether using a nonstick hinged or fixed mold, is to use enough plastic wrap to line the mold before filling it so that it hangs over the mold. After the terrine has been chilled and compressed, place an overturned serving platter on top of the mold, turn it right-side up, and then remove the terrine mold and plastic wrap.

To serve, line a platter with tender greens such as baby spinach, frisée, or oak-leaf lettuce. Herb sprigs also make an attractive platter decoration. For ease of serving, cut half of the terrine into slices and arrange them over crostini. Surround the unsliced terrine with crostini and serve with sauce on the side.

Alternatively, arrange slices drizzled with a light vinaigrette over a bed of greens as a small plated hors d'oeuvre.

If you are planning to make a terrine the main event at your gathering, serve it with several other hors d'oeuvres that complement it well. The texture, flavor, and color contrast of the following selections work especially well with any of the terrines:

Crispy Asparagus Straws (page 286) and Cherry Tomatoes with Haricots Verts (page 306)

Fontina Risotto Balls (page 304) and Cherry Tomatoes with Olive Salad (page 306)

Chèvre Grapes (page 302) and Lady Apples with Celeriac Salad (page 306)

Prosciutto-Wrapped Shrimp (page 341) and Grilled Beef Rolls (page 342)

Mango Crab Stacks (page 273) and B-L-Tea Sandwiches (page 316)

Deviled Quail Eggs with Fines Herbes, Pickled Ginger, and Wasabi Caviar (page 359) and Warm Spicy Kalamata Olives (page 356)

In the warmer seasons, offer glasses of Pimm's Cup (page 427), champagne, or Orange-Rosemary Cordial (page 440) and sparkling water over ice. In cooler months, substitute Red Sangria (page 428) or Ginger Fever (page 429) for Pimm's Cup.

Serve the terrine with Simple Crostini (page 243), Classic Bread Points (page 244), or Endive Petals (page 231).

## NORI STACKS WITH SMOKED SALMON

**MAKES 28 STACKS** | photograph on page 29

*The ingredients for this recipe can be purchased at an Asian market, or look in the Asian section of your grocery store. Wasabi caviar is flying fish roe to which wasabi, the fiery green Japanese horseradish, has been added.*

1½ cups sushi rice

3 tablespoons rice wine vinegar

2 teaspoons sugar

2 teaspoons mirin (Japanese rice wine)

2 teaspoons sake or water

1½ teaspoons kosher salt

4 7½ × 8-inch nori sheets

1½ teaspoons wasabi paste or 2 teaspoons
  wasabi powder combined with 1 teaspoon
  water

8 ounces thinly sliced smoked salmon

1 ounce pickled ginger, cut into narrow strips

1 ounce prepared wasabi caviar or Homemade
  Wasabi Caviar (page 326), or golden caviar,
  or salmon roe

Scallion-Soy Dipping Sauce (page 342)

**1** Place the rice and 2 cups of water in a medium saucepan; bring to a boil over high heat. Reduce the heat to low and simmer, covered, until the water has absorbed, 14 to 16 minutes.

**2** Meanwhile, combine the vinegar, sugar, mirin, sake, and salt in a small saucepan. Warm the mixture over medium-low heat until the sugar and salt are dissolved, about 2 minutes. Set aside.

**3** Transfer the cooked rice to a large mixing bowl. Slowly add the vinegar mixture to the warm cooked rice, stirring constantly, until all of the vinegar mixture is incorporated into the rice. Let cool completely, stirring occasionally.

**4** Toast the nori sheets to enhance their flavor: Using tongs, pass each sheet over a gas flame, flipping and turning until it crisps and darkens in color. Both changes will be slight so watch carefully; this should take only 30 seconds to 1 minute. (If only an electric burner is available, heat to medium, place a sheet of nori directly on the burner, flipping and turning for 30 seconds to 1 minute.)

**5** Place a sheet of toasted nori, shiny-side down, on a dry, clean work surface. Dampen your fingers with water to prevent the rice from sticking to your hands and spread 1 cup lightly packed rice onto the nori. Make sure to spread the rice evenly and all the way to the edges of the sheet. Wet your fingers again and dab ½ teaspoon of the wasabi paste over the layer of rice and spread it thin.

**6** Place a thin layer of smoked salmon over the rice, trimming the edges to fit the sheet of nori, top with a second sheet of nori, shiny side down, and gently smooth the top layer with a rolling pin. Pressing down firmly seals the layers and makes them easier to cut. Repeat the process 2 more times, creating a total of 3 layers, ending with a final sheet of nori, shiny-side up this time. Wrap with plastic wrap and refrigerate for a minimum of 4 hours; overnight is best. Using a very sharp, wet knife, trim the edges of the nori stack to measure 6 × 7 inches. Clean the knife and re-wet between each slice. Slice the nori stack into 1 × 1½-inch pieces. Garnish each piece with the strips of ginger and a dollop of wasabi caviar. Serve with the dipping sauce.

## SEA SCALLOPS WITH MINTED PEA PURÉE ON POTATO CHIPS

**MAKES 2 DOZEN** | photograph on page 24

*The purée may be made a day ahead and kept in an airtight container in the refrigerator. Return the purée to room temperature before serving. A thick-cut, good-quality packaged unsalted potato chip, or any other neutral-flavored base, such as Toasted Brioche Rounds (page 242), Classic Toast Points (page 244), or Pita Cups (page 242), works fine for these.*

2½ tablespoons extra-virgin olive oil

1 garlic clove, minced

1 shallot, finely chopped

1 small leek, white and pale green parts, cut into ¼-inch pieces, well washed (see Note, right)

½ teaspoon kosher salt, or more to taste

⅛ teaspoon freshly ground black pepper, or more to taste

1 cup (5 ounces) frozen peas, thawed

2 tablespoons homemade chicken stock or low-sodium canned chicken broth, skimmed of fat, or water

2 tablespoons chopped fresh mint, plus 2½ tablespoons chiffonade for garnish

12 medium sea scallops, sliced in half crosswise

24 Homemade Potato Chips (page 247)

**1** In a medium skillet, heat 1 tablespoon of the oil over low heat. Add the garlic, shallots, leeks, salt, and pepper. Cook until very soft but not browned, 8 to 10 minutes. Add the peas, raise the heat to medium, and cook, stirring, until the peas are cooked through, 3 to 5 minutes.

**2** Transfer half the pea mixture to the bowl of a food processor. Add the chicken stock and ½ tablespoon of oil. Pulse until the mixture is a coarse purée, about 20 pulses. Transfer the purée to a medium bowl. Process the remaining half of the peas until very smooth, about 30 seconds. Stir into

the coarsely puréed peas. Add the chopped mint. Adjust the seasoning with salt and pepper. Set aside.

**3** Heat the remaining tablespoon of oil in a medium skillet over medium-high heat. Season the scallops with salt and pepper. Add the scallops to the hot pan, and sear until golden brown, 1 to 2 minutes per side.

**4** Place 1 teaspoon of the pea purée on each of the potato chips and top with a scallop. Garnish with the shredded mint. Serve immediately.

---

**TECHNIQUE** | Cleaning Leeks

A member of the allium family, leeks are the restrained, shy relatives of onions and garlic—far less pungent, but no less flavorful. Available year-round in most parts of the country, they vary enormously in size; the smaller the leek, the more tender the stalk. Before using, trim the tiny roots that hang off the root end and trim the thick leaf end. Leeks grow into the soil, so they retain lots of dirt in their layers and leaves. Always wash them thoroughly before proceeding with a recipe.

The best way to ensure that every bit of dirt is washed from leeks is to cut them first into the size that is called for in the recipe. Generally they are halved lengthwise first, then sliced crosswise into ¼-inch-thick pieces. Transfer the leek pieces to a large bowl of cold water, stir, and let stand for 5 minutes to let dirt and sand settle to the bottom. Lift leeks out of the water with a slotted spoon and drain on paper towels.

## POMMES ANNETTE

**MAKES 2 DOZEN** | photograph on page 37

*A bite-size version of the classic French pommes Anna, these taste best when the potatoes are sliced so thin that they're almost transparent. Eight mini muffin tins, each with 6 openings measuring 1½ inches in diameter and ½ inch deep (see Sources, page 486), are needed if you bake these delicate potato hors d'oeuvres all at once; one goes on top, to press the potato slices down into the compact shape. Bake them in batches if you have fewer tins. If fingerling potatoes are not available, use another small, white potato, such as Yukon Golds. If the potato slices are too large to fit in the muffin tins, use a 1¼-inch round cookie cutter to trim them. Pommes Annette may be made 3 to 4 hours ahead and reheated in a 350° F. oven for 5 minutes, or until hot.*

2 tablespoons unsalted butter, room temperature,
    plus 1 tablespoon melted butter
24 small sprigs fresh thyme, plus 1½ teaspoons
    fresh thyme leaves
18 to 24 fingerling potatoes, skin on
5 ounces fresh goat cheese
Kosher salt and freshly ground black pepper

**1** Preheat the oven to 350° F. with the rack in the center. Using some of the melted butter, generously butter 4 of the mini muffin tins. Place 1 sprig of thyme in the bottom of each cup.

**2** Using a mandoline, cut the potatoes into ¹⁄₁₆-inch-thick slices (about 240). Using a pastry brush, butter both sides of 24 of the potato slices with the room-temperature butter. Place the slices over the thyme sprigs to make the first layer. Top each slice with about ⅛ teaspoon of the goat cheese, and season generously with salt and pepper. Make 9 more layers, alternating unbuttered potato slices with the goat cheese; only the top and bottom potato slices are buttered. Sprinkle a few thyme leaves on the last layer of goat cheese. Finish with one last slice of buttered potato on top of each cup.

**3** Cut a piece of parchment paper to fit over each muffin tin. Brush the paper generously with the remaining melted butter. Place the parchment, butter-side down, over the potatoes in the tin. Place a second muffin tin of the exact same size on top of the parchment and press down. Place a large cast-iron or other ovenproof skillet on top to compress the potatoes and place in the oven.

**4** Bake for 30 minutes. Remove the weight, the top muffin tin, and the parchment paper. Bake the potatoes for 8 to 10 minutes more, until golden brown. Let cool slightly, 2 to 3 minutes. Carefully run a knife around the inside of each cup. Using a butter knife, gently remove each Pommes Annette and turn over onto a serving platter.

## GRAVLAX, CRÈME FRAÎCHE, AND CAVIAR NAPOLEONS

**MAKES 3 DOZEN** | photograph on page 27

*These are so delicate, they literally melt in your mouth. Assemble them just before serving.*

¾ cup crème fraîche
6 ounces thinly sliced salmon gravlax, cut into
    1-inch pieces
1 recipe Potato Wafers (page 246)
1 ounce black caviar (see page 380)
2 large sprigs fresh dill

**1** Place the crème fraîche in a medium bowl and whisk until it thickens slightly, 1 to 3 minutes.

**2** Place 1 piece of the salmon onto a potato wafer and top with ¼ teaspoon of the crème fraîche. Place another potato wafer over the first layer and repeat with the salmon and crème fraîche. Cover with a final potato wafer and a piece of salmon. Garnish with ⅛ teaspoon of the caviar and a sprig of dill. Continue with the remaining ingredients. Serve immediately.

**MAKES 3 DOZEN** | photograph on page 23

## TECHNIQUE | Working with Mangos

The best way to determine whether a mango is ripe is to sniff the stem end; it should be fragrant and slightly sweet-smelling. Choose mangos with taut skin that shows some yellow or red and that gives slightly when pressed. If a mango is very firm and is not aromatic, leave it at room temperature for a few days to ripen.

When precisely cut pieces of mango are called for in a recipe, it is much easier to peel the mango before trimming it away from the pit. Some mangos can be easily peeled by hand; others require using a very sharp paring knife. Cut a thin slice off the bottom of the mango to create a flat surface. Stand the mango on a cutting board stem-end up. Beginning at the stem, run the knife to the bottom of the mango, trimming away the skin as you work around it.

Shaped like a flattened oval, the mango has two soft cheeks on either side of the pit, which runs from the top to the bottom of the fruit. To trim the fleshy cheeks away, place a very sharp knife at the top of the mango, slightly off center. Slice off one of the rounded cheeks in a clean, single cut, running the knife along the pit as you cut; some flesh will invariably cling to the pit. Repeat on the other side. You may be able to carve off a bit more flesh from the narrow edge of the pit, but the two halves account for the yields in all of the recipes in this book. Cut the halves as directed in each recipe.

Wasabi-spiked mayonnaise binds the crab and mango in these stacks. Wasabi, or Japanese horseradish, is available in paste and powder forms in Asian markets or in the Asian section of the grocery store. If you buy wasabi powder, add enough water to form a smooth paste.

⅓ cup plus 2 tablespoons homemade (page 315) or prepared mayonnaise

1¾ teaspoons wasabi paste or 2½ teaspoons wasabi powder combined with about 1¼ teaspoons water

6 ounces lump crabmeat, picked over for cartilage

1 small red bell pepper, seeds and ribs removed, cut into ¼-inch dice to yield ½ cup

2 tablespoons chopped fresh cilantro

2 tablespoons fresh lemon juice

Kosher salt

3 large, ripe mangos, sliced ¼ inch thick (see Note, left)

1 recipe Toasted Brioche Rounds (page 242)

**1** In a medium bowl, combine the mayonnaise and the wasabi paste; remove ¼ cup of the mixture to a separate bowl and reserve. Add the crabmeat, bell pepper, cilantro, and lemon juice to the remaining mayonnaise and mix well. Add salt to taste. Cover tightly with plastic wrap and refrigerate.

**2** Use a 1½-inch round cookie cutter to cut out 36 rounds from the mango slices. Cut the leftover mango pieces into a small dice for garnish. Spread some of the reserved wasabi mayonnaise onto each slice of brioche and top with a mango round. Top with 1 teaspoon of the crabmeat salad. Garnish with diced mango. Serve immediately.

## GRILLED SWORDFISH ON GINGER-JALAPEÑO RICE CAKES

**MAKES 2 DOZEN** | photograph on page 45

*Buy swordfish with firm, glistening, almost translucent flesh. Grill the swordfish just before serving.*

¼ cup homemade (page 315) or prepared
    mayonnaise
¼ cup chopped fresh cilantro, plus extra
    for garnish
Kosher salt and freshly ground black pepper
1 large shallot, finely chopped
1 teaspoon prepared chili paste
1 tablespoon fresh lime juice
2 tablespoons extra-virgin olive oil, plus more
    for the grill
13 ounces fresh swordfish
1 recipe Ginger-Jalapeño Rice Cakes (page 246)
1 medium jalapeño pepper, thinly sliced
    crosswise

**1** In a small bowl, combine the mayonnaise, 2 tablespoons of the chopped cilantro, and salt and pepper to taste. Cover and refrigerate until ready to use.

**2** In another small bowl, combine the shallot, chili paste, lime juice, and the remaining 2 tablespoons of cilantro. Slowly whisk in the olive oil until incorporated.

**3** Place the swordfish in a shallow, nonreactive bowl and cover with the chili-lime marinade. Refrigerate and allow to marinate for 30 minutes, turning once.

**4** Heat a lightly oiled grill pan over medium-high heat, or lightly oil a grill rack and prepare a grill. Grill the swordfish for 5 minutes, turn, and cook until the fish is just opaque in the center, 2 to 4 more minutes. When cool enough to touch, cut the swordfish into ¼-inch-thick slices that measure about 1 × 1¼ inches, to fit on the rice cakes. Set aside.

**5** Heat the oven to 400° F. Arrange the rice cakes on a baking sheet. Heat until warm, 4 to 6 minutes. Remove and spread lightly with the cilantro mayonnaise. Top with a piece of swordfish and garnish with a thin slice of jalapeño and a leaf of cilantro.

## PETIT CROQUE MONSIEUR

**MAKES 2 DOZEN** | photograph on page 48

*The classic French grilled ham and cheese sandwich cut into halves or quarters makes a very substantial hors d'oeuvre. I've added pear slices and a dab of pear compote, which are well suited to the Black Forest ham and Gruyère cheese. Forelle pears are the perfect size for these little sandwiches, but other varieties may be substituted and cut to fit.*

4 tablespoons unsalted butter
6 ripe but still firm Forelle or large Seckel pears,
    2 cut into ¼-inch dice, and 4 cut crosswise
    into ¼-inch slices
1 teaspoon sugar
1 tablespoon balsamic vinegar
24 very thin slices white sandwich bread or Pain
    de Mie (page 238), crusts removed
¼ cup plus 2 tablespoons coarse whole-grain
    mustard
8 ounces thinly sliced Black Forest or other ham
8 ounces thinly sliced Gruyère cheese

**1** In a medium skillet over medium heat, melt 1 tablespoon of the butter. Add the diced pears and cook, stirring, until just tender, 1 to 2 minutes, depending on ripeness. Increase the heat to medium-high. Sprinkle the pears with the sugar and cook until golden brown and caramelized, 5 to 7 minutes. Add the vinegar and swirl the pan until the liquid is absorbed. Remove from the heat and transfer the pears to a plate. Set aside.

**2** Melt 1 tablespoon of butter in the same skillet over medium heat. Working in batches if needed, add the pear slices and cook until lightly browned, 3 to 4 minutes on each side. Set aside.

**3** Use the remaining 2 tablespoons of butter to spread over one side of each slice of bread. Lay the buttered side down on the work surface and spread the other side generously with the mustard. Slice the bread in half diagonally. Assemble each half-sandwich, butter-side facing out, with 1 slice of pear, 2 slices of ham, and 2 slices of cheese.

**4** Working in batches, cook 5 to 6 sandwich halves in a medium skillet over medium heat. Cook until the cheese is melted and the sandwiches are golden brown, 1½ minutes per side. Garnish each half with 1 teaspoon of the diced pears. Serve hot.

## MAPLE-GLAZED DUCK BREAST ON SWEET POTATO GAUFRETTES

**MAKES 4 DOZEN** | photograph on page 35

*Kumquats are generally available nine months out of the year; pomegranates have a much shorter season. For a brief period from October through December, both are available at the same time in the market. When pomegranates are not available, use fresh herbs such as oregano or thyme with the kumquats and chives for the garnish.*

8 kumquats, sliced crosswise into ⅛-inch-thick rounds

1 cup sugar

1 pound duck breast

Kosher salt and freshly ground black pepper

1 tablespoon olive oil

1½ tablespoons maple syrup

1 recipe Sweet Potato Gaufrettes (page 249)

1 pomegranate, seeded

Fresh chives, cut into 1-inch lengths, for garnish

**1** Bring a small pot of water to a boil. Add the kumquats and blanch them for 30 seconds. Transfer the kumquats to a colander and rinse under cool running water to stop the cooking. Set aside.

**2** In a small saucepan over medium heat, dissolve the sugar with 1 cup of water and bring to a boil. Add the kumquats and simmer over low heat, until the kumquats are transparent, about 10 minutes. Drain and arrange the kumquats on a cooling rack. Set aside.

**3** Preheat the oven to 425° F. Remove the skin and fat from the duck breast. Season with salt and pepper to taste. Add the olive oil to a medium ovenproof skillet over medium-high heat. Add the duck breast and sear for 2 minutes on one side. Turn the breast over, brush with 1 tablespoon of the maple syrup, and transfer to the oven. Cook for 8 minutes for medium rare, brushing the breast halfway through cooking with the remaining syrup. Remove the breast from the pan and set aside to rest for 5 minutes before slicing.

**4** To assemble, thinly cut the breast crosswise into ¼-inch-thick slices. Cut each to fit the Sweet Potato Gaufrettes. Place 1 piece of duck on a gaufrette and top with the candied kumquat, pomegranate seeds, and fresh chives.

## JERK CHICKEN SANDWICHES WITH MANGO CHUTNEY

**MAKES 2 DOZEN** | photograph on page 43

*Homemade Jamaican jerk sauce calls for 15 ingredients and is worth making if you have the time. If you don't, buy a good prepared version and customize it by adding garlic, hot chili peppers, fresh orange juice, vinegar, and ginger to suit your taste.*

16 ounces (1¾ cups) homemade (recipe
    follows) or prepared jerk sauce
1½ pounds boneless, skinless chicken breasts
1 bunch garlic chives or regular chives
    (optional)
1 teaspoon olive oil
1 recipe Tostones (page 249)
1 recipe Mango Chutney (page 399)

**1** Pour the jerk sauce into a medium nonreactive bowl; do not dilute with water. Add the chicken to the sauce, turn to coat well, cover, and refrigerate for 1 hour or up to 24 hours.

**2** Bring a small pot of water to a boil. Using a pair of tongs, grasp the bunch of chives and quickly dip them in and out of the water. Set in ice water or run under cold water to stop the cooking.

**3** Preheat the oven to 375°F. Heat a lightly oiled large grill pan, or heavy skillet, over medium-high heat or prepare a grill. Place the chicken on the hot grill (do not wipe off the marinade). Sear the chicken, brushing on extra sauce as needed, 1½ to 2 minutes per side. Transfer the chicken to a roasting pan. Cook the chicken in the oven until cooked through, about 10 minutes. Remove and set aside until cool enough to handle. Cut into bite-size pieces that will fit on the tostones, about 1¼ × ½ inches.

**4** Place a piece of chicken on a tostone and top with about ½ teaspoon of the chutney. Top with another tostone and tie together with a blanched chive, if desired. Trim the ends of the chive. Serve with the remaining chutney on the side.

## JERK SAUCE

**MAKES 2 CUPS** | photograph on page 43

*The sauce should be spicy, but if you like yours less so, remove the seeds and ribs from the jalapeño before mincing.*

3 tablespoons allspice
3 tablespoons packed dark brown sugar
1½ teaspoons ground nutmeg
¾ teaspoon ground cinnamon
1 tablespoon kosher salt
¾ teaspoon dried red pepper flakes
3 tablespoons fresh orange juice
3 tablespoons rice wine vinegar
1 tablespoon Worcestershire sauce
1 tablespoon soy sauce
12 scallions (large bunch), white and light green
    parts, finely chopped
6 large shallots, minced
3 garlic cloves, minced
2 tablespoons grated fresh ginger
3 large jalapeño peppers, minced

**1** In a small bowl, combine the allspice, brown sugar, nutmeg, cinnamon, salt, and pepper flakes. In another small bowl, combine the orange juice, vinegar, Worcestershire, and soy sauce. Set both bowls aside.

**2** In the bowl of a food processor, combine the scallions, shallots, garlic, ginger, and jalapeños and pulse until finely chopped. Add the spice mixture and the orange juice mixture. Pulse until the sauce is well combined but still has some texture. The mixture will be pastelike. The jerk sauce will keep, tightly covered, in the refrigerator for up to 3 weeks.

During a recent visit to Jamaica, I happened upon a charming little roadside jerk pork shack, one of the many all over the island. Inside the shack was a jerk seasoning expert, who inspired me to make my own version of classic Jamaican jerk sauce.

Jerk sauce is actually a seasoning that is rubbed into meat before it is grilled. The word "jerk" is thought to have originated from the native Peruvian word *ch'arki*. The Spanish changed the term to a word that was more sensible to them, *charqui*, a word for dried meat. This term entered the English language as "jerk" or "jerky."

The actual technique of jerking was developed by Jamaican slaves, called Maroons, who escaped from British plantations on the island. Hidden in the mountainous jungle, they would cook seasoned pork until it was very dry, so it could be preserved in the tropical climate. They also cooked the meat over very low fires, which were less detectable to the British who might be hunting for the escaped slaves. Over time, this method evolved until the pork no longer needed to be cooked until dry. It is still cooked over a low fire, but it may now be served juicy and very spicy.

The exact sauce ingredients vary with each cook, but they generally include chilies, thyme, cinnamon, allspice, sugar, garlic, and onions. A thicker jerk sauce will be rubbed into the meat, while more liquid versions are used as a marinade. Jerk is used on pork, chicken, and beef before and during grilling.

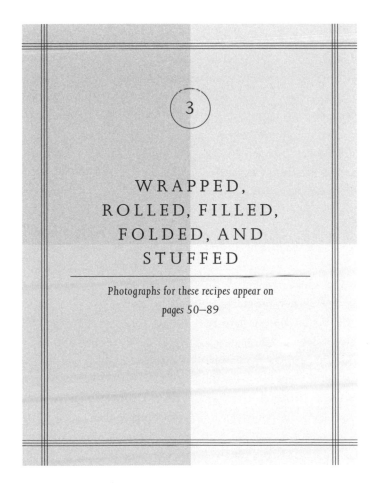

# 3

# WRAPPED, ROLLED, FILLED, FOLDED, AND STUFFED

Photographs for these recipes appear on
pages 50–89

THERE IS SOMETHING INHERENTLY APPEALING ABOUT HORS D'OEUVRES THAT CONSIST OF ONE FOOD ENCASED IN ANOTHER. PERHAPS IT IS BECAUSE THEY RESEMBLE BEAUTIFULLY WRAPPED PACKAGES, OR THAT THEY CARRY AN ELEMENT OF SURPRISE.

Whether wrapped, rolled, folded, filled, or stuffed, these decorative, delicious bundles are particularly inviting. Every country in the world has some tradition of food presented in this fashion. Some of the preparations I present here are, in their original incarnations, served as substantial snacks or even entrées rather than little bites. To convert them into hors d'oeuvres, I have simply miniaturized them, which transforms them into something quite new and different. Tiny versions of Morocco's chicken bisteeya, diminutive empanadas from South America, and coin-size classic French crepes all fit into this category.

Sometimes it's not so much a matter of scaling down, though, as dividing up a standard-sized batch among many small containers. I spoon Welsh rarebit into tiny toasted breadboxes, for example, serve a quick-to-make but startlingly deep-flavored cassoulet in crunchy croustades, put tangy scallop ceviche into toasted corn cups, and cradle calamari salad in mini pita halves. Tartlet shells flavored with sesame and orange zest, poppy seeds, or Parmesan and freshly ground black pepper are pretty, practical containers for fillings such as lemon chicken salad or pieces of tuna sliced from a large steak.

Another approach that works very well—particularly when you're cooking for larger groups—is to offer a single dish in many versions to create a sense of opulence. After scooping out the insides of red and yellow cherry tomatoes, for instance, I introduce five different fillings featuring different regional tastes, from the Mexican flavors of Grilled Corn and Shrimp Salad to the Italian bread salad called panzanella. In the same way, I recast that cocktail party standby, stuffed mushrooms, by using unusual fillings, such as broccoli rabe and pancetta, creamy polenta, and leek, fennel, and goat cheese. At times I simply like to put my own stamp on a classic finger food, such as Asian dumplings filled with a new flavor combination like scallops, arugula, and lemongrass.

For a quick stuffed hors d'oeuvre, you can make a container of one food and fill it with several others. Endive leaves make excellent nests for chèvre, port-glazed figs, and pecans, for example, while Globe grape halves rimmed with crushed pistachios and filled with chèvre are both cunning and delicious.

As you read through the recipes in this chapter, you will find that a single little package is large enough to combine an inspired mix of many flavors, textures, and colors. The key to creating successful hors d'oeuvres in this category, however, is to keep the flavors clean and distinct.

# POTSTICKERS

**MAKES 2 DOZEN** | photograph on page 66

*Named for their tendency to stick to the pot, potstickers are one of my favorite street snacks in New York City's Chinatown. It was there that I watched the Chinese women cooking them in giant pans, allowing the dumplings to sear to a very deep brown without disturbing them too much, then adding the broth, which loosens the potsticker and steams the top side. The filling may be made a day ahead and stored in an airtight container in the refrigerator.*

¼ ounce dried black or shiitake mushrooms

1 tablespoon sesame oil

1 teaspoon minced fresh ginger

½ teaspoon five-spice powder

2 ounces fresh shiitake mushrooms, stems
    removed, roughly chopped to yield ½ cup

1 medium carrot, cut into ¼-inch dice

1 medium leek, white and light green parts,
    finely chopped to yield ¼ cup, well washed
    (see page 271)

4 scallions, white and light green parts, finely
    chopped to yield ¼ cup

1 tablespoon dry sherry

1 tablespoon low-sodium soy sauce

Kosher salt and freshly ground black pepper

8 ounces ground pork

24 round potsticker wrappers (see page 283)

3 tablespoons canola oil

Scallion-Soy Dipping Sauce (page 395)

**1** Place the dried mushrooms in a small bowl and cover with ½ cup very hot water. Let sit for 20 minutes, until the mushrooms are full and soft. Drain and discard the liquid. Roughly chop the mushrooms. Set aside.

**2** Heat the sesame oil in a medium skillet over medium heat. Add the ginger and cook until very fragrant, about 15 seconds. Stir in the five-spice powder, the reconstituted mushrooms, and the shiitake mushrooms, and cook for 1 minute, stirring constantly. Add the carrots, leeks, and scallions and stir to combine. Add the sherry and stir well. Add the soy sauce and salt and pepper to taste. Transfer to a bowl to cool slightly, 5 to 10 minutes. Stir in the pork.

**3** Line a baking sheet with parchment paper. Work on one dumpling at a time, keeping the remaining wrappers covered with plastic wrap so they don't dry out. Place about 2 teaspoons of the filling in the middle of a wrapper. Using your fingers, moisten the edges of the wrapper with water. Fold in the middle to form a taco shape and squeeze the edges together to seal the dumpling. Pinch small pleats along one side only of the sealed edge, slightly wetting your fingers to help seal the pleats. Place the filled potsticker on the baking sheet and cover with plastic wrap. Repeat with the remaining ingredients until all the wrappers are filled.

**4** Heat 1½ tablespoons of the canola oil in a medium cast-iron skillet over medium-high heat for 3 to 4 minutes. Arrange half of the potstickers, pleat-side up, snugly together in the heated pan. Cook, shaking the pan once, until the dumplings are deep golden brown on the bottom, 1 to 2 minutes. Carefully add 1 cup of hot water, partially cover, and cook for 4 to 5 minutes. Reduce the heat to medium and cook until the bottoms of the potstickers are dark brown and very crisp and all the water has evaporated, 5 to 6 minutes. Slide a spatula under the potstickers to loosen them from the pan. Serve this batch of potstickers immediately, or place them on a baking sheet, cover loosely with foil, and keep in a warm oven. Wash and dry the skillet and repeat with the remaining canola oil and potstickers. Serve warm with the dipping sauce.

## SCALLOP, ARUGULA, AND LEMONGRASS DUMPLINGS

**MAKES 2 DOZEN** | photograph on page 66

*Dumplings can be cooked in any steamer, whether the classic collapsible metal insert or bamboo steamer basket, or a double boiler with a steamer rack. A lining of lettuce leaves provides moisture and prevents dumplings from sticking. The dumplings can be shaped 2 to 3 hours before steaming, covered with plastic wrap, and refrigerated.*

1 tablespoon plus ½ teaspoon peanut oil

1 garlic clove, minced

½ teaspoon minced fresh ginger

1 tablespoon low-sodium soy sauce

2 scallions, white and green parts, finely chopped

4 canned water chestnuts, roughly chopped

1 1-inch piece of fresh lemongrass, pounded and minced to yield ¾ teaspoon, or ¾ teaspoon grated lemon zest

Kosher salt

3 cups loosely packed arugula leaves, well washed

½ ounce rice vermicelli noodles (see Sources, page 487)

2 tablespoons chopped fresh cilantro

6 ounces bay scallops, muscle removed, roughly chopped

24 round dumpling wrappers (see page 283)

Lettuce leaves to line the steamer

Scallion-Soy Dipping Sauce (page 395)

**1** Heat 1 tablespoon of the peanut oil in a small skillet over medium heat. Add the garlic and ginger and cook until sizzling, about 30 seconds. Remove from the heat and stir in the soy sauce, scallions, water chestnuts, and lemongrass. Transfer the mixture to a bowl and set aside.

**2** Bring a large pot of lightly salted water to a boil. Add the arugula and blanch just until wilted, about 15 seconds. Drain and rinse with cold water to prevent the arugula from cooking further. Squeeze all excess water from the arugula and roughly chop. Set aside.

**3** Bring a small pot of lightly salted water to a boil. Add the noodles, return the water to a boil, and cook until tender, about 2 minutes. Drain, roughly chop into 2-inch pieces, and set aside, tightly covered with plastic wrap, until ready to use.

**4** In the bowl of a food processor, combine the cilantro and two thirds of the arugula. Process until puréed. Add half of the scallops and the remaining ½ teaspoon of peanut oil, and process just until combined and pastelike. Pieces of scallop should still be visible. Transfer to a bowl and stir in the ginger-garlic mixture. Add the remaining third of the arugula, the remaining scallops, and the reserved noodles. Stir well to combine. Season with salt to taste.

**5** Line a baking sheet with parchment paper. Work on one dumpling at a time, keeping the remaining wrappers covered with plastic wrap so they don't dry out. Place about 2 teaspoons of the filling in the middle of a wrapper. Using your fingers, moisten the edges of the wrapper with water. Bring the two edges together to form a taco shape and pinch them together to seal the dumpling. Place the filled dumpling on the baking sheet and cover with plastic wrap. Repeat with the remaining ingredients until all the wrappers are filled.

**6** Set a steamer basket in a wok or shallow saucepan and add enough water to just cover the bottom of the basket. Remove the steamer basket from the pan and bring the water to a simmer over low heat. Arrange the lettuce leaves to cover the bottom of the steamer basket. Working in batches if necessary, arrange the dumplings on the lettuce, in the steamer basket, being careful that the dumplings do not touch, as they might stick together. Place the whole steamer into the simmering water. Cover and steam until cooked through, 7 to 10 minutes. Serve immediately with the Scallion-Soy Dipping Sauce.

---

**NOTE** | Dumpling Wrappers

The freezer section of the supermarket yields many useful staples for making hors d'oeuvres, including dumpling wrappers, paper-thin sheets of dough found where Asian foods are sold (see photograph, page 62). The back of each package usually has an ingredient list in English. The wrappers can be made with or without eggs. The flour used can be white, whole wheat, or rice. Wrappers are either round or square and are made in varying degrees of thickness. These different wrappers are interchangeable in any of the steamed dumpling recipes. Potsticker wrappers are labeled in various ways but are all generally the same. For example, in Japanese they are called gyoza; in Chinese, wonton skins. Shao mai wrappers are about ½ inch smaller than the other kinds of wrappers. When making dumplings, fill one at a time and keep the remaining wrappers covered with plastic wrap so that they do not dry out. To order dumpling wrappers by mail, see Sources, page 487.

---

# CRABMEAT SOUP DUMPLINGS

**MAKES 6 DOZEN** | photograph on page 69

*These dumplings made Joe's Shanghai in New York City's Chinatown famous. Once you master the proper method of eating these, you'll be hooked. Take a bite, sip the broth inside, then eat the savory filling. The mystery lies in how the sip of soup gets inside.*

5 large parsley stems
1 teaspoon whole black peppercorns
3 sprigs fresh thyme
2 bay leaves
4 pounds chicken backs, necks, and wings
1 3-pound chicken, cut into 16 pieces
1 large onion, cut in half
Kosher salt and freshly ground black pepper
8 ounces lump crabmeat, picked over for
    cartilage
1 garlic clove, minced
1½ tablespoons chopped fresh flat-leaf parsley
2 tablespoons snipped fresh chives
1 tablespoon grated lemon zest
6 dozen wheat-cake wrappers (3½ inches round)
    or other dumpling wrapper (see Note, left)
Lettuce leaves to line the steamer

**1** Wrap the parsley stems, peppercorns, thyme, and bay leaves in a square of cheesecloth and tie with kitchen twine to make a bouquet garni. Set aside. Using a meat cleaver or large chef's knife, chop the chicken backs, necks, and wings into smaller pieces. Transfer all of the chicken pieces to a large stockpot. Add the reserved bouquet garni, the onion, and enough water just to cover the chicken, about 3 quarts. Be careful not to add too much water or the stock will be too diluted to gel. Cover and bring to a medium simmer over medium heat. Uncover and cook at a low simmer, skimming the top every 20 minutes or so, for

CONTINUED ON FOLLOWING PAGE

3½ hours. Do not let it boil. Drain the stock and discard all of the solids.

**2** Place the stock into a smaller saucepan and cook over high heat until reduced by half, 30 to 40 minutes. Season with salt and pepper to taste. Drain the liquid through a very fine strainer and pour it into a shallow 8-inch square cake pan. Cool the stock at room temperature. Cover the stock with plastic wrap and refrigerate until completely chilled, about 6 hours or overnight. Once chilled, skim the fat off the top. The stock should be thick and gelatinous. If the stock has not sufficiently gelled, transfer to the freezer for 4 to 6 hours. The stock may be made up to this point, tightly covered and refrigerated for up to 3 days or frozen for 3 to 4 months. If frozen, remove the stock about 20 minutes before using to thaw slightly.

**3** To make the dumplings: In a medium bowl, stir together the crabmeat, garlic, parsley, chives, and lemon zest. Season the mixture generously with salt and pepper.

**4** Work on one dumpling at a time, keeping the remaining wrappers covered with plastic wrap so they don't dry out. Moisten the edge of a wrapper. Place a heaping teaspoon or cube of the chilled stock into the center of one wrapper. Top the stock with a scant teaspoon of the crab filling. Bring the edges of the wrapper upward, pleating as you go, creating a small purse. Firmly pinch together the top of the purse to seal it. Filled dumplings that sit too long at room temperature will get soggy, so either steam them as they are made, in batches of 8 to 10, or store them in the freezer. In an airtight container, dumplings will keep 3 to 4 days in the freezer. Steam dumplings directly from the freezer.

**5** To steam the dumplings: Set a steamer basket in a wok or shallow saucepan and add enough water to just cover the bottom of the basket. Remove the steamer basket from the pan and bring the water to a simmer over low heat. Arrange the lettuce leaves to cover the bottom of the steamer basket. Working in batches if necessary, arrange the dumplings on the lettuce, being careful that the dumplings do not touch, as they might stick together. Place the whole steamer into the simmering water. Cover and steam until the wrappers are cooked through and the filling is hot, 7 to 10 minutes. (Timing is the same for frozen dumplings.) Serve the dumplings immediately in small plates or Asian soup spoons (see Sources, page 486) to catch the soup.

## SHRIMP AND BEAN SPROUT SHAO MAI

**MAKES 2 DOZEN** | photograph on page 66

*Shao mai, literally "to bake and to sell," are actually not baked but steamed dumplings. The filling may be made a day ahead, stored in an airtight container, and refrigerated. The dumplings themselves can be shaped several hours ahead, covered, and refrigerated.*

9 ounces medium shrimp, peeled and deveined (see page 340), and roughly chopped

1 large egg white

1¼ teaspoons chili oil

1¾ teaspoons sesame oil

2 teaspoons low-sodium soy sauce

2 tablespoons finely chopped fresh cilantro

1 small shallot, minced

1½ ounces bean sprouts, chopped in half, to yield ¾ cup

1 garlic clove, minced

3 canned water chestnuts, roughly chopped

¾ teaspoon kosher salt

Freshly ground black pepper

1 large bunch chives (about 30)

24 shao mai wrappers (see page 283)

Lettuce leaves to line the steamer

**1** In the bowl of a food processor, combine half the shrimp, the egg white, chili oil, sesame oil, and soy sauce. Process until smooth. Transfer the mixture to a bowl. Stir in the cilantro, shallots, bean sprouts, garlic, water chestnuts, remaining shrimp, the salt, and pepper to taste.

**2** Bring a medium pot of water to a boil. Using tongs, quickly dip the bunch of chives in and out of the boiling water to blanch. Set in ice water or run under cool water to stop the cooking.

**3** Line a baking sheet with parchment paper. Work on one dumpling at a time, keeping the remaining wrappers covered with plastic wrap so they don't dry out. Place one wrapper on the work surface. Place 2 teaspoons of the filling in the center. Using your fingers, moisten the edges of the wrapper with water. Gather up the corners of the wrapper with your fingers to form a bundle. Cinch the wrapper ½ inch below the edge to make a waist. (Some of the filling should bulge up a bit.) Tie a chive around the waist of the shao mai and trim the edges of the chive. Alternatively, shape the dumplings as in step 5 of Scallop, Arugula, and Lemongrass Dumplings, page 282. Place the filled dumpling on the baking sheet and cover with plastic wrap. Repeat with the remaining ingredients until all the wrappers are filled.

**4** Set a steamer basket in a wok or shallow saucepan and add enough water to just cover the bottom of the basket. Remove the steamer basket from the pan and bring the water to a simmer over low heat. Arrange the lettuce leaves to cover the bottom of the steamer basket. Working in batches if necessary, arrange the dumplings on the lettuce, in the steamer basket, being careful that the dumplings do not touch, as they might stick together. Place the whole steamer into the simmering water. Cover and steam until cooked through, 7 to 10 minutes. Serve immediately.

## SPICY TUNA ROLLS

**MAKES 5 DOZEN** | photograph on page 51

*Sushi-quality tuna, purchased from a reputable fishmonger, is a must for these glistening jewels. Black sesame seeds provide a striking contrast, but white can be used as well.*

1 pound very fresh yellowfin tuna steak, cut into
    ¼-inch dice
3 tablespoons snipped fresh chives
2 tablespoons sesame oil
¼ cup low-sodium soy sauce
2 tablespoons rice wine vinegar
½ teaspoon kosher salt, or more to taste
¼ teaspoon freshly ground black pepper, or more
    to taste
¼ cup homemade (page 315) or prepared
    mayonnaise
1 teaspoon chili paste
3 Japanese or kirby cucumbers
1 teaspoon black sesame seeds, toasted
    (see page 386)

**1** In a medium bowl, combine the tuna, chives, sesame oil, soy sauce, vinegar, salt, and pepper. Cover tightly with plastic wrap and refrigerate.

**2** Mix the mayonnaise and chili paste in a small bowl, cover, and refrigerate.

**3** Using a mandoline, slice the cucumbers lengthwise as thinly as possible into approximately 5-inch lengths. Season with salt and pepper to taste. Place 1 heaping teaspoon of the tuna tartar on one end of the cucumber slice. Roll up. The cucumber, when very thinly sliced, will stick together and stay rolled without a toothpick. Continue making rolls with the remaining ingredients.

**4** Fill a pastry bag fitted with a small (#3) tip, or a resealable plastic bag with the corner snipped off, with the spicy mayonnaise. Top each roll with a small dollop of the mayonnaise and a sprinkling of the toasted sesame seeds.

## CRISPY ASPARAGUS STRAWS

**MAKES 2 DOZEN** | photograph on page 72

*Choose thicker green, purple, or white asparagus with tightly packed tips for these crunchy hors d'oeuvres; pencil-thin asparagus will overcook in the oven. You may prepare the asparagus in advance, then set it aside on a baking sheet and refrigerate until ready to bake.*

24 asparagus spears, woody ends trimmed

6 sheets of phyllo dough, thawed if frozen

3 tablespoons unsalted butter, melted

12 thin slices prosciutto (about 6 ounces total),
      cut in half crosswise

4 ounces Parmesan cheese, grated on the
      medium holes of a box grater

**1** Place the asparagus in a steamer basket over 1 inch of boiling water. Cover tightly and steam until just al dente and bright green, about 2 minutes. Transfer to a colander to cool.

**2** Preheat the oven to 450° F. with the rack in the center. Line a baking sheet with parchment paper and set aside. Place 1 sheet of phyllo on a dry surface. Keep the remaining sheets covered with a clean, slightly damp towel. Brush lightly with melted butter and cut into 4 rectangular pieces, each 5 × 7 inches.

**3** Place 1 piece of prosciutto on the phyllo, lining it up along 1 short edge of the rectangle. Arrange an asparagus spear on top of the prosciutto along the same short edge of the rectangle, letting the tip lay exposed beyond the top edge of the dough by ¾ inch or so. Sprinkle with ½ teaspoon Parmesan. Roll up and secure the edge of the dough with additional butter, if necessary. Repeat with the remaining ingredients, transferring the straws onto the prepared baking sheet. The straws may be made 1 to 2 hours ahead up to this point, covered with plastic wrap, and refrigerated.

**4** Before baking, sprinkle the top of the straws with the remaining cheese. Cover the asparagus tips with foil to protect them from the heat. Bake until golden brown, 5 to 8 minutes. Serve warm, either whole or sliced into bite-size pieces.

## JICAMA AND GREEN PAPAYA SUMMER ROLLS

**MAKES ABOUT 2 DOZEN** | photograph on page 63

*In tropical countries, green papayas are often used as vegetables, which is how I use them here. Rice vermicelli noodles and Vietnamese spring roll wrappers are available at Asian markets and many grocery stores. The rolls may be kept at room temperature, covered with a lightly dampened paper towel, for 1 hour after being assembled. Do not refrigerate the rolls or the rice paper will dry out and become brittle.*

½ cup rice wine vinegar

2 tablespoons sugar

2 teaspoons kosher salt

1 small seedless cucumber

1 medium carrot

1 small jicama

1 large green papaya, peeled, halved (seeds
      discarded)

1 teaspoon fresh lemon juice

2 teaspoons chopped fresh cilantro

1 teaspoon canola oil

1 ounce rice vermicelli noodles

6 8½-inch Vietnamese dried rice spring roll
      wrappers

8 leaves Bibb lettuce, torn into smaller pieces,
      ribs removed

Peanut Dipping Sauce (page 395)

**1** In a small saucepan, combine the vinegar, sugar, and 1 teaspoon of the salt. Cook, stirring, over medium heat until the sugar dissolves, 1 to 2 minutes. Remove from the heat. Set aside and let cool completely.

**2** Slice the cucumber lengthwise using a mandoline or a chef's knife into long ⅛-inch-thick strips. Cut each strip lengthwise into ⅛-inch-wide pieces. Slice the carrot and the jicama lengthwise in the same way. Reserve. Cut the papaya lengthwise into ⅛-inch pieces. Cut each piece lengthwise into ⅛-inch-wide pieces. In a large bowl, combine the cucumber, carrot, jicama, and papaya. Toss gently with the reserved vinegar mixture, lemon juice, and cilantro. Set aside.

**3** Bring a medium pot of water to a boil. Add the canola oil, noodles, and the remaining teaspoon of salt. Boil until the noodles are tender, about 2 minutes. Drain and rinse under cold water. Leave the noodles in cool water until ready to use, so they won't stick together.

**4** Just before filling the rolls, transfer the vegetable mixture to a colander to drain. Gently press out the liquid. Drain the noodles and arrange them on a baking sheet, loosely covered with a damp paper towel.

**5** To assemble: Set up a large shallow bowl of very hot water. Slip a spring roll wrapper into the water. When the wrapper becomes pliable, after about 45 seconds, remove it from the water and lay it flat on a paper towel. Place 2 to 3 pieces of lettuce on the bottom half of the wrapper. Arrange ¼ packed cup of the vegetables over the lettuce. Spread out 1 heaping tablespoon of the noodles over the vegetables. Roll the wrapper up, tucking in the ends as you roll and rolling as tightly as possible. Repeat this procedure with the remaining wrappers. Trim off the ends of the rolls. Cut each roll in half in the middle. Then cut each of the 2 halves into 2 pieces on an angle to make a total of 4 pieces. Continue with the remaining rolls. Stand the rolls flat on their ends and serve with Peanut Dipping Sauce.

## SCALLOP CEVICHE WITH AVOCADO PURÉE IN TOASTED CORN CUPS

**MAKES ABOUT 3½ DOZEN** | photograph on page 60

*Ceviche is a traditional Spanish recipe that "cooks" fish or shellfish in the acid from vinegar and citrus. This recipe must be made the day before you plan to serve it, the shellfish requires at least 16 hours in the vinegar and citrus. The Toasted Corn Cups may be made on the same day you make the ceviche, but the avocado purée should be prepared just before assembling.*

¼ cup plus 2 tablespoons fresh lime juice
½ cup fresh orange juice
1 tablespoon cider vinegar
5 tablespoons chopped fresh cilantro
1 large jalapeño pepper, sliced into thin rounds
1 small red onion, sliced into thin rings
¼ pound bay scallops
1 blood orange
1 orange
1 lime
1 ripe avocado
Kosher salt and freshly ground black pepper
2 recipes Toasted Corn Cups (page 243)

**1** In a medium bowl, combine the ⅓ cup lime juice, the orange juice, vinegar, 2 tablespoons of the cilantro, the jalapeño, and half of the red onion. Cut the scallops in half crosswise. Stir the scallop halves into the marinade. Cover and refrigerate for 16 to 24 hours, stirring once or twice.

**2** Section the blood orange, the orange, and the lime, and remove the membranes. Cut each piece of sectioned fruit into 2 or 3 smaller pieces. Place the pieces in a small bowl. Cut the remaining onion rings into about 1-inch pieces, and add to the bowl. Add the remaining 3 tablespoons of the cilantro to the bowl. Set aside.

CONTINUED ON FOLLOWING PAGE

**3** When ready to assemble, peel the avocado, cut it into chunks, and place in the bowl of a food processor. Add the remaining 2 tablespoons lime juice and purée until smooth, about 20 seconds. Season with salt and pepper to taste. Place the avocado purée in a resealable plastic bag.

**4** Strain the liquid from the ceviche. Cut each scallop into quarters. Set aside. Cut off a corner of the plastic bag. Pipe about 1 teaspoon of avocado purée into each corn cup. Top with 2 pieces of the scallops and garnish with the citrus, cilantro, and red onion mixture. Serve right away.

## CASSOULET CROUSTADES

**MAKES 6 DOZEN** | photograph on page 56

*The flavors of this quick version of cassoulet are inspired by the Gascogne classic, which requires elaborate preparation, including homemade duck confit, and long cooking time. Spoon the cassoulet into the croustades just before serving. I use cured sausage flavored with garlic (see Sources, page 487), often labeled in French, saucisson a l'ail.*

8 ounces dried navy or cannellini beans

2 7-ounce legs prepared duck confit (see
  Sources, page 487)

1 teaspoon whole black peppercorns

2 bay leaves

1 whole clove

½ pound cured garlic sausage, cut into ½-inch
  dice

1 small onion, finely chopped

3 garlic cloves, minced

1 tablespoon tomato paste

10 sprigs fresh thyme

2 cups homemade chicken stock or low-sodium
  canned chicken broth, skimmed of fat

1 medium carrot, cut into ¼-inch dice

3 recipes Golden Croustades (page 243)

**1** Rinse the beans in a colander. Transfer the beans to a medium saucepan filled with water. Cover and bring to a boil. Remove from the heat and let sit, covered, for 1 hour. Drain and reserve.

**2** Preheat the oven to 375° F. with the rack in the center. In a medium ovenproof skillet over medium-high heat, sear the duck confit for 5 minutes, to render the fat. (Save the rendered duck fat for another use.) Transfer to the oven and cook until crispy, 15 to 20 minutes. Transfer the duck to a plate to cool. Shred the meat and cover to keep moist. Reserve.

**3** Wrap the peppercorns, bay leaves, and clove in a small piece of cheesecloth and tie with kitchen twine to make a bouquet garni. Set aside. In a large skillet over medium heat, cook the sausage until crispy, about 10 minutes. Add the onion and cook until transparent, about 5 minutes, scraping up any bits of brown in the pan. Add the garlic and cook until softened, 2 to 3 minutes. Add the tomato paste and cook 1 minute. Add the drained beans, 5 sprigs of the thyme, the stock, and the bouquet garni. Cover and bring to a boil. Reduce to a simmer and cook over low heat for 30 minutes. Add the carrots. Cover, and continue to cook until most of the liquid is absorbed and the beans are tender, 20 to 30 minutes. (If the cassoulet is still soupy, remove the cover and continue to simmer until most of the liquid is absorbed.)

**4** Remove the bouquet garni and the thyme sprigs. Spoon a scant ¾ tablespoon into each croustade. Top each with pieces of duck confit and thyme leaves from the remaining sprigs. Serve immediately.

## SAVORY TARTLETS

vegetables in each tartlet, reserving the liquid. Top each with seared tuna, and garnish with chives and orange zest. Before serving, drizzle the tops with a little of the remaining vinaigrette.

### SEARED TUNA IN SESAME-ORANGE TARTLETS

**MAKES 3 DOZEN** | photograph on page 86

*Sear the tuna just until both sides color slightly, the inside should glisten.*

4 ounces ¾-inch-thick yellowfin tuna steak
    (4½ × 5 inches)
2 tablespoons sesame oil
Kosher salt and freshly ground black pepper
1 tablespoon rice wine vinegar
1 tablespoon fresh orange juice
1½ teaspoons grated fresh ginger
3 tablespoons extra-virgin olive oil
1 small yellow bell pepper, seeds and ribs
    removed, cut into matchsticks
1 small seedless cucumber, peel on, cut into
    matchsticks
1 recipe Sesame-Orange Tartlet Shells (page 233)
1 tablespoon snipped fresh chives
2 tablespoons grated orange zest

**1** Brush the tuna with 1 tablespoon of the sesame oil and season generously with salt and pepper. In a skillet over medium-high heat, sear the tuna on both sides until the surface is light brown, 1 to 1½ minutes per side. Remove from the heat and let the tuna rest for 5 minutes.

**2** In a small bowl, whisk together the vinegar, the remaining tablespoon of sesame oil, the orange juice, and the ginger. Whisk in the olive oil until combined. Season generously with salt and pepper. Toss with the bell pepper and cucumber.

**3** Using a very sharp knife, slice the tuna into ⅛-inch-thick slices. Lay the slices flat and cut them into approximately ¾ × 1½-inch rectangles, to fit in the tartlet shells. Arrange a few pieces of the

### LEMON CHICKEN SALAD IN POPPY SEED TARTLETS

**MAKES 3 DOZEN** | photograph on page 86

*Lemon Chicken Salad filling may also be used on Classic Toast Points (page 244) or Simple Crostini (page 243), or in toasted Pita Cups (page 242).*

2 cups homemade chicken stock or low-sodium
    canned chicken broth, skimmed of fat
1 7-ounce skinless, boneless chicken breast
1½ tablespoons fresh lemon juice
3 tablespoons homemade (page 315) or
    prepared mayonnaise
1 tablespoon chopped fresh chervil, plus leaves
    for garnish
Kosher salt and freshly ground black pepper
1 recipe Poppy Seed Tartlet Shells (page 233)
8 red seedless grapes, thinly sliced

**1** Place the chicken stock in a small saucepan and bring to a simmer over medium-high heat. Add the chicken breast, reduce the heat to low, and poach until the breast is cooked through, 8 to 10 minutes. Remove the chicken breast and let cool.

**2** Shred the chicken into small pieces and place in a medium-size bowl. Stir in the lemon juice, mayonnaise, chervil, and salt and pepper to taste. Cover with plastic wrap and refrigerate until ready to use. This filling may be made 1 day ahead.

**3** Using a small spoon, place about 1 teaspoon of the chicken salad in each tartlet shell. Garnish with grape slices and chervil leaves.

**TECHNIQUE** | Dried Mushrooms

Dried mushrooms are essential in a well-stocked pantry. To use them they must first be rehydrated—a simple process that must be done properly to get good results.

In their dried state, mushrooms look hard, dry, and rather unappetizing. Depending on the variety of mushroom, they may come whole, sliced, or in small pieces. All varieties keep very well if stored in a cool, dry place, but it is best to use them within 6 months.

Place the dried mushrooms in a medium heatproof bowl. Pour enough boiling water over them to cover by 1 inch, and let them steep in the water for 20 to 30 minutes. To test the mushrooms, squeeze a few of them with your fingers; when they are properly rehydrated they will be soft and tender. If they are not, allow them to continue soaking.

When the mushrooms are rehydrated, you have 2 valuable ingredients—the mushrooms and the resulting soaking liquid, which is wonderful in soups, stocks, or sauces. Separate the mushrooms from the liquid by pouring them through a fine sieve lined with cheesecloth; the cheesecloth will catch the very fine silty powder. The strained liquid may be kept in the refrigerator, in an airtight container, for 3 days, or frozen for up to 3 months. If the mushrooms in the sieve are covered with the powder, rinse them quickly under cool water. Use the mushrooms as directed.

*Use this filling on Simple Crostini (page 243) or Classic Toast Points (page 244) if you prefer.*

½ ounce dried porcini mushrooms
¼ ounce dried morels
2 tablespoons unsalted butter
1 small leek, white and green parts, cut into
    ¼-inch rings, well washed (see page 271)
1 garlic clove, minced
3 tablespoons dry white wine
3 ounces button or cremini mushrooms, wiped
    clean, stems removed, cut into ¼-inch slices
1½ ounces chanterelle or oyster mushrooms,
    wiped clean, stems trimmed, cut into pieces
1½ ounces enoki mushrooms, trimmed
Kosher salt and freshly ground black pepper
1 recipe Parmesan-Pepper Tartlet Shells (page 234)
2 ounces Parmesan cheese, grated on the large
    holes of a box grater to yield ¾ cup

**1** Rehydrate the porcini mushrooms and morels (see Note, left).

**2** Drain the mushrooms, reserving the porcini liquid and discarding the morel liquid. Finely chop the porcinis, and cut the morels into ¼-inch slices.

**3** Heat the butter in a medium skillet over medium-low heat. Add the leeks and garlic and cook until soft, 3 to 5 minutes. Turn the heat up to medium-high and add the wine. Simmer until reduced by half, 1 to 3 minutes. Add the mushrooms and 3 tablespoons of the porcini soaking liquid and cook until the mushrooms are cooked through and most of the liquid has evaporated, 6 to 8 minutes. Add salt and pepper to taste. Keep warm.

**4** Spoon about 1 teaspoon of the warm mushroom mixture into each tartlet shell. Garnish with the Parmesan, and serve warm.

## PASTRY DOUGH TARTLETS

I use fluted tartlet molds for the following two savory tarts: a narrow, deep pan, measuring 2¼ inches across and ¾ inch deep, for the Swiss Chard, Shallot, and Parmesan Tartlets, the other shallow, measuring about 2¾ inches across and ⅜ inch deep, for the Tomato, Basil, and Olive Tartlets. Basic pastry dough tarts freeze beautifully if blind baked (see page 232).

## SWISS CHARD, SHALLOT, AND PARMESAN TARTLETS

**MAKES 2½ DOZEN** | photographs on pages 80 and 81

*These tartlets are best when served right out of the oven.*

1 tablespoon unsalted butter
1 small shallot, minced
1 1-pound bunch Swiss chard, leaves well
    washed, roughly chopped
Kosher salt and freshly ground black pepper
3½ ounces Parmesan cheese, grated on the large
    holes of a box grater to yield 1¼ cups
3 large eggs, lightly beaten
⅓ cup plus 1 tablespoon milk
2 teaspoons grated lemon zest
1 recipe Basic Pastry Dough Tartlet Shells
    (page 232)

**1** Preheat the oven to 400° F. Melt the butter in a large skillet over medium heat. Add the shallots and cook until translucent, about 2 minutes. Do not brown. Stir in the Swiss chard and continue to cook until wilted, about 2 minutes. Add the salt and pepper to taste. Remove from the heat and transfer to a medium bowl. In a separate bowl, stir together 1 cup of the cheese, the eggs, milk, and lemon zest.

**2** Place about 1 teaspoon of the chard mixture in each cooled tartlet shell. Top each with 2 teaspoons

of the cheese mixture. Transfer to 2 baking sheets. Bake until set, 20 to 25 minutes, rotating trays halfway through for even browning. Transfer the tartlets to a wire rack to cool slightly. Remove each tartlet from the pan, sprinkle with the remaining cheese, and serve warm.

---

**NOTE** | Filled Tartlet Shells

---

Baked tiny tartlets, filled with a variety of ingredients, are delicious hors d'oeuvres. Any of these fillings could form the basis of a miniature quiche or could be served as is in tartlet shells.

- Small cubes of eggplant, sautéed in olive oil with oregano
- Small cubes of zucchini, sautéed in olive oil with rosemary
- Small cubes of zucchini, sautéed in butter with tarragon
- Diced red bell pepper, sautéed in butter
- Spinach, steamed and chopped
- Diced tomatoes and sage
- Sliced sun-dried tomatoes and slivers of fresh or smoked mozzarella
- Sautéed chopped scallions mixed with cream cheese
- Steamed asparagus tips and diced prosciutto or crabmeat
- Chopped shiitake mushrooms, sautéed in butter with fresh flat-leaf parsley
- Cubed artichoke hearts, sautéed in olive oil
- Brie and fresh chopped herbs
- Grated cheese and herbs
- Crabmeat Filling (page 452)
- Curried Onions (page 454)

## TOMATO, BASIL, AND OLIVE TARTLETS

**MAKES 2½ DOZEN** | photographs on pages 80 and 81

*Emmentaler is a cow's-milk cheese with a nutty, mild flavor. Any Swiss-style cheese with small holes may be substituted.*

4 ounces Emmentaler cheese, grated on the large
    holes of a box grater to yield 1⅓ cups
4 medium vine-ripened tomatoes, seeded and
    chopped into ¼-inch pieces
½ cup plus 2 tablespoons thinly sliced basil
2 ounces (about 25) black olives, pitted, thinly
    sliced into strips
3 large eggs
⅓ cup plus 1 tablespoon milk
Kosher salt and freshly ground black pepper
1 recipe Basic Pastry Dough Tartlet Shells
    (page 232)

**1** Preheat the oven to 400° F. In a medium bowl, toss together the cheese, tomatoes, 2 tablespoons of the basil, and the olives. In a small bowl, whisk together the eggs and the milk. Add salt and pepper to taste.

**2** Fill each tartlet with 1 teaspoon of the tomato mixture. Top each with 2 teaspoons of the egg mixture. Transfer the shells to 2 baking sheets. Bake until the filling is golden and set, 25 to 30 minutes, rotating the baking sheets halfway through for even browning. Transfer the tartlets to a wire rack to cool slightly. Remove each tartlet from the pan, sprinkle with the remaining basil, and serve warm.

## CALAMARI SALAD IN PITA CUPS

**MAKES 4 DOZEN** | photograph on page 77

*Calamari is delicious and tender if cooked properly, tough and rubbery if not. I undercook calamari ever so slightly because it continues to cook when removed from the heat. To check for doneness, slice a ring from the calamari body; the inside of the ring should be opaque throughout. When buying squid whole, ask your fishmonger to remove the innards.*

*The salad can be made a day in advance, tightly covered, and refrigerated until ready to assemble.*

1 pound whole squid, well washed
1 teaspoon olive oil
Kosher salt and freshly ground black pepper
¼ cup fresh lemon juice
¼ cup chopped fresh flat-leaf parsley
1 teaspoon paprika
2 small garlic cloves, minced
6 tablespoons extra-virgin olive oil
1 15-ounce can chickpeas, drained (1½ cups)
1 small red onion, cut into ¼-inch dice
1 small tomato, cut into ¼-inch dice
1 seedless cucumber, peel on, cut into
    ¼-inch dice
1 cup plain yogurt
1 teaspoon ground cumin
1 recipe Pita Cups (page 242)
½ cup black olive tapenade

**1** Using a sharp knife, cut the squid tentacles away from the bodies and set aside. Heat a grill pan, or a heavy skillet, over medium-high heat. Brush with olive oil. Season the calamari with salt and pepper. Grill the bodies until opaque, about 1 minute on each side, and the tentacles for about 30 seconds on each side. Let cool. Cut the bodies crosswise into ¼-inch rings and chop the tentacles into smaller pieces. Cover and refrigerate.

**2** In a medium bowl, combine the lemon juice, parsley, ½ teaspoon of the paprika, and the garlic. Whisk in the olive oil until combined. Season with salt and pepper to taste. Add the chickpeas, red onion, tomato, cucumber, and reserved calamari to the vinaigrette.

**3** In a bowl, combine the yogurt with the cumin and the remaining paprika. Spread ½ teaspoon yogurt on each pita cup. Top with 1 teaspoon calamari salad and a dollop of the reserved aioli mixture.

## WELSH RAREBIT IN TOASTED BREADBOXES

**MAKES 4 DOZEN** | photograph on page 59

*A bite-size version of the British classic, this Welsh rarebit requires no knife and fork. Cheese has a tendency to become greasy if allowed to sit too long after it has melted. As a result, this recipe does not double well. Make only one recipe at a time to fill the 48 breadboxes, and once the mixture is ready, fill the boxes right away.*

1 recipe Toasted Breadboxes (page 244)
1 tablespoon unsalted butter
1 tablespoon all-purpose flour
6 ounces Cheddar cheese, grated on the large
    holes of a box grater to yield 3 cups
2 tablespoons lager or amber beer
1 teaspoon Worcestershire sauce
1 teaspoon dry mustard
Pinch of cayenne pepper
1 large egg, lightly beaten
12 cherry tomatoes, thinly sliced, for garnish

**1** Preheat the oven to 375° F. with the rack in the center. Line a rimmed baking sheet with parchment paper. Arrange the breadboxes on the baking sheet, and set aside.

**2** Bring 1 inch of water to a low simmer in the bottom of a double boiler. Place the butter and flour in the top of the double boiler and cook, stirring, until the mixture forms a paste, 2 to 3 minutes. Add the cheese, beer, Worcestershire, dry mustard, and cayenne. Stir to combine. Cook, stirring constantly, until the mixture is completely melted and smooth, 2 to 4 minutes. Whisk the egg into the cheese mixture until smooth. Keep the cheese mixture in the double boiler over low heat while proceeding.

**3** Using a small spoon, place ½ to 1 teaspoon of the cheese mixture into one breadbox and return breadbox to the baking sheet. Working quickly, repeat this process with the remaining cheese mixture, occasionally whisking it to keep it smooth. Bake until the cheese has puffed up and is slightly golden, 4 to 6 minutes. Garnish each with a tomato slice and serve immediately.

## FRICO TACOS WITH MÂCHE

**MAKES 2 DOZEN** | photograph on page 73

*Mâche, a delicate salad green with a nutlike flavor, may also be called lamb's lettuce, field salad, or corn salad. Delicate salad greens such as frisée or mizuna may be substituted; shred the leaves to fit in the frico tacos.*

4 teaspoons fresh lemon juice
1 small shallot, minced
1 teaspoon Dijon mustard
¼ cup extra-virgin olive oil
Kosher salt and freshly ground black pepper
4 small bunches mâche, leaves picked to yield
    about 2 cups
1 recipe Asiago Frico (page 192), taco-shaped

**1** In a small bowl, whisk together the lemon juice, shallots, and mustard. Whisk in the olive oil. Add salt and pepper to taste.

**2** Gently toss the mâche with the vinaigrette. Carefully place the mâche into the frico tacos and serve. Assemble as close to serving time as possible.

## EMPANADITAS

The smallest member of the family of Spanish and Mexican turnovers, which includes the family-size empanada gallica and the single-serving empanada, empanaditas are just the right size for a filling hors d'oeuvre. Because the dough is especially rich, I fill the tiny pouches with assertively seasoned fillings so that the flavors carry through the savory crust.

For an authentic shape and look, flute the sealed edge in the same way you would a piecrust, by using your forefinger to push the dough into the filling. Brushing the entire surface with egg wash creates a beautiful, glossy finish.

Empanaditas may be made 3 to 4 hours ahead and reheated in a 275° F. oven.

## ESCAROLE AND FONTINA EMPANADITAS

**MAKES 4 DOZEN** | photograph on page 79

2 tablespoons unsalted butter

1 large shallot, minced

2 garlic cloves, minced

1 large head escarole (about 1 pound), well washed, still damp, and finely chopped

Kosher salt and freshly ground black pepper

2½ ounces fontina cheese, grated on the large holes of a box grater to yield about ⅔ cup

1 large egg

1 tablespoon milk

1 recipe Empanada Dough (page 240)

**1** Heat the butter in a large skillet over medium heat. Add the shallots and garlic and cook until soft, about 1 minute. Increase the heat to medium-high and add the escarole. Cook until the escarole is just wilted, about 4 minutes. Add salt and pepper to taste, and spread the escarole onto a flat pan to cool. When cool, drain off any excess liquid from the pan and stir in the cheese.

**2** Preheat the oven to 375° F. Line a baking sheet with parchment paper. In a small bowl, lightly beat together the egg and milk. Set aside. Roll the dough out to a thickness that is between $\frac{1}{16}$ inch and $\frac{1}{8}$ inch. Using a 3¼-inch cookie cutter, cut out 48 rounds, rerolling the dough one time. Place the rounds onto the baking sheet, cover with plastic wrap, and refrigerate for 20 minutes.

**3** Place a scant tablespoon of the filling in the center of 1 circle. Use your finger to brush a little of the egg wash onto the inner rim of the circle. Fold the circle in half, forming a half moon. Pinch the edges together with your fingers, and use a fork to seal the empanadita. Using your forefinger, push the sealed edge of the dough toward the filling to form the fluted edge. Brush the top of the empanadita with the egg wash and place on the parchment-lined baking sheet. Repeat with all of the empanaditas and bake until the dough is golden, 15 to 20 minutes. Serve warm.

## CHICKEN, APPLE, AND CHEDDAR EMPANADITAS

**MAKES 4 DOZEN** | photograph on page 79

1 small Granny Smith apple, cut into ¼-inch
    pieces
1 tablespoon fresh lemon juice
1 tablespoon unsalted butter
1 small red onion, finely chopped
2 garlic cloves, minced
1 8-ounce boneless, skinless chicken breast, cut
    lengthwise into thin strips
2 teaspoons finely chopped fresh rosemary
2½ ounces white Cheddar cheese, grated on the
    large holes of a box grater to yield about
    ⅔ cup
Kosher salt and freshly ground black pepper
1 large egg
1 tablespoon milk
1 recipe Empanada Dough (page 240)

**1** Toss the apples with the lemon juice in a small bowl. Set aside.

**2** Heat the butter in a medium skillet over medium heat. Add the onions and garlic and cook until soft, about 3 minutes. Add the apples and lemon juice and cook, stirring, for about 2 minutes, until the apples begin to soften. Increase the heat to medium-high and add the chicken pieces. Cook, stirring frequently, until the chicken is just cooked through, about 5 minutes. Transfer the mixture to a bowl to cool. When the chicken is cool enough to handle, shred it into small pieces. Stir in the rosemary and cheese. Add salt and pepper to taste.

**3** Proceed as in steps 2 and 3 in the Escarole and Fontina Empanaditas recipe (page 294).

## BEEF EMPANADITAS

**MAKES 4 DOZEN** | photograph on page 79

¼ cup pine nuts
2 tablespoons olive oil
1 small onion, minced
2 teaspoons grated fresh ginger
1 pound lean ground sirloin
2 medium tomatoes, seeds removed, cut into
    small dice
½ teaspoon ground cinnamon
½ teaspoon ground cumin
½ teaspoon ground coriander
¼ cup dried cherries, roughly chopped
1 teaspoon red chili flakes
1⅓ cups tomato juice
4 teaspoons sugar
Kosher salt and freshly ground black pepper
1 large egg
1 tablespoon milk
1 recipe Empanada Dough (page 240)

**1** Heat the oven to 375° F. Place the pine nuts on a baking sheet and toast until golden, about 4 minutes. Transfer to a bowl and set aside.

**2** Heat the olive oil in a medium saucepan over medium heat. Add the onions and ginger and cook until soft, about 2 minutes. Add the beef and cook, stirring, for 2 minutes. Add the tomatoes, cinnamon, cumin, coriander, cherries, and chili flakes and cook, stirring occasionally, until the beef is cooked through, about 5 minutes. Add the tomato juice, sugar, and salt and pepper to taste. Simmer for 12 minutes over low heat. Stir in the pine nuts and set aside.

**3** Proceed as in steps 2 and 3 in the Escarole and Fontina Empanaditas recipe (page 294).

## BISTEEYA

**MAKES 7 DOZEN** | photograph on pages 82 and 83

*This is my version of a famous Moroccan specialty of savory ingredients, traditionally pigeon or chicken meat, wrapped in phyllo dough then topped with cinnamon and confectioners' sugar. Bisteeya is typically made in one large pan and cut into pieces, but for hors d'oeuvre portions I find that muffin tins work best. If you prefer not to use muffin tins, the phyllo can be bundled around the filling like a Chinese beggar's purse, or it can be formed into a long strudel-like roll that can be cut into thin slices after baking. Bisteeya can be made 1 day in advance, covered tightly, and refrigerated, or frozen for up to 1 week.*

1 cup (2 sticks) plus 2 tablespoons unsalted butter

1 small onion, finely chopped

1 small (3½-pound) chicken cut into 8 pieces, plus giblets (not the liver)

4 garlic cloves, smashed

⅓ cup finely chopped fresh flat-leaf parsley

Pinch of saffron threads

¼ teaspoon ground turmeric

1 teaspoon kosher salt

½ teaspoon freshly ground black pepper

1 tablespoon grated fresh ginger

2 3-inch cinnamon sticks

1½ cups slivered almonds, lightly toasted

2 teaspoons ground cinnamon, plus extra for dusting

¼ cup plus 2 tablespoons confectioners' sugar, plus extra for dusting

½ cup golden raisins

2 tablespoons fresh lemon juice

6 large eggs, lightly beaten

1 1-pound box phyllo dough (30 sheets), thawed if frozen

**1** Melt 2 tablespoons of the butter in a large saucepan over medium heat. Add the onions and cook, stirring, until they just begin to brown, 8 to 10 minutes. Add the chicken pieces and giblets, 2 cups of water, the garlic, parsley, saffron, turmeric, salt, pepper, ginger, and cinnamon sticks. Cover and bring to a boil. Reduce the heat and simmer, covered, until the chicken pieces are cooked through, about 40 minutes.

**2** Meanwhile, place 1 cup of the toasted almonds in the bowl of a food processor and pulse just until coarsely ground. In a medium bowl, combine the ground almonds with the ground cinnamon and the confectioners' sugar and set aside. Coarsely chop the remaining almonds and set aside.

**3** Remove the chicken with a slotted spoon and set aside to cool. Remove and discard the giblets, cinnamon sticks, and garlic cloves from the liquid. Place the remaining sauce over high heat and cook until it is reduced to about 1 cup, 18 to 20 minutes. Reduce the heat to low. Meanwhile, shred the chicken into small pieces, discarding the skin and bones. Transfer the chicken to a bowl and moisten it with ½ cup of the reduced sauce. Cover loosely and set aside.

**4** Over medium-low heat, add the raisins and the lemon juice to the remaining reduced sauce and cook, stirring, until the raisins plump, 2 to 3 minutes. Slowly add the beaten eggs to the sauce, stirring constantly until the eggs set, 4 to 6 minutes. The mixture will look curdled. Stir in the ½ cup of chopped almonds and set aside.

**5** Preheat the oven to 375°F. with the rack in the center. Place the 2 sticks of butter in a small pan over low heat until melted. Butter the bottom and sides of 2 mini muffin tins, with each of 9 openings measuring 2 inches in diameter. Place 1 sheet of phyllo on a dry surface, and keep the remaining sheets covered with a clean, slightly damp towel. Brush lightly with melted butter, top with a second sheet, and brush again with butter. Finish with a third sheet and brush with butter. Transfer to a bak-

Phyllo (Greek for "leaf") is a tissue-paper-thin sheet of pastry, made only of flour and water. Used in Greek and Middle Eastern savory and sweet recipes, phyllo (also spelled "filo") can be found frozen in supermarkets and fresh in Greek markets. (Packages labeled as strudel leaves may also be used.) Use fresh phyllo if you can find it. Frozen phyllo must be thawed in the refrigerator overnight before using. It should not be refrozen. The phyllo called for in these recipes is packaged in 30 sheets per 1-pound box. Be sure to check the package you buy. If you are in a rush, frozen phyllo may be defrosted at room temperature in about an hour, but it may be more difficult to work with.

To work with the sheets, unfold the dough and lay it flat on a work surface. Remove as many sheets as the recipe calls for plus one or two additional sheets for good measure. Return the remaining sheets to the box and refrigerate for another use. Cover the phyllo sheets on the work surface with a damp dish towel so that they do not dry out. (Because the sheets of dough are so thin, they dry out very easily and then cannot be salvaged.) To form the pastry, brush the thin sheets one by one with melted butter or oil as indicated in the recipe before layering or folding them around the filling. Depending on the recipe, I sprinkle or brush the layers with ingredients such as crushed nuts, flavored oils, and truffle butter.

When working with phyllo, rips or tears are common; just mend the torn area by brushing it with the melted butter or oil and then patching it with another piece of phyllo. If the entire package of phyllo is torn or cracked in the same place throughout the layers, alternate the way you arrange the sheets on top of each other.

All dishes made with phyllo are baked until the pastry becomes crisp and flaky. They may be eaten warm or at room temperature.

---

ing sheet and refrigerate until the butter hardens, about 10 minutes. With a 3½-inch cookie cutter, cut out 9 rounds from the phyllo. With a 2-inch cookie cutter, cut out 9 more rounds from the same layers of phyllo. Place one 3½-inch circle in each of the openings of the mini muffin tins. Layer ½ tablespoon of the chicken, 1 teaspoon of the egg mixture, and ½ teaspoon of the almond-sugar mixture into each phyllo cup. Lay the 2-inch circle over the top of each filled cup. Fold the edges of the larger round over the small layer to seal and brush the top with melted butter.

**6** Bake until the phyllo is golden, 10 to 12 minutes. Remove the bisteeya from the pans right away. Sprinkle the top of each cup with cinnamon and sugar. Set the pans aside to cool. Butter the bottom and sides of the pans and continue making phyllo cups until all the ingredients are used. Serve warm or at room temperature. The bisteeya pastries may be put together completely 1 day ahead and kept in an airtight container in the refrigerator. Bake them as needed no more than 2 hours before serving. To reheat, bake in a 300° F. oven just until warm, about 10 minutes.

## PLUM WINE FLANK STEAK IN GREEN TEA CREPES WITH PLUM WINE SAUCE

**MAKES ENOUGH TO FILL ABOUT 2 DOZEN CREPES** | photograph on page 84

*Flank steak is among the least expensive cuts of beef, yet it is most delicious when marinated. It becomes tender enough to wrap in delicate Green Tea Crepes, then eaten out of hand.*

½ cup plum wine

½ teaspoon kosher salt

1 teaspoon grated fresh ginger

2 garlic cloves, minced

3 tablespoons low-sodium soy sauce

½ teaspoon chili paste

2 tablespoons fresh lime juice

¼ cup honey

1½ pounds flank steak

3 tablespoons prepared plum sauce

4 scallions, green and white parts, cut into matchsticks

¼ medium jicama (about 6 ounces), cut into ¼-inch-thick matchsticks, about 2½ to 3 inches long

1 recipe Green Tea Crepes (page 237)

**1** In a medium bowl, combine the wine, salt, ginger, garlic, soy sauce, chili paste, lime juice, and honey. Stir well to combine. Place the marinade in a shallow nonreactive dish. Add the flank steak to the marinade, turning the beef to coat well with marinade. Cover with plastic wrap and marinate 4 to 6 hours, or overnight, in the refrigerator.

**2** Heat a large grill pan or an outdoor grill to medium-high heat. Remove the steak from the marinade, reserving the marinade. Wipe off excess marinade from the steak. Place the steak on the grill and cook for 4½ to 5 minutes. Turn the steak and cook another 4 minutes for medium-rare. (Timing will depend on the exact thickness of the cut of meat and the strength of the heat source.) Transfer the meat to a plate to cool slightly.

**3** Place the reserved marinade in a small saucepan and bring to a boil. Reduce the marinade by half. Reduce the heat to medium and whisk in the plum sauce. Transfer the sauce to a small serving dish.

**4** Slice the steak across the grain into very thin slices. Serve on a platter with the scallions, jicama, plum sauce, and crepes.

## CURRIED VEGETABLES IN CURRY CREPES

**MAKES ENOUGH TO FILL ABOUT 2 DOZEN CREPES** | photograph on page 85

*The filling can be made 6 to 8 hours ahead. Reheat it in a large skillet over medium heat for 5 minutes or until it is warm throughout.*

2 large baking potatoes, cut into ¼-inch-thick strips lengthwise, placed in cool water

¼ cup olive oil

2 small yellow onions, thinly sliced

1 tablespoon grated fresh ginger

4 small garlic cloves, minced

1½ teaspoons ground cumin

1 tablespoon curry powder

¼ teaspoon cayenne pepper

2 teaspoons whole mustard seed, lightly toasted (see page 386)

2 medium red bell peppers, seeds and ribs removed, cut into ¼-inch matchsticks

2 medium yellow bell peppers, seeds and ribs removed, cut into ¼-inch matchsticks

Kosher salt

1 recipe Curry Crepes (page 236)

**1** Drain the potatoes. Heat 3 tablespoons of the olive oil in a large skillet over medium-high heat. Add the potatoes and cook, stirring constantly, until they begin to soften, 5 to 7 minutes. Add the onions and reduce the heat to medium. Continue to cook, stirring until the onions have softened, 4 to 6 minutes. Stir in the ginger and the garlic. Pour 1 cup of water into the pan, reduce the heat to medium-low, and cover. Let simmer, covered, until most of the water has been absorbed, 5 to 7 minutes.

**2** Remove the cover and add the cumin, curry, cayenne, and 1 teaspoon of the mustard seed to the pan. Stir and add the remaining tablespoon of olive oil. Increase the heat to medium and add the bell peppers. Cook, stirring, until the peppers just begin to soften, 5 to 7 minutes. Add salt to taste and transfer to a bowl. Sprinkle with the remaining teaspoon of mustard seed. Serve warm with the crepes.

## LIMA BEAN FALAFEL FRITTERS IN LETTUCE CUPS

**MAKES 2½ DOZEN** | photograph on page 61

*If some of the Bibb leaves are too large, tear them in half. The inner leaves will be just the right size.*

8 ounces frozen lima beans

¼ cup coarsely chopped fresh flat-leaf parsley

¼ cup coarsely chopped fresh cilantro

1½ cups canned chickpeas, rinsed and drained

1 garlic clove, minced

1 teaspoon ground cumin

½ teaspoon ground turmeric

1½ teaspoons kosher salt

½ medium red onion, finely chopped

1 large hot red chili pepper, seeds and ribs
    removed, minced

1 tablespoon fresh lime juice

3 tablespoons all-purpose flour

1½ quarts peanut oil, for frying

4 heads Bibb lettuce, leaves separated

6 cherry tomatoes, quartered

Tahini-Yogurt Sauce (page 398)

1 tablespoon sesame seeds, toasted
    (see page 386)

**1** Bring 1 cup of water to a boil in a medium saucepan. Add the lima beans and return water to a boil. Cook the beans for 5 minutes and drain. Rinse with cold water to prevent the beans from cooking further. Set aside to dry.

**2** In the bowl of a food processor, process the parsley and the cilantro until fine. Add the chickpeas, lima beans, garlic, cumin, turmeric, salt, ¼ cup of the red onions, the chili pepper, and the lime juice. Pulse until the mixture forms a paste and is fairly smooth. Add the flour and pulse to combine. Transfer the mixture to a bowl and set aside. The falafel mixture may be made up to 1 day in advance and refrigerated in an airtight container.

**3** Heat the oil in a deep 6-inch saucepan, or an electric fryer, until a frying thermometer registers 365° F. Drop 1 tablespoon of the falafel mixture into the oil in batches of 6. Fry until the mixture is dark golden, about 30 seconds. Transfer the completed fritters to paper towels to drain and repeat with the remaining mixture.

**4** Serve each fritter in a lettuce cup, garnished with the remaining onions, the tomatoes, a dollop of tahini sauce, and a sprinkling of sesame seeds. Serve the remaining tahini sauce on the side.

## STUFFED MUSHROOMS

Stuffed mushrooms, often filled with a mixture of crabmeat and bread crumbs, are perhaps one of the most familiar and best-loved hors d'oeuvres—and for good reason. They are perfectly shaped, charming containers for all kinds of interesting fillings, and their woodsy undertone is just subtle enough to gently flavor whatever they are carrying. For perfect stuffed mushrooms, chose the freshest white mushrooms you can find, free of blemishes and about the size of a silver dollar in diameter. Serve them hot.

## LEEK, FENNEL, AND GOAT CHEESE STUFFED MUSHROOMS

**MAKES 2 DOZEN** | photograph page 54

*Fennel, also called anise, has a slight licorice flavor. Fennel bulbs vary greatly in size, depending on the season. Buy a very small bulb, about 1 pound, for this recipe.*

1 tablespoon unsalted butter
¼ of a small fennel bulb, trimmed, thinly shaved on a mandoline, and roughly chopped
1 small leek, white and light green parts, cut into 1-inch pieces, well washed (see page 271)
¾ teaspoon ground coriander
Kosher salt and freshly ground black pepper
4 ounces fresh goat cheese
1 recipe Golden Mushroom Caps (page 230)

**1** Heat the butter in a medium skillet over medium heat. Add the fennel and the leeks and cook until softened, 5 to 8 minutes. Add the coriander and season with salt and pepper to taste. Transfer to a large plate to cool. Reserve 2 tablespoons for garnish.

**2** Heat the oven to broil with the rack in the center. Mash the goat cheese into the leek-fennel mixture until well combined. Use a small spoon to fill each mushroom cap with the filling. Place the caps on a baking sheet and broil until hot throughout, about 1 minute. Garnish each with a bit of the reserved leek-fennel mixture. Serve hot.

## BROCCOLI RABE AND PANCETTA STUFFED MUSHROOMS

**MAKES 2 DOZEN** | photograph on page 54

*Broccoli rabe, also referred to as broccoli di rape, is a pleasantly bitter, leafy cousin to broccoli. I especially like it combined with pancetta, an assertively flavored Italian bacon cured with salt and spices that is generally available in the deli section of the grocery store.*

1 ounce sliced pancetta or bacon, cut into ½-inch dice
1 medium shallot, minced
1 recipe Golden Mushroom Caps (page 230) with the stems reserved, cleaned, and finely chopped
1 garlic clove, minced
2 tablespoons dry white wine
1 pound broccoli rabe, trimmed to leaves and florets only, roughly chopped
Kosher salt and freshly ground black pepper
1 tablespoon fresh thyme

**1** Preheat the oven to 400° F. with the rack in the upper position. Heat a medium skillet over medium-high heat. Add the pancetta and cook until beginning to crisp, 4 to 6 minutes. Reduce the heat to medium and add the shallots. Cook until softened and translucent. Add the mushroom stems and the garlic and cook for 3 more minutes. Add the wine and the broccoli rabe, cover, and let steam for 4 minutes, until the broccoli rabe is bright green. Remove the cover and cook until the liquid has evaporated, 1 to 2 minutes. Season with salt and pepper to taste. Remove from the heat.

**2** Using a small spoon, fill each mushroom cap with the filling. Place the caps on a baking sheet. Bake until the mushrooms are hot throughout, 2 to 4 minutes. Garnish with the thyme and serve hot.


## POLENTA STUFFED MUSHROOMS

**MAKES 2 DOZEN** | photograph on page 54

*Pecorino-Romano is an aged Italian sheep's-milk cheese with a sharp, intense flavor (see Cheese Glossary, page 419). It is worth searching out this cheese, but if you can't locate it, you can use Parmesan cheese.*

½ cup plus 3 tablespoons milk

¼ teaspoon kosher salt

1½ teaspoons fresh thyme

¼ cup quick-cooking polenta

1 ounce Pecorino Romano cheese, grated on the
    small holes of a box grater to yield ½ cup

1 tablespoon unsalted butter

1 recipe Golden Mushroom Caps (page 230)

**1** Heat the oven to broil with the rack in the upper position. Meanwhile, place ⅓ cup of the milk, ½ cup of water, the salt, and ½ teaspoon of the thyme in a medium saucepan. Bring to a boil. Slowly pour in the polenta, whisking constantly. Cook, stirring, about 2 minutes, until the polenta thickens. Stir in all but 2 tablespoons of the cheese, the remaining milk, and the butter.

**2** Using a small spoon, quickly spoon the polenta into the mushroom caps. Garnish each cap with the remaining cheese. Place the caps on a baking sheet. Broil until the cheese is golden, about 1 minute. Garnish with the remaining thyme. Serve hot.


## PORCINI STUFFED MUSHROOMS WITH CAMEMBERT

**MAKES 2 DOZEN** | photograph on page 54

*Porcinis, also known as cèpes, are among my favorite wild mushrooms. They are available fresh in late spring or autumn and dried year-round. When using dried, rehydrate them before incorporating into the recipe (see page 290).*

1 tablespoon unsalted butter

1 recipe Golden Mushroom Caps (page 230)
    with the stems reserved, cleaned, and
    roughly chopped

1 small shallot, minced

4 ounces fresh porcini mushrooms, roughly
    chopped (or 1 ounce dried porcini,
    rehydrated, plus 3 ounces white button
    mushrooms)

2 tablespoons dry white wine

Kosher salt and freshly ground black pepper

3 ounces Camembert cheese

**1** Heat the butter in a medium skillet over medium heat. Add the mushroom stems and shallots and cook until the shallots are translucent, 2 to 4 minutes. Add the porcini mushrooms and cook for 1 to 3 minutes. Add the white wine, scraping up any bits that may be on the bottom of the pan, and cook until the wine has evaporated, 1 to 3 minutes. Season with salt and pepper to taste and remove from the heat.

**2** Heat the oven to broil with the rack in the center. Use a small spoon to fill each mushroom cap with the filling. Place the caps on a baking sheet and set aside.

**3** Slice the Camembert into 24 small pieces, each slice just large enough to cover about half of the filling. Set aside. Broil the filled mushroom caps until hot throughout, 2 to 3 minutes. Remove and place a cheese slice on each mushroom. Serve hot.

## GOLDEN RAVIOLI WITH ARRABBIATA SAUCE

**MAKES 2 DOZEN** | photograph on page 57

*Inspired by the toasted ravioli found on almost every menu in the Italian section of St. Louis known as the Hill, this hors d'oeuvre is actually fried. Not surprisingly, it is always a favorite. Prepared ravioli is in the freezer section of most supermarkets and is available in a variety of flavors. Gently separate the ravioli from one another while frozen, and then thaw in the refrigerator or bring to room temperature. I serve arrabbiata, a classic spicy Italian tomato sauce, with cheese-filled ravioli, but fresh pesto sauce is a delicious dipping sauce, too.*

1 quart peanut oil, for frying

24 fresh basil leaves, washed and dried very well

½ cup yellow cornmeal

24 1¾- to 2-inch square or round cheese-filled ravioli

Kosher salt

Arrabbiata Sauce (page 394)

**1** Heat the oil in a 6-inch-deep saucepan, or electric fryer, until a frying thermometer registers 365° F. Place 1 or 2 basil leaves on a long-handled slotted spoon. Stand back from the hot oil and carefully slip the leaves into the oil and fry until translucent, about 10 seconds. Work very carefully; the hot oil tends to splatter. Remove the leaves with the slotted spoon and drain on paper towels. Continue until all basil leaves are fried. Set aside.

**2** Let the oil return to 365° F. Meanwhile, place the cornmeal in a large shallow bowl. Working in batches, dredge 6 ravioli in the cornmeal, shaking off any excess. Carefully slip the ravioli into the hot oil, and fry, turning once, until the ravioli are golden, 1 to 2 minutes. Remove and drain on paper towels. Repeat with the remaining ravioli, skimming the surface of the oil occasionally to remove any dark bits. Place the ravioli in a large bowl and garnish with the fried basil and salt. Serve warm with the Arrabbiata Sauce. Ravioli may be made up to 3 or 4 hours ahead and reheated in a 300° F. oven for 10 minutes.

## CHÈVRE GRAPES

**MAKES 2 DOZEN** | photograph on page 76

*You may use grapes with seeds if you wish, since the centers get scooped out anyway. In fact, larger seeded grapes make a more dramatic appearance. The goat cheese may be piped into each grape individually, but the cheesecloth method that I use gives it the texture of artisan-made cheese.*

¼ cup salted pistachio nuts, toasted and finely chopped

1 recipe Grape Cups (page 230)

5 ounces fresh goat cheese, chilled

**1** Place the nuts in a small bowl. Dip the rim of each grape into the nuts.

**2** Take 1 level teaspoon of the goat cheese and place in the center of a small square of cheesecloth. Twist the cheesecloth slightly, pinching the cheese into a ball. Unwrap the cheese but leave it on the cheesecloth. Holding the ball with the cheesecloth, transfer it into a grape cup and pull away the cheesecloth. Continue until all the grapes are filled, using a fresh square of cheesecloth or rinsing and squeezing out all water, as needed. Chill until ready to serve. May be made 6 to 8 hours ahead.

## FONTINA RISOTTO BALLS

**MAKES 3 DOZEN** | photograph on page 89

*These crispy balls are a great use for any kind of leftover risotto. They are also the perfect make-ahead hors d'oeuvre. They can be prepared and cooked 1 day in advance and simply reheated in the oven before serving, or they can be formed and refrigerated, uncooked, 2 days in advance. Mozzarella is a good alternative to the fontina.*

4 cups homemade chicken stock, or low-sodium
    canned chicken broth, skimmed of fat
1 tablespoon extra-virgin olive oil
2 large shallots, finely chopped to yield ⅓ cup
1 cup Arborio rice
½ cup dry white wine
1 teaspoon kosher salt, or more to taste
Freshly ground black pepper
2 tablespoons chopped fresh flat-leaf parsley
1 ounce Parmesan cheese, grated on the small
    holes of a box grater to yield ¼ cup
1 ounce fontina cheese, cut into 36 ¼-inch cubes
½ cup all-purpose flour
2 large eggs, lightly beaten
½ cup yellow cornmeal
2 quarts peanut oil, for frying

**1** Bring the chicken stock to a simmer in a medium saucepan over medium heat. Keep covered and warm on low heat.

**2** Heat the olive oil in a medium saucepan over medium heat. Add the shallots and cook until translucent, 2 to 3 minutes. Add the rice to the pan and cook, stirring, until the edges of the rice become translucent, 1 to 2 minutes. Add the wine and cook, stirring, until nearly all the wine is absorbed into the rice, 2 to 3 minutes. Add 1 cup of the stock and ½ teaspoon of the salt and cook, stirring constantly, until nearly all of the stock is absorbed, 3 to 5 minutes. Continue adding stock, ½ cup at a time, stirring constantly, until the rice is creamy but still firm, about 20 minutes. Add the remaining salt and season with pepper to taste. Stir in the parsley and the Parmesan. Remove from the heat and transfer to a large bowl. Allow the rice to cool completely, stirring occasionally. Cover with plastic wrap and refrigerate until firm and thoroughly chilled, 3 to 4 hours or overnight. The mixture must be cold before proceeding with the recipe.

**3** Line 2 baking sheets with parchment paper and set aside. Place 1 generous tablespoon of the risotto in the palm of your hand and form it into a shallow cup. Place 1 cube of the fontina in the center of the rice. Enclose the cheese with the risotto to form a ball. It is important to keep the cheese in the center. Place the risotto ball onto one of the baking sheets. Repeat with the remaining risotto and fontina. (The risotto balls may be covered with plastic wrap and refrigerated overnight at this stage.)

**4** Place the flour in a shallow bowl, and season with salt and pepper to taste. Place the eggs and cornmeal in 2 separate shallow bowls. Roll the risotto balls first in the flour, gently shaking off any excess. Dip the balls into the egg mixture, then lightly coat with the cornmeal. Place them on the second baking sheet and refrigerate, covered with plastic wrap, until ready to use.

**5** Heat the peanut oil in a large saucepan, or an electric fryer, until a frying thermometer registers 365°F. Carefully slip 6 risotto balls into the hot oil, and fry until golden, 1 to 2 minutes. Repeat until all the balls are cooked, skimming the surface of the oil occasionally to remove any dark bits. Drain the risotto balls on paper towels and keep warm in the oven until ready to serve.

## FILLED TOMATOES

The fillings for Cherry Tomato Cups should be arranged so that the ingredients just peek out of the top for the cleanest and most attractive presentation. Once filled, the tomatoes may be kept in the refrigerator in an airtight container for 2 to 3 hours. Return them to room temperature before serving. Serve them on a surface that prevents them from rolling around, such as a bed of chives or rock salt.

## CHERRY TOMATOES WITH PANZANELLA

**MAKES 4 DOZEN** | photograph on page 75

*To fill these cherry tomatoes, I make a miniaturized version of the Italian tomato-moistened bread salad called panzanella.*

4 ounces (about 4 slices) country bread or
    ciabatta, crusts on
1 small seedless cucumber, cut into ¼-inch dice
    to yield ¼ cup
1 small red onion, cut into ¼-inch dice to yield
    ¼ cup
2 tablespoons extra-virgin olive oil
1 small garlic clove, minced
2 tablespoons red wine vinegar
2 tablespoons capers, drained and roughly
    chopped
¼ cup shredded fresh basil
Kosher salt and freshly ground black pepper
10 cherry tomatoes, cut into ½-inch dice
2 recipes Cherry Tomato Cups (page 229)

Grill or toast the bread slices. Break the bread into pieces small enough to fit into the Cherry Tomato Cups to yield about 1¼ cups. Transfer the bread to a medium bowl. Add the cucumber,

onion, olive oil, garlic, vinegar, capers, basil, salt and pepper to taste, and the diced tomatoes. Toss together to combine. Use a small spoon to fill the cherry tomatoes and serve.

## CHERRY TOMATOES WITH WHITE BEAN PURÉE

**MAKES 2 DOZEN** | photograph on page 75

*Canned cannellini beans are a staple in my pantry. Puréed with garlic and herbs, it can be swabbed on Simple Crostini (page 243), slathered on crudités (page 374), or piped onto or into vegetables, as I do here.*

1 15-ounce can cannellini beans, drained
1½ tablespoons extra-virgin olive oil
1 garlic clove, minced
1 bunch sage (24 whole leaves plus 4 leaves
    minced)
2 teaspoons fresh lemon juice
Kosher salt and freshly ground black pepper
2 tablespoons peanut oil, for frying
1 recipe Cherry Tomato Cups (page 229)

**1** In the bowl of a food processor, combine half of the beans, the olive oil, garlic, the minced sage leaves, and the lemon juice. Purée until smooth. Add the remaining beans and pulse just until they are coarsely chopped. Add salt and pepper to taste.

**2** Heat the peanut oil in a small saucepan over medium heat. Add the whole sage leaves and fry, working in batches if necessary, until they become firm and the bubbles die down, 10 to 15 seconds. Transfer to paper towels to drain.

**3** Using a pastry bag or a resealable plastic bag with the corner snipped off, pipe the white bean purée into the cherry tomatoes. Garnish with a fried sage leaf and serve.

## CHERRY TOMATOES WITH GRILLED SHRIMP AND CORN

**MAKES 2 DOZEN** | photograph on page 75

3 tablespoons fresh lime juice

1 teaspoon ground coriander

1½ tablespoons extra-virgin olive oil, plus extra
   for the grill

10 medium shrimp, peeled and deveined
   (see page 340)

Kosher salt and freshly ground black pepper

1 ear fresh corn, husk and silk removed

1 small jalapeño pepper, seeds and ribs removed,
   minced

1 large shallot, finely diced

1 tablespoon chopped fresh cilantro, plus 24
   leaves for garnish

1 recipe Cherry Tomato Cups (page 229)

**1** In a small bowl, combine 2 tablespoons lime
juice, ½ teaspoon coriander, 1 tablespoon olive oil,
and the shrimp. Add salt and pepper to taste and
allow to marinate in the refrigerator, covered with
plastic wrap, for 30 minutes.

**2** Heat a grill pan, or grill, over medium-high
heat and brush with olive oil. Lightly brush the
corn with the remaining ½ teaspoon olive oil, and
sprinkle with salt and pepper. Grill the corn, rotating, until it is golden and slightly brown, 12 to 18
minutes. Remove the shrimp from the marinade
and grill until opaque and cooked through, 2 to 4
minutes. Discard the marinade.

**3** Chop the shrimp into ¼-inch pieces and place
in a medium bowl. Cut the corn kernels off the ear.
Add to the bowl. Toss in the jalapeño, shallots,
cilantro, and the remaining lime juice and ground
coriander. Season with salt and pepper to taste. Use
a small spoon to fill the cherry tomatoes with the
mixture. Garnish with cilantro leaves and serve.

## CHERRY TOMATOES WITH ROQUEFORT AND WATERCRESS

**MAKES 2 DOZEN** | photograph on page 75

*Roquefort is a sheep's-milk blue cheese from France with a
particularly rich, creamy texture and pungent flavor. Other
blue cheeses such as Maytag Blue, Bleu d'Auvergne, Cabrales,
or Danish Blue may be substituted.*

1 tablespoon white wine vinegar

2 ounces Roquefort cheese

1½ tablespoons canola oil

1 small bunch watercress, leaves coarsely
   chopped to yield about ½ cup, plus more for
   the garnish

1 small seedless cucumber, finely diced to make
   ⅓ cup

1 tablespoon snipped fresh chives

Kosher salt and freshly ground black pepper

1 recipe Cherry Tomato Cups (page 229)

**1** In the bowl of a food processor, combine the
vinegar and half of the cheese. Pulse until smooth.
Slowly add the oil, blending until smooth and
thick. (Consistency will be thinner than mayonnaise.) Transfer the mixture to a medium bowl. Stir
in all but 2 tablespoons of the cheese.

**2** Just before serving, fold in the watercress,
cucumber, and chives. Season with salt and pepper
to taste. Use a small spoon to fill the cherry tomatoes with the mixture. Garnish with watercress
leaves and the reserved cheese and serve.

## CHERRY TOMATOES WITH MIXED OLIVE SALAD

**MAKES 2 DOZEN** | photograph on page 75

*Select any combination of oil- or brine-cured olives, such as Nyons, Picholine, or niçoise. The olive salad is delicious spread on Simple Crostini (page 243).*

4 ounces (about ¾ cup) whole mixed olives
1 stalk celery, strings removed, cut into ¼-inch
    dice to yield ¼ cup
1 small red onion, finely chopped to yield ¼ cup
1 tablespoon extra-virgin olive oil
1 teaspoon fresh lemon juice
1 teaspoon fresh thyme
Kosher salt and freshly ground black pepper
1 recipe Cherry Tomato Cups (page 229)

Pit the olives and coarsely chop to yield about ½ cup. Transfer to a medium bowl. Add the celery, onion, olive oil, lemon juice, thyme, and salt and pepper to taste. Toss well to combine. Use a small spoon to fill the cherry tomatoes and serve.

## CHERRY TOMATOES WITH HARICOTS VERTS

**MAKES 2 DOZEN** | photograph on page 75

*Haricot vert is French for "green bean," but the term refers to a specific green bean that is very thin and narrow. Their size allows them to fit perfectly into Cherry Tomato Cups.*

1¼ teaspoons kosher salt, plus more to taste
4 ounces (about 36) haricots verts, bottom stem
    trimmed
1 small shallot, minced
1 teaspoon Dijon mustard
1 teaspoon red wine vinegar
2 teaspoons fresh lemon juice
¼ cup extra-virgin olive oil

Freshly ground black pepper
1 recipe Cherry Tomato Cups (page 229)

**1** Bring a large pot of water to a boil. Add 1 teaspoon of the salt to the water. Blanch the haricots verts in the boiling water just until bright green, 2 to 3 minutes. Immediately transfer the haricots verts to a large bowl filled with ice water to stop the cooking process. Once completely cool, drain. Cut the haricots verts into quarters. Set aside.

**2** To make the vinaigrette, combine the shallots, mustard, vinegar, lemon juice, and remaining ¼ teaspoon salt in a medium bowl. Slowly whisk in the olive oil. Season with salt and pepper to taste. Place the haricots verts into the cherry tomatoes, drizzle with the vinaigrette, and serve.

## LADY APPLES WITH CELERIAC SLAW

**MAKES 2 DOZEN** | photograph on page 88

*Lady apples are available throughout the winter; slices of crisp apples or firm pears may be used as a base for the salad at other times of the year. The filled lady apples keep in the refrigerator for up to 12 hours. Celeriac is also called celery root; buy a small head, about 1 pound, for this recipe.*

1 cup sugar
2 lady apples, peel on
1½ teaspoons vegetable oil
3 tablespoons walnut halves
⅓ of a small head of celeriac
2 tablespoons fresh lemon juice, rinds reserved
2 tablespoons dried cranberries, chopped
¼ cup homemade (page 315) or prepared
    mayonnaise
1 tablespoon chopped fresh tarragon
Kosher salt and freshly ground black pepper
1 recipe Lady Apple Cups (page 229)

**1** Preheat the oven to 175°F. Bring the sugar and 1 cup of water to a simmer in a medium saucepan over medium heat, stirring occasionally. Meanwhile, slice the apples ¹⁄₁₆ inch thick on a mandoline and set aside. When the sugar is completely dissolved, place 5 or 6 slices of the apple into the sugar syrup and simmer for 20 seconds. Remove the slices with a slotted spoon and drain on a wire rack. Continue until all the apple slices are completed.

**2** Brush a baking sheet with the vegetable oil. Arrange the apple slices on the sheet. Bake until the apples are crisp, about 2 to 2½ hours. Set the apple chips aside or place in an airtight container at room temperature until ready to use.

**3** Heat the oven to 350°F. Place the walnuts on a baking sheet; toast for 5 to 8 minutes, until fragrant and light brown. Set aside.

**4** Peel the celeriac and rub with the reserved lemon rinds to prevent discoloring. Thinly slice the celeriac on the mandoline. Cut the slices into a thin julienne, 2 inches long. In a large bowl, toss the celeriac with the lemon juice. Coarsely chop the walnuts and add to the celeriac.

**5** In a small bowl, combine the cranberries, mayonnaise, and tarragon. Add the mixture to the celeriac and walnuts. Add salt and pepper to taste. Place about 1 tablespoon of the salad into each Lady Apple Cup. Garnish each with an apple chip just before serving.

## ENDIVE WITH GOAT CHEESE, FIG, AND HONEY-GLAZED PECANS

**MAKES 3 DOZEN** | photograph on page 71

*This simple hors d'oeuvre is prettiest when made with fresh figs, but dried figs may also be used when fresh are out of season. Plump them in 3 tablespoons of warm water and 1 tablespoons of port for 5 minutes.*

¾ cup (3 ounces) pecan halves

5 tablespoons honey

8 ounces fresh goat cheese, at room temperature

½ cup port wine

1 recipe Endive Petals (page 231)

4 leaves frisée, torn into smaller pieces

9 whole fresh figs, cut into ¾-inch wedges

**1** Preheat the oven to 350°F. Line a baking sheet with parchment paper. In a small bowl, toss the pecans with 2 tablespoons of the honey. Place them in a single layer on the baking sheet. Bake for 4 minutes; then stir and continue baking until shiny, 3½ to 4 minutes. Set aside to cool.

**2** Using two demitasse spoons or small teaspoons, form 36 quenelles (see photograph, page 70) from the goat cheese: Hold 1 spoon in each hand with ½ teaspoon of the cheese in 1 spoon. Shape the cheese by turning one spoon against the other lengthwise, transferring the cheese back and forth between the spoons. Continue with the remaining cheese.

**3** Place the port and remaining honey in a small stainless-steel saucepan. Cook over low heat until the mixture is reduced by half and is thick and syrupy, about 5 minutes.

**4** Fill each endive leaf with a sprig of frisée, a pecan half, a cheese quenelle, 1 piece of fig, and a drizzle of the port reduction.

# TWICE-BAKED TRUFFLED POTATOES

**MAKES 2 DOZEN** | photograph on page 55

*I like the elongated shape of white creamer potatoes for this recipe because their shape mimics that of the baked potato, but any small potato will work. White truffle oil is wonderfully aromatic and flavorful; its perfume infuses the air as you drizzle it onto the potatoes. If in season, fresh white truffles may be shaved thinly over the top for the ultimate garnish.*

1¼ pounds small white creamer potatoes or
    new potatoes
2 ounces pancetta or bacon, cut into 1-inch pieces
1 ounce Asiago cheese, grated on the small holes
    of a box grater to yield a scant ½ cup
1 teaspoon kosher salt
¼ teaspoon freshly ground black pepper
¼ cup heavy cream, scalded
3 fresh sage leaves, finely chopped
2 teaspoons snipped fresh chives
2 teaspoons white truffle oil (see Note, below)
2 cups rock salt
¼ ounce shaved white truffles, for garnish
    (optional)

**1** Heat the oven to 375° F. with the rack in the center. Place the potatoes on a baking sheet and bake until soft when pierced with the tip of a knife, 20 to 35 minutes depending on type and exact size of potatoes. Set aside. Keep the oven at 375° F.

**2** Meanwhile, cook the pancetta in a small skillet over medium-high heat until crisp, 4 to 6 minutes. When cool, cut the pancetta into ⅛-inch dice.

---

**NOTE** | Truffle Oil

One of the most rare, expensive foods in the world, and undoubtedly the most prized of all fungi, fresh black and white truffles are traditionally reserved for special occasions. But their wonderfully earthy flavor can be found in a more affordable liquid form in high-quality olive oils into which the essence of the truffles has been infused. Through a rather complicated distillation process, the intense essence is extracted from the scraps of fresh truffles by placing them in a metal dish set over another filled with pure alcohol. The alcohol is heated and the vapor that rises from the truffles travels through a very cold condensing tube, which crystallizes the vapors. When the vapors are returned to room temperature, a liquid results, which is then combined with extra-virgin olive oil. The very best bottles of truffle oil always contain pieces of the distilled truffle scraps, which further intensify the flavor of the oil. Avoid truffle oils made with artificial flavors; they generally cost the same and offer none of the intensity of the natural version. Store truffle oil as you would any cooking oil—in a cool dark place or in the refrigerator. Though a bottle of truffle oil may seem pricey, a little drizzle goes a very long way: it transforms a dish. Truffle oil is available in specialty food shops and through mail order (see Sources, page 487).

In addition to flavoring Robiola Pizza (page 309), Twice-Baked Truffled Potatoes (above), and Crumbled Parmigiano-Reggiano with Truffle Oil (page 201), truffle oil can be lightly drizzled on the Stuffed Mushrooms (page 300), Wild Mushroom and Fontina Pizza (page 254), Morels with Roasted Garlic Purée Crostini (page 331), and the Sautéed Chicken Liver Crostini (page 330).

**3** When the potatoes are cool enough to handle but still warm, cut them in half lengthwise. Use a small melon baller to scoop out the centers, reserving the shells with a ⅛-inch border to keep the potatoes stable. Pass the scooped-out potato filling through a ricer or a food mill fitted with a medium disk. Alternatively, push the filling through a sturdy sieve. Immediately transfer the potato filling to a medium bowl. Add all but 2 tablespoons of the cheese. Add the salt and pepper. Pour in the scalded cream. Use a spatula to stir in the pancetta, sage, chives, and 1 teaspoon of the truffle oil.

**4** Spoon 1 teaspoon to 1 tablespoon of the potato mixture into the 24 nicest-looking shells; the amount will vary with the size of the potatoes. Discard the unused shells. Sprinkle each potato with the remaining cheese. Spread the rock salt onto a rimmed baking sheet. Arrange the potatoes on top and return to the oven until warm throughout and browned lightly on top, 10 to 15 minutes. Remove from the oven and drizzle with the remaining truffle oil. Garnish with shavings of white truffles, if desired. Spoon the rock salt onto a serving tray, arrange the warm potatoes on it, and serve.

## ROBIOLA PIZZA WITH WHITE TRUFFLE OIL

**MAKES THREE 10-INCH PIES; 48 PIECES**

**TOTAL** | photograph on page 87

*I first tasted this remarkable filled pizza years ago at Pino Luongo's Le Madri, a stylish Italian restaurant in New York City, but many chefs have created their own versions since then. It is worth seeking out the slightly tart, soft robiola cheese (see Sources, page 487) and white truffle oil for this special hors d'oeuvre. Fresh robiola, which I use here, is made in Italy's Piedmont region and should not be confused with the aged variety, which is produced in Lombardy. Alternatively, substitute 6 ounces of soft goat cheese or ricotta cheese*

*seasoned with freshly ground black pepper. Because the pizza cooks at high heat, make sure the oven is very clean, or it will smoke. For the very best flavor, serve these as they come out of the oven.*

1 recipe Pizza Dough (page 239)
All-purpose flour, for dusting
Cornmeal, for dusting
14 ounces fresh robiola cheese
1½ teaspoons extra-virgin olive oil
1 tablespoon white truffle oil (see page 308)

**1** Place a pizza stone on a rack in the lower third of the oven. Preheat the oven to 500° F. for at least 30 minutes. Divide the pizza dough into 6 equal balls. Keep the unused dough covered, at room temperature, while you work. On a lightly floured surface, use your hands to shape 2 of the dough balls into 8-inch rounds, about ⅛ inch thick. Place 1 round directly on top of the other and roll with a rolling pin until the round is 10 inches in diameter. Use a large fork to prick liberally the entire surface.

**2** Sprinkle cornmeal onto a wooden pizza peel or an inverted baking sheet and transfer the dough to it. Slide the pizza round onto the heated stone in the oven. Bake for 5 to 8 minutes, until it begins to brown. Remove from the oven to a work surface.

**3** Using a kitchen towel, hold the top of the hot pizza with one hand and use a long serrated knife to split the pizza in half horizontally. Remove the top layer to create an open-faced pizza crust. Spread one third of the robiola cheese on the bottom the crust and replace the top. Brush the top of the dough very lightly with ½ teaspoon of the olive oil. Return to the oven and bake until the pizza is golden brown, 5 to 7 minutes. Drizzle 1 teaspoon of the truffle oil over the top. Using a chef's knife, cut into 16 wedges and serve immediately. Repeat with the remaining ingredients until all 3 pizzas have been made.

# 4

## TEA SANDWICHES, CLASSIC CANAPÉS, AND SIMPLE CROSTINI

*Photographs for these recipes appear on pages 90–109*

France the basis for a collection of canapés, some classic and some innovative, and from Italy the inspiration for a handful of simple but very flavorful crostini. I've also updated all three approaches so they are perfectly suited to my informal entertaining style.

Tea sandwiches, for example, need not be limited to the usual combinations—the triangle of crustless white bread layered with butter, cucumber, and watercress. While there is certainly a place on the tea tray for this classic, here I've expanded the ingredient list to include such items as Italian prosciutto on marble bread that has been spread with a rich port-fig butter, and curried egg salad topped with thin-sliced radishes and peppery radish sprouts. Watercress still appears in my tea sandwich collection, but I combine it with creamy, slightly tangy goat cheese and garnish one edge of the bread with pungent snipped chives. The only convention you need follow when creating tea sandwiches is to enclose the fillings between two slices of fresh bread. As you'll see from these examples, the ritual of afternoon tea is only one of many occasions when finger sandwiches are appropriate to serve guests.

Similarly, canapés like Chopped Egg and Asparagus Canapés or Smoked Salmon Flower Canapés with Dill Butter are rather traditional, classically satisfying combinations. They are made using the technique that defines canapés: They are always prepared open-faced, and the bread is either toasted or dried, depending on the weight of the topping. Other recipes for canapés, while prepared using this technique, take advantage of new tastes and ingredients that have recently come into our culinary repertoire. Carrot Cumin Canapés, for instance, introduce a typical Tunisian flavor pairing, and one of my very favorites, Wasabi Caviar and Daikon Canapés, with their translucent white disks of daikon covering half-spheres of bright green wasabi caviar and layered on white bread rounds, are unusual, starkly beautiful, and wonderfully flavorful.

Crostini are little rounds or squares of bread that are brushed with olive oil, toasted in the oven, then topped with savory ingredients. Here I layer them with everything from the popular combination of tomato, mozzarella and basil to richly indulgent pâté de foie gras with caramelized plums.

All of these sandwiches also provide terrific outlets for creative expression. Working with various kinds of breads and forming half-circles, diagonal lines, concentric circles, stripes, dots, and mounds with assorted topping ingredients, you can make a display of sandwiches that are as dazzling to behold as they are delicious to eat.

All of the recipes for tea sandwiches and canapés are made the classic way: the filling is spread on the bread slice from edge to edge and is then cut into desired shapes (see photographs, pages 91-105). There will be some waste when the sandwiches are trimmed this way, but it is the only way to achieve very tailored-looking hors d'oeuvres. Alternatively, the bread can be cut into desired shapes first and the fillings arranged more loosely on them —a piece of smoked salmon can be folded to fit on the shape, for example—which creates a different, less structured look and little waste.

Tea sandwiches and canapés can be cut into many shapes; use cutters with the approximate dimensions given in the recipes. For example, the flower-shaped Smoked Salmon Tea Sandwiches (page 318) call for a 2-inch-wide cutter. Use this as a guideline if choosing a different shape; otherwise, the yield will be different.

There are several different breads you can use to make tea sandwiches and canapés. When I was catering, I used the large pullman loaves made by a local baker, or I made my own Pain de Mie (page 238). These are good choices if you are planning for a large gathering, since this very firm bread can be sliced horizontally (see page 92) and the sandwiches prepared in an assembly-line fashion. You can slice the bread this way yourself, or ask your baker to slice the bread for you with the machine set on melba or thin slice. Cutters (see Sources, page 486) are essential for creating uniform pieces from these long slices of bread. For smaller gatherings, I use the small party loaves that are presliced and found in the bread or deli section of most grocery stores. Party loaves are generally available in pumpernickel, rye, and whole wheat. These slices can be trimmed to the appropriate size with either a serrated knife or a cutter. The very thinly sliced packaged white and whole-wheat sandwich bread found in grocery stores is another option. These slices can also be trimmed to the appropriate size with either a serrated knife or a cutter, and a pair of slices is large enough to yield 2 tea sandwiches or 4 canapés.

Bread cut into small pieces will dry out quickly. Cover the slices with damp towels or plastic wrap while you assemble the hors d'oeuvres. Tea sandwiches can be prepared up to 1 hour in advance, covered with slightly moistened paper towels, wrapped in plastic wrap, and refrigerated. Canapés should be assembled as close as possible to serving time. Cover them with slightly moistened paper towels and keep at room temperature until ready to serve.

Prolong the freshness of tea sandwiches by overlapping them slightly or arranging them in neat piles (see Breadbox Buffet, page 102, Sesame-Crusted Chicken Salad Tea Sandwiches, page 95, and Assorted Tea Sandwiches, page 91). Arranged this way, less of the surface of the bread is exposed to the air while they are being served. Canapés, on the other hand, are best presented in single layers, placed close together, on low, flat trays. Arrange a variety of them on the same tray to create an interesting pattern (see page 99).

## LEMON CRAB SALAD TEA SANDWICHES

**MAKES 2 DOZEN** | photograph on page 91

*Be sure to use the full amount of lemon zest and fresh lemon juice in this filling. It may seem excessive, but it is the key to the incredibly fresh flavor of this sandwich.*

12 ounces lump crabmeat, picked over for cartilage
¼ cup plus 2 tablespoons homemade (page 315) or prepared mayonnaise
2 tablespoons grated lemon zest
2 tablespoons fresh lemon juice
4 scallions, white and light green parts only, thinly sliced crosswise
Kosher salt and freshly ground black pepper
1 1-pound loaf of brioche, or other dense white bread, sliced into 24 ¼-inch-thick slices
1 small head (4 ounces) of red oakleaf lettuce or other baby lettuce

**1** Place the crabmeat in a medium bowl and combine it with 2 tablespoons of the mayonnaise, the lemon zest, lemon juice, and scallions. Season generously with salt and pepper. Set aside.

**2** Spread the brioche slices with the remaining ¼ cup mayonnaise. Arrange a layer of lettuce leaves over each brioche slice. Spread the crab salad over half the slices. Close each sandwich with the remaining prepared brioche. Trim the crusts. Cut each sandwich into 2 even rectangles.

## TARRAGON SHRIMP SALAD TEA SANDWICHES

**MAKES 2 DOZEN** | photograph on page 91

*Tarragon has a very distinctive flavor, so you must be careful how you use it. But when it is right, as in this sandwich, it is perfect. The mayonnaise will turn a beautiful green only if you use a food processor. It tastes just as delicious, however, if you whisk it together by hand.*

1 pound medium shrimp, heads removed (see page 340)
1 tablespoon kosher salt, plus more to taste
¼ cup plus 2 tablespoons homemade (page 315) or prepared mayonnaise
2 tablespoons Dijon mustard
¼ cup finely chopped fresh tarragon
Freshly ground black pepper
24 very thin slices of white sandwich bread
1 small bunch of baby lettuce, torn into small pieces to yield about 2 cups

**1** Bring 3 cups of water to a boil in a medium saucepan. Add the shrimp and salt. Let simmer, covered, until the shrimp are just cooked through and opaque, 30 seconds to 2 minutes. Drain the shrimp. Set aside to cool, then peel and devein.

**2** In the bowl of a small food processor, combine the ¼ cup mayonnaise, mustard, and tarragon. Process until smooth. Season generously with salt and pepper. Transfer to a small bowl, cover, and refrigerate until ready to use.

**3** Once the shrimp are completely cooled, chop them into ¼-inch pieces and place in a bowl. Toss with 3 tablespoons of the reserved mayonnaise mixture. Spread the bread slices with the remaining mayonnaise. Spread about 2 tablespoons of shrimp salad on each of 12 bread slices. Top each with a layer of baby lettuce, then top with the remaining bread slices. Trim the crusts. Cut each sandwich on the diagonal to make 24 triangles.

## CLASSIC HOMEMADE MAYONNAISE

**MAKES 2½ CUPS**

*Use light olive oil to make the mayonnaise for delicately flavored foods such as tea sandwiches. Use richly flavored extra-virgin olive oils for a more assertive version.*

1 cup light olive oil

1 cup vegetable or safflower oil

2 large eggs

¼ teaspoon dry mustard

¾ teaspoon kosher salt, plus more to taste

2 tablespoons fresh lemon juice

Combine the oils in a large glass measuring cup. Place the eggs, mustard, and the ¾ teaspoon of salt in the bowl of a food processor. Process until the mixture is foamy and pale, about 1½ minutes. With the machine running, add the oil, drop by drop, until the mixture starts to thicken (about ½ cup of oil total); do not stop the machine at this point or the mayonnaise may not come together. Add the remaining oil in a slow, steady stream. When all of the oil has been incorporated, slowly add the lemon juice. Taste and adjust the mayonnaise for seasoning. Fresh mayonnaise can be kept, refrigerated, in an airtight container for up to 5 days.

*Note:* Because of the slight risk of bacterial poisoning, the USDA advises against the consumption of raw eggs by pregnant women, young children, and anyone with a weakened immune system.

---

**NOTE** | Homemade Mayonnaise

Homemade mayonnaise is a revelation to those who have never tried it; the flavor and texture are far superior to anything available in stores. Making mayonnaise is much easier now that we have food processors, but I still whisk mine in a bowl if I have time. I prefer to use whole eggs, not just the yolks, for a lighter texture.

Mayonnaise is actually an emulsion formed when certain components of the egg yolks disperse the molecules of the oils to form a thick, creamy mixture. The secret to a successful mayonnaise is to start out very slowly, adding the oil literally drop by drop. This keeps the egg yolks from being overwhelmed by too much oil.

By varying the ingredients, you can create endless variations of mayonnaise. Substitute a flavored vinegar such as tarragon or sherry for the lemon juice, for instance, or alter the flavor by trying different olive oils. Just as when making the Compound Butters (pages 391–394), seasonings or chopped fresh herbs may be added to the mayonnaise after it is made. Use these flavored mayonnaises when making tea sandwiches or canapés.

## B-L-TEA SANDWICHES

**MAKES 2 DOZEN** | photograph on page 91

*This tea sandwich takes advantage of the spiciness of peppered bacon (see Sources, page 487), the tenderness of lamb's lettuce (mâche), and the concentrated flavor of sun-dried tomatoes to update the classic BLT. Sun-dried tomatoes are available packed in olive oil or packaged dried in cellophane bags. Those packed in olive oil do not need rehydrating.*

1½ pounds thick-sliced hickory-smoked
    peppered bacon

24 (4 ounces) sun-dried tomatoes

1 cup homemade (page 315) or prepared
    mayonnaise

Kosher salt and freshly ground black pepper

24 ¼-inch-thick slices of rye bread or 48 slices
    of party rye

6 ounces lamb's lettuce (mâche) or other baby
    lettuce leaves, enough to make about 2
    loosely packed cups

**1** Heat the oven to 375°F. with the rack in the center. Arrange the bacon strips in a single layer without touching on 2 baking sheets and bake, one at a time, in the oven for 10 minutes each. Remove and drain off the fat. Continue to bake until the bacon is crisp, another 10 minutes. Drain and let cool on paper towels. Crumble the bacon into small pieces, about ½ inch each. Set aside.

**2** Meanwhile, heat 3 cups of water in a small saucepan until almost boiling. Place the sun-dried tomatoes in a medium bowl and cover with the very hot water. Allow the tomatoes to soak until they are soft, about 20 minutes. Drain, pat dry, and finely chop. Combine the tomatoes and the mayonnaise. Season generously with salt and pepper.

**3** Spread each bread slice with the mayonnaise mixture. Generously sprinkle half of the bread slices with the bacon. Arrange the mâche over the bacon, sprinkle with pepper, and top with the remaining bread. Trim the crusts. Slice each in half and serve.

## SERRANO HAM TEA SANDWICHES

**MAKES 7 DOZEN** | photograph on page 91

*Serrano translates as "from the sierra," a reference to the mountainous region where these famous raw hams are cured. The hams are dried in the cool air of the mountains in Andalusia, Spain. I like to use a Spanish cheese to go with this ham, such as Suspiro de Cabra, a semisoft aged goat cheese (see Cheese Glossary, page 416). However, any goat cheese that has been aged long enough, and is therefore firm enough to slice, may be used.*

*To make these sandwiches with a pullman loaf or Pain de Mie (see Note, page 238), you will need a 1⅞-inch square cookie cutter and a 1½-inch flower cutter (see Sources, page 486). If you would like to make fewer sandwiches or cannot find pullman loaves, 2 variations follow using different breads.*

1 whole-wheat pullman loaf, sliced horizontally
    into ¼-inch-thick slices

1 white pullman loaf or Pain de Mie (page 238),
    sliced horizontally into ¼-inch-thick slices

6 tablespoons unsalted butter, at room
    temperature

2¼ pounds thinly sliced Serrano ham

14 ounces Suspiro de Cabra or other semisoft
    aged goat cheese

**1** Spread half of each of the whole-wheat and white bread slices with the butter. Using the square cookie cutter, cut out squares from all of the slices. Set the buttered squares aside.

**2** Using the flower cutter, cut out flowers from the unbuttered squares. Return one flower to each square, alternating the white flowers within the whole-wheat squares, and the whole-wheat flowers within the white squares. Set aside.

**3** Using the square cutter, cut the ham and place a square on each buttered bread square. Use all of the scraps of ham to make enough squares. Slice the cheese as thinly as possible and trim to fit the bread. Place over the ham. Top with the flower bread square. Repeat with the remaining ingredients, arrange the sandwiches on a platter, and serve.

## VARIATION 1

### MAKES 2 DOZEN

*To make these sandwiches with presliced party loaves, you will need a 1⅞-inch square cookie cutter or a serrated knife and a 1½-inch flower cutter (see Sources, page 486). For this version, I prefer to use party pumpernickel rather than larger slices from loaf pumpernickel. The delicate ham is much easier to arrange on smaller pieces of bread.*

  24 slices of party pumpernickel bread

  24 slices of party whole-wheat bread

  3 tablespoons unsalted butter, at room temperature

  4 ounces thinly sliced Serrano ham

  4 ounces Suspiro de Cabra or other semisoft aged goat cheese

Follow the above recipe, substituting the slices of party bread for the pullman loaf or Pain de Mie. If you don't have a square cutter, use a serrated knife to trim the slices to 1⅞-inch squares.

## VARIATION 2

### MAKES 2 DOZEN

*If using very thinly sliced sandwich bread, you will need a 1½-inch square cutter or serrated knife so you can cut 2 tea sandwiches per slice. Use a 1⅛-inch round cookie cutter rather than the larger flower-shaped cutter (see Sources, page 486).*

  6 ¼-inch-thick slices of whole-wheat bread

  6 ¼-inch-thick slices of white sandwich bread

  6 tablespoons unsalted butter, at room temperature

  10 ounces thinly sliced Serrano ham

  6 ounces Suspiro de Cabra or other semisoft aged goat cheese

**1** Spread 3 of the whole-wheat bread slices and 3 of the white bread slices with butter. Cover the buttered slices with slices of ham and cheese. Using the square cookie cutter or a serrated knife, cut out 2 squares from all of the bread slices. Set aside the bread squares with ham and cheese.

**2** Using the round cookie cutter, cut out the center of each unbuttered square. Return one round to each ham and cheese square, alternating the white rounds within the whole-wheat squares and the whole-wheat rounds within the white squares, and serve.

To create a breadbox buffet, take inspiration from the sizes, shapes, and flavors of the loaves themselves. The bowl-like containers are made from crusty boules and the elongated versions from pullman loaves (see page 238). The soft centers are cut away and either sliced to make the tea sandwiches (pullman loaf) or used to make croutons or bread crumbs for a later use (see page 321). **HOW TO MAKE THE BOXES** You'll need dense sandwich-type bread with a relatively sturdy crust (see photograph, page 104). **1** Slice off the top of the loaf with an electric carving knife. To cut the inner block of bread from the crust "box," cut around the sides of the inner block, making vertical incisions ¾ of an inch from the crust. **2** To remove the inner block from the pullman loaf, turn it on its side and make an incision along one side only, ¾ inch from the bottom crust, being careful not to pierce the crust on the other sides. Remove the inner block of bread, and slice it, using the electric knife again for the cleanest possible cut. To remove the inside of the boule, turn the loaf on its side and, using an electric carving knife, slice the top of the bread off the loaf, about a third of the way down. Remove the top and, using your hands, pull the bread from the inside. Brush away any remaining crumbs inside the boule. **3** Arrange tea sandwiches in the breadboxes so that they overlap slightly (see photograph, page 105).

## SMOKED SALMON TEA SANDWICHES

**MAKES 2 DOZEN** | photograph on page 91

*Vary the flavor of this tea sandwich by using different Compound Butters (pages 391–394). Lemon-Dill Butter or Watercress Butter are delicious with smoked salmon.*

24 ¼-inch-thick slices of pumpernickel bread or
    48 slices of party pumpernickel
4 ounces Ginger-Cilantro Lime Butter (page
    392), at room temperature
8 ounces thinly sliced smoked salmon

**1** Spread all of the bread slices generously with the butter. Place slices of the smoked salmon in an even layer on half of the bread slices. Top with the remaining bread slices. Using a 2-inch flower-shaped cookie cutter, cut out the tea sandwiches.

**2** Remove the top slice of bread from each flower. Using a ¾- to ⅞-inch round biscuit cutter, cut a circle from the center of each, remove the circle, and discard. Replace the slice, butter-side down, on the flower. Arrange the tea sandwiches on a tray and serve.

## GOAT CHEESE AND CHIVE TEA SANDWICHES

**MAKES 2 DOZEN** | photograph on page 91

*Dipping one edge of these sandwiches in chopped chives provides a sharp accent and also makes them look quite special. Be sure that you choose a soft, creamy goat cheese so it spreads easily.*

8 ounces fresh goat cheese

24 very thin slices of white sandwich bread, crusts removed

1 medium bunch of watercress leaves, enough to make about 2 lightly packed cups

2 bunches of fresh chives, finely snipped to make ½ cup

2 tablespoons homemade (page 315) or prepared mayonnaise

**1** Spread the goat cheese liberally on all of the bread slices. Arrange the watercress leaves in an even layer on 12 of the bread slices. Top each of these slices with a second slice of bread, goat cheese side down.

**2** Place the chives in a small shallow bowl. Halve each sandwich on the diagonal. Using a small spatula, carefully spread mayonnaise along the long side of one tea sandwich, and then dip this long edge into the chopped chives. Repeat with each tea sandwich.

## CURRIED EGG SALAD TEA SANDWICHES

**MAKES 2 DOZEN** | photograph on page 91

*Spicy radish sprouts give a nice bite to these tea sandwiches, but you can also substitute other sprouts, such as alfalfa, for crunch and texture.*

4 large eggs

3½ tablespoons homemade (page 315) or prepared mayonnaise

1 teaspoon curry powder

1 teaspoon Dijon mustard

Kosher salt and freshly ground black pepper

3 medium radishes

24 ¼-inch-thick slices of whole-wheat bread or 48 whole-wheat party slices, crusts removed

1 cup (2 ounces) radish sprouts

**1** Place the eggs in a medium pan of cool water. Bring to a low simmer and cook the eggs for 10 minutes, stirring once or twice to ensure even cooking. Drain the eggs and rinse under cool water to prevent further cooking. Peel the eggs and set them aside until completely cool.

**2** In a small bowl, combine 2½ tablespoons of the mayonnaise, the curry powder, and the mustard. Season generously with salt and pepper. Mix well. Chop the eggs into approximately ¼-inch dice and gently stir them into the mayonnaise mixture. Adjust seasoning with salt and pepper.

**3** Using a mandoline or vegetable peeler, thinly slice the radishes into transparent circles and set aside.

**4** Spread half of the bread slices with the egg salad. Spread the other half of the bread slices with the remaining mayonnaise. Close the sandwiches. Use a 2-inch round cookie cutter to cut out 2 sandwiches from each large sandwich or 1 sandwich from each small sandwich. Insert 1 or 2 radish slices and some radish sprouts into each sandwich.

## SESAME-CRUSTED CHICKEN SALAD TEA SANDWICHES

**MAKES 2 DOZEN** | photograph on page 95

*These Asian-flavored sandwiches, with their half crust of toasted sesame seeds, make a particularly dramatic appearance when lined back-to-back to form a long pyramid. Don't skip toasting the sesame seeds, since it deepens their flavor. The chicken salad may be made a day in advance and kept in an airtight container in the refrigerator.*

1 medium onion, skin on, sliced in half

6 black peppercorns

1 bay leaf

2 sprigs fresh thyme

1 3½-pound chicken, giblets removed, rinsed
    and patted dry

½ cup plus 2 tablespoons homemade (page 315)
    or prepared mayonnaise

1 tablespoon dark sesame oil

2 tablespoons finely chopped fresh cilantro

2 tablespoons snipped fresh chives

3 scallions, white and light green parts only,
    thinly sliced crosswise to yield ¼ cup

Kosher salt and freshly ground black pepper

24 very thin slices of white sandwich bread

10 tablespoons (1¼ sticks) unsalted butter, at
    room temperature

¼ cup sesame seeds, toasted (see page 386)

Mizuna leaves, for garnish

**1** Place the onion, peppercorns, bay leaf, and thyme in a large pot. Add the chicken to the pot with just enough cold water to cover. Cover and bring to a simmer. Then uncover and cook for 1 hour. Drain the chicken, reserving the cooking liquid, and set the chicken aside to cool. Discard the seasonings and refrigerate or freeze the stock for future use. When the chicken is cool enough to handle, remove the skin and discard. Shred the meat from the chicken and then chop it very fine. Refrigerate, covered, until well chilled.

**2** In a small bowl, mix together the mayonnaise and sesame oil. Add this to the chicken and combine well. Add the cilantro, chives, and scallions and combine well. Add salt and pepper to taste. Refrigerate, covered, until ready to use.

**3** Spread each bread slice with butter, reserving some butter for garnishing. Spread an even layer of chicken salad onto half of the slices of bread. Top with the other half of the slices to make sandwiches. Trim the crusts. Cut each sandwich on the diagonal. Arrange the sandwiches long-edge down in a row to form a horizontal pyramid. Spread the remaining butter along one side of the pyramid. Spread the toasted sesame seeds along the buttered edge to cover. Garnish the platter with mizuna leaves and serve.

## PROSCIUTTO AND PORT-FIG BUTTER TEA SANDWICHES

**MAKES 2 DOZEN** | photograph on page 91

*Prosciutto and figs are a classic Italian flavor combination, and the port adds another layer of richness. Two-colored marble bread blends rye and pumpernickel for a very attractive look, but if you can't find marble, substitute white or rye.*

3 ounces Port-Fig Butter (page 393), at room
    temperature

12 ¼-inch-thick slices of marble bread

3 ounces thinly sliced prosciutto

Generously butter all of the slices of bread. Place the prosciutto in an even layer over 6 of the bread slices. Top each with a second slice of bread, butter-side down. Trim the crusts. Cut each sandwich into 4 squares and serve.

Bread crumbs have two very appealing characteristics: they are very simple to make, and they are a very economical use of good, fresh bread or any unsweetened bread. I like to make my tea sandwiches and canapés no larger than two bites, so depending on the bread you use, there are always varying amounts of bread scraps left over. Freeze the bread in a resealable plastic storage bag until you have a few handfuls' worth. If you are making a lot of hors d'oeuvres, you will have enough bread scraps right away.

There are two basic categories of bread crumbs: fresh and dry. For fresh, simply remove the crusts, place the bread in the bowl of a food processor, and process until fine. For dry bread crumbs, you must first place the bread in a 250° F. oven until fully dried, 12 to 15 minutes. Let the bread cool, then transfer to the food processor and process until fine.

Bread crumbs can be made the same way from darker breads. These somewhat earthier crumbs add an interesting flavor to gratins and breaded meats.

In addition to their other virtues, bread crumbs also store very well. If placed in an airtight container in the refrigerator, they will keep nicely for 1 week; in the freezer, they will keep for 6 months. Never use stale bread to make bread crumbs, because they will taste just that way—stale.

## TUNA NIÇOISE FICELLES

**MAKES 2 DOZEN** | photograph on page 94

*By using ficelles, which are very thin baguettes, you can include all of the wonderful fresh tastes of a classic Salade Niçoise in an hors d'oeuvre.*

3 large eggs
2 tablespoons red wine vinegar
5 tablespoons extra-virgin olive oil
6 flat anchovy fillets, chopped
2 tablespoons capers, drained
1 medium shallot, grated
Kosher salt and freshly ground black pepper
2 6-ounce cans chunk white tuna, drained and flaked
2 24-inch-long ficelles or other thin baguettes
1 small head of red oakleaf lettuce or other baby lettuce
10 ounces plum tomatoes, quartered and oven dried (see page 257)
¾ cup (4 ounces) oil-cured black olives, pitted and roughly chopped

**1** Place the eggs in a medium pan of cool water. Bring to a low simmer and cook the eggs for 10 minutes, stirring once or twice to ensure even cooking. Drain the eggs and rinse under cool water to prevent further cooking. Peel the eggs and set aside until completely cool. Slice thin crosswise.

**2** Place the vinegar in a small stainless-steel bowl. Slowly whisk in the olive oil. Add the anchovies, capers, and shallots. Season with salt and pepper to taste. Add the tuna and toss to combine.

**3** Split each ficelle lengthwise without cutting all the way through. Fold the loaves open like a book and arrange the lettuce leaves along the inside. Spoon the tuna mixture evenly onto the lettuce, and top with the egg slices, tomatoes, and olives. Close the ficelle and cut each into twelve 2-inch sandwiches.

## CHOPPED EGG AND ASPARAGUS CANAPÉS

**MAKES 2 DOZEN** | photograph on page 99

*I like to use the pumpernickel bread that comes presliced and packaged in cellophane, usually sold in the deli section of the grocery store, for these canapés. You can also use the smaller loaves of party pumpernickel, which require little more than removing the crusts. Select the thinnest asparagus spears you can find, since they are the most tender—perfect for these delicate canapés.*

24 ¼-inch-thick slices of pumpernickel bread, or 24 slices of party pumpernickel

6 large eggs

Kosher salt and freshly ground black pepper

12 thin asparagus spears

3 tablespoons finely chopped fresh tarragon

½ cup homemade (page 315) or prepared mayonnaise

**1** Heat the oven to 300° F. Arrange the bread slices on 2 baking sheets. Place the bread slices in the oven to dry out and toast slightly, 5 to 7 minutes per side. Transfer to cool on a wire rack.

**2** Place the eggs in a medium pan of cool water. Bring to a low simmer and cook the eggs for 10 minutes, stirring once or twice to ensure even cooking. Drain the eggs and rinse under cold water to prevent further cooking. Peel the eggs. Remove the egg whites and save them for another use, such as making egg salad.

**3** Place the cooked yolks in a fine mesh sieve. Using a rubber spatula, press the egg yolks through the sieve into a bowl. Set aside.

**4** Bring a large saucepan of lightly salted water to a boil. Add the asparagus and blanch just until bright green and tender, 30 seconds to 1 minute.

Drain and place under cold running water to prevent further cooking. Pat dry. Cut the tip of each spear into a 2½-inch length. (Save the remaining spears for snacking.) Slice each tip in half lengthwise so they will lie flat on the canapés. Set aside.

**5** In a small bowl, combine the tarragon, the mayonnaise, and salt and pepper to taste. Spread each bread slice with the mayonnaise mixture. Sprinkle the yolks generously over each slice. Using a 2-inch square cookie cutter, or a serrated knife, cut out 24 canapés. Place 1 slice of asparagus diagonally over each canapé and serve.

## LENTIL AND FETA CHEESE CANAPÉS

**MAKES 2 DOZEN** | photograph on page 99

*Beluga lentils are small, black, and look like dark, delicious caviar. Look for them in specialty food stores (see Sources, page 487). If they are unavailable, use French Le Puy lentils instead; they are also very tasty and hold their shape well when cooked. As for the feta cheese, try to find a creamy variety so it will blend well with the cream cheese.*

2 cups homemade chicken stock or low-sodium canned broth, skimmed of fat

1 small onion, peel on, cut in half

1 bay leaf

1 sprig fresh thyme

⅓ cup beluga or French green lentils, picked over and rinsed

2 tablespoons extra-virgin olive oil

1 tablespoon red wine vinegar

Kosher salt and freshly ground black pepper

6 tablespoons (2 ounces) mild feta cheese

¼ cup (2 ounces) cream cheese, at room temperature

1 roasted red bell pepper (see page 266)

24 ¼-inch-thick slices of whole-wheat bread, or 24 slices of party whole-wheat

**1** Place the stock, 1 cup water, onion, bay leaf, and thyme in a medium saucepan. Add the lentils and bring to a simmer over high heat. Reduce the heat to medium-low, partially cover, and simmer until the lentils are tender, 25 to 30 minutes. Drain the lentils, discarding the onion, bay leaf, and thyme. Transfer the lentils to a small bowl and gently toss with the olive oil and vinegar. Add salt and pepper to taste. Cover and refrigerate until cool, about 1 hour. The lentils may be made 1 day ahead and kept, in an airtight container, in the refrigerator.

**2** In the bowl of a food processor, combine the feta and the cream cheese. Process until smooth. This cheese mixture may also be made a day ahead; cover and refrigerate until ready to use.

**3** Slice the roasted pepper into 2½ × ⅛-inch julienne strips. Set aside.

**4** Heat the oven to 300° F. Arrange the bread slices on 2 baking sheets. Place the bread slices in the oven to dry out and toast slightly, 5 to 7 minutes per side. Transfer to cool on a wire rack.

**5** Spread each bread slice with the feta cheese mixture. Using a 2-inch square cookie cutter, or a serrated knife, cut out 24 canapés. Place the straight edge of a blade of a large kitchen knife diagonally across half of the canapé. Spread 1 teaspoon of the reserved lentils over the exposed cheese, using the straight edge of the knife as a barrier from spilling the lentils over the entire canapé. Place 1 slice of bell pepper diagonally along the edge of the lentils. Repeat with the remaining canapés. Serve immediately.

## TAPENADE AND GOAT CHEESE CANAPÉS

**MAKES 2 DOZEN** | photograph on page 100

*Select a creamy goat cheese for easy spreading.*

> 4 ounces (about 10) Bella di Cerignola or other large green olives, pitted
>
> 4 ounces niçoise olives, pitted
>
> 6 tablespoons (3 ounces) fresh goat cheese, at room temperature
>
> ¼ cup (2 ounces) cream cheese, at room temperature
>
> 24 very thin slices of white sandwich bread

**1** Set aside 2 large green olives and 5 niçoise olives for the garnish. Place the remaining green olives in the bowl of a food processor. Pulse just until very finely chopped, 20 to 30 seconds. Transfer to a small bowl. Wipe out the bowl of the processor and add the niçoise olives. Pulse just until very finely chopped, 20 to 30 seconds. Transfer to a second small bowl. Set aside.

**2** In a small bowl combine the goat cheese and cream cheese until smooth. Set aside.

**3** Heat the oven to 300° F. Arrange the bread slices on 2 baking sheets. Place the bread slices in the oven to dry out and toast slightly, 5 to 7 minutes per side. Transfer to cool on a wire rack.

**4** Spread each bread slice with the goat cheese mixture. Using a 2¼-inch round cookie cutter, cut out 24 canapés. Place the straight edge of a large kitchen knife along the diameter of the canapé. Spread 1 teaspoon of green or black chopped olives over half of the cheese, using the knife as a guide. Repeat with remaining canapés. Thinly slice the reserved olives. Garnish each canapé with green or black olives. Serve immediately.

## CARROT CUMIN CANAPÉS

**MAKES 2 DOZEN** | photograph on page 99

*In Tunisia, carrots are a dietary staple and are often mixed with earthy cumin; it is a culinary combination that works perfectly together. You can prepare the carrot-cumin purée 2 to 3 hours ahead and keep it, covered, in the refrigerator.*

4 medium carrots, cut into 2-inch pieces to
    yield 1 cup
½ teaspoon ground cumin
6 tablespoons canned vegetable broth or water
Kosher salt and freshly ground black pepper
1 cup peanut oil, for frying
2 medium shallots, thinly sliced lengthwise
1 medium leek, white and green parts only, cut
    lengthwise into very thin julienne, well
    washed and patted dry (see page 271)
12 very thin slices of white sandwich bread
1 tablespoon whole cumin seeds

**1** Place the carrots in a steamer basket over 1 inch of boiling water and cover tightly. Steam until fork-tender, 8 to 10 minutes. Transfer the carrots to the bowl of a food processor. Add the ground cumin and 4 tablespoons of the stock. Purée until the mixture is very smooth, adding the remaining 2 tablespoons of stock as necessary to make the purée spreadable but not runny. Add salt and pepper to taste. Transfer to a bowl and set aside to cool.

**2** Heat the oil in a skillet, or an electric fryer, over medium heat until a frying thermometer registers 360°F., or until a shallot placed in the oil sizzles. Add the shallots, in batches, and cook until golden, 20 to 30 seconds. Transfer to paper towels. Add the leeks, in batches, to the oil and fry until golden, 20 to 30 seconds. Transfer to paper towels. Set aside.

**3** Heat the oven to 300°F. Arrange the bread slices on a baking sheet. Place the bread slices in the oven to dry out and toast slightly, 5 to 7 minutes per side. Transfer to cool on a wire rack.

**4** Increase the heat to 375°F. Place the cumin seeds on a small rimmed baking sheet and toast until fragrant, 3 to 5 minutes. Transfer to a small bowl.

**5** Spread each bread slice with the carrot purée. Trim the crusts. Slice in half and garnish with the shallots, leeks, and toasted cumin seeds. These canapés are best served as soon as possible.

## ROASTED RED PEPPER HUMMUS CANAPÉS

**MAKES 4 DOZEN** | photograph on page 100

*Roasted peppers and garlic enriches the flavor of these canapés, as does tahini, a paste made from ground sesame seeds. Be sure to stir the tahini well before adding it.*

3 large roasted red bell peppers (see page 266)
3 heads of roasted garlic (see page 265), puréed
1 15-ounce can chickpeas, drained (1½ cups)
2 tablespoons fresh lemon juice
3 tablespoons tahini paste
2 tablespoons extra-virgin olive oil
1 teaspoon kosher salt
24 ¼-inch-thick slices of pumpernickel bread

**1** Coarsely chop 1 of the peppers. Slice the 2 remaining peppers into ⅛ × 1½-inch pieces and reserve. Transfer the chopped pepper to the bowl of a food processor. Add 2 teaspoons of the garlic purée and process until smooth. Add the chickpeas, lemon juice, tahini paste, olive oil, and salt. Process until smooth. Transfer to a bowl and set aside.

**2** Heat the oven to 300°F. Arrange the bread slices on 2 baking sheets. Place the bread slices in the oven to dry out and toast slightly, 5 to 7 minutes per side. Transfer to cool on a wire rack.

**3** Spread each bread slice with the hummus. Trim the crusts. Slice each canapé in half on the diagonal. Garnish with the pepper strips and a dollop of the garlic purée.

## GRILLED ZUCCHINI CANAPÉS

**MAKES 2 DOZEN** | photograph on page 98

*Look for a creamy Greek or French feta to make very smooth eggplant purée.*

1 small eggplant (10 ounces)
2½ ounces creamy feta cheese
Kosher salt and freshly ground black pepper
12 ¼-inch-thick slices of pumpernickel bread
6 ounces baby zucchini, or 2 6-ounce zucchini
1 tablespoon olive oil
2 large roasted red bell peppers (see page 266)

**1** Heat the oven to 400°F. with the rack in the center. Place the whole eggplant on a baking sheet and roast until the skin buckles and the flesh is cooked throughout, 30 to 40 minutes. Remove the eggplant and slice open.

**2** Scrape away all of the cooked eggplant flesh from the skin and place it in the bowl of a food processor. Process until as smooth as possible. Set aside to cool. Crumble in the feta cheese and process until blended. The mixture should equal about 1 cup. Season generously with salt and pepper and set aside.

**3** Meanwhile, reduce the oven heat to 300°F. Arrange the bread slices on a baking sheet. Place the bread slices in the oven to dry out and toast slightly, 5 to 7 minutes per side. Transfer to cool on a wire rack. Cut each slice into a 2½ × 3-inch piece.

**4** Using a mandoline or vegetable peeler, cut the zucchini lengthwise into ⅛-inch-thick slices. Heat a grill pan or outdoor grill over medium-high heat. Brush the zucchini slices lightly with olive oil. Working in batches, grill the slices until tender, about 2 minutes each side until light grill marks appear. Remove and set aside.

**5** Cut the peppers into approximately 2½ × 3-inch pieces. Generously spread each bread slice with the reserved eggplant purée. Place a roasted pepper piece over the purée. Arrange 4 baby zucchini slices on top of the red pepper, parallel with the short end of the bread. (If using regular zucchini slices, cut them first into 3-inch lengths and then arrange 4 pieces, slightly overlapping, on each bread slice.) Trim the crusts. Using a sharp knife, cut each piece lengthwise into 2 rectangles.

---

**NOTE** | Canapé Trays

A tray of canapés should offer a variety of flavors and textures. Arrange those with assertively flavored ingredients together so as not to overpower more delicately flavored hors d'oeuvres. Here are some of my favorite canapé combinations.

Beluga Lentil and Feta Cheese

Smoked Salmon Flower and Herb Butter

Westphalian Ham and Celeriac Remoulade

Carrot-Cumin with Fried Shallots and Leeks

Clams and Curry Butter

Olive Tapenade with Goat Cheese

Shrimp, Cucumber, and Dill Butter

Beef Carpaccio

Grilled Zucchini

Roasted Red Pepper Hummus

Taramasalata with Assorted Caviars

Smoked Salmon Cream Cheese and Cucumber

Wasabi Caviar and Daikon

Chopped Egg and Asparagus

This version of wasabi caviar duplicates the piquant flavor of the purchased variety (see Sources, page 487), though the color is not as vibrant. In a small bowl, sift ¾ teaspoon wasabi powder into 1 ounce golden caviar. Mix well and set aside for 15 minutes.

## WASABI CAVIAR AND DAIKON CANAPÉS

**MAKES 2 DOZEN** | photograph on page 101

*This is one of my very favorite canapés. I love the unusual colors, its serene appearance, and the way its Japanese flavorings are at once delicate and satisfying. Slice the daikon very thin, so that you can see the caviar right through it.*

24 very thin slices of white sandwich bread
1 small daikon radish, at least 2 inches in
    diameter
¾ cup (6 ounces) cream cheese, at room
    temperature
2½ ounces prepared wasabi caviar or homemade
    (see Note, above)

**1** Heat the oven to 300° F. Arrange the bread slices on 2 baking sheets. Place the bread slices in the oven to dry out and toast slightly, 5 to 7 minutes per side. Transfer to cool on a wire rack.

**2** Using a mandoline, thinly slice the daikon into ¹⁄₁₆-inch rounds. Use a 1¾-inch round cookie cutter to cut each daikon slice into uniform rounds. Cover with damp paper towels and set aside.

**3** Spread each bread slice with an even layer of the cream cheese. Use a 2¼-inch round cookie cutter to cut out 24 canapés. Working one at a time, place a small piece of parchment, or wax, paper over half the canapé. Spread ½ teaspoon of the caviar over the exposed cream cheese and then lift off the paper. Place a round of daikon on the top of each canapé. Serve immediately.

## TARAMASALATA AND CAVIAR CANAPÉS

**MAKES 2 DOZEN** | photograph on page 99

*Taramasalata is a creamy, pink spread made from pale orange carp roe, lemon juice, bread crumbs, and other seasonings. A wonderful Greek standard, very good prepared taramasalata is now available in glass jars in specialty food stores as well as in the gourmet section of many supermarkets (see Sources, page 487).*

24 very thin slices of white sandwich bread
½ cup (about 4 ounces) prepared taramasalata
1 bunch of mâche or other baby lettuce leaves
½ ounce assorted caviar, such as black or golden
1 tablespoon grated lemon zest

**1** Heat the oven to 300° F. Arrange the bread slices on 2 baking sheets. Place the bread slices in the oven to dry out for 3 minutes on each side. Remove. Cut into 24 rounds using a 2¼-inch round cookie cutter. Return to the oven until firm to the touch, 3 to 4 minutes, but not brown. Transfer to cool on a wire rack.

**2** Spread each bread slice with the taramasalata. Garnish each with mâche leaves, a small dollop of caviar, and lemon zest. These canapés are best served right away.

## BEEF CARPACCIO CANAPÉS

**MAKES 2 DOZEN** | photograph on page 99

*The trick with carpaccio is to make sure that the beef is sliced paper thin. The best way to do this is to ask your butcher to slice it. If that is not possible, put the tenderloin in the freezer until it is firm but not completely frozen, at least 1 hour, and slice it as thin as you can with a mandoline or very sharp slicing knife.*

1 cup peanut oil, for frying

1½ tablespoons capers, drained and patted dry

1 small garlic clove, minced

½ cup homemade (page 315) or prepared mayonnaise

Kosher salt and freshly ground black pepper

24 very thin slices of white sandwich bread

1 pound beef tenderloin, sliced into 24 paper-thin slices, each at least 2¼ inches in diameter, chilled

1 small bunch of arugula leaves (about 1½ cups), cut into ribbons

1 ounce Parmesan cheese, thinly shaved

**1** Heat the oil in a small saucepan, or an electric fryer, until a frying thermometer registers 360° F. Add the capers and fry until they blossom, 20 to 30 seconds. Transfer to paper towels to drain. Set aside.

**2** In a small bowl, combine the garlic and the mayonnaise. Add salt and pepper to taste. Cover with plastic wrap and refrigerate until ready to use.

**3** Heat the oven to 300° F. Arrange the bread slices on 2 baking sheets. Place the bread slices in the oven to dry out and toast slightly, 5 to 7 minutes per side. Transfer to cool on a wire rack.

**4** Spread each bread slice with the reserved mayonnaise. Place 1 slice of the chilled beef in the center of each slice. Use a 2¼-inch round cookie cutter to cut out 24 canapés. Garnish each with arugula ribbons, Parmesan, and fried capers, and serve.

## WESTPHALIAN HAM AND CELERIAC RÉMOULADE CANAPÉS

**MAKES 2 DOZEN** | photograph on page 99

*Celeriac, also known as celery root, makes a crisp, light slaw when dressed with the classic French rémoulade sauce, which I like to make without anchovies. Either prosciutto or Serrano makes a fine substitution for the classic German Westphalian ham.*

3 tablespoons homemade (page 315) or prepared mayonnaise

1 cornichon, roughly chopped

8 capers, drained

½ teaspoon Dijon mustard

½ teaspoon finely chopped fresh flat-leaf parsley

¾ teaspoon finely chopped fresh tarragon

¼ teaspoon kosher salt

¼ small bulb celeriac

24 very thin slices of white sandwich bread

½ cup (4 ounces) cream cheese, at room temperature

8 ounces Westphalian ham sliced into 24 paper-thin slices, each at least 2¼ inches in diameter, chilled

**1** In a small food processor, combine the mayonnaise, cornichon, capers, and mustard. Blend until the capers and cornichon are in very small pieces. (If blending by hand, chop the ingredients very fine and combine.) Add the parsley, tarragon, and salt. Blend just to combine and transfer the mayonnaise to a medium bowl.

**2** Slice the celeriac into ⅛-inch pieces with a mandoline or a chef's knife. Cut the slices into matchsticks 1½ to 2 inches long and toss them into the mayonnaise mixture. Cover with plastic wrap and set aside in the refrigerator.

CONTINUED ON FOLLOWING PAGE

**3** Heat the oven to 300°F. Arrange the bread slices on 2 baking sheets. Place the bread slices in the oven to dry out and toast slightly, 5 to 7 minutes per side. Transfer to cool on a wire rack.

**4** Spread each bread slice with the cream cheese. Arrange 1 ham slice in the center of each bread slice. Use a 2-inch square cookie cutter, or a serrated knife, to cut out 24 canapés. Garnish each canapé with the celeriac rémoulade. Serve.

## SMOKED SALMON FLOWER CANAPÉS

**MAKES 2 DOZEN** | photograph on page 100

*Either a flower-shaped or round cookie cutter will work well here. To add variety of taste and color, use different Compound Butters, such as Watercress Butter (page 391).*

> 12 ¼-inch-thick slices of pumpernickel bread, or 24 slices of party pumpernickel
> 3 ounces Dill Butter (page 393), at room temperature
> 6 ounces thinly sliced smoked salmon
> 24 small sprigs fresh dill

**1** Heat the oven to 300°F. Arrange the bread slices on a baking sheet. Place the bread slices in the oven to dry out and toast slightly, 5 to 7 minutes per side. Transfer to cool on a wire rack.

**2** Spread each bread slice with the butter. Arrange a single layer of smoked salmon over each slice. Use a 2-inch flower-shaped cookie cutter to cut out 24 canapés, 2 from each slice. Garnish each canapé with a sprig of dill and serve.

## SMOKED SALMON CREAM CHEESE AND CUCUMBER CANAPÉS

**MAKES 2 DOZEN** | photograph on page 99

*Use a mandoline to make uniform cucumber slices.*

> ½ cup (3 ounces) roughly chopped smoked salmon
> ½ cup (4 ounces) cream cheese, at room temperature
> 1 tablespoon fresh lemon juice
> 1 teaspoon prepared horseradish, or more to taste
> 12 very thin slices of white sandwich bread
> 2 large seedless cucumbers, peel on

**1** In a small bowl, use a fork to combine the salmon, cream cheese, lemon juice, and horseradish. Set aside, covered in plastic wrap, in the refrigerator until ready to use.

**2** Heat the oven to 300°F. Arrange the bread slices on a baking sheet. Place the bread slices in the oven to dry out and toast slightly, 5 to 7 minutes per side. Transfer to cool on a wire rack.

**3** Generously spread each bread slice with the salmon cream cheese. Using a mandoline or a vegetable peeler, thinly slice the cucumbers lengthwise about ⅛ inch thick. Arrange the cucumber slices, overlapping slightly, on each bread slice. Trim the crusts. Slice each canapé in half on the diagonal with a sharp knife. Repeat with the remaining canapés. Serve slightly chilled.

## CLAM AND CURRY BUTTER CANAPÉS

**MAKES 2 DOZEN** | photograph on page 98

*Curry and seafood are a particularly delicious combination. Curry powder, a staple of Indian cuisine, is a blend of 20 different spices, herbs, and seeds. Because it is quite intense, it is ideal for seasoning bite-size hors d'oeuvres, where small bites need big flavor.*

½ cup dry white wine

1 tablespoon unsalted butter

1 tablespoon kosher salt

24 littleneck or Manila clams, scrubbed

24 very thin slices of white sandwich bread

3 ounces Curry Butter (page 392), at room temperature

1 small bunch of fresh chives, cut into 3-inch lengths

**1** In a medium saucepan, combine the wine, butter, and salt. Add ½ cup of water, cover, and bring to a simmer. Add the clams to the pan and cook, covered, until the shells open, 8 to 10 minutes. Remove the clams with a slotted spoon, reserving the broth, and let cool enough to handle. Take the clams from the shells. Discard the shells. Place ½ cup of the broth into a small bowl and add the clams to keep them from drying out. Set aside at room temperature while proceeding.

**2** Heat the oven to 300°F. Arrange the bread slices on 2 baking sheets. Place the bread slices in the oven to dry out and toast slightly, 5 to 7 minutes per side. Transfer to cool on a wire rack.

**3** Spread each bread slice with the butter. Use a 2-inch oval, or round, cookie cutter to cut out 24 canapés. Drain the clams. Place 4 chives across each oval and trim the ends with kitchen shears. Place a clam in the center of each canapé and serve.

## SHRIMP, CUCUMBER, AND DILL BUTTER CANAPÉS

**MAKES 2 DOZEN** | photograph on page 97

*By slicing the shrimp lengthwise, the graceful curve of the shrimp is left intact, which makes for a very pretty canapé. If you use standard packaged thinly sliced white sandwich bread, each slice measures 3 × 3½ inches with the crusts removed, so 4 canapés can be cut from each slice.*

⅓ cup dry white wine

1 tablespoon kosher salt

12 medium shrimp, heads removed (see page 340)

6 very thin slices of white sandwich bread, crusts removed

3 ounces Shallot-Parsley Butter (page 391), at room temperature

1 seedless cucumber

1 small bunch of fresh dill, sprigs removed

**1** Place the wine, 2 cups of water, and the salt in a medium saucepan. Bring to a simmer and add the shrimp. Cook, covered, until the shrimp are opaque and cooked through, about 1 minute. Drain the shrimp. Set aside to cool, then peel and devein.

**2** Heat the oven to 300°F. Arrange the bread slices on a baking sheet. Place the bread slices in the oven to dry out and toast slightly, 5 to 7 minutes per side. Transfer to cool on a wire rack.

**3** Spread each bread slice with the shallot butter. Using a mandoline or vegetable peeler, thinly slice the cucumber lengthwise. Place 2 cucumber slices side by side to cover the surface of a bread slice. Trim the crusts. Arrange sprigs of dill over the cucumber. Cut 2 shrimp in half lengthwise and evenly space the 4 shrimp halves on the slice. Cut each piece of bread into quarters. Repeat with the remaining ingredients and serve.

## PÂTÉ DE FOIE GRAS WITH CARAMELIZED PLUM CROSTINI

**MAKES 2 DOZEN** | photograph on page 108

*Pâté de foie gras, a specialty of the Alsace and Perigord regions of France, is a very rich goose liver pâté. Here I combine it with sweet caramelized plums for a crostini suitable for very special occasions.*

½ tablespoon unsalted butter
2 ripe red plums, sliced into ¼-inch pieces
1 tablespoon sugar
1 tablespoon port wine
1 teaspoon olive oil
8 ounces pâté de foie gras, sliced ¼ inch thick
    and cut to fit crostini
24 Simple Crostini (page 243)
2 tablespoons fresh thyme

**1** Heat a large skillet over medium-high heat. Add the butter, then add the plums. Cook, stirring occasionally, until the plums begin to soften, 3 to 4 minutes. Sprinkle the sugar over the plums and cook, turning occasionally, until both sides have caramelized, about 2 minutes. Add the port to the pan and cook, stirring, until all the liquid has been absorbed, about 30 seconds. Carefully transfer the plums to a dish and set aside.

**2** Heat a large skillet over medium-high heat until very hot. Brush lightly with olive oil. Place about 4 pieces of the foie gras in the skillet and sear the foie gras, about 10 seconds per side (the pâté will begin to melt if heated too long). Immediately transfer the foie gras to the crostini and top each with 2 plum slices. Repeat with the remaining foie gras. Garnish each crostini with a sprinkle of fresh thyme.

## SAUTÉED CHICKEN LIVER CROSTINI

**MAKES 2 DOZEN** | photograph on page 109

*Pancetta, an Italian bacon that has been cured with salt and spices, has an earthy flavor that perfectly complements chicken liver and sage. If unavailable, regular bacon may be used.*

1 teaspoon olive oil
1 medium shallot, minced to yield 2 tablespoons
10 ounces pancetta, cut into ¼-inch dice
1 bay leaf
12 ounces chicken livers, cleaned and deveined
2 tablespoons Marsala wine
Kosher salt and freshly ground black pepper
¼ cup peanut oil, for frying
24 sage leaves, from 1 bunch
24 Simple Crostini (page 243)

**1** Heat the olive oil in a medium skillet over medium heat. Add the shallot and pancetta and cook until the pancetta is crisp, 6 to 8 minutes. Remove 3 tablespoons of the pancetta pieces and set aside.

**2** Increase the heat to high. Add the bay leaf and the livers to the remaining shallots and pancetta in the pan. Cook until the livers are brown on the outside and barely pink in the center, about 2 minutes. Add the Marsala to the pan and cook, scraping the bottom of the pan with a spoon, until the liquid has evaporated, about 30 seconds. Add salt and pepper to taste. Transfer immediately to a dish to cool slightly.

**3** Heat the peanut oil in a small saucepan over medium heat. Add the sage leaves, in batches, and fry until the leaves are firm and the bubbles die down, 10 to 15 seconds. Transfer to paper towels to drain. (Any large leaves may be crumbled to fit on top of the crostini.)

**4** Remove the livers from the pancetta mixture. Roughly chop the livers until they begin to hold together. Season with salt and pepper to taste. Combine all the livers back into the pancetta mixture. Place about 1 tablespoon of the pancetta-liver mixture on each crostini. Garnish with the reserved pancetta and a fried sage leaf.

## MOREL AND ROASTED GARLIC POTATO CROSTINI

**MAKES 2 DOZEN** | photograph on page 109

*Morels come from the same family as the truffle and have a distinctively smoky, nutty flavor. They are generally available fresh in the months of April through July (see Sources, page 487), but if you can't get fresh ones, substitute dried or use another variety of mushrooms.*

24 medium fresh morels, trimmed and wiped
    clean, or 1½ ounces dried
1 head of garlic
2 medium Idaho potatoes (12 ounces)
¼ cup plus 1 tablespoon heavy cream, at room
    temperature
Kosher salt and freshly ground black pepper
1 tablespoon unsalted butter
2 tablespoons fresh rosemary
24 Simple Crostini (page 243)

**1** If using dried morels, place them in a medium bowl. Heat 3 cups of water almost to a boil and pour it over the morels. Let sit until the morels have softened, 10 to 15 minutes. Drain and discard the liquid. Reserve the morels.

**2** Heat the oven to 425°F. Slice the top quarter off the head of garlic and discard. Wrap the garlic and the potatoes together in a foil pouch. Cook until the garlic cloves are soft, 35 to 45 minutes. Remove the garlic and keep cooking the potatoes until fork-tender, about 10 minutes more. Squeeze

the garlic out of each clove and into a small bowl. Smash with a fork until smooth and set aside to cool. Reduce the oven temperature to 275°F.

**3** Peel the potatoes and place them in a medium bowl. Using a fork, mash the potatoes with 2 tablespoons of the roasted garlic. Thin the mixture slightly with the heavy cream until the consistency is spreadable. Add salt and pepper to taste. Set aside.

**4** Heat the butter in a medium skillet over high heat. Add the morels and cook until browned and softened slightly, 3 to 6 minutes. Add the rosemary and salt and pepper. Remove from the heat.

**5** Spread about 1 tablespoon of potato mixture on each crostini. Place on a baking sheet and heat until the potato is warm throughout. Top each with a warm morel. Serve right away.

## TOASTED GOAT CHEESE AND SHREDDED BEET CROSTINI

**MAKES 2 DOZEN** | photograph on page 108

*Beets are wonderful when grated and served raw, but they do tend to dry out. Serve this crostini as soon as you assemble it.*

12 ounces fresh goat cheese
24 Simple Crostini (page 243), untoasted
1 small beet, finely grated on a box grater to
    yield ⅓ cup

Heat the oven to broil with a rack in the upper third. Working with one crostini at a time, slice a ¼-inch disk from the goat cheese and place it on the crostini. Using your finger, rub a little olive oil on top of the goat cheese. Arrange the crostini on a baking sheet and place them under the hot broiler. Rotate the pan after 2 minutes and continue to broil until the cheese begins to soften and the edges turn golden, 3 to 5 minutes total. Garnish each crostini with the grated beet.

## STEAK AU POIVRE CROSTINI

**MAKES 2 DOZEN** | photograph on page 106

*Green peppercorns, which are the soft, underripe berry of the pepper plant, are usually preserved in brine. They are not as sharp as mature, dried black peppercorns, but have a wonderfully refreshing pungency all their own.*

12 very thin slices of white sandwich bread,
    crusts removed
3 tablespoons unsalted butter, at room
    temperature
2½ tablespoons olive oil
1 pound center-cut beef tenderloin, trimmed
Kosher salt and freshly ground black pepper
¼ cup Cognac or brandy
1½ cups homemade beef stock or canned
    beef broth, skimmed of fat
2 tablespoons heavy cream
¼ cup green peppercorns in brine, drained

**1** Heat the oven to 425°F. Cut each bread slice into 2 rectangular pieces. Brush each side with butter and place on a baking sheet. Bake until golden and toasted on both sides, 3 to 4 minutes per side. Transfer to a rack to cool.

**2** Heat 2 tablespoons of the olive oil in a medium ovenproof skillet over high heat. Rub the tenderloin with the remaining ½ tablespoon of olive oil and season generously with salt and pepper. Add the beef to the pan and sear on all sides until brown, about 2 minutes per side. Place in the oven and roast until medium rare, 7 to 10 minutes. Transfer the beef to a baking sheet to rest. Cover with foil.

**3** Meanwhile, reheat the skillet over high heat for 30 seconds. Remove the skillet from the flame, add the Cognac, return to the heat, and ignite. Stand back and as the flames die, stir with a wooden spoon to loosen any particles in the bottom of the pan. After the Cognac has reduced to 1 tablespoon,

add the beef stock, simmering until reduced to ½ cup, 12 to 15 minutes. Stir in the cream and the peppercorns. Set aside.

**4** Using a very sharp knife, slice the tenderloin as thin as possible into 24 pieces. Place 1 slice, about ½ ounce, on each crostini. Top each with the warm sauce and peppercorns. Serve.

## CAPRESE CROSTINI

**MAKES 2 DOZEN** | photograph on page 108

*Tomatoes, mozzarella, and basil are the ingredients in the classic Italian insalata caprese. Small cherry tomatoes are just the right size for these crostini. Select red or yellow pear-shaped tomatoes if they are available.*

24 cherry tomatoes (about 9 ounces), sliced in
    half lengthwise
Kosher salt and freshly ground black pepper
8 ounces fresh salted mozzarella cheese, cut into
    ¼-inch pieces
24 Simple Crostini (page 243)
¼ cup fresh basil leaves, cut into chiffonade
    (from ½ of a bunch)

**1** In a medium bowl, toss together the tomatoes and salt and pepper to taste. Set aside to marinate at room temperature for 10 to 15 minutes.

**2** Scatter the tomato halves and mozzarella pieces onto each crostini. Garnish each with fresh basil and sprinkle with salt and pepper. Serve.

Compound butters (pages 391–394) are very versatile. For an added layer of flavor, spread them on Simple Crostini (page 243) before adding the crostini toppings. Here are some flavor combinations that I particularly like.

**WATERCRESS BUTTER**

Toasted Goat Cheese and Shredded Beet

Caprese

Morel and Roasted Garlic Potato

Steak au Poivre

**ORANGE-TARRAGON BUTTER**

Pâté de Foie Gras and with Caramelized Plum

Toasted Goat Cheese and Shredded Beet

Sautéed Chicken Liver

**SUN-DRIED TOMATO AND ROSEMARY BUTTER**

Caprese

Steak au Poivre

**ANCHOVY BUTTER**

Caprese

Sautéed Chicken Liver

Morel and Roasted Garlic Potato

Steak au Poivre

**LEMON-CHIVE BUTTER**

Toasted Goat Cheese and Shredded Beet

Sautéed Chicken Liver

Morel and Roasted Garlic Potato

Steak au Poivre

Fava Bean and Pecorino

# FAVA BEAN AND PECORINO CROSTINI

**MAKES 2 DOZEN** | photograph on page 107

*Fresh fava beans in their pods are available sporadically throughout the spring and early summer months. The same beans are available frozen year-round in Middle Eastern markets. If you are unable to find either fresh or frozen favas, substitute one 10-ounce package (1¾ cups) of frozen large lima beans. The fava paste may be made a day in advance and kept in an airtight container in the refrigerator. Refrigerate the whole favas in a separate small container. Buy the Pecorino in an 8-ounce chunk to make shaving it easier.*

2 pounds fresh fava beans, removed from pods (about 1¾ cups)

1 tablespoon extra-virgin olive oil

1 tablespoon chopped fresh mint

2 teaspoons fresh lemon juice

Kosher salt and freshly ground black pepper

24 Simple Crostini (page 243)

Pecorino cheese, for garnish

**1** Bring a medium pot of water to a boil and add the fava beans. Boil for 5 minutes, then drain, and rinse under cold water. Using your fingers, peel the outer skin off the beans and discard. Separate 3 tablespoons of fava beans and set them aside.

**2** Place the remaining favas, olive oil, mint, lemon juice, and salt and pepper to taste in the bowl of a food processor and quickly pulse to create a thick, chunky paste. Transfer the fava mixture to a small bowl and taste for seasoning.

**3** Spread 1 teaspoon of fava paste onto each crostini. Garnish each crostini with the remaining whole favas. Using a vegetable peeler, thinly shave the Pecorino cheese over each crostini. Sprinkle with freshly ground black pepper and serve.

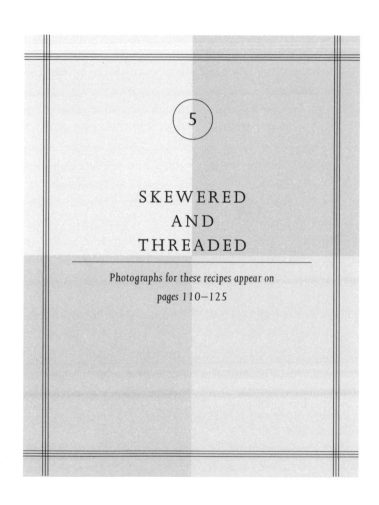

$5$

# SKEWERED
# AND
# THREADED

Photographs for these recipes appear on
pages 110–125

SKEWERED AND THREADED HORS D'OEUVRES ARE IDEAL FINGER FOOD FOR ONE SIMPLE REASON: EACH SERVING COMES EQUIPPED WITH A HANDLE. I USE THE SKEWERING TECHNIQUE FOR FOODS THAT MIGHT OTHERWISE BE TOO MESSY TO EAT WITH YOUR FINGERS.

As for the skewers themselves, my primary rule is not to limit them to toothpicks. Although they are perfectly fine to use, look for alternatives onto which you can thread ingredients. Woody-stemmed herbs are ideal, for example, because they not only provide an unusual skewer, they also perfume the food that is cooked on them. This is true of my Grilled Shiitake Mushrooms on Rosemary Skewers, for instance, where the needles on the portion of the rosemary stems that emerge from the mushrooms are the garnish. In the same vein, I use sliced stalks of sweet sugarcane to skewer chicken and tropical fruit squares.

There are also many types of toothpicks from which to choose. My Moroccan Salmon Skewers, for example, are pierced with Asian toothpicks with tiny bamboo handles. I thread Grilled Beef Rolls on long, rather thick toothpicks with small turned handles, while Roasted Root Vegetable Skewers are slipped onto square-sided wooden toothpicks, and long round wooden picks hold together Shrimp Gumbo Skewers. Unique skewers and toothpicks can be found in Asian and specialty food shops and are also available by mail (see Sources, page 486). One note of caution: Always be sure that, before threading food onto them for grilling, you soak wooden skewers in cool water for at least 30 minutes. This prevents them from burning while the food is cooking.

In addition to varying the material used as the skewer, I also like to vary the size of the portion.

Sometimes I fashion large skewers for guests to pull individual servings from, as with the Skewered Bocconcini Sandwiches. Other times, a skewer should provide just enough for an individual sampling, such as a single large prosciutto-wrapped shrimp on a wooden skewer or a meatball served Asian-style. This even works well with foods that people are used to eating in large portions, such as salmon, which I have cut into bite-size squares and encrusted with fennel seeds.

One of my very favorite recipes in this collection is a skewer I call Figs in a Blanket. Taking inspiration from Pigs in a Blanket (cocktail franks in a dough crust), I poach figs in a thyme-scented red wine, wrap them in thin slices of pork tenderloin, thread them onto a skewer, broil them, then bathe them in a warm balsamic glaze. The familiar form and slightly unusual but delicious combination of ingredients work perfectly with each other. This is exactly the kind of innovation that skewers inspire, and one of the reasons they make such delightful hors d'oeuvres.

In the recipes in this chapter, I have skewered just about everything—from root vegetables, mushrooms, and fruit to beef, chicken, and shrimp—taking inspiration from sources as far-ranging as Japanese negamaki, New Orleans seafood gumbo, and the Greek stuffed grape leaves known as dolmades. I encourage you to experiment with new ideas, too, by merely looking at your favorite recipes in a slightly different way.

## SKEWERED BOCCONCINI
## SANDWICHES

**MAKES 2 DOZEN** | photograph on page 121

*Ficelle are very thin, almost stringlike, baguettes. Thin slices are perfect for sandwiching bocconcini, literally translated from Italian as "mouthful," a term that refers not to their small size but to their deeply satisfying flavor. The bay leaves are not meant to be eaten, so simply put them aside as you pull the hors d'oeuvres from the skewers. Before assembling, soak six 8-inch wooden skewers in cool water for 30 minutes.*

30 bay leaves, preferably fresh

1 ficelle, cut into 48 ¼-inch-thick slices

12 balls fresh bocconcini cheese, at room
    temperature, halved

3 tablespoons extra-virgin olive oil

Kosher salt and freshly ground black pepper

6 tablespoons unsalted butter

6 flat anchovy fillets, minced

3 tablespoons capers, drained

1 tablespoon fresh lemon juice

1 tablespoon grated lemon zest

2 tablespoons chopped fresh flat-leaf parsley

**1** Heat the oven to 325°F. and line a baking sheet with parchment paper. Skewer 1 bay leaf, 1 slice of bread, 1 piece of cheese, and another bread slice. Continue skewering until 4 "sandwiches" are formed on each skewer, beginning and ending with a bay leaf. Place the skewers on the baking sheet. Brush each skewer with olive oil and season with salt and pepper. Bake, turning the skewers halfway through, for 7 minutes, or until the cheese is warmed through but not melted.

**2** Meanwhile, in a small saucepan, melt the butter over medium heat. Add the anchovies and stir until well combined. Add the capers, lemon juice, zest, and parsley. Spoon the warm mixture over the warm skewers. Remove the skewers and serve with lots of napkins to catch the drips.

## GRILLED SHIITAKE
## MUSHROOMS ON
## ROSEMARY SKEWERS

**MAKES 2 DOZEN** | photograph on page 113

*Shiitake mushrooms that are 2 to 2 ½ inches in diameter will hold up best on skewers. Be sure that the rosemary stems are sturdy enough to hold the mushrooms, and leave the needles attached to the portion of the stem that emerges from the top of the mushroom.*

¼ cup balsamic vinegar

½ cup extra-virgin olive oil

2 tablespoons chopped fresh rosemary, plus 12
    10-inch stems for skewering

½ teaspoon kosher salt

¼ teaspoon freshly ground black pepper

48 2- to 2½-inch-diameter shiitake mushrooms
    (about 1¾ pounds), wiped cleaned and
    stems removed

**1** Place the vinegar in a small bowl; whisk in the oil. Add the rosemary, salt, and pepper. In a shallow nonreactive dish, arrange the mushrooms, stem-side down, in an even layer. Brush each mushroom cap with the marinade and set aside. Cover the dish with plastic wrap and let sit at room temperature for 15 to 20 minutes.

**2** Trim the rosemary stems to about 5 inches in length. Thread the rosemary, stem-end first, cross-wise through 2 of the mushrooms, removing rosemary needles if needed to skewer. Heat a grill pan over medium-high heat until warm. Cook the skewered mushrooms, stem-side up, on the grill for about 6 minutes, until subtle grill marks appear. Serve warm with the remaining vinaigrette on the side, if desired.

## ROASTED ROOT VEGETABLE SKEWERS

**MAKES 7 DOZEN** | photograph on page 112

*For even roasting, the vegetables should be as uniform in size as possible and blanched first. Blanching also reduces the roasting time; if the tiny vegetables are exposed to heat for too long, they will shrivel and become unattractive. You will need 7 dozen toothpicks for these skewers and, to avoid burning them, you should soak them in cool water for 15 minutes before threading the vegetables onto them.*

1 medium turnip, cut into ½-inch cubes
2 medium parsnips, cut into ½-inch cubes
1 large taro root, cut into ½-inch cubes
    (optional)
1 medium Idaho potato, cut into ½-inch cubes
1 medium sweet potato, cut into ½-inch cubes
2 medium carrots, cut into ½-inch cubes
1 medium beet, cut into ½-inch cubes
2 tablespoons extra-virgin olive oil
Kosher salt and freshly ground black pepper
2 tablespoons fresh rosemary, roughly chopped
Bagna Cauda (page 390)

**1** Preheat the oven to 425°F. Bring a large pot of water to a boil. Add the turnips and blanch for 30 seconds. Use a slotted spoon to remove the turnips and transfer to a bowl of ice water to cool. Drain thoroughly and set aside. Using the same boiling water, repeat this procedure with the parsnips, taro, potato, sweet potato, and carrots, blanching the vegetables in the order above. Lastly, blanch the beets for 3 minutes in the boiling water, then transfer to a bowl of ice water to cool. Drain thoroughly and set aside, keeping the beets separate.

**2** Place all of the vegetables except the beets in a medium bowl and toss with all but ½ teaspoon of the olive oil. And salt and pepper to taste. In a separate bowl, toss the beets with the remaining oil and salt and pepper. Skewer 4 different vegetables

onto a 2½-inch toothpick. Continue, alternating the vegetables used, until none remain. Place the skewers on two 12 × 17-inch baking sheets and sprinkle with the rosemary. Roast, turning the skewers over after 15 minutes and rotating the pans in the oven for even browning, until the vegetables are golden and begin to shrink, 15 to 25 minutes. Serve warm with the Bagna Cauda.

## TROPICAL CHICKEN ON SUGARCANE SKEWERS WITH PEANUT-PLANTAIN DIPPING SAUCE

**MAKES 3 DOZEN** | photograph on page 117

*You may use canned or fresh sugarcane in this recipe (see Sources, page 487). If using fresh sugarcane, use a paring knife to peel and carefully slice the stalks lengthwise into skewers 4 to 6 inches long. For canned sugarcane, cut each cylinder lengthwise into 6 to 8 pieces. Whichever you use, you will need 36 skewers. Any wooden or bamboo skewers may also be substituted.*

½ cup dark rum
½ teaspoon ground allspice
1 cup prepared pineapple juice
1 cup fresh orange juice (3 to 4 oranges)
2 scotch bonnet or other small hot fresh chili
    peppers, seeds and ribs removed, minced
2 tablespoons packed dark brown sugar
1 tablespoon fresh lemon juice
½ cup peanut oil
1½ pounds skinless, boneless chicken breasts,
    cut into 1¼-inch pieces
1 unripe papaya, cut into 1¼-inch pieces
1 unripe mango, cut into 1¼-inch pieces
1 unripe pineapple, cut into 1¼-inch pieces
2 firm avocados, cut into 1¼-inch pieces
1 very ripe plantain, sliced

**1** In a medium saucepan, combine the rum, all-spice, pineapple juice, orange juice, peppers, brown sugar, lemon juice, and peanut oil. Bring to a boil, reduce the heat to low, and simmer until the mixture has reduced to 1¼ cups, 25 to 35 minutes. Remove from the heat and cool. (The marinade may be kept, tightly covered, in the refrigerator for 1 day.) Place half of this marinade in the bowl of a food processor. Divide the remaining marinade between 2 nonreactive baking dishes. Set aside.

**2** Arrange 1 piece of chicken on a skewer with 2 pieces of the fruit, with the exception of the plantain. Alternate the papaya, mango, pineapple, and avocado with the chicken on the skewers, until all the ingredients are used. Transfer the skewers to the 2 dishes with the marinade, turning to coat. Cover with plastic wrap and refrigerate for 30 minutes.

**3** Heat a grill pan on the stove over medium heat, or prepare an outdoor grill. Meanwhile, add the plantain to the marinade in the food processor. Process until smooth. Transfer to a serving bowl and set aside.

**4** Remove the skewers from the marinade and place on the heated grill, in batches if necessary. Baste with the remaining marinade. Cook until the chicken is cooked through, 5 to 7 minutes per side. Serve on a platter with the reserved sauce.

## MOROCCAN SALMON SKEWERS
**MAKES 2½ DOZEN** | photograph on page 114

*Grinding whole seeds is a bit of a chore, but fresh-ground spices are much more flavorful than the preground version. The spice mixture may be stored in an airtight container at room temperature for up to 3 days. You will need 2½ dozen toothpicks.*

1½ teaspoons whole cumin seeds
1 teaspoon whole coriander seeds
2 teaspoons whole fennel seeds
1 teaspoon kosher salt
⅛ teaspoon freshly ground black pepper
1¾ pounds salmon fillet, skin removed, cut into
      ¾-inch-square pieces
Citrus Dipping Sauce (page 395)

**1** Preheat the oven to 400°F. In a mortar and pestle combine the cumin, coriander, and fennel seeds. Grind until the coriander seed is just broken. Alternatively, whole seeds may be placed in a spice grinder and pulsed just until coriander is broken; do not overprocess. The spices may also be crushed using a heavy cast-iron skillet. Transfer the seeds to a small bowl and toss with the salt and pepper.

**2** Dip 1 side of the salmon into the spice mixture to coat heavily. Repeat with all of the salmon squares.

**3** Heat a large ovenproof skillet over medium heat. Do not add any oil. Place the salmon squares, spice-side down, into the pan. Cook until the spices are dry, golden, and toasted, about 4 minutes. Immediately transfer the pan to the oven to cook until the salmon is just cooked through, about 30 seconds. Transfer the salmon bites to a serving platter and skewer with toothpicks. Serve warm with the dipping sauce.

Whether simply piled on crushed ice and served with a spicy cocktail sauce, halved and tucked into a tea sandwich, or wrapped in prosciutto and skewered, shrimp is among the most popular hors d'oeuvres. By following a few simple purchasing and preparation guidelines, you can be assured you are serving the freshest, most perfectly cooked shrimp to your guests.

**BUYING** Along the Gulf Coast and in other shrimp fishing regions, it's sometimes possible to buy fresh-caught shrimp; however, most shrimp that is sold in retail markets has been frozen at sea directly after it is caught. This is known as flash-frozen shrimp. Due to modern freezing technology, the difference in taste between fresh and frozen shrimp is virtually indiscernible. I always buy shrimp frozen, since thawed shrimp keeps just 1 day. Frozen shrimp is sold in 1-pound bags or in bulk (4.4-pound blocks and 5-pound blocks). If you buy in bulk, thaw the amount of shrimp you plan to use from the block by running a section under cold water. Place the remaining block of shrimp back in the freezer, tightly double-wrapped in plastic wrap and labeled with the date. The shrimp can be frozen 3 to 4 months.

When buying shrimp, look for those that feel firm and have a pleasant smell. Avoid shrimp with black spots, a gritty texture, or yellowed shells and those that smell of ammonia. I prefer buying shrimp in the shell with the heads removed. While it is less work to purchase those that have already been peeled and deveined, shrimp cooked in their shells retains more flavor, color, and texture than the shelled version.

**COOKING** Always cook shrimp in generously salted, boiling water. Well-salted water brings out the natural flavor of the shrimp. Use kosher salt, which is additive free, for pure salt flavor. Depending on the size of the shrimp, cooking time can take anywhere from 1½ to 4 minutes. The best way to determine whether shrimp is cooked is to watch as it cooks; the shrimp should be pink and opaque in the center. To check for doneness, remove a shrimp from the cooking water and slice it open at the thickest part. The flesh should be moist and white, slightly tinged with pink; if it's gray and translucent, it is undercooked. If the flesh is tough to cut through, the shrimp has been overcooked. Once cooked, quickly pass the shrimp through cold running water to prevent the shrimp flesh from becoming tough and flavorless.

**PEELING AND DEVEINING** Once it is cool enough to handle, hold the shrimp with the legs facing up. Using your thumb and forefinger, peel the shell away from the head of the shrimp on the inside curve in 2 or 3 sections. Although it isn't necessary, I remove the black vein that runs the length of the shrimp. To expose the vein, use a sharp paring knife to make a shallow cut along the outside curve of the shrimp from the head to the tail. This will expose the vein, which can then be pulled out with the tip of a knife or with your fingers. Quickly rinse the shrimp under cold water and pat dry. Cooked shrimp can be stored in an airtight container for up to 2 days in the refrigerator. It is best not to freeze cooked shrimp; they will lose flavor and their texture becomes mushy when thawed.

## PROSCIUTTO-WRAPPED SHRIMP

**MAKES 2 DOZEN** | photograph on page 116

*Wrapping intensely flavored prosciutto around the body of the shrimp seals in the subtle taste of anise-flavored sambuca and the shrimp's natural juices. As the wrapped shrimp cooks, the prosciutto shrinks tightly around it, giving the finished hors d'oeuvre a much more interesting appearance. It is important to use large shrimp here, since only one goes on each skewer. Before assembling, soak twenty-four 6- to 8-inch skewers in water for at least 30 minutes.*

24 large shrimp (about 1½ pounds), tails on,
    peeled and deveined (see Note, left)
½ cup sambuca liqueur
¼ cup extra-virgin olive oil
¼ cup fresh rosemary
Kosher salt and freshly ground black pepper
8 paper-thin slices prosciutto, about 3½ ounces

**1** Arrange the shrimp in an even layer in a large nonreactive dish. Pour the sambuca, olive oil, 2 tablespoons of the rosemary, and salt and pepper to taste, over the shrimp. Use your fingers to toss the shrimp in the marinade and coat well. Cover with plastic wrap and let marinate for 15 minutes in the refrigerator, turning the shrimp halfway through.

**2** Gently sprinkle the shrimp with the remaining rosemary. Cut each prosciutto slice lengthwise into thirds. Wrap 1 slice of prosciutto snugly around the center of each shrimp. Thread 1 wrapped shrimp onto each skewer through the head and tail.

**3** Heat a grill pan or a heavy skillet over medium-high heat, or prepare an outdoor grill. Cook the shrimp, in batches, until the prosciutto is crispy and the shrimp is opaque and cooked through, about 1½ minutes per side. Serve warm.

## SHRIMP GUMBO SKEWERS

**MAKES 2 DOZEN** | photograph on page 124

*To serve these colorful skewers, cook 2 cups of long-grain white rice according to the package instructions, then spread the cooked rice on a 16-inch platter and set the skewers on top. Before assembling, soak twenty-four 8- to 10-inch wooden skewers in water for at least 30 minutes.*

24 medium shrimp (about 12 ounces), tails on,
    peeled and deveined
12 baby yellow squash, cut in half crosswise
24 red cherry tomatoes
12 baby okra, cut in half crosswise
8 baby zucchini, cut in thirds crosswise
¼ cup extra-virgin olive oil
Kosher salt and freshly ground black pepper
Creole Dipping Sauce (page 388)

**1** Thread 1 shrimp and 1 piece each of squash, tomato, okra, and zucchini onto each skewer. Brush each skewer lightly with the olive oil, and add salt and pepper to taste.

**2** Heat a large grill pan over medium-high heat, or prepare an outdoor grill. Place the skewers on the grill. Cook until the shrimp are opaque and cooked through, about 4 minutes per side. Place the skewers on the rice and serve with the warm dipping sauce.

## GRILLED BEEF ROLLS WITH SCALLION SOY DIPPING SAUCE

**MAKES 2½ DOZEN** | photograph on page 111

*Similar to Japanese negamaki, these beef rolls include crisp, colorful bell peppers. For an attractive presentation, a bit of the peppers and scallion should peek out from inside the beef.*

1 cup low-sodium soy sauce

½ cup packed light brown sugar

2 pounds beef tenderloin, well trimmed

Kosher salt and freshly ground black pepper

4 scallions, green tops cut into 3-inch lengths
 and sliced lengthwise; whites cut into
 ⅛-inch rings

3 bell peppers (one each of green, red, and
 yellow), trimmed, seeded, and cut into
 long, thin matchsticks

1 teaspoon olive oil

**1** In a small bowl, whisk together the soy sauce and the brown sugar until dissolved; set aside. Cut the tenderloin crosswise into ¼-inch-thick slices. Trim off any fat or connective tissue. Place 1 slice between 2 pieces of plastic wrap. Using the flat side of a meat pounder, evenly pound out the slice, keeping it roughly in a rectangular shape, until it is ⅛ inch thick. Do not overpound the slices or they will begin to disintegrate. Remove the plastic wrap and transfer the thin slice to a large plate. Continue until all the beef is pounded.

**2** Dip 1 slice of beef in the soy sauce mixture and place it on a clean surface. Sprinkle with salt and pepper. Place 2 pieces of scallion green and 1 piece of each pepper across the shorter length of the beef, so that the vegetables extend over both edges by about ¾ inch. Roll up lengthwise, and skewer near the edges with 2 toothpicks. Set aside. Repeat with the remaining beef and vegetables.

**3** Lightly brush a grill pan with olive oil and heat until hot, or heat the oven broiler. Grill or broil the

beef rolls, brushing with the sauce and turning, until medium rare, 2 to 4 minutes. Cut each roll in half, or cut any rolls that are a little longer into 3 pieces. In a small saucepan bring the remaining sauce to a boil for 3 to 5 minutes. Pour into a small bowl, add the scallion rings, and serve on the side.

## BEEF BULGOGI IN LETTUCE LEAVES WITH SOY-GINGER DIPPING SAUCE

**MAKES 2 DOZEN** | photograph on page 123

*Bulgogi, a classic Korean beef dish, is served here in a manner inspired by the spring rolls of Vietnam. The best way to eat these is to pick up the lettuce leaf, dip the skewered meat into the sauce, then wrap the leaf around the whole thing and slide it off the skewer. Before assembling, soak twenty-four 8- or 10-inch skewers for at least 30 minutes.*

1 cup low-sodium soy sauce

3 large garlic cloves, minced

1 tablespoon grated fresh ginger

1 tablespoon sugar

¼ teaspoon freshly ground black pepper

3 tablespoons sesame seeds, toasted (see
 page 386) and crushed

1 tablespoon sesame oil

¼ cup sake, plum wine, or white wine

6 scallions, white and light green parts only

1¼ pounds filet mignon (piece should be at least
 5 inches long)

24 Bibb lettuce leaves (about 3 heads)

1 small seedless cucumber, peel on, cut into thin
 matchsticks

1 carrot, cut into thin matchsticks

**1** In a large nonreactive bowl, combine the soy sauce, garlic, ginger, sugar, pepper, sesame seeds, sesame oil, and sake. Finely chop 3 of the scallions and add them to the marinade. Set aside.

**2** Slice the filet into ¼-inch-thick pieces, cutting lengthwise with the grain. Trim the pieces to approximately 5-inch lengths. Cut each 5-inch piece lengthwise into 1- to 1½-inch pieces, depending on the exact width of the meat. You should have 24 pieces. Transfer the meat strips to the marinade and cover with plastic wrap. Allow to marinate at room temperature for 1 hour.

**3** Heat the oven to 275°F. Heat a large grill pan over high heat, or prepare an outdoor grill. While the pan is heating, thread a piece of meat onto each skewer, piercing the meat about 6 times so that it stretches along the length of the skewer. Place the meat on the grill and cook until medium-rare, about 1 minute per side. Transfer the meat to a baking sheet and place in the oven to keep warm, for no longer than 30 minutes.

**4** Arrange the lettuce leaves on a serving platter and cut 2 of the remaining scallions into matchsticks. Fill each leaf with the cucumber, scallion, and carrot matchsticks. Cover the leaves, and keep cool until ready to use.

**5** Bring the remaining marinade to a boil in a small saucepan. Boil the sauce for 1 minute, then transfer it to a serving dish. Thinly slice the remaining scallion crosswise and add it to the sauce.

**6** Place the bulgogi skewers in the lettuce and serve warm or at room temperature with the sauce.

## LAMB AND COUSCOUS DOLMADES WITH MINTED YOGURT SAUCE

**MAKES 2½ TO 3 DOZEN** | photograph on page 119

*Dolmades, the classic Greek grape leaf roll with a rice filling, also works well with a tangy filling of pine nuts, couscous, and feta cheese. As you prepare the dolmades, soak 36 bamboo picks (see Sources, page 486) or wooden skewers (4 to 6 inches) in cool water to soak.*

¼ cup pine nuts

½ cup homemade beef stock or canned beef broth, skimmed of fat

1 tablespoon unsalted butter

⅓ cup couscous

1 lemon, zested and juiced

1 small tomato, cut into ¼-inch dice

2 tablespoons chopped fresh mint

2 ounces feta cheese, crumbled

1 small seedless cucumber, peel on, cut into ¼-inch dice

Kosher salt and freshly ground black pepper

14 ounces boneless loin of lamb, trimmed of fat

15 imported grape leaves packed in vinegar brine (see page 231)

½ teaspoon ground cumin

3 tablespoons olive oil, plus extra for grilling

½ cup plain yogurt

**1** Heat the oven to 375°F. Place the pine nuts on a baking sheet and toast until golden, 3 to 5 minutes. Set aside and leave the oven on.

**2** Bring the beef stock to a simmer in a small saucepan. Add the butter and stir in the couscous. Cover the pot and remove from the heat. Let sit for 5 to 10 minutes. Fluff the couscous with a fork and transfer to a medium bowl. Stir in the reserved pine nuts, lemon zest, lemon juice, tomatoes, 1 tablespoon of the mint, the feta cheese, and all but 3 tablespoons of the cucumber. Add salt and pepper to taste. Cover and set aside to cool.

**3** Slice the lamb into fifteen ½-inch-thick pieces. Place the lamb between 2 sheets of plastic wrap and pound gently, using the flat side of a meat pounder, until the lamb has become twice as thin and has almost doubled in size when flat. Repeat with the remaining lamb slices and set aside while you fill the grape leaves.

CONTINUED ON FOLLOWING PAGE

**4** Remove any thick center ribs from the grape leaves. Lay the leaves flat on a work surface. Place 1½ tablespoons of the couscous filling onto the bottom part of the grape leaf and roll, tucking in the edges, until the grape leaf forms a firm, cylindrical shape. Repeat with the remaining couscous and grape leaves. The dolmades can be made up to this point and kept, tightly covered, in the refrigerator for up to 1 day.

**5** In a small bowl combine the cumin, olive oil, and salt and pepper to taste. Brush both sides of 1 lamb slice with the flavored oil. Place the rolled grape leaf at the bottom edge of a piece of lamb and roll together. Skewer the roll with two picks, one at either end and one in the middle. Repeat with the remaining ingredients.

**6** Heat a grill pan over high heat and brush with olive oil, or prepare a grill. Place the dolmades on the grill and cook, turning once, until browned and grill marks are visible, about 2 minutes per side. Transfer to a baking sheet and finish cooking in the oven until cooked through, 5 to 8 minutes.

**7** Meanwhile, in a small bowl, mix the yogurt with the remaining mint and cucumber. To serve, cut each dolmade in half, or cut any larger rolls into thirds and skewer the third roll. Serve with the sauce on the side.


## ASIAN MEATBALLS ON SNOW PEA PICKS

**MAKES 4 DOZEN** | photograph on page 125

*Meatballs are an important part of classic Chinese cooking. They come in all varieties and in all sizes, from the huge Lion's Head meatball that serves a large group to small pork meatballs that may be served either crispy-fried or stewed. This Chinese tradition inspired these skewered meatballs, which are lighter in texture and spicier in flavor than the classic version. The meatballs may be formed 1 day ahead and kept in the refrigerator uncooked and covered with plastic*

*wrap. The skewered snow peas may be prepared 6 to 8 hours ahead and kept in an airtight container in the refrigerator. After cooking, keep the meatballs warm in the oven and the snowpeas cold in the refrigerator until just ready to serve; the contrast in temperatures is part of the effect of the dish.*

1 pound ground pork
6 ounces sweet Italian sausage, removed from casing
2 teaspoons freshly grated ginger
1 small shallot, minced
¼ cup finely chopped water chestnuts
4 teaspoons low-sodium soy sauce
1 tablespoon roughly chopped fresh cilantro
Kosher salt
5 ounces snow peas (at least 48)
1 teaspoon cornstarch
1 garlic clove, minced
½ cup homemade chicken stock or low-sodium canned broth, skimmed of fat
2 teaspoons packed dark brown sugar
½ teaspoon chili paste

**1** Preheat the oven to 400° F. In a medium bowl, use a fork to combine the pork, sausage, 1 teaspoon of the ginger, shallot, water chestnuts, 2 teaspoons of the soy sauce, and the cilantro. Use your hands to form the mixture into 1-inch balls, placing the meatballs in a large roasting pan.

**2** Cook the meatballs in the roasting pan for 20 to 25 minutes, shaking the pan every 5 minutes to rotate the meatballs and brown the sides evenly.

**3** Meanwhile, bring a large saucepan of salted water to a boil. Add the snow peas to the water and cook just until bright green, about 30 seconds. Drain the snow peas and immediately transfer them to an ice bath to prevent further cooking. Drain and set aside.

**4** Remove the roasting pan from the oven and transfer the meatballs to a medium bowl. Set aside. In a small bowl, whisk the cornstarch with 1 tablespoon of water. Set aside. Place the roasting pan, and any collected fat, over medium heat. Add the garlic and remaining ginger to the pan. Cook, stirring with a wooden spoon, for 30 seconds. Add the chicken stock to the pan, stirring up any cooked-on bits that have collected on the bottom of the pan. Stir in the remaining soy sauce, the brown sugar, and the chili paste. Bring the mixture to a boil, whisk in the cornstarch mixture, and simmer until thickened, about 1 minute. Pour the warm sauce over the meatballs. (The meatballs may be held in the sauce in the roasting pan, covered with foil, over very low heat for 1 hour.)

**5** Skewer each snow pea with a toothpick. Serve the skewers alongside the warm meatballs.

## FIGS IN A BLANKET

**MAKES 3 DOZEN** | photograph on page 122

*A play on words and looks with the classic "pigs in a blanket," this version exquisitely combines the flavors of salty and sweet. You may use whole dried apricots as a substitute for the dried figs in this recipe. You will need 6 ounces, about 25 apricots. Poach the apricots until just softened, about 5 minutes, then cut each one in half to use in the pork rolls. You will need 3 dozen toothpicks for these skewers.*

8 ounces dried Calimyrna figs (about 10 figs)
2 cups dry red wine
1 sprig fresh thyme, plus more for garnish
3 whole black peppercorns
⅓ cup honey
½ cup plus 2 tablespoons balsamic vinegar
2 tablespoons packed dark brown sugar
1 2-inch cinnamon stick
Kosher salt
1 12-ounce pork tenderloin, trimmed of excess
    fat and silverskin
Freshly ground black pepper

**1** In a medium saucepan, combine the figs, wine, thyme, peppercorns, and honey. Bring to a boil, reduce the heat to low, and simmer gently until softened, 8 to 10 minutes. Transfer the figs with a slotted spoon to a small bowl and set aside until cool enough to handle. Reserve the liquid in the pan. Cut the figs into quarters and set them aside.

**2** Add ½ cup of the vinegar, the brown sugar, cinnamon stick, and a pinch of salt to the liquid. Simmer until it is thickened and syrupy, 15 to 20 minutes, being careful not to scorch the sauce. Remove from the heat and stir in the remaining vinegar. Divide the sauce into 2 small bowls and set aside.

**3** Cut the tenderloin crosswise into ½-inch slices. Using the side of a chef's knife, flatten each slice into an oval that is about 1½ × 3 inches in size and ⅛ inch thick. Slice each oval lengthwise into 2 strips. Season the strips with salt and pepper to taste. (As you cut toward the end of the tenderloin, the slices will become smaller; these smaller slices can be flattened, but there is no need to cut them in half lengthwise.) There should be about 40 slices.

**4** Heat the oven to broil with the rack in the center. Place a fig quarter, cut-side down, on a slice of pork. Lift up each end of pork and overlap the 2 ends over the fig. (Make sure the fig sticks out at each end of the roll, trimming the pork if necessary.) Transfer the roll, seam-side down, to a rimmed baking sheet. Repeat with the remaining ingredients. Brush the bundles with half of the glaze. Broil until cooked through, about 3 minutes. To serve, skewer a toothpick through each bundle. Brush the rolls with the remaining glaze, or arrange them on a serving platter and drizzle with the glaze. Serve warm.

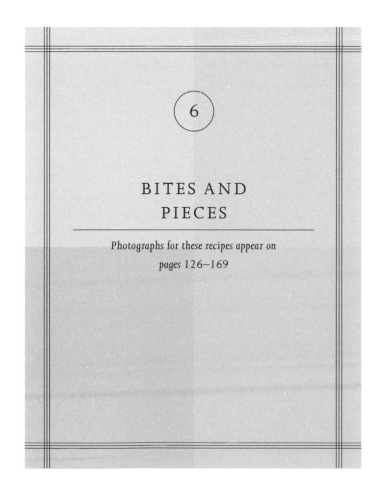

# 6

# BITES AND PIECES

*Photographs for these recipes appear on pages 126–169*

instills a sense of bounty. This doesn't mean you must present your guests with a huge variety of different foods. Although there is nothing wrong with that, an abundance of one item can also look stunning in its simplicity. This way of presenting hors d'oeuvres requires less work and is anything but fussy. Instead, it conveys a feeling of relaxed elegance that is appropriate for almost any gathering.

The "bites and pieces" approach often works best when similar foods are set out together in bowls and on platters. For example, I like to fill various styles of white bowls and cups with seasoned cashews, peanuts, macadamias, pecans, and mixed nuts, and set them beside one another on a table. A selection of various types of olives that have been marinated with wonderful flavor combinations such as lavender and Herbes de Provence or fennel and orange makes an equally beguiling display. Glass and ceramic trays lined with rows and rows of soft Pretzel Bites also prove irresistible; my recipe makes twenty-one dozen, and you can be sure every last one will be eaten. In the same fashion, a rough-hewn board topped with bowls of Crunchy Split Pea Bites and Spiced Chickpeas, or an earthenware bowl of steamed fresh soybeans, will convey an earthy but elegant simplicity.

Bread sticks are another wonderful casual hors d'oeuvre. The recipe for yeast bread sticks in this chapter, which includes six flavor variations, is a favorite of mine because the sticks are sturdy enough to make extra long and can be arranged upright in cylindrical containers for a dramatic presentation. There is also a quick version of bread sticks, with variations that change the color completely simply by adding flavorings such as beet, tomato, or carrot juice.

Icebox Crackers, easy to prepare in a variety of flavors, are among the ultimate make-ahead hors d'oeuvres; the dough logs for these crackers can be kept in the freezer to be sliced and baked as needed. The dough for flavorful, savory biscotti can also be prepared up to a month in advance and kept frozen.

Some of my bites and pieces derive luster from their luxe nature. Quail eggs, for instance, seem special because of their diminutive size. I hard-boil and devil these tiny eggs, top them with a variety of ingredient combinations, then present them on an array of colorful linen napkins.

The classic hors d'oeuvre in the bites and pieces category is, of course, crudité. While the idea may seem overused, there is a reason the concept is so popular; if properly done, crudités are a feast for the eye. I arrange long, narrow vegetables such as green and white asparagus and haricots verts upright in a bowl, or drape fiddlehead ferns off the edge of a bowl filled with dip. Leave the vegetables as close to their natural state as possible; carrots are far more appealing, for example, with their green tops still on. Seafood, such as shrimp and crab claws, will contribute drama and variety to a crudité display. For more elegant crudités, cut vegetables into flower shapes and pipe them with flavored cream cheeses.

Depending on the party, you can plan a menu entirely from this chapter, or you can use the recipes to balance a more formal selection.

## MOLASSES-GLAZED COCKTAIL RIBS

**MAKES ABOUT 3 DOZEN** | photograph on page 136

*Have your butcher slice the rack of ribs in half lengthwise for these small cocktail ribs. I like to use harissa, a fiery sauce from Tunisia traditionally served with couscous, in unconventional ways, as with these bite-size ribs. It comes in a tube, can, or jar and can be found in gourmet or Middle Eastern grocery stores. Avoid using a pan deeper than the one indicated below or the ribs may steam and take much longer to cook.*

¼ cup cider vinegar

2 tablespoons unsulphured molasses

⅔ cup maple syrup

½ cup Dijon mustard

¼ cup harissa

2 pounds baby back or spare ribs, cut in half
    lengthwise and cut into individual ribs

Kosher salt and freshly ground black pepper

**1** Place the vinegar, molasses, maple syrup, mustard, and harissa in a large bowl and mix to combine. Add the ribs and allow to marinate for 1 hour, covered, in the refrigerator.

**2** Heat the oven to 375°F. Transfer the ribs from the marinade to 2 rimmed baking sheets, reserving the marinade. (Any ovenproof pans with 1-inch-high sides may be used.) Season the ribs with salt and pepper to taste. Cook the ribs, basting twice during the first half hour with the remaining marinade, turning the ribs over after a half hour. The ribs should cook for a total of about 45 minutes, until glazed and cooked through. Do not baste in the last 10 minutes of cooking. Discard any remaining marinade. Serve warm.

## SWEET PEPPERED BACON BITES

**MAKES ABOUT 2 DOZEN** | photograph on page 140

*Slab bacon or thick-cut bacon (see Sources, page 487) is a must for these delicious bites. If your butcher doesn't carry the peppered version, coarsely grind pepper over plain slab bacon. I recommend asking your butcher to slice the slab bacon for you. Its cooking time will vary considerably depending on its thickness and the amount of marbling.*

8 ounces peppered slab bacon, sliced into
    ⅛-inch-thick pieces

½ cup packed light brown sugar

2 teaspoons olive oil

**1** Heat the oven to 375°F. Line a rimmed baking sheet with parchment paper and place the strips of bacon on it. Using your hands, coat both sides of the bacon with a thick layer of sugar. Lightly brush a sheet of parchment paper with oil. Place the paper, oiled-side down, over the bacon. Place a smaller baking sheet on top of the paper and bacon, and weigh it down with a heavy ovenproof skillet.

**2** Bake for 10 minutes. Remove from the oven, set aside the baking sheet and weight, and carefully drain off the fat. Return the bacon to the oven, with the top baking sheet and weight in place, and bake for 10 to 15 minutes more, or until the bacon is crisp and caramelized. Remove the baking sheet and weight and the top piece of parchment. Using a spoon, drizzle the caramel that will have accumulated in the pan over the bacon slices. Return to the oven without the top pan for 1 to 2 minutes, until the caramel is spread evenly over the bacon. Remove the bacon to a wire rack until cool enough to handle. Cut each slice into 2-inch pieces. Serve at room temperature. To reheat, place in a warm oven for 2 to 4 minutes.

## ORANGE-HONEY GLAZED BLACK FOREST HAM AND BISCUITS

**SERVES 12 TO 24** | photograph on page 169

*Garnish this succulent ham with kumquats and fresh bay leaves. I love the small, fully cooked ham from Karl Ehmer Quality Meats (see Directory, page 489). Check the ham often as it cooks; the sweet glaze must be used for basting throughout the heating time or it will burn. Serve these tiny sandwiches with your favorite sweet-hot mustard. You will have more biscuits than you need to make these. Set all of them out and offer them with any of the Compound Butters (pages 391–394).*

½ cup honey

1 tablespoon fresh orange juice

½ teaspoon grated orange zest

1 2- to 2½-pound "fully cooked" Black Forest ham

24 whole cloves

White Cheddar, Sage, and Buttermilk Biscuits or Sweet Potato Biscuits (recipes follow), split

**1** Preheat the oven to 350° F. with the rack in the center. In a small bowl, combine the honey, orange juice, and zest. Set aside.

**2** Remove the strings from the ham and rinse the ham under cool water. Pat dry and place the ham in a 9 × 13-inch roasting pan. Using a sharp knife, score the top of the ham in a diamond pattern, cutting ¼ inch deep. Place the cloves in the center of each diamond. Using a basting brush, gently brush the ham with half of the honey mixture.

**3** Bake the ham, basting with the remaining mixture every 10 minutes, for 30 minutes. After 30 minutes, baste the ham with the juices from the bottom of the roasting pan. Add enough water to just cover the bottom of the pan if it becomes too dry. Cook until the ham has darkened and the edges of the meat are crispy, 10 to 20 minutes more. Transfer to a serving platter and serve with the biscuits and mustard.

## WHITE CHEDDAR, SAGE, AND BUTTERMILK BISCUITS

**MAKES 3½ DOZEN** | photograph on page 169

2 cups all-purpose flour

1 teaspoon kosher salt

4 teaspoons baking powder

½ teaspoon cream of tartar

1 tablespoon sugar

8 tablespoons (1 stick) unsalted butter, chilled, cut into small pieces

3¼ ounces white Cheddar cheese, grated on the medium holes of a box grater to yield 1 cup plus 2 tablespoons

10 fresh sage leaves, cut into thin strips

⅔ cup buttermilk

**1** Preheat the oven to 400° F. Line a 12 × 17-inch baking sheet with parchment paper. Set aside.

**2** In a large bowl, combine the flour, salt, baking powder, cream of tartar, and sugar. Using your fingers or a pastry cutter, cut the butter into the flour mixture. Combine until the mixture resembles coarse meal. Stir in 1 cup of the Cheddar and the sage. Using a fork, add the buttermilk and combine until the buttermilk is just incorporated. The mixture will be crumbly.

**3** Turn out the dough onto a lightly floured surface. Use your hands to lightly press it together until the dough is a scant ¾ inch thick. Using a 1½-inch round cookie cutter, cut out rounds and transfer them to the prepared baking sheet. Rework the remaining scraps of dough to cut out more rounds. Transfer them to the baking sheet. Sprinkle each biscuit with the remaining cheese. Bake until golden brown, 10 to 12 minutes.

## SWEET POTATO BISCUITS

**MAKES 5 DOZEN** | photograph on page 169

1 pound (about 4 medium) sweet potatoes

2½ cups all-purpose flour

4 teaspoons baking powder

2 tablespoons sugar

1 teaspoon kosher salt

¼ teaspoon cayenne pepper

8 tablespoons (1 stick) unsalted butter, chilled,
    cut into small pieces

¼ cup milk

**1** Preheat the oven to 400°F. with 2 racks. Line two 12 × 17-inch baking sheets with parchment paper. Prick the sweet potatoes in several spots with a fork and transfer to one of the baking sheets. Bake until easily pierced with the tip of a knife, 40 to 60 minutes. When cool enough to handle, cut open the sweet potatoes and scoop out the flesh. Press the flesh through a sieve or mesh strainer. Set aside the flesh.

**2** In a large bowl, combine the flour, baking powder, sugar, salt, and cayenne. Using your fingers or a pastry cutter, cut the butter into the flour mixture. Combine until the mixture resembles coarse meal.

**3** Whisk together the milk and the sweet potato. Using a fork, stir this mixture into the flour mixture until well combined.

**4** Turn out the dough onto a lightly floured surface. Use your hands to lightly press it together until the dough is a scant ½ inch thick. Using a 1½-inch round cookie cutter, cut out rounds and transfer them to one of the prepared baking sheets. Rework the remaining scraps of dough to cut out more rounds. Transfer to the second baking sheet. Bake until golden brown, 12 to 14 minutes.

## A SELECTION OF SAUSAGES AND WURSTS

**SERVES 36** | photograph on page 138

*Handmade, freshly smoked link sausages are available at most butcher shops. Ask your butcher for exact cooking instructions for each sausage; most are precooked but taste better when grilled until slightly charred. Plan to serve 1 pound of sausage for 12 people. Kovbasa, a Ukrainian kielbasa, is available coarsely cut (krayana) and finely ground (siekana).*

½ cup Kosciusco (spicy brown) mustard

½ cup Pommery (French grainy) mustard

½ cup extra-strong Polish mustard

½ cup honey mustard

½ cup Pommery "Moutarde du Lion" mustard

½ cup horseradish mustard

½ pound weisswurst

½ pound bratwurst

1 pound kovbasa krayana sausage

1 pound kovbasa siekana sausage

½ pound kabanos sausage

1 long loaf crusty bread, thinly sliced

**1** Spoon the mustards into individual serving bowls and set aside. Using kitchen shears or a sharp knife, cut the sausage links apart, if attached.

**2** Heat a grill pan or heavy skillet over medium heat until hot. Working in batches, grill the weisswurst, bratwurst, and kovbasa sausage links, turning as needed until they are slightly charred all over and are hot. Timing will vary depending on the sausage, 5 to 10 minutes. Slice each sausage on the diagonal into ¼- to ½-inch pieces.

**3** Meanwhile, bring a medium pot of water to a boil. Drop the kabanos into the water and boil for 10 minutes. Transfer to a cutting board and slice on the diagonal into ¾-inch pieces.

**4** Arrange the sausage slices on a large platter. Serve with the mustards and bread and with toothpicks for skewers.

## CRISPY CHORIZO WITH CABRALES AND APPLES

**SERVES 6** | photograph on page 137

*Assertively seasoned cured chorizo sausage is not only wonderful when combined with cheese, as in the Chorizo and Manchego Cheese Quesadilla (page 259), but delicious when eaten in small bites along with tart green apples and Cabrales, an aged Spanish blue cheese that is similar to, if more intensely flavored and a bit more crumbly than, other blue cheeses. I recommend ordering Cabrales (see Sources, page 487) if you can't find it at your local cheese counter. Serve this dish with hard cider, sherry, or your favorite aperitif.*

3 Granny Smith or other tart apples

1 lemon, quartered

4 links (10 ounces) of cured chorizo sausage, cut into ¼-inch-thick rounds

12 ounces Cabrales cheese

Core each apple and slice into 8 wedges. Rub the wedges with the lemons to prevent discoloration. Set aside. Heat a large skillet over medium-high heat. Cook the chorizo rounds in batches, until slightly crispy and warm, about 4 minutes per side. Serve warm, with the apples, cheese, and hard cider or other beverage of choice.

## CLASSIC CRAB CAKES

**MAKES ABOUT 2½ DOZEN** | photograph on page 164

*I have been serving these crab cakes ever since I can remember; they are always the first thing to disappear from the hors d'oeuvre tray.*

12 ounces lump crabmeat, picked over for cartilage

2 slices white bread, broken into very small crumbs

1 tablespoon Dijon mustard

1 teaspoon Worcestershire sauce

2 teaspoons Old Bay seasoning

2 medium jalapeño peppers, seeds and ribs removed, minced

3 tablespoons finely chopped fresh cilantro

1 large egg, lightly beaten

1 large shallot, minced

2 tablespoons homemade (page 315) or prepared mayonnaise

Zest of 1 lemon

Freshly ground black pepper

3 to 4 tablespoons canola oil

Chili-Lime Aïoli (page 397)

**1** Preheat the oven to 400° F. Line a 12 × 17-inch baking sheet with parchment paper. Set the baking sheet aside.

**2** Combine the crabmeat and the bread in a medium bowl. Set aside. In another medium bowl, mix together the mustard, Worcestershire, Old Bay, jalapeños, cilantro, egg, shallots, mayonnaise, and lemon zest. Add the mayonnaise mixture to the crabmeat and stir to combine. Season with pepper to taste.

**3** Using your fingers, shape about 1½ tablespoons of the crab mixture into half-dollar-size rounds. Continue with the remaining crab mixture.

**4** Heat 3 tablespoons of the canola oil in a large skillet over medium heat. Working in batches of 6 to 8, place the crab cakes in the skillet and cook until golden brown on the bottom, 30 seconds to 1 minute. Turn the crab cakes and cook until golden brown, about 1 minute more. Transfer the crab cakes to a paper towel to absorb the oil. Transfer the crab cakes to the prepared baking sheet. Bake for 10 minutes, or until golden brown. The crab cakes may be held in a warm oven for 30 minutes, or cooled and reheated at serving time. Serve warm with the Chili-Lime Aïoli.

## BAKED MUSSELS

**MAKES 4 DOZEN** | photograph on page 132

*Buy more mussels than you need for this recipe, since those that do not open upon steaming should be discarded. The bread crumbs can be made up to 3 days in advance and stored in an airtight container at room temperature.*

3 slices of white sandwich bread, crusts removed

1 large shallot, finely chopped

2 garlic cloves, minced

¾ cup dry white wine

2 bay leaves

4 tablespoons unsalted butter

1½ teaspoons kosher salt

48 mussels (about 1 pound), scrubbed, de-
    bearded, and washed clean (see Note, right)

2 tablespoons finely chopped fresh flat-leaf
    parsley

**1** Heat the oven to 275°F. Place the bread on a wire rack. Place the rack onto a baking sheet and place in the oven. Cook until the bread feels dry to the touch but has no color, 5 to 7 minutes. Remove the baking sheet from the oven and let cool. Break the bread into very small crumbs. Set aside. Raise the heat to 450°F.

**2** Place the shallots, garlic, wine, bay leaves, butter, salt, and ½ cup of water in a medium saucepan over medium heat. Bring to a simmer. Add the mussels to the pan and cover tightly with a lid. Cook, shaking the pan occasionally, until the shells open, 2 to 3 minutes. Transfer the mussels with a slotted spoon to a separate bowl. Increase the heat to high. Cook until the liquid has reduced by half, about 6 minutes. Strain the liquid through a fine sieve into a small bowl and set aside.

**3** Break off the top shell of each mussel and discard. Using a small fork, loosen the mussels in the shells without removing them. Place the mussels, in their shells, on a wire rack set over a baking sheet. (The wire rack helps them stand upright during baking.) Spoon ½ teaspoon of the cooking liquid over each mussel.

**4** Combine the parsley with the bread crumbs in a small bowl. Sprinkle each mussel with 1 teaspoon of the bread crumb mixture. Place the mussels in the oven and cook until the bread crumbs turn golden, about 5 minutes. Serve warm.

---

**NOTE** | Preparing Mussels

Today, most of the mussels you find at the fishmarket are cultivated—grown in the sea on plastic mesh bags filled with large gravel. As a result, they are much easier to clean than wild mussels, which are typically covered in grit. Discard those that have broken shells, feel very heavy (indicating that they may be full of sand) or very light and loose (indicating that they are dead), or that are very wide open. Mussels that are slightly open are healthy if they snap shut quickly when tapped.

Store mussels in a bowl in the refrigerator, covered with a wet towel to prevent them from drying out. They can be refrigerated for up to 2 days. Never store the mussels in tap water; it will kill them.

To prepare them, place the mussels under cold running water and, using a stiff scrub brush, remove any grit and sand. Using your thumb and forefinger, grasp the dark weedy growth (the beard) protruding from between the mussel shells and tug it from the mussel. Since mussels die after their beards are removed, do this as close to cooking time as possible.

Served raw on the half shell, oysters are among the most wonderful of all culinary treats. Briny, fresh, and luxurious on the tongue, they taste like the very essence of the ocean.

Most oyster fanciers have heard the old saying that these bivalves should be eaten only in months spelled with the letter "R." In other words, according to this cautionary maxim, oysters should not be eaten from May through August. In the days before refrigeration, this was very good advice, since oysters, like all seafood, spoil quickly in hot weather. But although this is no longer a concern, oysters still are not at their best during the summer. This is the time in which they spawn, which makes them a bit softer and more fatty than they are at other times of the year. The very best oysters are those harvested during fall and winter months.

While it is usually safe to ask your local fishmonger for an oyster recommendation, I find it more interesting to understand the possible choices. That way, I can mix and match oysters to suit the tastes of my guests and the formality of the occasion.

The wide variety of oyster names can be confusing, but there are actually only five species available in the United States. All of the scores of individual varieties fall into one of these categories.

By far the three most widely available species are the familiar Atlantic oysters, which are grown along the East Coast as well as the Gulf Coast; the round, flat-shelled European oysters, grown primarily in the Northwest; and the

deeply scalloped Pacific oysters, grown along the West Coast. The two other species available in the United States are the half-dollar-size Olympia, grown only in the Northwest and rarely available anywhere else, and the kumamoto, long considered a Pacific oyster but recently declared a distinct species.

Each of these species is also referred to by other names. Atlantic oysters, for example, are often called eastern oysters, Pacifics may be called Japanese, and Europeans are called flats or Belons. Within each of the five species, there are dozens of individual varieties, each named after the particular geographic location where it was grown and harvested. Among the best-known Atlantic oysters (see photograph, page 154), for example, are the Blue Point from Long Island, the Malpeque from Prince Edward Island in Canada, and the eponymous Martha's Vineyard oyster from Massachusetts. Snow Creek is one of the most readily available of the Pacific oysters, and the Cape Nedick variety is harvested in Maine.

DISTINGUISHING VARIETIES It is not always easy to distinguish the various species of oyster from the profiles of their shells, but you can make an educated guess. Atlantic oysters resemble rounded triangles, opening out from the hinge, with a light scalloping along the outer edge. The edges of Pacific oysters' shells tend to be more deeply scalloped, and the scalloped ridges along the top of the shell are also more pronounced. European oysters are flat and almost round. Olympias are also rather round and flat, but are much smaller than Europeans. Kumamotos, while larger than Olympias, are like a miniature version of the Pacific oysters.

The exact taste of an individual variety of oyster is determined by the environment where it was grown; climate, water quality, and the age and condition of the growing beds are all important factors. But within each species there are also some common flavor characteristics. Atlantic oysters are particularly briny and crisp on the tongue, with a lightly fishy aftertaste. Flats are also quite briny, but have a distinct, pleasantly metallic finish. Pacific oysters have a less salty flavor and are often described as fruity and a bit sweet. Kumamotos (see photograph, page 156) and Olympias have slight but distinct differences from the Pacifics; kumamotos are generally a bit more complex and quite mild, with a very creamy texture, while Olympias have a particularly clean flavor.

While it is interesting to know all of this, it is not essential. You should try the many different varieties until you find out what you like best, but as with other seafood, the most important principle when selecting oysters is to buy what is freshest.

When buying oysters, make sure they are tightly closed. If any of the shells are partially open, rap them sharply with a knife or spoon; if they still don't close, discard them. When you open oysters, the liquid inside the shell should be clear or slightly milky, and the only odor should be the same as you would smell when inhaling a lovely sea breeze.

**STORING** Although it might seem like common sense to store oysters in water, this will actually kill them, since they must have oxygen to stay alive. Instead, store them in the refrigerator with the larger half facing down, covered with a damp cloth or a layer of seaweed. You should eat them within three days, although I think it is best to eat them the day they are purchased. With oysters, as with all seafood, fresher is better.

**PREPARING AND SERVING OYSTERS** First scrub all of the oysters well with a brush. Then place a folded towel in the palm of your hand and, holding each oyster with the cupped side facing down, use an oyster knife to pry into the oyster's hinge and pop off the top shell. Then use a knife to scrape the oyster from the bottom shell. If any bits of shell have gotten into the oyster, remove them. Place the half shell on a bed of crushed ice or even coarse sea salt, being careful that neither water nor the salt accidentally gets into the oysters.

Of course, it is easier to have a fishmonger shuck the oysters for you, a task that most of them will be quite willing to do. Since oysters begin to lose their full flavor after two hours or so, arrange to have the oysters shucked just before you pick them up for your party.

While it is fun to have several different kinds of oysters for your guests to sample and compare, even a single variety, sitting plump and shiny on a bed of chopped ice, provides a wonderful temptation. As for accompaniments, I like to serve oysters with not only Classic Mignonette Sauce, but also with Sake-Lime Sauce, Hot Sesame and Chili Sauce, and Lemon-Tabasco Sauce (page 396).

Olives of all kinds are a staple in my pantry. They are the perfect "bite" to serve with drinks before dinner. Don't throw out the flavored oil marinades from the olive recipes; they make delicious additions to vinaigrettes. Slowly whisk 3 tablespoons of the oil into 1 tablespoon of tarragon or balsamic vinegar. Season with salt and pepper. Refrigerate for up to 1 week until ready to use.

## MIXED PROVENÇAL OLIVES WITH PRESERVED LEMON AND OREGANO

**MAKES 2 CUPS** | photograph on page 130

*Preserved lemons, which can be found in gourmet grocery stores and many Middle Eastern markets, give these olives a tart flavor and refreshing citrus aroma (see Sources, page 487). Fresh lemon zest makes a fine substitute; make wide strips of zest from one lemon and use in place of the preserved lemon.*

8 to 10 ounces (2 cups) assorted olives, such as niçoise, Nyons, and Picholine
4 pieces preserved lemon, sliced into 1¼-inch pieces
¼ cup white wine vinegar
½ cup extra-virgin olive oil
1 tablespoon fresh lemon juice or brine from preserved lemons
2 teaspoons dried oregano

**1** Place the olives in a medium bowl.
**2** In a small saucepan, combine the lemon, vinegar, olive oil, and lemon juice. Bring to a simmer and add the oregano. Pour over the olives and let them marinate at room temperature for at least 2 hours. The olives may be made 1 week ahead and kept refrigerated in an airtight container. Return to room temperature before serving.

## FRENCH OIL-CURED OLIVES WITH LAVENDER AND HERBES DE PROVENCE

**MAKES 2 CUPS** | photograph on page 130

*Herbes de Provence—which typically includes basil, fennel seed, marjoram, thyme, rosemary, sage, and summer savory— is usually found in the herb section of specialty food stores. Lavender, a member of the mint family, lends pungency to the mix.*

8 to 10 ounces (2 cups) French oil-cured black olives such as Nyons
½ cup extra-virgin olive oil
¼ cup red wine vinegar
1 tablespoon Herbes de Provence
1 teaspoon dried lavender

**1** Place the olives in a medium bowl.
**2** In a small saucepan, combine the olive oil, vinegar, herbs, and lavender. Bring to a simmer. Pour the warm mixture over the olives and let them marinate at room temperature for at least 2 hours. The olives may be made 1 week ahead and kept refrigerated in an airtight container. Return to room temperature before serving.

## WARM SPICY KALAMATA OLIVES

**MAKES 2 CUPS** | photograph on page 130

*Sun-dried red bell peppers are sold near the dried fruit in gourmet stores.*

8 to 10 ounces (2 cups) kalamata olives
¼ cup cider vinegar
½ cup extra-virgin olive oil
2 tablespoons sun-dried red bell peppers, or 3 tablespoons sun-dried tomatoes, thinly sliced
1 small whole dried chili pepper
1 teaspoon red pepper flakes

1 Place the olives in a medium bowl. (If using the sun-dried tomatoes, place them in a medium bowl, cover with very hot water, and leave to plump for 15 minutes. Drain and use.)

2 In a small saucepan, combine the vinegar, olive oil, red bell peppers, chili, and red pepper flakes. Bring to a simmer. Pour the warm mixture over the olives and let them marinate at room temperature for at least 2 hours. The olives may be made 1 week ahead and kept refrigerated in an airtight container. Return to room temperature before serving.

## PICHOLINE OLIVES WITH ROASTED GARLIC AND RED ONION

MAKES 2 CUPS | photograph on page 130

*Picholine olives are one of the most well-known varieties exported from France. They are easily recognized by their shiny, green skins and elongated shape. Cured in brine with a high salt content, they are much more salty than other brine-cured varieties.*

8 to 10 ounces (2 cups) Picholine olives
½ cup plus 1 tablespoon extra-virgin olive oil
4 garlic cloves, thinly sliced lengthwise
¼ cup plus 2 tablespoons champagne vinegar
½ small red onion, thinly sliced
2 bay leaves
1 tablespoon mixed (red, white, green) peppercorns, slightly crushed

1 Place the olives in a medium bowl.

2 Heat 1 tablespoon of the olive oil in a small skillet over medium-low heat. Add the garlic and cook just until golden, about 2 minutes. Transfer the garlic to a paper towel and cool. Set aside.

3 Bring 2 tablespoons of the vinegar and the red onion to a simmer in a small saucepan over medium heat. Continue to cook until reduced by half, to 1 tablespoon. Add the remaining ½ cup olive oil, ¼ cup vinegar, the bay leaves, and the peppercorns and bring to a simmer. Stir in the garlic. Pour the warm mixture over the olives and let them marinate at room temperature for at least 2 hours. The olives may be made 1 week ahead and kept refrigerated in an airtight container. Return to room temperature before serving.

## PICKLED BELLA DI CERIGNOLA OLIVES WITH FENNEL AND ORANGE

MAKES 2 CUPS | photograph on page 130

*Bella di Cerignola are huge, meaty olives from southern Italy that are cured in ashes. They are available both green and ripe, but I prefer the green version for the sweet, dense flesh.*

8 to 10 ounces (2 cups) Bella di Cerignola olives
¼ cup fresh orange juice
1 tablespoon grated orange zest
½ cup (about 1½ ounces) shaved fennel
½ cup extra-virgin olive oil
¼ cup tarragon vinegar
1 teaspoon whole fennel seeds, lightly toasted

1 Place the olives in a medium bowl.

2 In a small saucepan, combine the orange juice, the zest, and the fennel. Bring to a simmer and cook until the mixture has reduced to a syrupy consistency, about 5 minutes. Add the olive oil, vinegar, and fennel seeds. Pour the warm mixture over the olives and let them marinate at room temperature for at least 2 hours. The olives may be made up to 2 weeks ahead and kept refrigerated in an airtight container. Return to room temperature before serving.

## MIXED OLIVES WITH CAPER BERRIES

**MAKES 2½ CUPS** | photograph on page 131

8 to 10 ounces (2 cups) assorted olives, such as
    niçoise, Nyons, kalamata, Picholine, and
    Bella di Cerignola
½ cup caper berries
1 teaspoon red pepper flakes
1 head roasted garlic (see page 265), cloves
    peeled and left intact
1 sprig fresh thyme, picked
1 sprig fresh rosemary, picked

In a large bowl, combine the olives, caper berries, red pepper flakes, and garlic. Transfer to a serving bowl and garnish with the thyme and rosemary.

## HARD-BOILED AND DEVILED QUAIL EGGS

**MAKES 2 DOZEN HALVES** | photograph on page 127

*Tiny quail eggs, which have long been popular in Asian cuisines, are now available in gourmet stores as well as Chinese markets. Use half of the hard-boiled eggs for deviling and leave the remaining yolks intact for seasoning and garnishing.*

12 quail eggs
2 tablespoons homemade (page 315) or
    prepared mayonnaise
Kosher salt and freshly ground black pepper

**1** Prepare an ice bath in a large bowl. Set aside. Place the quail eggs in a medium saucepan and cover with several inches of cold water. Place the pan, covered, over high heat, stirring occasionally, until just before the water comes to a boil. Uncover, reduce to a simmer, and cook for 2 minutes, stirring the eggs gently several times to ensure even cooking. Immediately transfer the eggs, with a slotted spoon, to the ice bath. Let cool completely, about 5 minutes. Pat dry one egg at a time and peel (see Note, page 359). Place the peeled eggs in a bowl. Cover with plastic wrap and refrigerate until ready to use. The eggs made be prepared up to this point 6 hours in advance.

**2** Cut the eggs in half lengthwise. To make the deviled eggs, remove the yolks from 12 halves and place them in a small bowl. Using the back of a fork, mash the yolks until they are completely smooth. Stir in the mayonnaise, and season with salt and pepper to taste. Using a small pastry bag fitted with a ⅜-inch tip (a resealable plastic freezer bag with a corner snipped out may also be used), pipe the yolk mixture into the empty egg halves. For the remaining 12 halves, decorate and season as desired, or use the suggestions that follow.

## SEASONINGS AND GARNISHES FOR QUAIL EGGS

**EACH SERVING SUGGESTION IS FOR 12 EGG HALVES (6 EGGS)** | photograph on page 127

### TARRAGON MAYONNAISE

5 tablespoons coarsely chopped fresh tarragon,
    plus 12 sprigs for garnish
½ cup homemade (page 315) or prepared
    mayonnaise

Combine the tarragon and the mayonnaise in the bowl of a food processor or in a blender. Process until the mayonnaise is green. Transfer the mayonnaise to a pastry bag fitted with a number 7 tip. Pipe out dollops of tarragon mayonnaise on each egg half and garnish each with a sprig of tarragon.

### CAVIAR AND CRÈME FRAÎCHE

1 tablespoon crème fraîche
¼ ounce (about 2 teaspoons) caviar

Top each egg half with a dollop of crème fraîche and garnish with caviar.

### NUTMEG AND SEA SALT

¼ teaspoon freshly ground nutmeg
¼ teaspoon coarse sea salt

Sprinkle each egg half with a dusting of nutmeg followed by a pinch of sea salt.

### FINES HERBES

½ teaspoon finely chopped fresh tarragon
½ teaspoon finely chopped fresh flat-leaf parsley
½ teaspoon finely chopped fresh chervil
½ teaspoon finely snipped fresh chives

Sprinkle each egg half with a pinch of each of the herbs.

### ANCHOVY

6 small anchovy fillets, sliced into 12 1½-inch-
   long strips

Top each egg half with one of the rolled strips of anchovy.

### KALAMATA OLIVES

2 kalamata olives, pitted, each cut into 8 strips

Top each egg half with 1 to 2 strips of olive.

### BACON AND THYME

1 6-inch-long slice of cooked bacon, crumbled
¼ teaspoon fresh thyme

Sprinkle each egg half with bacon and thyme.

### CURRY-CUMIN

¼ teaspoon curry powder
¼ teaspoon toasted cumin seeds (see page 386)

Sprinkle each egg half with curry powder. Top each with a sprinkling of cumin seeds.

### PICKLED GINGER AND WASABI CAVIAR

12 ½ × ¾-inch slices pickled ginger
2 teaspoons prepared wasabi caviar or
   homemade (see page 326)

Top each egg half with a strip of pickled ginger and a dollop of caviar.

---

**NOTE** | Peeling and Storing Quail Eggs

Quail eggs appear very fragile and delicate, but in fact they have a much tougher membrane under the shell than hen's eggs, which makes them more difficult to peel. To peel a hard-boiled quail egg, lightly tap it all around on a work surface, then roll it gently along the surface with the palm of your hand. The shell will begin to crack. At this point, carefully peel the egg by gently pulling away the membrane with the shell attached.

Once peeled, the eggs may be held up to 6 hours in an airtight container in the refrigerator.

To prepare them for piping, cut the eggs in half lengthwise using a very sharp knife. Clean off any yolk that clings to the knife as you slice each egg. Once halved, the eggs may be stored, wrapped in plastic touching the cut surface of each egg, in an airtight container for up to 2 hours. Garnish with herbs and spices just before serving. Arrange the eggs on chilled ceramic or china platters, which will help keep the eggs cool. For a colorful presentation, arrange the eggs on a platter spread with toasted sesame seeds, rock salt, or fresh chives.

## SEASONED
## NUTS AND LEGUMES

To make the most flavorful toasted nuts, you must begin with the very freshest. Since there is really no way to tell how fresh a nut is from looking at it, the best precaution is to buy from a purveyor who sells in volume (see Sources, page 487).

Each of these recipes makes about 5 cups. In my experience, each guest will eat about ¼ cup of these mixes. That means if you are serving only one type, you will need one recipe for every twenty guests. Of course, if you want to be sure that you have plenty, make ½ cup per guest.

To make a real visual impact, I sometimes pick one type of nut and serve a huge bowl full of it. Pistachios (see photograph, page 142) are perfect for this purpose, since they have a beautiful shape and a lovely color and are easily shelled. When serving an hors d'oeuvre as simple as this, choose a very striking bowl for serving.

## GINGER-SCENTED PECANS
**MAKES 5 CUPS** | photograph on page 141

5 cups pecan halves

½ cup sugar

2 teaspoons kosher salt

1 teaspoon ground ginger

2 tablespoons honey

2 teaspoons canola oil

**1** Heat the oven to 325°F. Place the nuts in a single layer on 2 rimmed baking sheets. Toast until the nuts are fragrant, 10 to 15 minutes, rotating the pans halfway through cooking. Meanwhile, combine the sugar, salt, and ginger in a small bowl and set aside.

**2** Combine the honey, 2 tablespoons of water, and the oil in a large saucepan and bring to a boil over high heat. Reduce the heat to medium and add the roasted pecans. Cook, stirring once or twice, until all of the liquid has evaporated, 3 to 5 minutes. Transfer the mixture to a bowl, add the sugar mixture, and toss until well combined. Spread the nuts in a single layer on a sheet of parchment paper to cool. These pecans may be kept in an airtight container at room temperature for 1 week.

## WARM MIXED NUTS WITH
## ROSEMARY AND SHALLOTS
**MAKES 5 CUPS** | photograph on page 141

*Once seasoned, these nuts taste best if eaten that day.*

5 cups mixed nuts, such as walnuts, cashews, almonds, pecans, and hazelnuts

1 tablespoon extra-virgin olive oil

2 small shallots, thinly sliced crosswise into rings to yield about ¼ cup

3 garlic cloves, thinly sliced lengthwise

2 tablespoons unsalted butter

¼ cup coarsely chopped fresh rosemary

¼ teaspoon cayenne pepper

1 tablespoon firmly packed dark brown sugar

1 tablespoon kosher salt

**1** Heat the oven to 350°F. Place the nuts in a single layer on 2 rimmed baking sheets. Toast until the nuts are golden and fragrant, 8 to 12 minutes, rotating the pans halfway through cooking. Transfer the nuts to a large bowl and set aside.

**2** Heat the olive oil in a small skillet over medium heat. Add the shallots and garlic; fry until golden, 3 to 5 minutes. Transfer the shallots and garlic to paper towels. Set aside.

**3** Melt the butter and pour it over the nuts. Add the rosemary, cayenne, brown sugar, and salt and stir well to combine. Toss in the crispy garlic and shallots. Serve warm. The nuts may be reheated in a 300°F. oven for 10 minutes.

## TOASTED PEANUTS WITH INDIAN SPICES

**MAKES 5 CUPS** | photograph on page 141

*If you can't find black onion seeds (see Sources, page 487), black sesame seeds may be substituted.*

1 tablespoon ground cumin

1 tablespoon ground coriander

2½ teaspoons kosher salt

1 tablespoon sugar

¼ teaspoon freshly ground black pepper

⅛ teaspoon cayenne pepper

2 large egg whites

5 cups shelled, unsalted peanuts

3 tablespoons black onion seeds

**1** Heat the oven to 300°F. Line 2 rimmed baking sheets with parchment paper. In a small bowl, combine the cumin, coriander, salt, sugar, black pepper, and cayenne. Set aside.

**2** In a medium bowl, beat the egg whites with a small whisk until frothy. Whisk in the reserved spice mixture. Stir in the peanuts and the black onion seeds.

**3** Spread the nut mixture in single layers onto the baking sheets and bake, stirring the nuts and rotating the pans halfway through cooking, until the nuts are dry and toasted, 20 to 25 minutes. Spread the nuts in a single layer on parchment paper to cool. These peanuts may be kept in an airtight container at room temperature for 1 week.

## COCONUT CURRY MACADAMIA NUTS

**MAKES 5 CUPS** | photograph on page 141

1½ teaspoons ground ginger

1½ teaspoons ground cumin

1½ tablespoons curry powder

½ teaspoon cayenne pepper

¼ cup packed dark brown sugar

¾ teaspoon kosher salt

2 large egg whites

5 cups macadamia nuts

1 cup large or small coconut flakes

**1** Heat the oven to 300°F. Line 2 rimmed baking sheets with parchment paper. In a small bowl, combine the spices, brown sugar, and salt. Set aside.

**2** In a medium bowl, beat the egg whites with a small whisk until frothy. Whisk in the reserved spice mixture. Stir in the nuts and the coconut flakes. Spread the mixture in a single layer onto the baking sheets. Bake, stirring the nuts and rotating the pans halfway through cooking, until the nuts are dry, 20 to 25 minutes. Transfer to parchment paper to cool. The nuts may be kept in an airtight container at room temperature for 1 week.

> **TECHNIQUE** | Toasting Nuts
>
> Toasting not only crisps nuts, it also releases their essential oils, bringing out their fullest flavors. The easiest way to toast just about any kind of nut is to place them in a single layer on a rimmed baking sheet in a 350°F. oven and bake them until they are golden, 8 to 12 minutes. Give the pan a shake midway through roasting to make sure the nuts roast evenly.

## HONEY-ROASTED ALMONDS

**MAKES 5 CUPS** | photograph on page 141

*As with other nuts, roasting almonds brings out their full flavor by releasing their oils.*

1 cup honey
2 teaspoons Chinese five-spice powder
5 cups whole almonds, skin on

**1** Heat the oven to 300° F. Line 2 rimmed baking sheets with parchment paper. Warm the honey in a medium saucepan over medium heat until it becomes thin and easy to pour. Stir in the five-spice powder and the almonds.

**2** Spread the mixture in a single layer onto the baking sheets. Bake, rotating the pans halfway through cooking, until the nut mixture has darkened in color, 45 to 55 minutes. Immediately spread the almonds in a single layer on parchment paper. Set aside to cool. The almonds may be kept in an airtight container at room temperature for 1 week.

## SPICY PAPRIKA CASHEWS

**MAKES 5 CUPS** | photograph on page 141

*I like to make these nuts fairly spicy, but you can raise or lower the heat by adjusting the amount of cayenne.*

1 tablespoon kosher salt
2 tablespoons cayenne pepper
1½ teaspoons paprika
½ cup sugar
2 large egg whites
5 cups unsalted cashews

**1** Heat the oven to 300° F. Line 2 rimmed baking sheets with parchment paper. In a small bowl, combine the salt, cayenne, paprika, and sugar and set aside.

**2** In a medium bowl, beat the egg whites with a small whisk until foamy. Whisk in the spice mixture. Stir in the nuts. Spread the cashews in a single layer onto the baking sheets. Bake for 15 minutes. Reduce the oven temperature to 250° F., rotate the pans in the oven, and cook for 10 more minutes. Immediately spread the cashews in a single layer on parchment paper. Set aside to cool. These cashews may be kept in an airtight container at room temperature for 1 week.

## HONEY-ROASTED SEED AND NUT CLUSTERS

**MAKES 2½ DOZEN 1-INCH CLUSTERS** | photograph on page 141

*I use more honey and corn syrup than is used for the firm, brittle version of these; it makes these sweet, salty clusters wonderfully soft and chewy.*

⅔ cup pine nuts
⅔ cup pumpkin seeds
⅔ cup sunflower seeds
¼ cup sugar
4 teaspoons kosher salt
4 teaspoons honey
4 teaspoons dark corn syrup
2 teaspoons canola oil

**1** Heat the oven to 300° F. Mix the pine nuts, pumpkin seeds, and sunflower seeds and spread them on a rimmed baking sheet. Toast until golden, 10 to 15 minutes. Set aside.

**2** In a small bowl, combine the sugar and salt. Set aside. In a small saucepan, combine the honey, corn syrup, 2 tablespoons of water, and the oil. Bring to a boil. Stir in the toasted nuts and seeds, and cook, stirring, for about 3 minutes. Stir in the sugar-salt mixture. Spread the entire mixture, in an even ¼-inch-thick layer, onto a baking sheet. Cool completely. Use a metal spatula to break the mixture into approximately 1-inch clusters. The clusters will keep at room temperature in an airtight container for up to 5 days.

## CRUNCHY SPLIT PEA BITES
**MAKES 1½ CUPS** | photograph on page 168

*These bites add a wonderful crunch to an hors d'oeuvre selection; match them with a juicy bite, such as marinated olives (pages 356–358) or cornichons, for a nice balance of textures. The peas are soaked in baking soda to maintain their color when cooked.*

1 cup dried green split peas
2 teaspoons baking soda
4 teaspoons sesame oil
4 teaspoons vegetable oil
Kosher salt

**1** Place the split peas in a large bowl and toss with the baking soda. Add 3 cups of water and cover the bowl with plastic wrap. Let the peas soak at room temperature for 4½ hours.

**2** Drain the split peas and thoroughly dry them with paper towels. Heat a large skillet over medium-high heat and add 2 teaspoons of the sesame oil and 2 teaspoons of the vegetable oil. Add half the peas and cook, stirring frequently, until they begin to turn golden brown in spots and become crunchy, 6 to 10 minutes. Transfer to a paper-towel-lined baking sheet. Season generously with salt. Repeat with the remaining oil and peas. When cool, the peas may be kept in an airtight container at room temperature for 3 days.

## SPICED CHICKPEAS
**MAKES 2 CUPS** | photograph on page 168

*I use the microwave to dry the chickpeas, which makes them crispy without using any additional fat for frying or sautéing. Use the rotating carousel in the microwave for even drying.*

2 teaspoons kosher salt
2 teaspoons paprika
1 teaspoon ground coriander
½ teaspoon chili powder
2 15-ounce cans chickpeas, rinsed and drained
    to equal 3 cups

**1** In a small bowl, combine the salt, paprika, coriander, and chili powder. On a double layer of paper towels, arrange half of the chickpeas in an even layer. Season with half of the seasoned salt mixture. Put the chickpeas on the paper towels in the microwave. Microwave on 80 percent power for 18 to 22 minutes altogether, stirring the chickpeas every 5 minutes. (If your microwave only has full power, use for the same amount of time, watching carefully for dryness.) When the chickpeas feel firm to the touch, remove them from the microwave. Set aside to cool.

**2** Repeat with the remaining chickpeas, using fresh paper towels. Toss the 2 batches together and serve. The seasoned chickpeas can made 2 days ahead and kept in an airtight container at room temperature.

## CHEDDAR-CORNMEAL ICEBOX CRACKERS

**MAKES 20 CRACKERS** | photograph on page 134

1 cup all-purpose flour

2 tablespoons yellow cornmeal

1¼ teaspoons kosher salt

¼ teaspoon cayenne pepper

Pinch of freshly grated nutmeg

2 tablespoons very cold unsalted butter, cut into
  small pieces

1 cup (2½ ounces) finely grated Cheddar cheese

¼ cup plus 1 tablespoon milk

**1** Combine the flour, cornmeal, salt, cayenne, and nutmeg in the bowl of a food processor. Pulse to combine. Add the butter and pulse until the mixture resembles coarse meal. Add the cheese and pulse until combined. With the machine running, add the milk. Process until the dough comes together and is well combined.

**2** Transfer the dough to a clean work surface. Shape the dough into a 2-inch-wide log. Wrap with plastic wrap and refrigerate for at least 24 hours.

**3** Heat the oven to 325° F. Slice the well-chilled log into ¼-inch-thick slices. Transfer the slices to a baking sheet and bake immediately, rotating the sheet halfway through cooking, until the crackers are golden brown and firm in the center, 25 to 35 minutes. (The crackers should not get too dark around the edges.) Transfer to a rack to cool. The crackers may be made a day ahead and kept in an airtight container at room temperature.

---

**NOTE** | Icebox Crackers

Cheese crackers differ from baked-dry crackers such as saltines in that they are made with a very rich, fine-textured dough. I like to keep the dough for these in the freezer, then slice and bake the crackers as I need them.

With a very short dough such as this, temperature is an important consideration at every stage of the process. It is best to start with butter that has been stored in the freezer.

Each of the 4 recipes here makes 1 log, 5½ inches long and 2 inches thick. The logs must be chilled in the refrigerator at least 24 hours before they are sliced and baked.

I generally slice the crackers ¼ inch thick, but they may be sliced as thin as ⅛ inch. The thinner the slices, the higher the yield and the shorter the baking time. Make each batch of uniform thickness and watch the time carefully when they are in the oven; the crackers should not be too dark around the edges.

Once you have put the slices of dough on the baking sheets, don't let them sit out for too long. The sliced dough should still be cool when put into the oven.

Wrapped in plastic wrap, the dough logs may be kept in the refrigerator for up to 2 weeks. For longer storage, wrap them in 2 layers of plastic wrap and freeze for up to 4 weeks. The crackers themselves may be made a day ahead and kept in an airtight container at room temperature. If necessary, crackers kept overnight may be recrisped in a 250° F. oven for 10 minutes.

## PARMESAN-ROSEMARY ICEBOX CRACKERS

**MAKES 20 CRACKERS** | photograph on page 134

¾ cup all-purpose flour

1 teaspoon kosher salt

Pinch of white pepper

2 teaspoons finely chopped fresh rosemary, plus extra sprigs for garnish

3 tablespoons very cold unsalted butter, cut into small pieces

1 cup (2½ ounces) finely grated Parmesan cheese

5 tablespoons sour cream

1 large egg white, lightly beaten

**1** Combine the flour, salt, pepper, and the chopped rosemary in the bowl of a food processor. Pulse to combine. Add the butter and pulse until the mixture resembles coarse meal. Add the cheese and pulse until combined. Add 1 tablespoon of the sour cream at a time, pulsing each time to combine. Process until the dough comes together and is well combined.

**2** Transfer the dough to a clean work surface. Shape the dough into a 2-inch-wide log. Wrap the log with plastic wrap and refrigerate for at least 24 hours.

**3** Heat the oven to 325°F. Slice the well-chilled log into ¼-inch-thick slices. Transfer the slices to a baking sheet. Dip a sprig of rosemary into the egg white and place it in the center of 1 cracker slice. Repeat with the remaining rosemary and crackers. Bake immediately, rotating the sheet halfway through cooking, until the crackers are golden brown and firm in the center, 25 to 35 minutes. (The crackers should not get too dark around the edges.) Transfer to a rack to cool. The crackers may be made a day ahead and kept in an airtight container at room temperature.

## BLUE CHEESE-PECAN ICEBOX CRACKERS

**MAKES 20 CRACKERS** | photograph on page 134

*Blue cheese is moist enough to bring this dough together, making the addition of milk or sour cream as in the other cheese crackers unnecessary. Any good-quality blue cheese, such as a Danish blue, would be good.*

2 ounces (¾ cup) pecan halves

¾ cup all-purpose flour

4 tablespoons very cold unsalted butter, cut into small pieces

3 ounces blue cheese, crumbled

**1** Heat the oven to 375°F. Place the pecans on a rimmed baking sheet and bake until fragrant, 3 to 5 minutes. Let cool. Transfer the pecans to the bowl of a food processor and pulse until finely ground. Transfer the ground pecans to a small bowl and set aside.

**2** Combine the flour and the ground pecans in the bowl of the food processor. Pulse briefly to combine. Add the butter and pulse until the mixture resembles coarse meal. Add the cheese and process until the dough comes together and is well combined.

**3** Transfer the dough to a clean work surface. Shape the dough into a 2-inch-wide log. Wrap the log with plastic wrap and refrigerate for at least 24 hours.

**4** Heat the oven to 325°F. Slice the well-chilled log into ¼-inch-thick slices. Transfer the slices to a baking sheet and bake immediately, rotating the sheet halfway through cooking, until the crackers are golden brown and firm in the center, 25 to 35 minutes. (The crackers should not get too dark around the edges.) Transfer to a rack to cool. The crackers may be made a day ahead and kept in an airtight container at room temperature.

## GRUYÈRE-THYME ICEBOX CRACKERS

**MAKES 20 CRACKERS** | photograph on page 134

1 cup all-purpose flour

1 teaspoon kosher salt

⅛ teaspoon freshly ground black pepper

1½ tablespoons chopped fresh thyme, plus extra sprigs for garnish

3 tablespoons very cold unsalted butter, cut into small pieces

1 cup (2½ ounces) finely grated Gruyère cheese

¼ cup plus 1 tablespoon milk

1 large egg white, lightly beaten

**1** Combine the flour, salt, pepper, and chopped thyme in the bowl of a food processor. Pulse to combine. Add the butter and pulse until the mixture resembles coarse meal. Add the cheese and pulse until combined. With the machine running, add the milk. Process until the dough comes together and is well combined.

**2** Transfer the dough to a clean work surface. Shape the dough into a 2-inch-wide log. Wrap the log with plastic wrap and refrigerate for at least 24 hours.

**3** Heat the oven to 325° F. Slice the well-chilled log into ¼-inch-thick slices. Transfer the slices to a baking sheet. Dip a sprig of thyme into the egg white and place it in the center of 1 cracker slice. Repeat with the remaining thyme and crackers. Bake immediately, rotating the sheet halfway through cooking, until the crackers are golden brown and firm in the center, 25 to 35 minutes. (The crackers should not get too dark around the edges.) Transfer to a rack to cool. The crackers may be made a day ahead and kept in an airtight container at room temperature.

## BREAD STICKS

### YEAST BREAD STICKS

**MAKES 5 DOZEN** | photographs on pages 144 and 146

*Yeast bread sticks take longer to make than the crackerlike quick bread sticks because the dough must rise, but their more complex textures and flavors are worth the effort. Because these sticks are stronger than quick bread sticks, they can be stretched longer and twisted into interesting shapes and can be used as dippers. This makes them the perfect stick to arrange upright in cylindrical containers for a dramatic presentation.*

1 ¼-ounce package active dry yeast (2 teaspoons)

2 cups warm water (110° F.)

1½ tablespoons honey

5 tablespoons olive oil, plus extra for brushing

5¾ cups all-purpose flour

½ cup finely grated Parmesan cheese

4 teaspoons kosher salt

**1** In a medium bowl, combine the yeast and ¼ cup of the warm water. Set aside to proof for 5 minutes. Meanwhile, in a small bowl, combine the remaining 1¾ cups warm water with the honey and the olive oil. Stir the honey mixture into the yeast. Set aside. Brush the inside of a large bowl with olive oil. Set aside.

**2** In another large bowl, combine the flour, Parmesan, and salt. Pour the wet yeast mixture over the dry flour mixture. Using your hands, combine until the flour mixture is completely incorporated; the dough will be sticky.

**3** Transfer the wet mixture to a lightly floured board. Knead the dough until soft and elastic, about 5 minutes. Transfer the dough to the reserved large bowl, brush the dough with olive oil, and cover with plastic wrap. Set aside in a warm place to rise until doubled in size, about 1½ hours.

**4** Heat the oven to 425°F. Divide the dough evenly into 4 batches. Wrap 3 batches in plastic wrap and set aside. Cut the remaining batch into 16 pieces (about 1 inch in diameter each). Using your fingers, roll one piece at a time on a lightly floured surface into 16-inch-long sticks. Transfer the sticks to 2 baking sheets, placing them about 1 inch apart. Cover with plastic wrap, set aside in a warm place, and let proof for 30 minutes. Repeat with another batch of dough and 2 more sheet pans. While the second batch is proofing, proceed with the first batch.

**5** Just before baking, brush each stick with olive oil and sprinkle with salt. Bake, rotating the sheets once, until lightly browned, 10 to 12 minutes. The bread sticks can be stored at room temperature in an airtight container for 2 to 3 days.

## FLAVORED YEAST BREAD STICKS
**MAKES 5 DOZEN** | photograph on page 144

*Adding herbs and spices to the Yeast Bread Sticks recipe (left) creates some delicious flavor variations. Unless otherwise instructed, each combination of flavoring ingredients is added to the recipe in step 2 along with the flour, Parmesan, and salt. Salt may also be sprinkled on any of the flavored bread sticks; simply sprinkle them with kosher salt just before baking.*

### LEMON-DILL STICKS
2 tablespoons grated lemon zest, finely chopped
2 tablespoons fresh dill, roughly chopped

### FENNEL STICKS
¼ cup whole fennel seeds, lightly toasted
(see page 386)

### CILANTRO, CHILI, AND LIME STICKS
¼ cup finely chopped fresh cilantro
1 tablespoon chili powder
2 tablespoons grated lime zest, finely chopped

### PAPRIKA-CAYENNE STICKS
2 teaspoons paprika
1 teaspoon cayenne pepper

### CURRY, TURMERIC, AND BLACK ONION SEED STICKS
2 teaspoons curry powder
½ teaspoon ground turmeric powder

Before rolling out the dough in step 4, sprinkle the work surface with ½ cup black onion seeds (see Sources, page 487).

### SAFFRON STICKS
In step 1, add ¼ teaspoon saffron threads to the yeast and ¼ cup warm water and let sit for the 5 minutes as the yeast proofs (the saffron threads will not dissolve completely).

## PROSCIUTTO-WRAPPED BREAD STICKS WITH CAVAILLON MELON AND FIGS
**SERVES 12** | photograph on page 149

24 paper-thin slices Prosciutto di Parma (about 10 ounces)
24 Yeast Bread Sticks (page 366)
2 Cavaillon or cantaloupe melons
12 large fresh Black Oregon figs

**1** Wrap 1 slice of prosciutto around each bread stick and set aside.

**2** Using a very sharp knife, cut away the stem end of the melons 2 inches from the top. Using a melon baller, scoop out the flesh of the melon and set aside.

**3** Arrange the bread sticks, melon, and figs on a platter and serve.

## CLASSIC QUICK STICKS

**MAKES 3 DOZEN** | photograph on page 144

*These quick sticks, along with all of the variations that fol-
low, may be made straight or may be twisted at either end. If
you prefer your sticks less salty, don't sprinkle them with salt
before baking.*

2 cups all-purpose flour
½ teaspoon kosher salt
1½ teaspoons baking powder
3 tablespoons solid vegetable shortening
2 tablespoons olive oil (optional)
½ cup sea salt or kosher salt (optional)

**1** Heat the oven to 350°F. In the bowl of a food
processor, pulse the flour, the salt, and the baking
powder to combine. Add the shortening and pulse
until the mixture resembles coarse meal. With the
machine running, gradually add between ½ and ¾
cup ice water until the dough comes together,
about 1 minute.

**2** Transfer the dough to a lightly floured surface.
Form the dough into a smooth rectangle, about
4 × 6 inches, with your fingers. Then roll out the
dough into an 8 × 10-inch sheet, ¼ inch thick. Cut
the dough lengthwise into ¼-inch-wide strips.

**3** Using your hands, gently roll each strip back
and forth into 16-inch-long sticks. For the twisted
version, grab each end of the dough strip with
your fingers and carefully stretch and twist the
strip in opposite directions. Arrange the sticks on
2 baking sheets, side by side but not touching. If
salting, brush each stick lightly with olive oil and
sprinkle with salt. Press the ends onto the baking
sheet to keep the sticks straight while they cook.
Bake until firm and cooked through, 14 to 18 minutes. Transfer the sticks to a wire rack to cool. Store
in an airtight container at room temperature for
2 to 3 days.

## CURRY-TURMERIC QUICK STICKS

1 teaspoon curry powder
½ teaspoon ground turmeric
½ cup black onion seeds

Pulse the curry and turmeric with the flour,
salt, and baking powder in step 1. Add ½ cup plus
1 tablespoon water for the liquid in the same step.
Before rolling out the dough in step 4, sprinkle the
work surface with the black onion seeds.

## CUMIN QUICK STICKS

2 teaspoons ground cumin

Pulse the cumin with the flour, salt, and baking
powder in step 1. Add ½ cup plus 1 tablespoon of
water for the liquid in the same step.

## CUMIN-PARMESAN QUICK STICKS

2 teaspoons ground cumin
½ cup finely grated Parmesan cheese

Pulse the cumin with the flour, salt, and baking
powder in step 1. Add ½ cup plus 1 tablespoon
water for the liquid in the same step. In step 3,
sprinkle the sticks with the Parmesan just after
brushing them with olive oil.

## VEGETABLE QUICK STICKS

**MAKES 3 DOZEN** | photograph on page 148

Flavored quick sticks are made by the simple addition of fresh vegetable juice to the Classic Quick Sticks recipe (left). They make a stunning presentation when arranged by color. The vegetable juices that I use to flavor and color the sticks can be purchased at juice bars or in health food stores, or made using an electric juice extractor. To make any of the flavored quick sticks, simply add the juice and the listed amount of water in place of the ½ to ¾ cup of water in step 1 of Classic Quick Sticks and proceed with the recipe. Each recipe makes about 3 dozen sticks.

### BEET QUICK STICKS

2 tablespoons beet juice, from 1 small beet

Combine the beet juice with ½ cup cold water.

### CARROT QUICK STICKS

¼ cup carrot juice, from 5 ounces (about 3) carrots

Combine the carrot juice with ¼ cup cold water.

### PARSLEY QUICK STICKS

½ cup parsley juice, unstrained, from 14 ounces of flat-leaf parsley

Strain the parsley juice through a fine mesh sieve. The resulting liquid should equal ¼ cup. Combine the ¼ cup parsley juice with ¼ cup plus 1 tablespoon water.

### TOMATO QUICK STICKS

1½ tablespoons tomato paste

Dissolve the paste in ½ cup plus 2 tablespoons water.

## PARMESAN PUFF PASTRY STRAWS

**MAKES ABOUT 3½ DOZEN** | photograph on page 144

The saltiness of Parmesan cheeses varies from wheel to wheel, so be sure to taste the cheese before adding it to the mixture. If it is salty, reduce the amount of added salt to 1 teaspoon.

1 recipe Puff Pastry (page 240), chilled
All-purpose flour for dusting
4 tablespoons unsalted butter, melted
5 ounces Parmesan cheese, grated on the small holes of a box grater to yield 1¼ cups
2 teaspoons kosher salt
1 large egg, lightly beaten

**1** Preheat the oven to 475°F. with the rack in the center. Place the chilled puff pastry on a lightly floured surface. Roll out the dough until it is about ⅛ inch thick, making a 24 × 26-inch piece. Use a sharp knife to trim the edges of the dough; this will help make the straws uniform as they cook. Brush the dough lightly with the melted butter. Sprinkle the dough with ¾ cup of the Parmesan and 1 teaspoon of the salt.

**2** With the short side of the dough facing you, fold the dough in half, bringing the top edge down toward you. Brush the surface of the dough with the egg. Sprinkle with the remaining 1 teaspoon salt and ½ cup Parmesan. Using a very sharp knife, cut the dough vertically into ½-inch-wide strips. Transfer 6 of the strips to a baking sheet, spacing them evenly apart. Grab each end of a dough strip with your fingers, and carefully stretch and twist the strip in opposite directions. Continue with the remaining strips of dough. (Unbaked dough should be stored in the refrigerator to stay cool. The straws may be twisted, covered with plastic wrap, and transferred on the baking sheets to the refrigerator before baking.)

CONTINUED ON FOLLOWING PAGE

**3** Bake until golden brown, 10 to 12 minutes. Remove and let the straws cool on the baking sheet for 5 minutes to firm up. Using both hands, transfer the sticks to a wire rack or serving platter.

## FLAVORED PARMESAN PUFF PASTRY STRAWS

**MAKES ABOUT 3½ DOZEN** | photographs on pages 144 and 147

*Poppy seeds, parsley, and red pepper flakes can be added to the Parmesan Puff Pastry Straws recipe (page 369) to add color, texture, and flavor variations.*

### PARMESAN-POPPY PUFF PASTRY STRAWS

1 tablespoon plus 1 teaspoon poppy seeds

Add 1 tablespoon of the poppy seeds when sprinkling on the Parmesan and salt in step 1. Sprinkle the remaining 1 teaspoon of poppy seeds onto the straws before baking.

### PARMESAN-PARSLEY PUFF PASTRY STRAWS

¾ cup finely chopped fresh flat-leaf parsley

Add ½ cup of the parsley when sprinkling on the Parmesan and salt in step 1. Sprinkle the remaining ¼ cup parsley onto the sticks before baking.

### PARMESAN-PEPPER PUFF PASTRY STRAWS

1 tablespoon plus 2 teaspoons red pepper flakes

Add 1 tablespoon of the red pepper flakes when sprinkling on the Parmesan and salt in step 1. Sprinkle the remaining 2 teaspoons of red pepper flakes onto the straws before baking.

## PRETZEL BITES

**MAKES 21 DOZEN** | photograph on page 143

*Don't let the quantity this recipe makes fool you into thinking there will be any of these addictive bites left for later. Season the pretzels as you like, using the amounts listed below as a guide. When grinding toasted seeds, do not overprocess them; they should remain coarse. Pretzel salt (see Sources, page 487) will not dissolve during baking, which will result in very traditional-looking pretzels, but kosher, sea, or coarse salt are fine substitutes.*

1 tablespoon sugar
1 ¼-ounce package active dry yeast
    (2 teaspoons)
5½ to 6 cups all-purpose flour
1 tablespoon kosher salt
2 teaspoons canola oil
1 teaspoon whole fennel seeds
1 teaspoon whole cumin seeds
1 teaspoon whole anise seeds
2 tablespoons baking soda
1 large egg beaten with 1 tablespoon of water,
    for the egg wash
2 tablespoons pretzel salt, or coarse or kosher
    salt, for sprinkling
1 tablespoon poppy seeds
1 tablespoon sesame seeds
2 tablespoons grated Parmesan cheese

**1** Pour 2 cups of hot water into the bowl of an electric mixer fitted with a dough hook. Add the sugar and stir to dissolve. When the water temperature on an instant-read thermometer registers 110°F., sprinkle the yeast evenly over the water. Let it sit for 5 minutes, until the mixture is foamy and creamy.

**2** With the mixer on low speed, beat in 1 cup of the flour until just combined. Beat in the kosher salt and slowly add 4 more cups of the flour just until combined. Beat on medium-low until the dough is pulling away from the sides of the bowl, about 1½ minutes. Add ½ cup more flour and beat on low speed, kneading the dough, for 1 minute. If the dough is still very wet and sticky, add ½ cup more flour and knead until combined, about 30 seconds. Transfer the dough to a lightly floured board and knead about 10 times until smooth.

**3** Coat the bottom and sides of a large mixing bowl with ½ teaspoon of oil. Transfer the dough to the bowl, turning the dough to coat with oil. Cover the bowl with a towel and leave in a warm place until the dough has doubled, 1 to 1½ hours.

**4** In a small bowl, combine the fennel seeds, cumin seeds, and anise seeds. Toast and grind (see page 386). Set aside.

**5** Preheat the oven to 450°F. Lightly oil 2 baking sheets with the remaining oil and set aside. Punch down the dough to remove any bubbles. Transfer to a lightly floured board. Knead once or twice. Divide the dough into 16 pieces (about 2½ ounces each). Cover the dough lightly with plastic wrap.

**6** Using the tips of your fingers, roll one piece at a time into an 18-inch-long strip, about ½ inch wide. Cut each strip into ¾-inch-long pieces. Transfer the pieces to the baking sheets. Cover with a damp kitchen towel as you work.

**7** Fill a large shallow pot with 2 inches of water and bring to a boil over high heat. Add the baking soda. Reduce the heat to a simmer. Using your hands or a large slotted spoon, transfer about 15 bites into the water. Poach for 1 minute, using the spoon to prevent the bites from sticking together. Use the slotted spoon to transfer the bites to a clean, dry baking sheet. Continue with the remaining bites. Arrange the bites evenly on the 2 oiled baking sheets.

**8** Working in batches of about 50, brush each bite with egg wash and sprinkle with coarse salt. Sprinkle each batch with a different flavoring: the poppy seeds, sesame seeds, Parmesan, and the spice mixture. Bake until golden brown, 12 to 15 minutes, rotating the baking sheets once for even browning. Transfer the bites to wire racks to cool slightly. Serve warm. Pretzel Bites are best when eaten the day they are made.

## BLUE CHEESE POPOVERS

**MAKES 4 DOZEN** | photograph on page 129

*Because this batter must be cold before pouring into the muffin tins, I usually make it 1 day in advance. Unlike traditional popover recipes, this simple version requires no hot pans or hot oil. Though the rise and fall of these mini popovers is less dramatic than that of the standard-size popover, the low profile is perfect for an hors d'oeuvre. Be sure to use mini muffin tins with 1½-inch-diameter openings across the top.*

2 large eggs
1 cup milk
2 tablespoons unsalted butter, melted, plus more
    for tins
1 cup all-purpose flour
½ teaspoon kosher salt
⅛ teaspoon freshly ground black pepper
1¼ ounces blue cheese, crumbled
1 tablespoon roughly chopped fresh thyme

**1** In a large bowl, whisk together the eggs, milk, melted butter, flour, salt, and pepper. Whisk until all of the lumps have disappeared. Whisk in the cheese and the thyme. Transfer the batter to an airtight container. The batter must be chilled; refrigerate for at least 2 hours or up to 1 day.

**2** Preheat the oven to 425°F. Generously butter the mini muffin tins. Fill each cup to the top with the chilled batter. Bake the popovers until golden and puffed, 15 to 18 minutes. Repeat until all the batter is used. Serve warm.

The sweet versions of biscotti—the crisp, twice-baked Italian cookies traditionally dipped in dessert wine or coffee—are most familiar, but the dough is very accepting of savory flavorings that are ideal for cocktail snacks. Biscotti are also perfect make-ahead party food. Once the dough has been formed into logs, it can be double-wrapped in plastic wrap and frozen for up to 1 month. To thaw, return the log to room temperature before proceeding with the recipe. Once baked, the biscotti will keep in an airtight container at room temperature for up to 1 week.

## BROWNED-BUTTER, LEMON, AND CAPER BISCOTTI

**MAKES 4 DOZEN** | photograph on page 158

*When butter is browned, it takes on a subtle nutty flavor, perfect in combination with tart lemon.*

8 tablespoons (1 stick) unsalted butter, cut into 8 pieces
2½ cups all-purpose flour
¼ teaspoon freshly ground black pepper
1½ teaspoons baking powder
2½ teaspoons kosher salt
2 large eggs
⅓ cup milk
3 tablespoons plus 1 teaspoon olive oil
¼ cup capers, drained, roughly chopped
Zest of 1 lemon
¼ cup finely chopped fresh flat-leaf parsley
1 large egg lightly beaten with 1 tablespoon water and a pinch of salt, for an egg wash

1 Place the butter in a small saucepan over medium heat. Cook the butter until it is dark brown and has a nutty aroma, 5 to 7 minutes, but do not allow it to burn. Set aside.

2 Place the flour, pepper, baking powder, and salt in the bowl of an electric mixer fitted with the paddle attachment. Combine on low speed. Slowly add the melted butter and combine until the mixture resembles coarse meal, about 1 minute.

3 In a small bowl, whisk together the eggs, milk, and 3 tablespoons of the olive oil. Gradually pour the milk mixture into the dough and mix until just combined. Add the capers, lemon zest, and parsley, and mix to combine. Turn the dough out onto a lightly floured surface.

4 Preheat the oven to 350°F. Grease a baking sheet with the remaining olive oil and set aside. Divide the dough into 4 equal parts. Roll each piece into a log measuring 1½ inches thick and about 7 inches long. Transfer the logs to the prepared baking sheet, cover with plastic wrap, and refrigerate until chilled, about 30 minutes.

5 Brush each log with the egg wash. Bake until the logs are light brown and feel firm to the touch, 30 to 40 minutes. Transfer the logs to a wire rack to cool, about 30 minutes. Reduce the oven to 250°F.

6 Using a serrated knife, slice the logs crosswise on a long diagonal into ¼-inch-thick pieces that are 3 to 4 inches long. Arrange the slices cut-side down on a wire rack set over a baking sheet and bake, turning the biscotti halfway through cooking time for even browning, until crisp, about 40 minutes. Cool completely and store in an airtight container at room temperature for up to 1 week.

## ORANGE, PISTACHIO, AND BLACK OLIVE BISCOTTI

**MAKES 4 DOZEN** | photograph on page 158

*Once the dough is made and chilled, the steps in the biscotti recipe are the same as for Browned-Butter, Lemon, and Caper Biscotti (page 372).*

2½ cups all-purpose flour

¼ teaspoon freshly ground black pepper

2 teaspoons baking powder

¼ teaspoon kosher salt

8 tablespoons (1 stick) unsalted butter, chilled, cut into 8 pieces

2 tablespoons plus 1 teaspoon olive oil

2 large eggs

½ cup milk

Zest of 1 orange

1 cup (8 ounces) shelled pistachio nuts

1 cup (6 ounces) oil-cured black olives, pitted and finely chopped

1 large egg lightly beaten with 1 tablespoon water and a pinch of salt, for an egg wash

**1** Place the flour, pepper, baking powder, and salt in the bowl of an electric mixer fitted with a paddle attachment. Combine on low speed. Add the butter and beat until the mixture resembles coarse meal.

**2** In a small bowl, whisk together the 2 table-spoons of the olive oil, the eggs, and milk. Gradually pour the milk mixture into the dough and mix until just combined. Add the orange zest, pistachios, and olives, and mix to combine. Turn the dough out onto a lightly floured surface.

**3** Proceed with step 4 of the recipe for Browned-Butter, Lemon, and Caper Biscotti (page 372).

## FENNEL AND GOLDEN RAISIN BISCOTTI

**MAKES 4 DOZEN** | photograph on page 158

*Since fresh spices and seeds have a rather short shelf life, buy them in small quantities if you can.*

2 tablespoons whole fennel seeds, toasted (see page 386)

2½ cups all-purpose flour

1 teaspoon baking powder

1 teaspoon kosher salt

¼ cup plus 2 tablespoons semolina

1 cup (5 ounces) freshly grated Parmesan cheese

12 tablespoons (1½ sticks) unsalted butter, chilled, cut into small pieces

2 large eggs

¼ cup milk

½ cup golden raisins, coarsely chopped

1 teaspoon olive oil

1 large egg lightly beaten with 1 tablespoon water and a pinch of salt, for an egg wash

**1** Finely grind 1 tablespoon of the fennel seed. Combine the ground and whole fennel seed, flour, baking powder, salt, and ¼ cup of the semolina in the bowl of an electric mixer fitted with the paddle attachment. Mix on low speed until combined. Add the Parmesan and mix in. Add the butter and beat until the mixture resembles coarse meal.

**2** In a small bowl, whisk together the eggs and milk. Gradually pour into the dough. Mix until just combined. Turn the dough out onto a lightly floured surface and knead in the raisins.

**3** Proceed as in step 4 of the recipe for Browned-Butter, Lemon, and Caper Biscotti (page 372). When the logs of dough are formed, sprinkle each with the remaining semolina and place on the baking sheet.

## CRUDITÉS

Classic crudités are traditionally composed of many different raw seasonal vegetables served with a dip. While a really good vegetable crudité served with Buttermilk Peppercorn Dip is one of my cocktail party standards, I've expanded the definition a bit to include a version that includes shrimp and crab claws (a good choice if this is the only seafood you are serving), another that "pickles" fresh vegetables in a delicious marinade, and finally, a crudité of a singular steamed vegetable, edamame, or fresh soybeans, seasoned with sea salt.

## VEGETABLE CRUDITÉS

**SERVES 12** | photograph on page 150

*Prepare the beans, celery, scallions, and carrots a day in advance; keep them stored with a damp paper towel in a sealed plastic bag.*

1 tablespoon kosher salt
4 ounces haricots verts or wax beans
1 bunch thin asparagus (about 16 ounces)
1 bunch celery (about 1 pound 10 ounces)
1 small jicama (about 5 ounces)
1 medium cucumber or 3 kirby cucumbers, peel on
2 bunches scallions
1 bunch carrots (about 12 ounces)
1 medium yellow squash (about 5 ounces)
1 medium zucchini (about 6½ ounces)
1 medium daikon (about 12 ounces)
12 cherry tomatoes
Buttermilk Peppercorn Dip (page 389)

**1** Prepare a large bowl of ice water and set aside. Bring a large pot of water to a boil and add the salt. Trim the beans and place in the boiling water. Blanch for 15 to 25 seconds until the color becomes bright green. Use a slotted spoon to transfer the beans to the ice water to cool. When cool, remove them from the ice water, pat dry with a paper towel, and set aside. Trim the woody ends from the asparagus and immerse in the boiling water. Blanch until bright green, about 30 seconds; transfer to the ice bath to cool. Remove them from the ice water, pat dry, and reserve.

**2** Separate the celery stalks and wash thoroughly. Using a vegetable peeler, peel away any tough, stringy fibers from the outside of each stalk. Trim the bottoms and tops off each stalk and set aside. Peel the jicama and cut into ¼-inch matchsticks, measuring 3 to 5 inches in length. Set aside. Wash the cucumbers very well and cut in half (if using regular cucumbers); cut the cucumber into spears, set aside. Trim the scallions to 9-inch lengths and set aside. Wash and peel the carrots and cut lengthwise into strips measuring ¼ inch in diameter. Set aside.

**3** Wash the squash and zucchini very well and slice ¹⁄₁₆ inch thick lengthwise, preferably on a mandoline. Peel the daikon and cut into ¹⁄₁₆-inch-thick slices lengthwise. Set aside all of the slices, covered with a damp towel, until serving time. Wash the cherry tomatoes and dry. Set aside.

**4** Place the beans, asparagus, celery, jicama, cucumbers, and carrots in serving glasses. Roll up the squash, zucchini, and daikon strips and place on the serving platter with the other vegetables. Place the tomatoes in a bowl or glass. Serve the crudités with the Buttermilk Peppercorn Dip.

The key to appealing crudités is simple: Buy impeccable seasonal produce and lots of it. My most successful crudité platters have been those with only a few carefully chosen vegetables—perfectly fresh—in generous quantities.

A French or Japanese mandoline (see Sources, page 486) is another key to creating interesting crudités; either style lets you slice vegetables super-thin, so you can present everything from yellow squash to jicama in imaginative ways.

Below are approximate amounts of each vegetable you will need to serve 12 to 48 people. If you can't find any one of these, be sure to make up for the quantity with a different vegetable.

|  | FOR 12 | FOR 24 | FOR 48 |
|---|---|---|---|
| Asparagus (1 bunch = 24 thin spears) | 1 bunch thin (1 lb.) | 2 bunches (2 lbs.) | 3 bunches (3 lbs.) |
| Carrots (with greens attached) (1 bunch = 6–8 carrots) | 1 bunch (12 oz.) | 2 bunches (1½ lbs.) | 4 bunches (3 lbs.) |
| Cherry tomatoes (1 pt. = 15 oz. = 24 tomatoes) | 7½ oz. | 15 oz. | 30 oz. |
| Daikon | 1 medium (12 oz.) | 1 large (1½ lbs.) | 2 large (3 lbs.) |
| Jicama | 1 small (5 oz.) | 1 medium (9 oz.) | 2 medium or 1 large (1½ lbs.) |
| Kirby cucumbers or regular | 3 Kirby (1 reg.) | 6 Kirby (3 reg.) | 12 Kirby (6 reg.) |
| Scallions (6–8 per bunch) | 2 bunches (6 oz.) | 4 bunches (12 oz.) | 8 bunches (24 oz.) |
| Wax beans or haricots verts | 4 oz. | 8 oz. | 16 oz. |
| Yellow squash (1 squash = 24 slices) | 1 squash (5 oz.) | 2 squash (10 oz.) | 4 squash (1¼ lbs.) |
| Zucchini (1 zucchini = 28 slices) | 1 zucchini (6½ oz.) | 2 zucchini (13 oz.) | 3 zucchini (1¾ lbs.) |

Working with a pastry bag and different decorating tips might seem somewhat daunting at first, but with a basic understanding of the technique and a little practice, piping decorative garnishes will undoubtedly become a favorite part of making hors d'oeuvres. To start, always work with a very clean pastry bag and pastry tips. A coupler, a two-piece insert for the tip of the pastry bag, is essential for piping, because it allows you to change decorating tips in the middle of piping. The coupler is much like a nut and bolt: The coupler tube is shaped like a conical bolt and the coupler nut is fitted to secure the pastry tip tightly to the pastry bag. To assemble the bag for piping, slide the coupler tube into the pastry bag and through the small opening. Position the decorating tip of your choice over the end of the coupler tube outside the bag. Secure the decorating tip by screwing on the fitted coupler nut. To change decorating tips, simply unscrew the nut and switch tips, then screw the nut back on.

To fill the pastry bag, cuff the rim of the top of the bag and, using a spatula, fill the bag halfway. Alternatively, place the bag, tip down, into a tall glass, fold the bag down over the rim of the glass, and scoop the filling into it. Never fill the bag more than halfway; any fuller and the bag becomes unwieldy. Once the bag is filled, unfold the cuff and gather the top edges of the bag together and twist with one hand. Use your other hand to push the filling down toward the tip. Continue to twist as you pipe to maintain pressure against the filling.

The most effective way to pipe is to hold the bag in your right hand (do the opposite if you are left-handed) with your thumb positioned at the top of the bag. Position your left hand slightly lower on the bag. Use your right hand to press out the filling and use your left hand for guidance.

The tips used on the Simple Piped Crudités (right) include:

Straight Tip #45
Open Leaf #352
Closed Star #30
Plain Round #2
Plain Round #4

## SIMPLE PIPED CRUDITÉS

**SERVES 12** | photograph on page 153

*Use a channel knife to make flower-shaped vegetables. It is available in most kitchenware stores (see Sources, page 486).*

1 bunch of celery
2 teaspoons kosher salt
1 dozen snow peas
3 medium radishes
1 seedless cucumber, peel on
1 medium daikon, peeled
18 baby carrots, peeled
3 heads endive
3 cups Flavored Cream Cheeses (right)
Chives and mint leaves, for garnish

**1** Separate the celery stalks and wash thoroughly. Using a vegetable peeler, peel away any tough, stringy fibers from the outside of each stalk. Cut each stalk into 4-inch-long pieces and set aside.

**2** Bring a large pot of water to a boil. Add the salt. Snip the tips off each snow pea and place into the boiling water. Blanch for 15 seconds. Drain and immediately rinse under cold water.

**3** Slice the radishes into ⅛-inch-thick rounds. Set aside. Working with a canelle knife, cut about 6 parallel evenly spaced grooves down the length of the cucumber. Slice the cucumber crosswise into ¼ inch thick rounds. Set aside. Using the canelle knife, slice about 8 parallel evenly spaced grooves down the length of the daikon. Slice into ¼-inch rounds and set aside.

**4** Slice the carrots in half lengthwise and set aside. Just before piping, separate the endive and trim the ends.

**5** Arrange the vegetables in single layers on large platters. Spoon the cream cheese into a pastry bag fitted with a pastry tip, or a freezer bag with the corner snipped off, and pipe the cream cheese onto the vegetables. Garnish with chives and mint leaves.

## FLAVORED CREAM CHEESES

**MAKES ABOUT 1 CUP EACH** | photograph on page 152

*Each combination below will make enough to pipe out cream cheese for about 28 of the largest crudités, such as the 4-inch-long celery strip, or 15 dozen of the smallest crudités, such as the cucumber slices. Combine the following ingredients in a medium bowl and mix until thoroughly incorporated. The cream cheeses will keep, tightly covered, in an airtight container in the refrigerator for 2 to 3 days.*

### DILL CREAM CHEESE

⅓ cup packed roughly chopped fresh dill
8 ounces cream cheese, at room temperature
½ teaspoon kosher salt

### CRÈME CHEESE

8 ounces cream cheese, at room temperature
2 ounces Homemade Crème Fraîche (page 394), or prepared

### WASABI CREAM CHEESE

8 ounces cream cheese, at room temperature
2 tablespoons wasabi paste

### BEET CREAM CHEESE

¼ cup beet juice, from 1 small beet or purchased
8 ounces cream cheese, at room temperature
½ teaspoon kosher salt

### CARROT-CARDAMOM CREAM CHEESE

¼ cup carrot juice, from 2 carrots or purchased
2 cardamom pods
8 ounces cream cheese, at room temperature
Kosher salt

Place the carrot juice and the cardamom in a small saucepan. Simmer for 10 minutes. Strain the juice and discard the cardamom. Let the juice cool. Add half of the carrot juice to the cream cheese and mix well. (Save the remaining juice for another use or use all of it if doubling the recipe.) Add salt to taste.

# SEAFOOD CRUDITÉS

**SERVES 12** | photograph on page 166

*I love to use chives and their edible lavender flowers as a colorful and delicious addition to my crudités. They have a mild onion flavor that makes them very versatile; they can also be used as a pretty garnish on a favorite dish or to dress up salads. Look for them in your local green market or super-market year-round. Buy the crab claws precooked at your seafood store.*

24 large shrimp (see page 340)

1 tablespoon plus 1 teaspoon kosher salt

24 cooked crab claws

4 ounces haricots verts, trimmed

24 thin green asparagus

24 white asparagus

24 sugar snap peas

24 fiddlehead ferns, washed and trimmed of
    papery particles

2 heads endive

1 head radicchio

1 medium fennel bulb, trimmed

2 large red bell peppers

2 large orange bell peppers

24 cherry tomatoes

24 baby carrots

24 ears baby corn, husks and silk removed

1 bunch flowering chives

1 bunch broccoli rabe flowers

1 bunch fresh flowering rosemary

1 lemon, sliced into 6 to 8 wedges

1 lime, sliced into 6 to 8 wedges

Chile-Lime Aïoli (page 397)

**1** Bring 2 cups of water to a boil in a medium saucepan. Add the shrimp and 1 tablespoon of the salt and cover. Let the shrimp cook until opaque, 1 to 3 minutes. Drain the shrimp and immediately place under cool running water to stop the cooking. Carefully peel and devein the shrimp, leaving the tail intact. The cooked shrimp may be refrigerated at this point in an airtight container for up to 4 to 5 hours.

**2** Using a mallet or a hammer, crack open the bottom part of each crab shell, leaving the black claw on. The shelled crab claws may be kept refrigerated in an airtight container for up to 4 to 5 hours.

**3** Prepare a large bowl of ice water and set aside. Bring a large pot of water to a boil and add the remaining 1 teaspoon salt. Add the haricots verts to the water and blanch for 15 seconds. Transfer to the ice water. When cool, pat dry with a paper towel and set aside. Trim the woody ends off the green asparagus and plunge into the boiling water. Blanch for 30 seconds, until bright green. Transfer to the ice bath to cool. Pat dry and reserve. Trim the woody ends off the white asparagus and plunge into the boiling water. Blanch for 30 seconds; transfer to the ice bath to cool. Pat dry and reserve. Blanch the sugar snap peas for 30 seconds; transfer to the ice bath. Pat dry and reserve. Steam the fiddleheads in 1 inch of the boiling water until tender, 4 to 6 minutes. Transfer to the ice bath to cool. Pat dry and reserve.

**4** When you are ready to assemble the crudités, separate the endive and radicchio leaves and trim the ends. Place on the serving platter. Slice the fennel into 1-inch wedges and place on the serving platter. Slice the bell peppers in half and carefully remove the seeds and ribs. Slice into 1-inch-thick pieces and add to the platter. Assemble all of the remaining ingredients, the shrimp and crab claws, and the blanched vegetables as you wish. Garnish with the flowering chives, broccoli rabe flowers, fresh flowering rosemary, lemons, and limes. Serve with the Chile-Lime Aïoli.

## VEGETABLES ESCABECHE

**SERVES 24 TO 48** | photograph on page 128

*Classic escabeche is poached or fried fish that is covered with a strong marinade and refrigerated for 1 day in order to flavor, almost pickle, the fish. I use this technique to marinate some of my favorite vegetables and for an alternative to traditional crudité. Marinate them in a pretty container for a dramatic presentation and serve on small plates. Fiddlehead ferns, available in early spring, and baby corn are optional. The vegetables can be refrigerated for up to 1 day.*

1 head cauliflower, washed and trimmed of
 leafy base
20 baby carrots, or 8 medium carrots
8 medium jalapeño peppers
2 medium red bell peppers
2 medium yellow bell peppers
2 medium green bell peppers
1 small fennel bulb, trimmed of leafy top and
 cored
4 celery stalks
4 ounces string beans, ends trimmed
1 large red onion, peeled and cut into ¼-inch
 slices
4 ounces fiddlehead ferns, washed and trimmed
 of papery skin (optional)
12 ears baby corn (about 3 inches long),
 shucked (optional)
6 cups white wine vinegar
1 tablespoon sugar
1 tablespoon kosher salt

**1** Trim the cauliflower into long florets and divide among 2 large mixing bowls. If using large carrots, cut into 4-inch batons and add to the bowls. If the carrots are very thick, first slice them lengthwise into quarters and then into batons. Slice the jalapeños in half lengthwise, leaving the seeds, ribs, and stems intact, and add to the bowls. Cut all of the bell peppers in half lengthwise and carefully

remove the seeds and stems. Brush away any stray seeds and slice the peppers into thick, hooked pieces, measuring about 1 inch in width. Combine with the other prepared vegetables. Slice the fennel into wedges measuring about 1 inch thick; add to the bowls. Slice the celery stalks in half lengthwise and into 4-inch sticks, combine with other vegetables. Add the string beans, onion, ferns, and corn to the bowls. You should have an even mix of vegetables in both bowls. Set aside.

**2** Combine the vinegar, sugar, salt, and 6 cups of water in a large saucepan and bring to a boil. Pour the hot vinegar mixture evenly into the 2 bowls and gently stir the vegetables. Cover with plastic wrap and let marinate for 2 hours, tossing every 30 minutes. Serve the vegetables at room temperature, or refrigerate, tightly covered, for up to 2 days and return to room temperature before serving.

## EDAMAME WITH SEA SALT

**SERVES 16** | photograph on page 165

*Edamame is the Japanese name for fresh (as opposed to dried) soybeans. They are available in Asian markets—fresh, from late spring to late fall, and frozen year-round. I always cook edamame in briny sea salt, then sprinkle a bit more on them just before serving. Unlike the fast-dissolving kosher salt, the denser granules of sea salt hold their shape on the warm beans to create a pretty presentation as well as excellent flavor.*

1 16-ounce bag edamame (fresh soybeans)
1 tablespoon sea salt

Bring a medium pot of water to a boil. Add the edamame and 1 teaspoon salt, return to a boil, and cook until the edamame are tender, 2 to 3 minutes. Drain well and transfer to a serving bowl. Sprinkle with the remaining salt, toss lightly, and serve.

An elegant and delicious hors d'oeuvre, caviar can be served simply on toast points or in an ensemble with blini, hard-boiled eggs, onions, and crème fraîche.

To put it most plainly, caviar is salted fish eggs, also known as fish roe. The most well-known caviar comes from the sturgeon that live in the Caspian Sea, which borders Iran and Russia. Russian caviar is processed with slightly more salt than Iranian and has a touch of borax added, which enhances the flavor and preserves the eggs longer. *Malossol* means "lightly salted" in Russian, and only roe in prime condition are prepared and labeled this way.

The three most prominent types of caviar are from beluga, osetra, and sevruga sturgeon. Beluga sturgeon, the rarest and largest of the three, produces the largest eggs, which are prized for their size, color, and delicate flavor. The color can vary from the highly regarded light gray to jet black. Osetra sturgeon has the widest variety of eggs. The young osetra produces large, dark golden eggs; as the fish ages, the eggs become a pale amber color and have a more subtle flavor. Sevruga tends to be the least expensive of the three caviars, primarily because it is the most common. The eggs, which range in color from gray to black, have the saltiest flavor of the three.

The term "caviar" is also used to describe the preserved eggs of other fish. Salmon caviar is a rich orange color and can be quite delicious. Golden caviar comes from whitefish; it is small and crunchy and is best used as a garnish. Pressed caviar is the thick, pastelike residue of eggs that were broken in processing. The flavor is very strong and is best suited to something mild like blini and sour cream.

When you are buying caviar, look for cans or jars that are vacuum-packed with a tight seal. Sealed caviar can be stored in the refrigerator for 2 to 3 months at about 37° F. When opened, caviar is good for only about 2 to 3 days. Lift the lid carefully when you open the can or jar; the fish eggs will be packed in and you won't want to lose a precious one. The eggs should have a healthy, shiny, slightly oily appearance and should be separate and firm. The aroma will be only that of the sea. Take the caviar out of the refrigerator about 30 minutes before serving; open the caviar when you are just about to serve it. Serve 1 to 2 ounces (3 to 4 teaspoons) of caviar per person, and keep it well chilled at all times.

There are a plethora of serving utensils for caviar, ranging from mother-of-pearl to wood. Steer clear of metal when serving caviar; the caviar will oxidize the moment it comes in contact with the metal, and its flavor will change.

As with any highly variable luxury product, it is best to buy caviar from only the most reputable places, whether they are local markets or mail-order sources (see Sources, page 487).

## BLINI WITH CAVIAR AND CRÈME FRAÎCHE

**SERVES 8** | photograph on page 162

Blini are the traditional Russian serving vehicle for sour cream, caviar, or smoked salmon. The small buckwheat pancakes are yeast-risen, which makes them nice and fluffy. If you like to pile your caviar on blini, be sure to have extra caviar on hand.

8 ounces Homemade Crème Fraîche (page 394)
    or prepared
2 ounces black caviar (see Note, left), or more
1 small white onion, finely diced
3 large hard-boiled eggs, whites and yolks
    separated and each passed through a sieve
1 recipe Buckwheat Blini (page 245)

Place the condiments in serving bowls. Keep the caviar well chilled. Serve the condiments with the warm blini.

## CAVIAR TOAST POINTS

**MAKES 2 DOZEN** | photograph on page 161

For larger parties, try using different types of caviar to make a colorful and enticing platter of canapés.

1 recipe Classic Toast Points (page 244)
2 tablespoons Homemade Crème Fraîche
    (page 394) or prepared
3½ ounces assorted caviar (see Note, left)

Spread each toast point with ¼ teaspoon of crème fraîche. Place ¾ teaspoon of caviar onto each toast point and gently spread to cover the entire toast. Serve immediately.

---

**NOTE** | Serving Caviar

Serving a variety of caviars not only looks beautiful and makes a stunning presentation, it is a good way to compare the flavors and avoid the cost of serving only the more expensive caviars. Lumpfish, salmon, whitefish, and trout roes are all excellent complements to beluga and osetra caviar.

The following hors d'oeuvres are simple to prepare, yet they are the among the most luxurious you can serve.

Spread Dill Cream Cheese (page 377) on Toasted Brioche Rounds (page 242) and spoon ½ teaspoon caviar over each.

Spoon ¼ to ½ teaspoon caviar into taco-shaped Asiago Frico (page 409)

Pipe Wasabi Cream Cheese (page 377) into Endive Petals (page 231) and spoon ¼ teaspoon caviar onto each

Pipe Crème Cheese (page 377) into Cherry Tomato Cups (page 229) and spoon ¼ teaspoon caviar on top of each

Spoon ¼ teaspoon caviar over raw oysters (page 354) and serve them with Classic Mignonette (page 396)

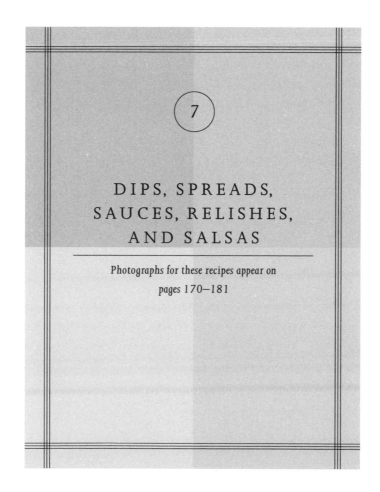

( 7 )

# DIPS, SPREADS, SAUCES, RELISHES, AND SALSAS

*Photographs for these recipes appear on pages 170–181*

THIS CHAPTER FEATURES RECIPES FOR THE SIMPLEST AND MOST ESSENTIAL KIND OF APPETIZER. AS THE TITLE IMPLIES, IT INCLUDES DISHES FOR DIPPING, SPREADING, TOPPING, DOLLOPING, AND ACCOMPANYING. CULTURES ALL OVER THE WORLD

have used various versions of dips, spreads, sauces, and relishes for centuries. Cooks love them because they are used in relatively small amounts, so they can contain intense flavors without becoming overpowering. They are also an important part of the culinary repertoire of everyone who enjoys giving parties, because most of them can be prepared at least a day or two ahead of time.

I find that many of my guests like to sample tried-and-true favorites as well as new creations, so I have included recipes for both here. The dips, for example, range from a traditional Hot Crab Dip to more adventurous Spicy Yellow Dhal Dip. My Black Bean Dip is a combination of both approaches—a classic recipe to which tangy goat cheese has been added for a new twist.

Salsas and relishes have become extremely popular in recent years, and with good reason: They are easy to make, provide a wonderful opportunity for combining interesting ingredients, and allow guests to experience flavor combinations of cuisines from around the world. To provide a good sampling, I have included recipes ranging from a classic Tropical Fruit Salsa to a rather exotic Adzuki Bean, Daikon, and Shiso Leaf Salsa to the deep, smoky-flavored Grilled Vegetable Salsa. I also love Mixed Tomato Salsa, in which I use tomatoes of various colors and sizes, and the Apple, Ginger, and Beet Salsa, which is a delightful combination of flavors, shapes, and colors.

One of my favorite recipes in this chapter is the Brandade with Garlic Confit; this French bistro classic comes from the chef at Balthazar restaurant in New York City. Once you try it, you will be singing the praises of salt cod, which is far more delicious than it sounds. You will also want to use the delectable and supremely easy garlic confit from this recipe in many different ways.

With their imaginative variations on a theme, the compound butters are all extremely versatile. They're also very easy to make, since the recipes require only that butter be mixed with one or more flavoring ingredients. The compound butters are a quick way to add a layer of flavor to tea sandwiches, canapés, and crostini, and since they can be made two to three days ahead and kept in the refrigerator, they are great for last-minute hors d'oeuvre preparations. I have included six recipes for them here, but you can use your imagination to create your own flavored butters.

A particularly easy and enjoyable way to begin a get-together is with a platter of sensational briny oysters served raw on the half shell. To make it even more festive, I like to set out three or four oyster sauces, each in a separate bowl, so my guests can enjoy a variety of tastes with their chilled shellfish. Again, I like to mix the traditional with the new, so I offer Classic Mignonette as well as Japanese-inspired Sake-Lime Sauce, piquant Hot Sesame and Chili Sauce, and bracing Lemon-Tabasco Sauce.

## HOT CRAB DIP

**MAKES 3½ CUPS** | photograph on page 179

*A longtime party favorite, this dip contains a number of assertive seasonings that balance the richness of the cheeses and the crab.*

3 tablespoons unsalted butter

2 medium shallots, minced

¼ teaspoon cayenne pepper

¾ teaspoon Old Bay seasoning

1½ teaspoons dry mustard

¾ cup half-and-half

8 ounces cream cheese, cut into small pieces

4 ounces sharp white Cheddar cheese, grated on the large holes of a box grater to yield 1¾ cups

3 tablespoons fresh lemon juice

2 teaspoons Worcestershire sauce

10 ounces lump crabmeat, picked over for cartilage

½ cup chopped fresh flat-leaf parsley

2 slices white bread, crusts removed, torn into ¼-inch pieces

½ teaspoon paprika

**1** Preheat the oven to 400°F. with the rack in the center. Melt 2 tablespoons of the butter in a medium saucepan over medium heat. Add the shallots and cook until soft, about 2 minutes. Add 1 tablespoon of water and simmer for 30 seconds. Stir in the cayenne, Old Bay, and dry mustard until well combined. Pour the half-and-half into the saucepan and bring to a simmer. Slowly whisk in the cream cheese, a few pieces at a time. When the cream cheese is fully incorporated, whisk in the Cheddar cheese a bit at a time. Stir the mixture for 2 minutes. Remove from the heat. Add the lemon juice and Worcestershire and stir to combine. Add the crabmeat and half of the parsley and stir.

**2** Transfer the mixture to a an ovenproof baking dish and sprinkle with the bread pieces. Dot the top of the bread pieces with the remaining tablespoon of butter. Sprinkle with the paprika. Bake for 18 to 22 minutes, until the bread pieces are golden and the dip is hot. Garnish with the remaining parsley and serve with Pita Cups (page 242), crudités (pages 374–378), or Classic Toast Points (page 244).

## SPICY YELLOW DHAL DIP

**MAKES 2 CUPS** | photograph on page 181

*Massur dhal is a variety of lentil distinguished by the fact that the tiny lentils are orange when raw, but turn yellow when cooked. They are a staple of Indian cooking and have a lovely, rich flavor. Both massur dhal and the curry leaves are available in Middle Eastern grocery stores and health food stores (see Sources, page 487).*

1 cup massur dhal lentils

¼ teaspoon ground turmeric

1 large shallot, chopped

¾ teaspoon kosher salt

2 tablespoons canola oil

2 garlic cloves, thinly sliced crosswise

2 small red chili peppers, fresh or dried

3 fresh curry leaves, optional

Indian-Spiced Pita Toasts (page 242)

**1** Place the lentils, turmeric, shallot, and 2¼ cups water in a saucepan. Cover and bring to a boil. Reduce the heat to low and simmer, partially covered, until the liquid is absorbed, about 20 minutes. Pass the dhal mixture through a food mill fitted with a medium disk into a medium bowl. Add the salt, stir well to combine, and keep warm. If using right away, transfer to a small serving bowl. (This may be made 1 day ahead up to this point and reheated just before serving.)

CONTINUED ON FOLLOWING PAGE

**2** Heat the canola oil in a small skillet over low heat. Add the garlic and the whole chili peppers and cook for 1 minute. Add the curry leaves and cook, stirring, until the garlic becomes golden but does not burn, 1 to 2 minutes. Spoon the garlic, chilies, and curry leaves onto the dhal with a slotted spoon, allowing some of the oil to drip onto it as well. Discard the remaining oil. Serve warm with Indian-Spiced Pita Toasts.

---

### TECHNIQUE | Toasting Seeds

Toasting whole seeds releases their flavor, adding a dimension to recipes that raw seeds do not. Although some recipes call for oil, I prefer to dry-toast the seeds, so no additional fat or oil is added to the recipe and the flavors of the toasted seeds remain clean and fresh.

To toast seeds, heat a heavy skillet, such as cast-iron, over medium-low heat. Add the seeds and shake the skillet gently to move the seeds around so that they toast evenly and do not burn. Toast the seeds until they are aromatic and barely take on color. Allow them to cool slightly and then transfer them to a spice grinder. Pulse the seeds to a fine powder, or as indicated in the recipe. In my kitchens, one coffee or spice grinder is always used exclusively to grind spices. To clean the spice grinder, simply insert a few pieces of fresh bread and grind. There is no need to wash the inside with water.

---

## BLACK BEAN DIP

**MAKES 1½ QUARTS** | photograph on page 180

*This recipe departs from the usual black bean dip by pairing the beans with tangy goat cheese. Don't substitute canned beans in this recipe; you will need the extra liquid from the cooked dried beans. If you want to add a little extra heat, stir a diced jalapeño pepper into the beans while they are cooling.*

2 cups dried black beans
1 medium onion, peel on, cut in half
1 head of garlic, cut in half crosswise, outer
  paper removed
1 tablespoon whole cumin seeds, toasted
  and ground (see page 386), to yield
  1 tablespoon
1 teaspoon cayenne pepper
Kosher salt and freshly ground black pepper
14 ounces fresh goat cheese
6 scallions, white and green parts, thinly sliced
  crosswise
¼ cup chopped fresh cilantro

**1** Place the beans in a deep medium saucepan and cover by 2 inches with water. Cover and bring to a boil over medium-high heat. Turn off the heat, leave covered, and let sit for 1 hour. Drain and rinse the beans. Return the beans to the pot. Fill the pot with cold water to cover the beans by 1½ inches. Add the onion, garlic, and cumin. Bring to a simmer over high heat. Reduce the heat to medium-low and simmer, uncovered, until the beans have begun to fall apart, about 1½ hours. Discard the onion and the garlic. Add the cayenne pepper and season with salt and pepper to taste. Transfer the beans and all their liquid to a bowl to cool.

**2** Heat the oven to 400° F. with the rack in the center. Place about a third of the black bean mixture into a deep baking or soufflé dish (about 1½ quarts) that can also be used for serving. Crumble a third of the goat cheese over the beans. Combine the scallions and the cilantro in a small bowl, reserving 2 tablespoons for garnish. Sprinkle a third of the scallion-cilantro mixture over the cheese. Repeat twice more to make 3 layers of beans and cheese, ending with a layer of the scallion-cilantro mix. (The dip can be prepared up to this point and refrigerated up to 1 hour ahead. If refrigerated, the dip will take a little longer to heat through.) Bake until the cheese begins to brown and the dip is hot, 20 to 25 minutes. If the top gets too dark, cover with foil and continue to cook. Garnish with reserved 2 tablespoons scallion-cilantro mix. Serve hot with corn chips.

## BRANDADE WITH GARLIC CONFIT

**MAKES 3½ CUPS** | photograph on page 171

*Brandade de morue is a favorite of mine on the menu at Balthazar, a Parisian-style brasserie in New York City. Balthazar's chef Riad Nasr shared with me his recipe of pounded salt cod (see Sources, page 487), puréed potatoes, and cream. Don't be put off by the unsightly look of salt cod; you will gain an appreciation for it after tasting this delicious dip. Serve this warm with Simple Crostini (page 243), store-bought flatbreads, or sourdough toast.*

1 pound salt cod, cut into large pieces

2 heads of garlic, halved crosswise, outer paper removed

2 bouquet garni each with: 2 bay leaves, 1 sprig fresh rosemary, 6 sprigs fresh thyme, and each tied together with kitchen twine

2 cups milk

½ cup olive oil

1 pound Yukon gold potatoes, peeled, quartered

Kosher salt

½ cup plus 2 tablespoons heavy cream, warmed

½ cup Garlic Confit (recipe follows)

**1** In a large bowl, soak the cod, covered with water, for at least 24 hours, changing the water every 2 to 3 hours. When ready to make the brandade, drain the cod.

**2** In a medium saucepan, place the cod with 1 head of the garlic, 1 bouquet garni, the milk, and 1 cup of water. Bring to a simmer over low heat. Simmer until the fish is flaky, 8 to 12 minutes. Discard the garlic and the bouquet garni. Using tongs, transfer the cod to a medium bowl. When cool enough to touch, flake apart. Set aside. Discard the milk.

**3** In a small saucepan, place the oil and the remaining garlic and bouquet garni. Over low heat, warm the oil for about 10 minutes. Strain the oil through a fine strainer. Discard the garlic and bouquet garni.

**4** Place the potatoes in a medium saucepan filled with water to cover. Add a generous pinch of salt. Cook the potatoes at a simmer over medium-low heat until fork-tender, 15 to 20 minutes. Drain.

**5** Preheat a serving bowl. Put the potatoes through a food mill fitted with a medium disk (or a ricer) while they are still warm. In the bowl of an electric mixer fitted with the paddle attachment, combine the potatoes and the reserved cod on low speed, just until incorporated. Gradually add the infused oil followed by the ½ cup of cream. Do not overmix or the potatoes will become pasty.

**6** Transfer the brandade to the preheated bowl. Garnish the warm brandade with the remaining 2 tablespoons warm cream and Garlic Confit. Serve warm with toasted croutons or bread. The brandade may be made 2 to 4 hours ahead. Reheat it in a 350° F. oven in a heatproof bowl, covered with foil, for 20 to 25 minutes. Stir halfway through warming time.

## GARLIC CONFIT

**MAKES ABOUT ½ CUP** | photograph on page 171

*Garlic confit is delicious spread on warm bread.*

½ cup olive oil
1 head of garlic, cloves separated and peeled

Place the oil and garlic cloves in a small saucepan over low heat. Cook until soft and golden brown, 45 to 50 minutes. Serve warm.

## CREOLE DIPPING SAUCE

**MAKES 1¾ CUPS** | photograph on page 124

*Make sure that you use whole canned tomatoes in this sauce; they have a much fuller flavor than the ground or puréed versions. Gumbo filé, a key ingredient in Creole cooking, is available in most grocery stores. Serve this sauce warm with Shrimp Gumbo Skewers (page 341) or any other New Orleans–style dish.*

3 tablespoons olive oil
1 small onion, cut into ¼-inch dice
2 garlic cloves, finely chopped
1 small green chili pepper, diced
1 15-ounce can whole tomatoes, coarsely
    chopped, juice reserved
1 sprig fresh thyme
2 bay leaves
½ teaspoon kosher salt
⅛ teaspoon freshly ground black pepper
1 teaspoon filé powder

**1** Heat the oil in a medium skillet over medium-low heat. Add the onion, garlic, and chili pepper and cook, covered, until translucent, 5 to 8 minutes. Add the tomatoes and their juice, thyme, bay leaves, salt, and pepper. Simmer until slightly thickened, 10 to 15 minutes. Stir in the filé and cook 5 minutes more. Remove the bay leaves and thyme sprig.

**2** Transfer half of the sauce to a blender and pulse just until broken down. Return sauce to the pan, mix well, and heat through to serve warm.

## TOASTED PEPITA DIP

**MAKES 2½ CUPS** | photograph on page 174

*Pepitas are edible pumpkin seeds that are very popular in Mexican cooking. When toasted, they develop a lovely, delicate flavor. Serve with sesame sticks, Simple Crostini (page 243), bread sticks (pages 366–370), or crudités (pages 374–378).*

2 tablespoons olive oil
2 garlic cloves, thinly sliced
2 cups (10 ounces) pepitas
1 15-ounce can whole, peeled tomatoes, juices
    squeezed out
1 teaspoon whole cumin seed, toasted and
    ground (see page 386)
1 bunch (4 ounces) scallions, white and green
    parts, roughly chopped
2 medium jalapeño peppers, seeds and ribs
    removed, roughly chopped
¼ teaspoon cayenne pepper
3 tablespoons fresh lime juice
Kosher salt and freshly ground black pepper

**1** Heat the olive oil in a medium skillet over medium heat. Add the garlic and cook until fragrant, about 30 seconds. Add the pepitas and cook, stirring frequently, until the seeds begin to pop and turn golden brown, 6 to 9 minutes. Transfer the mixture to a baking sheet to cool. Set aside 2 table-spoons of the seeds for a garnish.

**2** Place the pepitas and the garlic in the bowl of a food processor and process until fine, about 15 seconds, scraping down the sides of the processor as necessary. Using your hands, squeeze each tomato to release as much juice as possible. Discard the juice. Add the tomatoes, cumin, scallions, jala-peños, cayenne, and lime juice. Process the mixture until thoroughly combined and chunky (although the texture will also be creamy). Season with salt and pepper to taste. Serve immediately. The dip may be made a day ahead and kept in an airtight container in the refrigerator. Bring to room temperature before serving.

## WHITE BEAN AND MUSTARD GREENS DIP

**MAKES 1½ CUPS** | photograph on page 174

*This dip was inspired by the Spanish soup called Caldo Gallego. It can be made with other seasonal greens if mustard greens are not available, but choose slightly bitter ones such as dandelion greens, arugula, or broccoli rabe to keep the flavor profile similar. The cannellini bean purée may be made a day ahead and refrigerated. Wilt the greens up to 2 hours before serving, then add them to the prepared dip. Serve with Simple Crostini (page 243), crudités (pages 374–378), or Bread Sticks (pages 366–370).*

5 slices smoked bacon, cut into ¼-inch dice

2 garlic cloves, minced

¼ cup olive oil

2 ounces mustard greens, cleaned, roughly chopped

1 15-ounce can cannellini beans, drained with liquid reserved

1 tablespoon chopped fresh sage leaves

1 tablespoon fresh lemon juice

Kosher salt and freshly ground black pepper

Zest of 1 lemon

**1** In a medium skillet over medium heat, cook the bacon until it is brown and crispy. Using a slotted spoon, remove the bacon from the pan and set aside to drain on a paper towel. Pour off and discard all but 1 teaspoon of fat from the pan. Return the pan to the heat, add the garlic, and cook to soften, about 30 seconds. Add 1 tablespoon of the olive oil and the mustard greens, and reduce the heat to medium-low. Stirring occasionally, cook until the greens are tender, 15 to 30 seconds.

**2** Preheat a serving bowl. Place the beans, the sage, and the lemon juice in the bowl of a food processor. Process until combined. With the machine running, add the remaining oil through the feed tube. Season with salt and pepper to taste. If necessary thin out the bean purée with the reserved bean liquid. Stir in all but 1 tablespoon of the reserved mustard greens. Reserve 1 tablespoon of bacon for garnish. Fold in the remaining bacon and half the lemon zest. Transfer the mixture to the warm serving bowl and sprinkle with the remaining bacon, mustard greens, and lemon zest. The dip may be reheated in an ovenproof dish in a 275°F. oven until warm, 10 to 15 minutes. Serve warm.

## BUTTERMILK-PEPPERCORN DIP

**MAKES 1⅓ CUPS** | photograph on page 150

*Serve this refreshing dip with crudités (pages 374–378) or Homemade Potato Chips (page 247).*

1 cup sour cream

2 tablespoons buttermilk

1 teaspoon coarsely ground mixed peppercorns (black, pink, and green)

2 teaspoons minced chives

½ teaspoon finely chopped fresh thyme

1 large shallot, minced

½ teaspoon kosher salt

Place the ingredients in a medium bowl and stir well to combine. Serve immediately or store, covered, in the refrigerator, for up to 48 hours.

## ROASTED RED PEPPER AND EGGPLANT DIP

**MAKES 3 CUPS** | photograph on page 174

*I serve this Mediterranean-flavored dip with Simple Crostini (page 243).*

1 large (1¼ pounds) eggplant, cut in half
    lengthwise
2 large red bell peppers, halved, seeds and ribs
    removed
4 garlic cloves, peeled
2 tablespoons olive oil
¼ cup pine nuts, lightly toasted (see page 361)
1 teaspoon whole cumin seed, toasted and
    ground (see page 386)
¼ teaspoon red pepper flakes
¼ cup roughly chopped fresh cilantro
2 tablespoons fresh lemon juice
¼ cup roughly chopped fresh flat-leaf parsley,
    plus extra for garnish
Kosher salt and freshly ground black pepper

**1** Heat the oven to 475° F. Brush the eggplant, peppers, and garlic with the oil. Arrange them cut-side down on a baking sheet. Cook until the eggplant softens, the skin on the peppers separates, and the garlic is golden, 30 to 45 minutes.

**2** Transfer the eggplant to a wire rack to drain. Once cool enough to handle, remove the skins from the peppers. Use a large spoon to remove the seedy pulp from the eggplant. Discard the skins.

**3** Transfer the eggplant pulp, the peppers, and the garlic to the bowl of a food processor and pulse until combined. Add the pine nuts, cumin, pepper flakes, cilantro, lemon juice, and parsley. Process until smooth. Add salt and pepper to taste. Garnish the dip with some chopped parsley and serve. The dip can be refrigerated in an airtight container for up to 2 days. Return to room temperature before serving.

## BAGNA CAUDA

**MAKES 1 CUP** | photograph on page 112

*I discovered a delicious version of bagna cauda at Follonico, a lovely Tuscan restaurant in lower Manhattan. As soon as there is a chill in the air, Chef Alan Tardi offers this specialty of the Piedmont region of Italy on his menu. Presented fondue-style, the bagna cauda is served in special earthenware dishes set over votive-like candles to keep the bath hot. For dipping he chooses cool-weather vegetables, including roasted beets, blanched broccoli rabe, and endive, and crisp sticks of red and yellow bell pepper. In the Italian tradition, just before the last spoonfuls of bagna cauda are scooped away, a single quail egg is ceremoniously stirred into the remaining sauce and cooked until it is warmed, thickening the broth for a luxurious last few dips. Serve this with the Roasted Root Vegetable Skewers (page 338) or Vegetable Crudités (page 374).*

1 3-ounce jar flat anchovy fillets, rinsed and
    patted dry
6 medium garlic cloves, peeled
4 tablespoons unsalted butter, cut into small
    pieces
¼ cup extra-virgin olive oil
2 tablespoons fresh lemon juice

Place all of the ingredients in the bowl of a food processor and process until completely combined. Transfer the mixture to a small saucepan and bring to a simmer over medium heat. Transfer to a small bowl and serve immediately.

## COMPOUND BUTTERS

I love compound butters because they are easy to make, they are a wonderful way to add quick flavor to a whole range of dishes, and the flavor options are virtually limitless. In some instances, I find that a single flavoring ingredient, such as watercress or curry powder, dill or anchovies, works very well. At other times, I like to add combinations such as ginger, cilantro, and lime, or port and figs, or lemon and chives. Any of these butters can be made ahead and kept tightly wrapped in plastic wrap in the refrigerator for 2 to 3 days or for up to 1 month in the freezer.

## WATERCRESS BUTTER

**MAKES ONE 10-OUNCE 11 x 1-INCH LOG,
ENOUGH TO MAKE 6 DOZEN CANAPÉS OR TEA
SANDWICHES** | photograph on page 96

8 tablespoons (1 stick) unsalted butter, at room
    temperature
4 ounces (½ cup) fresh goat cheese, at room
    temperature
3 cups watercress leaves from 1 medium bunch
Kosher salt and freshly ground black pepper

**1** Place the butter, goat cheese, and watercress in the bowl of a food processor. Pulse until just combined, making sure the watercress is well chopped. Add salt and pepper to taste.

**2** Transfer the butter mixture to a sheet of parchment or wax paper. Roll into a 1-inch-wide log. Refrigerate until ready to use.

## SHALLOT-PARSLEY BUTTER

**MAKES ONE 5-OUNCE 7 x 1-INCH LOG,
ENOUGH TO MAKE 3 DOZEN CANAPÉS OR TEA
SANDWICHES** | photograph on page 96

*Be sure to chop the shallot very finely so that the compound butter is smooth.*

8 tablespoons (1 stick) plus ½ tablespoon
    unsalted butter, at room temperature
1 large shallot, minced to yield 3 tablespoons
1 tablespoon dry white wine
1 teaspoon kosher salt
1 tablespoon finely chopped fresh flat-leaf
    parsley

**1** Heat the ½ tablespoon butter over medium-low heat in a small skillet. Add the shallots and cook until soft, 1 to 2 minutes. Add the white wine and cook until the liquid has evaporated, about 30 seconds. Remove from the heat and stir in the salt. Cool completely.

**2** Place the remaining 8 tablespoons of the butter in a medium bowl. Add the shallot mixture and the parsley. Smash with the back of a fork or wooden spoon until well combined.

**3** Transfer the butter mixture to a sheet of parchment or wax paper. Roll into a 1-inch-wide log. Refrigerate until ready to use.

## GINGER-CILANTRO LIME BUTTER

**MAKES ONE 7-OUNCE 10 x 1½-INCH LOG,
ENOUGH TO MAKE 4 DOZEN CANAPÉS OR TEA
SANDWICHES** | photograph on page 96

8 tablespoons (1 stick) unsalted butter, at room
    temperature
2 ounces (¼ cup) cream cheese, at room
    temperature
1 tablespoon grated fresh ginger
1 tablespoon fresh lime juice
3 tablespoons chopped fresh cilantro
1 teaspoon kosher salt

**1** Place the butter, cream cheese, ginger, lime
juice, cilantro, and salt in the bowl of a food processor. Pulse just until the ingredients are combined, about 30 seconds. (Alternatively, the
ingredients may be placed in a medium bowl and
combined using the back of a fork or a wooden
spoon.)

**2** Transfer the butter mixture to a sheet of parchment or wax paper. Roll into a 1½-inch-wide log.
Refrigerate until ready to use.

## ANCHOVY BUTTER

**MAKES ONE 4-OUNCE 7 x 1-INCH LOG,
ENOUGH TO MAKE ABOUT 3 DOZEN CANAPÉS OR TEA
SANDWICHES** | photograph on page 96

5 medium flat anchovies, rinsed and patted dry
8 tablespoons (1 stick) unsalted butter, at room
    temperature

**1** Place the anchovies and the butter in the bowl
of a small food processor and blend until well
combined.

**2** Transfer the butter mixture to a sheet of parchment or wax paper. Roll into a 1-inch-wide log.
Refrigerate until ready to use.

## CURRY BUTTER

**MAKES ONE 4-OUNCE 7 x 1-INCH LOG,
ENOUGH TO MAKE 3 DOZEN CANAPÉS OR TEA
SANDWICHES** | photograph on page 96

*Curry butter tastes particularly good with chicken and
seafood.*

8 tablespoons (1 stick) unsalted butter, at room
    temperature
1¼ teaspoons curry powder
½ teaspoon kosher salt

**1** Place the butter, curry, and salt in a medium
bowl. Smash with the back of a fork or wooden
spoon until well combined.

**2** Transfer the butter mixture to a sheet of parchment or wax paper. Roll into a 1-inch-wide log.
Refrigerate until ready to use.

## ORANGE-TARRAGON BUTTER

**MAKES ONE 5-OUNCE 7 x 1-INCH LOG,
ENOUGH TO MAKE ABOUT 3 DOZEN CANAPÉS OR TEA
SANDWICHES** | photograph on page 96

8 tablespoons (1 stick) unsalted butter, at room
    temperature
1 tablespoon grated orange zest
1 tablespoon fresh orange juice
2 tablespoons finely chopped fresh tarragon
Kosher salt and freshly ground black pepper

**1** Place the butter, orange zest, orange juice, and
tarragon in a medium bowl and combine using the
back of a fork or a wooden spoon. Add salt and
pepper to taste.

**2** Transfer the butter mixture to a sheet of parchment or wax paper. Roll into a 1-inch-wide log.
Refrigerate until ready to use.

## DILL BUTTER

MAKES ONE 7-OUNCE 11 x 1-INCH LOG,
ENOUGH TO MAKE 4 DOZEN CANAPÉS OR TEA
SANDWICHES | photograph on page 96

8 tablespoons (1 stick) unsalted butter, at room
     temperature

2 ounces (¼ cup) cream cheese, at room
     temperature

1 teaspoon grated lemon zest

1 tablespoon fresh lemon juice

2 tablespoons chopped fresh flat-leaf parsley

2 tablespoons chopped fresh dill

½ teaspoon kosher salt

**1** Place the butter, cream cheese, lemon zest and
juice, parsley, dill, and salt in a medium bowl.
Smash with the back of a fork or wooden spoon
until well combined.

**2** Transfer the butter mixture to a sheet of parchment or wax paper. Roll into a 1-inch-wide log.
Refrigerate until ready to use.

## SUN-DRIED TOMATO AND ROSEMARY BUTTER

MAKES ONE 9-OUNCE 12 x 1-INCH LOG,
ENOUGH TO MAKE 6 DOZEN CANAPÉS OR TEA
SANDWICHES | photograph on page 96

*When they are softened, chop the sun-dried tomatoes fine so
that once they are mixed into the butter it will spread easily.*

10 sun-dried tomato halves

8 tablespoons (1 stick) unsalted butter, at room
     temperature

4 ounces (½ cup) fresh goat cheese, at room
     temperature

1 tablespoon finely chopped fresh rosemary

**1** Place the tomatoes in a medium bowl and
cover with very hot water. Allow to soak until the
tomatoes have softened, 5 to 10 minutes, then
drain. Finely chop the tomatoes and place them in
a medium bowl.

**2** Add the butter, goat cheese, and rosemary to
the sun-dried tomatoes. Use the back of a fork or
wooden spoon to combine all the ingredients.

**3** Transfer the butter mixture to a sheet of parchment or wax paper. Roll into a 1-inch-wide log.
Refrigerate until ready to use.

## PORT-FIG BUTTER

MAKES ONE 7-OUNCE 9 x 1-INCH LOG,
ENOUGH TO MAKE 4 DOZEN CANAPÉS OR TEA
SANDWICHES | photograph on page 96

4 large dried figs (3 to 4 ounces)

3 tablespoons port wine

8 tablespoons (1 stick) unsalted butter, at room
     temperature

½ teaspoon kosher salt

**1** Place the figs in the bowl of a food processor.
Pulse just until the figs are finely chopped, about
30 seconds. Transfer the figs to a small bowl. Set
aside.

**2** Heat the port in a small saucepan for about 1
minute to warm. Pour the port over the figs. Let
soak until the port is absorbed, 10 to 20 minutes.

**3** Place the butter in the bowl of the food processor. Add the figs and salt. Pulse just until well combined with no chunks of butter remaining.

**4** Transfer the butter mixture to a sheet of parchment or wax paper. Roll into a 1-inch-wide log.
Refrigerate until ready to use.

## LEMON-CHIVE BUTTER

**MAKES ONE 4½-OUNCE 7 x 1-INCH LOG,
ENOUGH TO MAKE 3 DOZEN CANAPÉS OR TEA
SANDWICHES** | photograph on page 96

8 tablespoons (1 stick) unsalted butter, at room
    temperature
1 tablespoon grated lemon zest
1 teaspoon fresh lemon juice
2½ tablespoons snipped fresh chives
½ teaspoon kosher salt

**1** Place the butter, lemon zest, lemon juice,
chives, and salt in a medium bowl and combine
with the back of a fork or wooden spoon.

**2** Transfer the butter mixture to a sheet of parchment or wax paper. Roll into a 1-inch-wide log.
Refrigerate until ready to use.


## HOMEMADE CRÈME FRAÎCHE

**MAKES 1 CUP** | photograph on page 162

*Crème fraîche is a thickened cream that has a slightly tart
flavor and very smooth texture. I prefer homemade, but prepared crème fraîche is sold in most supermarkets.*

1 teaspoon nonfat buttermilk, at room
    temperature, or 2 teaspoons sour cream, at
    room temperature
1 cup heavy cream, at room temperature

Pour the buttermilk and heavy cream into a clean
glass jar. It is important that the ingredients be at
room temperature. Place the lid on the jar and
shake the mixture to combine it well. Let the mixture stand at room temperature, uncovered, for
1 day, until it thickens. Place the lid back on the jar
and refrigerate for 8 hours before using. Crème
fraîche can be stored in an airtight container in the
refrigerator for up to 10 days.


## ARRABBIATA SAUCE

**MAKES 2 CUPS** | photograph on page 57

*Arrabbiata, literally translated, means "angry"; this classic
Italian spicy red sauce is named for its fierce heat. The perfect
accompaniment to Golden Ravioli (page 302), it is also delicious for dipping chunks of good-quality Italian bread or
crudités (pages 374–378). The sauce can be made ahead and
frozen in an airtight container. It also can be made more or
less fiery by adjusting the amount of red pepper.*

2 tablespoons olive oil
1 medium onion, finely chopped
2 garlic cloves, lightly crushed
1 28-ounce can whole, peeled Italian tomatoes
¾ teaspoon red pepper flakes, or to taste
1 tablespoon freshly grated Parmesan cheese
1½ teaspoons kosher salt
¼ teaspoon freshly ground black pepper

**1** Heat the olive oil in a large skillet over
medium-low heat. Add the onions and garlic and
cook, covered, stirring occasionally, until softened
and translucent, 6 to 8 minutes. Crush the tomatoes with your hands as you add them, with their
juice, to the skillet. Add the red pepper flakes.
Increase heat to medium and simmer, breaking up
the tomatoes more if needed with the back of a
spoon. Cook until the sauce has thickened, 25 to
30 minutes.

**2** Stir in the cheese, salt, and pepper. Serve immediately or cool to room temperature and freeze in
an airtight container for up to 3 weeks.

## PEANUT DIPPING SAUCE

**MAKES 1 CUP** | photograph on page 63

*Thin this sauce with warm water if it is too thick to lightly coat the Jicama and Green Papaya Summer Rolls (page 286).*

2 tablespoons peanut oil

1 small onion, finely chopped to yield ½ cup

2 garlic cloves, minced

1½ teaspoons chili paste

½ teaspoon curry powder

2 teaspoons kosher salt

¼ cup smooth peanut butter

¼ cup unsweetened coconut milk

2 teaspoons white wine vinegar

2 tablespoons packed dark brown sugar

¼ cup coarsely chopped roasted unsalted peanuts

¼ cup boiling water

**1** Heat the oil in a medium skillet over medium heat. Add the onions and garlic and cook until translucent, 3 to 5 minutes. Add the chili paste, curry powder, and salt. Stir to combine. Stir in the peanut butter, coconut milk, vinegar, brown sugar, and 2 tablespoons of warm water. Stir well and bring to a simmer. Let simmer for 1 to 2 minutes, stirring, until the sauce thickens and the peanut butter dissolves.

**2** Add 2 tablespoons of the peanuts to the sauce and then transfer it to a blender. Blend until smooth, adding 2 to 4 tablespoons of boiling water to help the sauce emulsify. Transfer it to a bowl. Let cool to room temperature. Before serving, garnish with the remaining peanuts. The sauce may be made 1 day ahead and refrigerated in an airtight container. (Press plastic wrap directly on top of the sauce to prevent a skin from forming.) Bring the sauce back to room temperature for 1 hour before serving.

## CITRUS DIPPING SAUCE

**MAKES 1 CUP** | photograph on page 114

*Kafir yogurt, which is a bit more tangy and much thicker than regular yogurt, is available in Middle Eastern grocery stores and gourmet food stores (see Sources, page 487). Serve it with the Moroccan Salmon Bites (page 339).*

2 tablespoons fresh lime juice

1 tablespoon fresh lemon juice

¼ cup fresh orange juice

Zest of 1 lime, 1 lemon, and 1 orange

½ cup kafir or sheep's-milk yogurt

½ cup plain yogurt

Kosher salt

**1** In a small saucepan over high heat, combine the lime, lemon, and orange juices with ½ teaspoon of the lime zest, ¼ teaspoon of the lemon zest, and ½ teaspoon of the orange zest. Boil to reduce until thick and syrupy, making about 1 tablespoon. Remove from the heat and let cool.

**2** In a medium bowl, combine the citrus syrup and the yogurts. Mix with a spoon until well combined. Season with salt to taste. Keep refrigerated until ready to use. Sprinkle the remaining zest over the top before serving.

## SCALLION-SOY DIPPING SAUCE

**MAKES ⅓ CUP** | photograph on page 111

*Use this easy-to-make dipping sauce for any of the dumplings or Asian hors d'oeuvres.*

¼ cup low-sodium soy sauce

1 scallion, white and green parts, thinly sliced crosswise to yield 2 tablespoons

Combine the soy sauce and scallions in a bowl and use as a dipping sauce.

## FOUR SAUCES FOR OYSTERS

### CLASSIC MIGNONETTE
MAKES ¾ CUP | photograph on page 157

*A must for serving with oysters.*

¼ cup plus 2 tablespoons red wine vinegar

2 tablespoons dry red wine

4 large shallots, minced to yield ½ cup

2 tablespoons fresh lemon juice

½ teaspoon kosher salt

½ teaspoon cracked black peppercorns, plus
    more to taste

Stir together all of the ingredients in a small
bowl. Let stand for at least 20 minutes to allow the
shallots to soften. Season with black peppercorns to
taste. Serve with oysters (see page 354).


### SAKE-LIME SAUCE
MAKES ⅔ CUP | photograph on page 157

3 tablespoons sake

¼ cup plus 2 tablespoons rice wine vinegar

Zest of 1 lime

2 tablespoons fresh lime juice

½ teaspoon kosher salt

3 scallions, white and pale green parts only, cut
    crosswise into ⅛-inch rings

¼ cup finely chopped fresh cilantro, plus 1 sprig
    for garnish

Combine the sake, vinegar, lime zest, lime juice,
and salt in a small bowl. Stir to combine. Garnish
with the scallions and cilantro. Serve with oysters
(see page 354).


### LEMON-TABASCO SAUCE
MAKES ¾ CUP | photograph on page 157

¼ cup dry white wine

¼ cup fresh lemon juice

2 teaspoons Tabasco sauce

3 large shallots, minced

½ teaspoon kosher salt

3 tablespoons extra-virgin olive oil

Lemon zest, for garnish

In a small bowl, stir together the wine, lemon
juice, Tabasco sauce, shallots, and salt. Slowly whisk
in the olive oil. Garnish with the lemon zest. Serve
with oysters (see page 354). The sauce can be prepared 1 day in advance, stored in an airtight container, and refrigerated.


### HOT SESAME AND CHILI SAUCE
MAKES 1 CUP | photograph on page 157

*This spicy sauce tastes delicious on chilled, raw oysters.*

¼ cup dark sesame oil

¼ cup hot chili oil

¼ cup sake

¼ cup fresh lime juice

2 small garlic cloves, minced

1½ teaspoons kosher salt

Dried chili pepper, for garnish

Stir together all of the ingredients except the
dried chili pepper in a small bowl. Garnish with
the dried chili pepper. Serve with oysters (see
page 354).

## FRESH COCKTAIL SAUCE

**MAKES 1½ CUPS** | photograph on page 178

*Horseradish root is so often purchased prepared that many people don't know how much better it is fresh. Use fresh and try this sauce with boiled shrimp—you will be amazed at the difference.*

   1 small horseradish root or ½ cup prepared
      horseradish
   1 cup ketchup
   1 tablespoon fresh lemon juice

**1** Peel the horseradish and grate on the fine holes of a box grater to yield ½ cup, plus more for garnish.

**2** Combine the ingredients in a medium bowl. Just before serving, sprinkle a little grated fresh horseradish over the top. The sauce can be refrigerated in an airtight container for up to 1 day.

## CHILI-LIME AÏOLI

**MAKES 1½ CUPS** | photograph on page 178

*Habanero chili peppers, also called Scotch Bonnets in the Caribbean, are the hottest chili peppers you can buy. They are available in yellow, orange, or red, depending on their state of ripeness. Be careful with them—they have a wonderful flavor but are approximately 60 times hotter than jalapeños.*

   1 garlic clove, minced
   1 teaspoon kosher salt
   1 large egg
   1 large egg yolk
   1 cup canola oil
   Zest of 1 lime
   2 tablespoons fresh lime juice
   2 orange or red habanero or other hot chili
      peppers, seeds and ribs removed, minced

Place the garlic and salt in the bowl of a food processor. Process until puréed. Add the egg and egg yolk and process, scraping down the sides of the bowl to combine the ingredients thoroughly. With the machine running, very slowly add the canola oil a few drops at a time at first, and then in a thin, steady stream; it will emulsify and thicken. Once the oil is added and the aïoli has formed, quickly pulse in the lime zest and the juice. Transfer to a bowl and stir in the peppers. The aïoli may be refrigerated in an airtight container for up to 1 day.

## CILANTRO-ALMOND RELISH

**MAKES 1 CUP** | photograph on page 178

*Toasting the almonds gives them a deeper flavor, but watch them carefully in the oven, as they tend to burn quickly.*

   ½ cup blanched almond slivers, plus 6 to 8 slices
      for garnish
   1 cup tightly packed fresh cilantro, plus 2 sprigs
      for garnish
   1 small garlic clove
   1 small jalapeño, seeds and ribs removed, minced
   ¼ cup fresh lime juice
   3 tablespoons sour cream
   3 tablespoons homemade (page 315) or
      prepared mayonnaise

**1** Heat the oven to 350° F. Place the almonds on a rimmed baking sheet and toast until golden, about 5 minutes. Transfer to a bowl or a plate and let cool.

**2** In the bowl of a food processor, combine the almonds, cilantro, garlic, and jalapeño. Process until a paste forms. Add the lime juice and process until just combined. Add the sour cream and mayonnaise and pulse until just combined. Transfer to a small bowl and garnish with the almond slices and cilantro sprigs. The relish may be refrigerated in an airtight container for up to 1 day.

## TARRAGON MUSTARD SAUCE

MAKES 1¼ CUPS | photograph on page 178

*Make this seafood dipping sauce 1 day before you plan to serve it to allow the flavors to blend.*

1 cup homemade (page 315) or prepared
    mayonnaise
2 tablespoons Dijon mustard
2 tablespoons whole-grain mustard
2 tablespoons finely chopped fresh tarragon, plus
    a few sprigs for garnish

Stir together the ingredients in a medium bowl. Garnish with tarragon sprigs. Serve with shrimp or Seafood Crudités (see page 378).

## TAHINI-YOGURT SAUCE

MAKES ⅔ CUP | photograph on page 61

*Serve this creamy, cool sauce with Lima Bean Falafel Fritters (page 299).*

1 garlic clove, finely chopped
2 tablespoons fresh lemon juice
¼ cup tahini
½ teaspoon kosher salt
1 tablespoon extra-virgin olive oil
⅓ cup plain yogurt
Toasted sesame seeds (see page 386), for garnish

In the bowl of a food processor, put the garlic, lemon juice, tahini, and salt. Process until combined. With the machine running, slowly add the olive oil through the feed tube. Add the yogurt and pulse until just combined and smooth. Garnish with sesame seeds. The yogurt sauce can be refrigerated in an airtight container for up to 1 day.

## APPLE-ONION COMPOTE

MAKES ¾ CUP | photograph on page 46

*Calvados is a dry apple brandy made in the Normandy region of France. It gives the compote a clean, sweet, apple flavor, but you may substitute apple cider brandy or water if Calvados is not available.*

1 small Granny Smith apple, peel on
1 tablespoon fresh lemon juice
1 tablespoon unsalted butter
½ tablespoon canola oil
1 small red onion, very thinly sliced
1 tablespoon plus 1 teaspoon sugar
1 tablespoon Calvados

**1** Dice the apple into ¼-inch pieces (about ½ cup) and toss with the lemon juice in a small bowl. Set aside.

**2** Heat the butter and the oil in a medium skillet over medium heat. Add the onions and cook, stirring, until the onions soften, about 4 minutes. Add the sugar and reduce the heat to medium-low. Let the onions cook, stirring occasionally, until they darken slightly (but do not let them brown) and become soft, about 10 minutes. Increase the heat to medium-high and add the apples. Cook for about 1 minute, stirring once. Add the Calvados, scraping up any browned bits from the bottom of the pan. Cook until most of the liquid has evaporated from the pan, about 30 seconds. Serve warm with the Celeriac Potato Pancakes. The compote may be refrigerated in an airtight container for up to 1 day. To reheat, combine the compote with 1 teaspoon of water in a small saucepan and cook over low heat until warm.

## GUACAMOLE

**MAKES 2½ CUPS** | photographs on pages 176–177

*My favorite guacamole was created by Josefina Howard and is served at her restaurant Rosa Mexicano in New York City. It is made fresh, tableside, right before your eyes in a Mexican lava stone molcajete, the traditional Mexican-style mortar. To remove the meat from the avocado, cut it in half, then, using a paring knife, cut just down to the peel in a crosshatch pattern on the separated halves, and slide the meat out with a spoon. Leave the seeds and ribs in the jalapeño if you like your guacamole hotter.*

1½ teaspoons kosher salt

1 small white onion, finely chopped

1 large jalapeño pepper, seeds and ribs removed if desired, minced

2 tablespoons finely chopped fresh cilantro, plus more to taste

3 ripe avocados

1 medium tomato, seeds removed, cut into ¼-inch dice

**1** In a medium bowl or molcajete, combine the salt, onion, jalapeño, and cilantro, using the back of a wooden spoon or a tejolote.

**2** Cupping the avocado with the palm of your hand, split it in half lengthwise and remove the seed. Slice it lengthwise into ⅛-inch strips, then crosswise to make ½-inch dice. Scoop out with a spoon. Add the avocado to the bowl and mix thoroughly into the paste. Add the tomatoes and cilantro, if desired, and serve with corn chips. The dip can be refrigerated in an airtight container, with a piece of plastic wrap laid directly on the guacamole to prevent it from discoloring, for up to 4 hours.

## MANGO CHUTNEY

**MAKES 1¾ CUPS** | photograph on page 43

*If you want the chutney to be milder, remove the seeds and ribs from the jalapeño.*

1 mango, peeled, pit removed (see page 273)

1 tablespoon olive oil

1 small shallot, finely diced

1 small red bell pepper, seeds and ribs removed, cut into ¼-inch dice to yield ½ cup

1 small jalapeño pepper, finely diced

2 tablespoons golden raisins

¼ teaspoon ground cinnamon

¼ cup fresh lime juice

2 teaspoons cider vinegar

1 tablespoon chopped fresh cilantro

**1** Place half of the mango into a blender or food processor and purée until smooth. Transfer the purée to a bowl. Dice the remaining mango into ¼-inch pieces and stir them into the mango purée. Set aside.

**2** Heat the oil in a large skillet over medium-low heat. Add the shallots and cook, covered, until translucent, about 4 minutes. Add the bell pepper, jalapeño, raisins, and cinnamon and cook until the peppers and jalapeño are tender, 5 to 8 minutes. Stir in the lime juice, vinegar, and reserved mango and cook until just heated through. Remove from the heat and cool. Stir in the cilantro. This may be stored in the refrigerator in an airtight container for up to 2 weeks.

## FRUIT AND VEGETABLE SALSAS

### TROPICAL FRUIT SALSA

**MAKES 5 CUPS** | photograph on page 172

*Add passion fruit or star fruit to this salsa for additional color and texture. If you use star fruit, be sure to cut off the very tips of the points, which are often hard.*

1 medium ripe papaya, cut into ½-inch dice
1 medium ripe mango, cut into ½-inch dice
    (see page 273)
½ pineapple, cut into ½-inch dice
1 medium jalapeño pepper, seeded and ribs
    removed, minced
1 small red onion, cut into ¼-inch dice
1 tablespoon chopped fresh cilantro
1 tablespoon grated lime zest
1 tablespoon fresh lime juice
Kosher salt to taste

In a medium bowl, combine all of the ingredients. Serve immediately. This may be made 1 hour ahead, without adding the papaya, and refrigerated. Add the papaya just before serving.

### APPLE, GINGER, AND BEET SALSA

**MAKES 4½ CUPS** | photograph on page 172

*This salsa has few ingredients, but every one brings a unique flavor to the whole. I particularly like the way the sweet beets play off the tart Granny Smiths and the aromatic ginger.*

2 medium beets, well washed
1 large Granny Smith apple, peel on
1 tablespoon fresh lemon juice
1 teaspoon minced fresh ginger
1 tablespoon red wine vinegar
1 tablespoon chopped fresh flat-leaf parsley
Kosher salt

**1** Place the beets in a small saucepan, cover with water by 2 inches, and bring to a simmer. Cook until the beets are fork-tender, 20 to 35 minutes, depending on the size of the beets. Drain and set aside until cool enough to handle. Peel. Chop into ¼-inch dice. Set aside.

**2** Chop the apple into ¼-inch dice. In a medium bowl, toss with the lemon juice to prevent browning. Add the reserved beets, the ginger, vinegar, and parsley to the apples and toss to combine. Season with salt to taste. This salsa may be made 3 to 4 hours ahead and kept, covered with plastic wrap, in the refrigerator.

### MIXED TOMATO SALSA

**MAKES 2¾ CUPS** | photograph on page 172

*Use the most colorful selection of tomatoes you can find for this classic pico de gallo.*

1 plum or regular tomato, cut into ¼-inch dice
12 yellow cherry tomatoes, cut into sixths
1 very small sweet onion, cut into ¼-inch dice
1 large jalapeño pepper, seeds and ribs removed,
    minced
1 serrano chili or ½ jalapeño pepper, seeds and
    ribs removed, minced
2 tablespoons chopped fresh cilantro
2 tablespoons fresh lime juice
½ teaspoon kosher salt, plus more to taste
¼ teaspoon freshly ground black pepper, plus
    more to taste

In a medium bowl, combine the tomatoes, onion, jalapeño, serrano, cilantro, lime juice, salt, and pepper. Adjust the seasoning with salt and pepper to taste. Cover with plastic wrap and let sit at room temperature for 1 hour to allow the flavors to blend.

## GRILLED VEGETABLE SALSA

**MAKES 1½ QUARTS** | photograph on page 172

*Roasting the bell peppers and grilling the corn and onion give this salsa a deep smoky flavor. Serve it with grilled or toasted bread or tortilla chips, or spooned over crostini.*

1 teaspoon olive oil
2 ears of fresh corn, husk and silk removed
1 small red onion, sliced into ½-inch-thick rings
4 plum tomatoes, cut lengthwise into quarters
    and oven-dried (page 257)
2 roasted large red bell peppers (page 266)
1 roasted large yellow bell pepper (page 266)
1 roasted large orange bell pepper (page 266)
3 ounces kalamata or oil-cured black olives,
    pitted, chopped to yield ½ cup
1 garlic clove, minced
¾ teaspoon ground cumin
2 tablespoons fresh lemon juice
Kosher salt and freshly ground black pepper
½ cup roughly chopped arugula or basil

**1** Prepare a grill or heat a lightly oiled grill pan over high heat. Place the corn and onions on the pan and grill, turning, until grill marks appear on all sides and the corn and onions are cooked through. The onions will take 5 to 8 minutes and the corn will need 15 to 20 minutes. Transfer to a plate to cool. When cool, cut the corn off the cob. Cut the onion rings into ½-inch pieces. Set aside.

**2** Chop the tomatoes into ½-inch pieces. Cut the peppers into ½-inch strips. Set aside.

**3** In a large bowl, combine the tomatoes with the peppers, corn, and onion. Stir in the olives, garlic, cumin, and lemon juice. Season with salt and pepper to taste. Allow the vegetables to marinate at room temperature for 1 hour. The salsa may be made up to this point and refrigerated in an airtight container for up to 6 hours. Return to room temperature and add the arugula just before serving.

## ADZUKI BEAN, DAIKON, AND SHISO LEAF SALSA

**MAKES 4½ CUPS** | photograph on page 172

*Adzuki beans are slightly sweet when cooked. Daikon is a large white radish, and shiso is an aromatic leaf of the mint and basil family. All of these ingredients are available in Japanese markets. This salsa is delicious on Crispy Wontons (page 248) and as a filling for Cucumber Cups (page 229).*

1 cup dried adzuki beans
1 medium onion, peel on, cut in half
1 bay leaf
1 2-inch piece of daikon or 5 medium radishes,
    cut into ¼-inch dice to yield ⅓ cup
4 scallions, white and light green parts, thinly
    sliced crosswise to yield ¼ cup
4 tomatillos, husks removed, cut into ¼-inch dice
2 plum tomatoes, cut into ¼-inch dice
3 fresh shiso leaves, cut into thin strips
1½ teaspoons canola oil
2½ teaspoons fresh lime juice
2½ teaspoons rice wine vinegar
½ teaspoon kosher salt
¼ teaspoon freshly ground black pepper

**1** Place the adzuki beans in a medium bowl and cover with water. Cover and let soak overnight. (Or, place the beans in a medium saucepan. Cover with water by 3 inches. Cover and bring to a boil. Turn off the heat and let sit, covered, for 1 hour.)

**2** Drain and rinse the beans. Place in a medium saucepan and cover with water by 1½ inches. Add the onion and bay leaf. Bring to a simmer. Simmer, uncovered, for 20 minutes, until the beans are tender but still hold their shape. Discard the onion and bay leaf. Drain and rinse the beans in cold water. Pat dry and transfer to a medium bowl. Add the remaining ingredients and stir. Let marinate for at least 1 hour, covered with plastic wrap, in the refrigerator. This may be made 4 to 6 hours ahead.

# FONDUE, FRICO, AND A SELECTION OF FINE CHEESES

Photographs for these recipes appear on
pages 182–201

CHEESE MAY BE THE SINGLE MOST POPULAR AND EFFORTLESS HORS D'OEUVRE OF ALL. WITH THE SPLENDID SELECTION OF ARTISANAL CHEESES AVAILABLE TO US TODAY, YOU CAN OFFER DIFFERENT AND INTERESTING VARIETIES EVERY TIME YOU ENTERTAIN.

There really are few things that are as easy to prepare yet at the same time as sophisticated and adventuresome as a cheese tray. When selecting cheeses to group together, one way to guarantee that your choices are compatible is to settle on a single defining characteristic, then choose all the cheeses from within that category. This makes for very interesting comparisons among the individual varieties, which guests will find entertaining as well as delicious.

Sometimes I like to pick cheeses that are all made from the same type of milk. Goat's-milk cheeses, for instance, have become very popular lately, so there is a wide selection available. Other times I select cheeses that are all produced in the same country. There are remarkable artisanal cheeses being made today not only in Spain, France, and Italy, but also in the United States. See the glossary at the end of this chapter for descriptions of some of these cheeses.

It is also a good idea to vary the flavor intensity of the cheeses when putting together a selection. Among goat cheeses, for example, I would include a mild cheese such as the Egg Farm Dairy Fresh Chèvre as well as a sharper-flavored version such as Valençay or Selles-sur-Cher.

When planning a cheese tray, I also consider the appearance of different varieties I might use, and try to vary colors and shapes. When choosing French cheeses, for example, I might include a snow-white cheese such as Bucheron, a orange-yellow cheese such as aged Mimolette, and a creamy cheese such as Morbier, with its fascinating interior dividing line made of vegetable ash. Besides color differences, cheeses come in a plethora of shapes, from fat wheels and flat disks to squares and rectangles.

The cheese trays pictured in this book are quite expansive and meant for a large group. Depending on the size of your gathering, two or three varieties, or even just one wheel of a very fine cheese arranged with nuts, fruits, olives, and some small slices of good crusty bread, make an impressive hors d'oeuvre presentation. When I use a single cheese in this way, I like all of the hors d'oeuvre components to be from the same general region. I might set out a Spanish cheese such as Queso de Murcia al Vino, for example, along with blood oranges, quince jelly, marinated Spanish olives, and almonds.

Melted cheese is another wonderful source for delicious hors d'oeuvres. Fortunately, the virtues of fondue have recently been rediscovered, and I like to serve both a classic three-cheese version and one permeated with the musky flavor of black truffles. My spicy Mexican take on fondue, Chile con Queso with Roasted Poblano Peppers, is always dipped to the bottom of the pot. Perhaps the most elegant hors d'oeuvre of all in this chapter is the quickest to prepare—Camembert baked right in its own little wooden box, then set out with French bread or a few sliced pears.

Among the most novel cheese hors d'oeuvres I make is frico, the lacy Italian cheese wafers that are nothing more than bite-size rounds of shredded cheese cooked just long enough to become crispy chips. Delicious plain or flavored with soft herbs and served on their own, frico can also be shaped to cradle delicate fillings and are sturdy enough to scoop light dips.

## CLASSIC SWISS FONDUE

**SERVES 10 TO 12** | photograph on page 186

*It is important to use 3 different varieties of Swiss cheese in this fondue to achieve the full range of flavor that makes it so delightful. Appenzeller or Comté may be substituted for any of the cheeses in this recipe, but do not omit the Kirsch, the cherry liqueur that gives this fondue its distinctive character.*

6 ounces Emmentaler cheese, grated on the large
    holes of a box grater to yield 2 cups
3 ounces Gruyère cheese, grated on the large
    holes of a box grater to yield 1 cup
4 ounces Vacherin Fribourgeois cheese, grated
    on the large holes of a box grater to yield
    1¼ cups
¼ cup plus 2 tablespoons all-purpose flour
3 cups dry white wine
2 garlic cloves, crushed
¼ cup Kirsch liqueur
Pinch of freshly grated nutmeg
Kosher salt and freshly ground black pepper

**1** In a medium bowl, toss the grated cheeses with the flour. Place the wine and the garlic in a medium saucepan over high heat. Bring the wine and the garlic to a boil, and reduce to a simmer and cook over low heat for 2 minutes.

**2** Gradually whisk in the cheese, 1 handful at a time, whisking constantly until the cheese melts before adding the next handful. After the last addition of cheese, add the Kirsch, the nutmeg, and the salt and pepper to taste.

**3** Transfer to a warm fondue pot. Serve immediately with chunks of fresh bread, apple wedges, or a variety of other fondue dippers (see photograph, page 187).

## FONTINA FONDUE WITH BLACK TRUFFLES

**SERVES 10 TO 12** | photograph on page 189

*This simple fondue is made special by the black truffle, which spreads its earthy aroma and rich flavor throughout the entire dish. Fresh bread chunks, button mushrooms, and artichoke hearts make delicious dippers for this fondue.*

1 pound fontina cheese, grated on the large holes
    of a box grater to yield 4½ cups
1 tablespoon cornstarch
1 cup Pinot Grigio or other dry white wine
4 tablespoons unsalted butter
1 ¼-ounce fresh black truffle
Kosher salt and freshly ground white pepper
White or black truffle oil (see page 308)
    (optional)

**1** In a medium bowl, toss the grated cheese with the cornstarch. Place the wine and the butter in a medium heavy-bottomed saucepan over medium heat. Bring the wine-butter mixture to a boil, and reduce the heat to a simmer.

**2** Gradually whisk in the cheese, 1 handful at a time, whisking constantly until the cheese melts before adding the next handful. Whisk over medium heat until well combined.

**3** Using a truffle shaver or mandoline, shave the truffle very thin and add to the saucepan, reserving 2 shavings for garnish. Using a spoon, fold the truffles into the mixture. Add salt and pepper to taste.

**4** Transfer to a warm fondue pot. Garnish with the reserved truffle, and drizzle with truffle oil to taste. Serve immediately with the desired fondue dippers (see photograph, page 187).

It was a cliché of modern American life that every bride and groom received a fondue set as a wedding gift, put it away without using it, then eventually passed it on to another couple for their wedding. Fortunately that cycle has been put to rest, as we have begun to remember how much fun and how delicious fondue is when made correctly.

The word "fondue" is derived from the French word *fondre*, which means "to melt." The dish, which originated in Switzerland, is basically a dip made from cheese melted with white wine and other flavorings and is traditionally served with chunks of toasted bread. It is commonly made and served in a pot called a caquelon, a wide, shallow, earthenware dish that absorbs and retains heat very well. Enameled cast-iron or stainless-steel pots are also good choices. Fondue can also be made over a double boiler, which gently heats the cheese over a simmering water bath.

The key to making successful fondue is to add the cheese to the hot liquid slowly so that each portion melts fully before the next is added, creating a silky-smooth dip. Fondue should always be prepared and held over low heat because cheese separates at high temperatures. Keeping the finished fondue warm at all times ensures that the texture remains smooth and even. Fondue sets have a small Sterno fuel can holder for this purpose, but you can achieve the same effect by placing the finished fondue mixture in an ovenproof container perched over several candles. Encourage guests to swirl their fondue dippers (see photograph, page 187) down to the bottom of the pot. This will not only ensure that the dipper gets nicely coated, but also will stir the mixture at the same time. Finally, be sure to serve the fondue as soon as it is made, since even when kept warm it will tend to separate a bit as it sits.

Fondue lends itself to informal entertaining. For a fondue party, make at least three different variations. Serve Classic Swiss Fondue (page 405) with boiled new potatoes sprinkled with freshly grated nutmeg, warm toasted walnuts, slices of tart Granny Smith apples, and chunks of fresh white, rye, and pumpernickel bread. Set out bottles of white wine and Kirsch for sipping. Fontina Fondue with Shaved Black Truffles (page 405) is particularly delicious with button mushrooms, artichoke hearts, grapes, blanched cauliflower, asparagus spears, pear slices wrapped in prosciutto, and cubes of focaccia. Champagne is a good accompaniment for this fondue. For Chile con Queso with Roasted Poblano Peppers (page 407), I arrange a platter of tortilla chips, grilled sausages, and Classic Toast Points (page 244) and serve it with Sangrias (page 428) and Blue Margaritas (page 430). Set out small dishes of toasted caraway, fennel, mustard, and sesame seeds near each pot. Guests can coat their dippers with the seeds just after swirling them in the cheese.

It is traditional to allow the thin layer of fondue that remains after guests have swirled the last bit of fondue out of the pot to sit over the heat until it becomes crisp. Considered a delicacy, the cheese wafer, known as *la religieuse*, is broken into pieces and passed to each guest.

## POACHED MOZZARELLA

**SERVES 8 TO 12** | photograph on page 196

*To serve this unusual dip, scoop out the melted mozzarella in tomato sauce and fork it onto slices of fresh bread. It is important to use an ovenproof baking dish that is wide enough so that the sauce is no more than 1 inch deep.*

1 tablespoon olive oil

3 garlic cloves, thinly sliced lengthwise

1 15-ounce can diced tomatoes with juices

1 15-ounce can crushed tomatoes with juices

1 bay leaf

4 leaves fresh basil

Kosher salt and freshly ground black pepper

1 1-pound ball lightly salted fresh mozzarella
cheese

1 1-pound loaf of coarse-textured peasant bread,
for cutting into pieces

**1** Preheat the oven to 300° F. Heat the olive oil in a large skillet over medium-low heat. Add the garlic and cook until it is golden, about 5 minutes. Do not let the garlic burn. Add the tomatoes, bay leaf, basil, and salt and pepper to taste. Simmer, stirring occasionally, until the sauce reduces slightly, 20 to 25 minutes.

**2** Transfer the sauce to an approximately 8-inch round ovenproof baking dish. Place the cheese in the middle of the sauce and transfer to the oven. Bake until the cheese has almost completely melted, 25 to 35 minutes. Sprinkle with pepper. Serve warm with the bread.

## CHILE CON QUESO WITH ROASTED POBLANO PEPPERS

**SERVES 10 TO 12** | photograph on page 197

*This Mexican version of fondue combines 2 cheeses and 2 peppers. I use manchego cheese for its sharp, nutty taste and Monterey Jack for its easy melting quality. The poblano peppers provide mostly flavor while the jalapeños supply the heat. If you like your food spicy, add more jalapeño.*

3 roasted medium-size poblano peppers
(see page 266)

1 roasted jalapeño pepper (see page 266)

1 tablespoon olive oil

1 medium onion, finely chopped

1 garlic clove, minced

½ teaspoon kosher salt

12 ounces lager beer

8 ounces manchego cheese, grated on the large
holes of a box grater to yield 2¼ cups

8 ounces Monterey Jack cheese, grated on the
large holes of a box grater to yield 3 cups

1 tablespoon cornstarch

½ teaspoon cumin seeds, freshly toasted and
ground (see page 386)

1 tablespoon fresh oregano

**1** Cut the peppers into thin strips. Set aside.

**2** Heat the oil in a medium saucepan over medium-low heat. Add the onions, garlic, and salt, and cook, covered, until soft. Add the beer, increase the heat to high, and bring to a boil.

**3** In a medium bowl, toss the 2 cheeses with the cornstarch. Reduce the heat to a simmer and gradually whisk in the cheeses 1 handful at a time, whisking constantly until the cheese melts before adding the next handful. When the cheese has melted, whisk in the roasted peppers.

**4** Transfer to a warm fondue pot. Garnish with the ground cumin and the fresh oregano. Serve immediately with blue or yellow corn chips or Miniature Flour Tortillas (page 235).

## FRICO

Frico are crisp, lacy cheese wafers, traditionally made in Italy with Montasio cheese, but Parmesan or Asiago are often used as a substitute. I experimented with many different cheeses and discovered that frico can actually be made with Cheddar and Gruyère. I also tried sprinkling various fresh herbs onto the cheese as it melts, and found that the more assertively flavored ones, such as thyme and marjoram, taste best.

## CHEDDAR FRICO

**MAKES 2 DOZEN 4-INCH FRICO** | photographs on pages 192–193

*Sharp cheddar is the best choice for these frico; the mild variety does not have enough flavor.*

10 ounces sharp Cheddar cheese, grated on the
    fine holes of a box grater to yield 5 cups
1 tablespoon all-purpose flour
2 teaspoons fresh thyme

**1** In a medium bowl, toss the cheese and the flour together. Heat a medium nonstick skillet over medium-low heat. Sprinkle 1½ tablespoons of the cheese into the pan to form a circle about 4 inches in diameter. (The Cheddar cheese melts together more so than other cheeses; sprinkle it into the pan so there is plenty of space between the pieces.)
**2** Sprinkle 1 or 2 leaves of the thyme over the cheese. Cook until the cheese is somewhat melted but not firm, 1½ to 2 minutes. Using a spatula, turn the cheese over and cook until it is firm and just slightly golden, 30 seconds to 1 minute more. Transfer the frico to a paper towel to cool. Repeat with the remaining cheese.

### NOTE | Making Frico

There are a few simple guidelines for making perfect frico. First, do not grate the cheese ahead of time. It will lose moisture and will not melt or spread out properly, which is essential to making good frico. Instead, grate the cheese just before you are ready to cook the frico.

When cooking frico, the exact timing will vary with the variety of cheese, the level of heat, and the weight of the pan. Frico should never be allowed to become too dark when cooking; when cooked until dark brown, the cheese loses much of its delicate flavor and becomes bitter. Until you become confident with your cooking method, it is best to make the frico one at a time to control the cooking of the cheese. It's rather like making crepes; expect the first few to be less than perfect. Use them as a guide to adjust the heat and achieve a perfect, evenly cooked wafer.

Any of the frico may be made and laid out flat on a paper towel to cool, or you can drape each frico over an ungreased rolling pin just as you lift it out of the pan. This will give the cooled frico a soft, rounded shape which looks pretty in a bowl or footed compote.

Frico make a delicious garnish on salads and are a nice alternative to croutons in soup. They may be stored at room temperature in an airtight container for 2 to 3 days.

## PARMESAN ROSEMARY FRICO

**MAKES 2 DOZEN 4-INCH FRICO** | photographs on pages 192–193

*Unlike the other frico varieties, the Parmesan version remains pale even when it is fully cooked.*

9 ounces Parmesan cheese, grated on the fine holes of a box grater to yield 4 cups
1 tablespoon all-purpose flour
1 tablespoon fresh rosemary needles from 1 large branch

**1** In a medium bowl, toss the cheese and the flour together. Heat a medium nonstick skillet over medium-low heat. Sprinkle 1½ tablespoons of the cheese into the pan to form a circle about 4 inches in diameter.

**2** Sprinkle 2 to 3 needles of the rosemary over the cheese. Cook until the cheese is somewhat melted but not firm, 1½ to 2 minutes. Using a spatula, turn the cheese over and cook until it is firm but not taking on any color, 30 seconds to 1 minute more. Drape the frico over a large rolling pin until cool. Repeat with the remaining cheese.

## MARJORAM GRUYÈRE FRICO

**MAKES 2 DOZEN 4-INCH FRICO** | photographs on pages 192–193

*Marjoram's cousin, oregano, may be substituted for the marjoram, but the flavor will be a bit sharper.*

9 ounces Gruyère cheese, grated on the fine holes of a box grater to yield 3½ cups
1 tablespoon all-purpose flour
1 tablespoon fresh marjoram

**1** In a medium bowl, toss the cheese and the flour together. Heat a medium nonstick skillet over medium-low heat. Sprinkle 1½ tablespoons of the cheese into the pan to form a circle about 4 inches in diameter.

**2** Sprinkle 1 or 2 leaves of the marjoram over the cheese. Cook until the cheese is somewhat melted but not firm, 1½ to 2 minutes. Using a spatula, turn the cheese over and cook until it is firm and golden around the edges, 30 seconds to 1 minute more. Transfer the frico to a paper towel to cool. Repeat with the remaining cheese.

## ASIAGO FRICO

**MAKES 2 DOZEN 4-INCH FRICO** | photographs on pages 192–193

*Asiago is an aged Italian cheese that is sweeter than Parmesan and not as sharp as Romano. It's one of my favorite cooking cheeses and is also a great component of a cheese board.*

9 ounces Asiago cheese, grated on the fine holes of a box grater to yield 3½ cups
1 tablespoon all-purpose flour

**1** In a medium bowl, toss the cheese and the flour together. Heat a medium nonstick skillet over medium-low heat. Sprinkle 1½ tablespoons of the cheese into the pan to form a circle about 4 inches in diameter.

**2** Cook until the cheese is somewhat melted but not firm, about 2 minutes. Using a spatula, turn the cheese over and cook until it is visibly firm and just taking on a little color, 30 seconds to 1 minute. Drape the frico over a large rolling pin or place on paper towels until cool. To make frico tacos, transfer the frico from the pan to a paper towel and hold it in the palm of your hand. Depress an offset spatula down the middle to form a taco shape (see photograph, page 192). Transfer to paper towels to cool. Repeat with the remaining cheese.

## HERBED AND SPICED GOAT CHEESE BALLS

**MAKES 3½ DOZEN** | photograph on page 200

*Any number of fresh herbs, spices, and nuts may be used to coat these creamy bites. Try rosemary and chopped nuts, for example, or walnuts, cilantro, and crushed mild Aleppo chili pepper. The goat cheese balls may be formed and refrigerated, unseasoned, in an airtight container for 1 day.*

1¼ pounds soft goat cheese

1 tablespoon finely chopped flat-leaf parsley

1½ tablespoons snipped fresh chives

1½ tablespoons fresh thyme

2 tablespoons chopped pecans, toasted
   (see page 361)

1 tablespoon freshly cracked black pepper

2 teaspoons paprika

2 teaspoons curry powder

2 tablespoons extra-virgin olive oil

1 teaspoon red pepper flakes

**1** Line a baking sheet with parchment paper. Form 1 tablespoon of the goat cheese into a small ball. Transfer to the baking sheet. Continue with the remaining cheese. Refrigerate the balls for 10 minutes to set slightly.

**2** In 5 separate small bowls, place the parsley, chives, thyme, pecans, and pepper. Roll about 6 balls in each of the 5 coatings and set aside. To make the paprika band, sprinkle the paprika in a straight thin line on a cutting board. Straighten the edges of the paprika with a knife. Roll 6 of the balls down the line to form the paprika strip. To make the curry dot on the 6 remaining balls, place the curry in a sieve, cover half of each ball with a wide knife, and sprinkle the curry over the other half.

**3** Pour the olive oil onto a serving platter. Sprinkle the oil with the red pepper flakes. Arrange the goat cheese balls on the platter and serve with toothpicks on the side.

## BAKED CAMEMBERT

**SERVES 10 TO 12** | photograph on page 188

*Baking the cheese in its own wooden box is simplicity itself. Serve with chunks of good-quality French bread or any of the fondue dippers (see photograph, page 187).*

1 round Camembert cheese, in a wooden box

Crisp baguette cut into chunks, for dipping

**1** Preheat the oven to 375° F. Remove and discard any paper labels from the front or sides of the cheese box. Unwrap the cheese and discard the wrapping. Place the cheese back in the box, cover with the lid, and place it on a baking sheet.

**2** Bake until the cheese is completely soft on the inside, 20 to 30 minutes. Transfer to a work surface and remove the lid of the box. Use a serrated knife to slice the top of the rind off the cheese and serve the cheese immediately with chunks of bread.

## CRUMBLED PARMIGIANO-REGGIANO WITH TRUFFLE OIL

**SERVES 2 DOZEN** | photograph on page 201

*Any cheese pieces too small to be served can be finely grated for use in Parmesan-Rosemary Icebox Crackers (page 365), Parmesan-Pepper Tartlet Shells (page 234), or in the Parmesan Puff Pastry Straws (pages 369–370). For the Parmesan knife, see Sources, page 486.*

3½ pounds Parmigiano-Reggiano cheese,
   at room temperature

White truffle oil for drizzling (see page 308)

Use a small Parmesan or paring knife to break the Parmigiano-Reggiano cheese into bite-size chunks. Place the chunks onto a serving platter and, just before serving, drizzle with the truffle oil to taste.

# GLOSSARY

## ASSORTED GOAT CHEESES
photograph on pages 190–191

**CABÉCOU** Cabécou ("little goat" in French dialect) originates in the Perigord region of France, but is also available from the Quercy, Languedoc, and Rouergue regions. It is a goat cheese with no rind and is sold in small, flat disks that are sometimes wrapped in chestnut leaves. Cabécou has a white, soft, creamy interior when young, and becomes hard and brown when aged. It can be creamy and sweet, but becomes very strong when overaged. Often sold macerated in plum brandy, it is lovely to serve with a fruity white wine or a Bordeaux.

**CAPRIOLE BANON** The American version of this classic French goat cheese is made in Indiana. It can also be made with cow's milk and is usually wrapped in chestnut or grape leaves that have been dipped in white wine, eau de vie, or brandy, and tied with ribbon or raffia. Sometimes Banon is made without the leaves, but it is then sprinkled with herbs or spices. The interior is soft, runny, and beige-colored, and tastes nutty and fruity. A young Banon is best served with fruity, lively red wines; a riper Banon should be served with a Rhône red.

**CAPRIOLE CROCODILE TEAR** This fresh goat cheese is known as a Crocodile Tear because of its unusual figlike shape. Produced in the Ohio River Valley, it is an aged goat cheese with a dense, creamy interior and an edible rind that is usually dusted with paprika.

**LE CHEVROT** This small, cylindrical raw goat's-milk cheese can be aged to please your personal tastes. As a young cheese it is soft, moist, and spreadable with flavors that are mild and sweet. As it ages, it becomes firm and chewy, tasting more nutty and piquant over time. Serve a dry white wine with the young Chevrot and a bolder red with the aged.

**CROTTIN DE CHAVIGNOL** Crottin is a raw goat's-milk cheese produced in the Berry region of France. It has a natural, edible rind and is shaped like a small barrel with a flat top and bottom, measuring about 2 inches high and 1½ inches in diameter. When young, this cheese has a stark white exterior and a soft snow-white interior with mild, tangy flavor. It should be served with crusty bread and white wine. When mature, Crottin de Chavignol has a beige exterior and a firm, white, chalky interior with a flavor that is nutty, robust, and meaty. Aged crottin can be shaved onto bread or into salads. This full-flavored product is considered one of the tastiest goat cheeses.

**EGG FARM DAIRY FRESH CHÈVRE** Made in Peekskill, New York, it is a soft, creamy, mild cheese that is lovely to spread on crusty white bread. Serve with dry white wine, pears, and nuts.

**PICO PICANDINE** A raw goat's-milk cheese produced by Picandine cheese farm in Saint-Astier, France, this cheese is soft and very nutty. Juicy and full-flavored with hints of spice, it weighs about 6 ounces and is sold as disks in wooden boxes.

**SAINTE-MAURE DE TOURAINE** Also known as Chèvre Long, this log-shaped cheese is made in the Touraine region of France. It is a soft goat cheese with a velvety rind, strong mold aroma, and full goat flavor. The rind may be ashed or not; it is edible either way. Sainte-Maure is packaged in paper and often has a piece of

When putting together a small selection of cheeses, follow the same principles that apply when assembling a more comprehensive cheese tray: Use cheeses with different textures, flavors, and even colors. When using only two or three cheeses, I mix and match among countries of origin and milk types. Different types of cheeses are also more or less appropriate depending on what other food is being served.

If you are serving cheeses as hors d'oeuvres before a meal, choose gently flavored cheeses so that they will not overwhelm your guests' taste buds. Soft-ripened cheeses, fresh goat cheese, and semisoft cheese of cow, goat, or sheep milk all fit nicely into this category.

If you are serving only hors d'oeuvres, the stronger, full-flavored varieties work best, such as aged, blue, or washed-rind cheeses.

If I am serving only wine and cheese, I like to combine both of the above approaches. That is, I will pair cheeses that have gentler flavors with lighter wines, then move on to the more aggressively flavored cheeses and fuller-bodied wines.

### COMBINATIONS WITH GENTLER FLAVORS

Egg Farm Dairy Fresh Chèvre (goat cheese)
Old Chatham Camembert (American)
Tetilla (Spanish)

Saint-Maure de Touraine (goat cheese)
Pavé d'Affinois (French)
Asiago (Italian)

Selles-sur-Cher (goat cheese)
Prince de Claverolle (French)
Queso de Murcia al Vino (Spanish)

Cabécou (goat cheese)
Wild Ripened Cheddar by Egg Farm Dairy (American)
Montasio (Italian)

Pico Picandine (goat cheese)
Fontina (Italian)
Bocconcini (Italian)

### COMBINATIONS WITH AGGRESSIVE FLAVORS

Capriole Banon (goat cheese)
Vella Dry Jack (American)
Great Hill Blue (American)

Morbier (French)
Maytag Blue (American)
Le Chevrot (goat cheese)

Bucheron (French)
Artisanal Aged Manchego (Spanish)
Cabrales (Spanish)

Capriole Crocodile Tear (goat cheese)
Reblochon (French)
Sally Jackson Sheep's Milk Cheese (American)

Crottin de Chavignol (goat cheese)
Mahón Artisano (Spanish)
L'Ami du Chambertin (French)

Wabash Cannonball (American)
Edel de Cléron (French)
Suspiro de Cabra (Spanish)

Vacherin Fribourgeois (Swiss)
Pecorino (Italian)
Parmigiano-Reggiano (Italian)

straw running from end to end through its center. It is often dipped in Chenin Rouge, the local wine, during aging. This cheese is very nice served at the end of a meal with a dry, fruity white wine, particularly one from the Touraine region.

**SELLES-SUR-CHER** Produced in the small town of Selles on the River Cher, this raw goat's-milk cheese has a black exterior, which may be either ash or powdered charcoal, and a perfectly white, firm interior. The flavor is slightly sour and salty, yet also sweet and moist. The texture is slightly hard and becomes heavy and melting in the mouth. The flavor is intense, so pair this cheese with fresh fruit for balance.

**VALENÇAY** The rind of this French goat cheese is usually covered in a natural, edible preservative coat of blue-black wood ash. It is shaped like a 4-sided, truncated pyramid, about 3½ inches high. The interior is white, and the flavor is sharp, soft, and nutty. As Valençay ages, the flavors become musty and strong. Serve this cheese with ripe, juicy plums and dry, crisp white wine.

## A SELECTION OF AMERICAN CHEESES
photograph on pages 198–199

**GRAFTON VILLAGE CHEDDAR** Grafton Village Cheddar is a raw milk cheese produced in Vermont. Cheddar is a cheese most often encountered in plastic in the supermarket dairy case, but this one is made in small batches and aged, producing a substantial flavor. The Grafton Village Special Reserve is a sharp, fruity Cheddar that derives a particularly deep flavor from its long aging process. A wonderful slicing cheese, it is a perfect complement to full-bodied red wines.

**MAYTAG BLUE** A staple of American cheeses, Maytag Blue has been produced by Maytag Dairy Farms in Iowa since 1941. Each 4-pound wheel is handmade from raw cow's milk and aged for 6 months. It has a sweet, nutty flavor and a creamy texture. Serve it with the traditional accompaniments: pears and walnuts.

**OLD CHATHAM CAMEMBERT** This square Camembert-style cheese is made with a combination of sheep's and cow's milk by the Old Chatham Sheepherding Co. in the Hudson River Valley. It is mild and creamy and must be served at room temperature, when its luscious texture and full flavor are at their peak. As with all fine cheeses, this Camembert should be eaten on its own. But if it becomes too runny to eat out of hand, serve it with wafer crackers.

**SALLY JACKSON** Sally Jackson's aged goat's-milk and sheep's-milk cheeses are handmade in the Okanogan Valley in Washington. Her mild and fruity sheep's-milk cheese is wrapped and aged in grape leaves, and is just right for the very best cheese board.

**VELLA DRY JACK** Produced by the Vella Cheese Company of California, this aged Jack cheese is packaged as an 8-pound, round-sided, flat-bottomed wheel. Its rind is coated with a mixture of vegetable oil, cocoa, and pepper, and it is aged for 2 years. The name "Jack" was given to the cheese by its originator, a Scot named David Jacks who ended up in California during the Gold Rush. The Vella Company added the word "dry" to convey its texture and aging. It is a sweet, fruity, sharp, and full-bodied cheese, wonderful served alone or grated into salads, pastas, soups, and stews.

**WABASH CANNONBALL** The Wabash Cannonball is produced by Capriole, Inc., in the Ohio River Valley region of Indiana. A goat's-milk cheese, Cannonball is robust in flavor and unusual in appearance; the name denotes the shape. The exterior is coated in ash, and the rind develops a wonderful flavor with age. This is lovely to serve with a chilled fruity white wine and figs.

**WILD RIPENED CHEDDAR BY EGG FARM DAIRY** Produced by Egg Farm Dairy in Peekskill, New York, this cheese is an aged Cheddar with a double heritage. The producers start with a Vermont Cheddar that has already been aged for 12 to 18 months and ripen it further at the Egg Farm Dairy. The result is an excellent smooth cheese—if less sharp and salty than an English Cheddar—that is suited to hearty, earthy red wines.

## A PRESENTATION OF FRENCH CHEESES
photograph on pages 184–185

**L'AMI DU CHAMBERTIN** Produced in Burgundy, L'Ami du Chambertin is a smooth cow's-milk cheese with a soft, reddish-brown edible rind that results from a bath in marc de Bourgogne (a French eau de vie). The small, flat, disk-shaped cheese is packed in a wooden box, and is similar to traditional Muenster. As with all fine cheeses, serve L'Ami du Chambertin at room temperature, when its pungent, earthy flavor is at its peak.

**BUCHERON** This goat's-milk cheese was one of the first French chèvres to be imported into the United States more than 25 years ago. Made from a combination of powdered milk and frozen curd, it has a soft, flaky interior and a velvety rind that sharpens with age. Serve this complex, very tangy chèvre with a selection of both a mild, firm cheese such as Pavé d'Affinois and a buttery cheese such as Prince de Claverolle.

**EDEL DE CLÉRON** This version of the well-known Vacherin cheese is made in the Franche-Comté region in France. It is characterized by the spruce bark wrapped around its perimeter and its soft, oozing interior. The texture is supple, creamy, fruity, a little tangy, and even a bit nutty. Serve with nuts, dried fruit, and bread.

**MIMOLETTE** Originating in Flanders and Normandy, Mimolette is an orange-colored, organically dyed cow's-milk cheese. The interior of Mimolette is firm and shot through with cracks and holes. Aged Mimolette is very dry, with a winey bite and a sharp, crisp finish; it is best served with full-bodied wine or beer. Mimolette is also available in a younger, milder, and moister version.

**MONTBRIAC** This is a creamy cow's-milk blue cheese with a Brie-like consistency. It has a luxurious, runny interior and a very mild flavor. Serve at room temperature with apples, pears, grapes, and sweet wines, such as Sauternes.

**MORBIER** A cow's-milk cheese with an inedible natural rind, Morbier is produced in the Franche-Comté region of France. It is made in 13- to 16-pound wheels. The soft brown rind of Morbier encases 2 creamy layers separated by a thin layer of blue vegetable ash; the bottom layer is made from the morning milking and the top is added on after the evening milking. Morbier has a subtle, nutty flavor and is best served with light, fruity red wines.

**PAVÉ D'AFFINOIS** This is a creamy French cow's-milk cheese characterized by its snow-white color, square shape, and grooved rind, which has a subtle mushroom flavor. The interior is firm and chalky, and the very center is extremely creamy, like Brie.

However you are planning to use cheese, and whatever cheese you select, it is important to know how to buy it as well as how to store it. In this regard, a trustworthy cheese merchant is virtually indispensable, but there are also some ground rules that will be helpful even if you are selecting cheeses on your own.

First, there is outward appearance. Unlike many other foods, when it comes to cheeses, a rough-looking exterior is often a sign of a wonderful product. This is because artisanal cheeses are almost always less smooth and "clean" looking than those made in factories. A handmade look means a handmade flavor.

The interior of a cheese is a different matter. Unless it is a blue cheese, there should be no mold on the interior, nor should there be any gray or pink discolorations, which are signs that the cheese is overripe.

Next comes the primary rule of cheese buying: Always taste before you buy. Any good cheese merchant will be willing to offer a sample, and tasting a cheese is the only way to know if you will enjoy it. This is particularly important when you are venturing into types of cheese that are new to you.

Unless you plan to eat the cheese the day you buy it, it should be wrapped and refrigerated. The best wrapping material is parchment paper, which slows down oxidation while allowing the cheese to breathe. If you don't have parchment paper, use wax paper, cheesecloth, or even aluminum foil. Avoid plastic wrap, as it completely seals out air.

At least an hour before serving the cheese, remove it from the refrigerator and allow it to come to room temperature. This is essential to the enjoyment of a fine cheese, since the rich, subtle flavors are considerably dampened when chilled. Leave the wrapping on the cheese until just before serving, however, so that the exposed surfaces don't dry out.

**PRINCE DE CLAVEROLLE** A somewhat firm sheep's-milk cheese made in the French Pyrenees, Prince de Claverolle is ivory on the inside and has a very buttery, fruity flavor. It is best served with a Bordeaux. Prince de Claverolle may also be labeled Istara, as it is undergoing a name change.

**REBLOCHON** This is a raw cow's-milk cheese with an intriguing history. Produced in the Savoie and Haute-Savoie regions of France, Reblochon is patois for the milk remaining in the cows after milking, which herdsmen intentionally withheld for themselves when landowners came to collect their pay in milk. They would then milk the cow a second time, which yielded a creamier, richer milk. Reblochon comes in small disks, usually wrapped with wood and paper. The rind is soft and brown, the interior creamy and white. Serve sweet, rich Reblochon with young, fruity red and white wines.

## THE SPANISH CHEESE BOARD
photograph on pages 194–195

**ARTISANAL AGED MANCHEGO** This aged cheese is made in La Mancha in central Spain, from the raw milk of the hardy sheep that roam this rugged terrain. Manchego has a very distinct rind; it is grayish-black with a herringbone pattern around the rim, a result of the cheese mold in which it is aged. The rind is typically cut away before serving. The interior is dotted with tiny holes. Its sharp, nutty flavor tastes good with dried figs and bold red wine, or, as is the tradition in Spain, with quince paste sprinkled with sugar and cinnamon.

**CABRALES** Spain's signature blue cheese, Cabrales is made from a mixture of cow's, sheep's, and goat's milk. It has been made in the caves of the Asturias region of northwest Spain for centuries. The rind is too salty to be edible, but the interior is a wonderful combination of flavors, textures, and colors—crumbly, buttery, and assertive. Cabrales is excellent served with hard cider, Spanish sherry, or bold, red Spanish wines. Crisp, tart apples and nuts also complement Cabrales nicely.

**MAHÓN ARTISANO** This cow's-milk cheese has been made on the island of Menorca for centuries. The orange-gold rind is achieved by rubbing the rind with a mixture of butter, olive oil, and paprika during its last month of maturation. Easily recognized on the exterior by its square, pillow shape and on the inside by its proliferation of tiny holes throughout, this nutty, firm cheese is best served with Spanish red wines and beer.

**QUESO DE MURCIA AL VINO (DRUNKEN GOAT)** This is a semisoft goat cheese with a dark red, inedible rind that is created by washing the cheese with the red wine made in the Murcia region of southeastern Spain. This cheese, which should be eaten very fresh, is tangy and strong and adds a colorful accent and bold flavor to the cheese board.

**SUSPIRO DE CABRA** Spanish for "goat's sigh," Suspiro de Cabra is a semisoft goat's-milk cheese with a luscious, creamy interior that becomes creamier as it matures. Full-flavored yet not overbearing, the earthy overtones and tangy bite of this cheese are best complemented by slices of cured chorizo, thin slices of Serrano ham, toasted almonds and walnuts (see page 361), figs, and dates. Bold red wines or very crisp white wines hold up to its assertive flavor.

**TETILLA** This is a semisoft cow's-milk cheese from the Galicia region just north of Portugal. Seductively shaped like a woman's breast (hence the cheese's name), it has a greenish-beige exterior and an inedible rind. A mellow, tangy flavor makes this cheese a natural accompaniment to many Spanish white wines and dry sherry. Tetilla is also wonderful served with fruit or raw vegetables.

## OTHER CHEESES USED IN THIS BOOK

**APPENZELLER** A cow's-milk cheese originating in northern Switzerland, Appenzeller has a pronounced, tangy, fruity flavor and strong aroma. The interior is speckled with holes, and the rind is cured with cider, white wine, and a mixtue of more than 20 herbs and spices, giving it a smooth, brownish finish. Appenzeller melts extremely well but is also lovely paired with fresh fruit, nuts, and light red and white wines.

**ASIAGO** This semifirm Italian cheese, made from partially skimmed cow's milk, has a mild, slightly fruity flavor. It has an inedible rind and a light beige interior with many small holes. When young, Asiago can be sliced and eaten, but after aging a year or more, it becomes hard and most suitable for grating. There are now, excellent domestically produced versions of the hard cheese. Asiago is lovely served with either light, fruity reds or bigger reds, such as Chianti.

**BOCCONCINI** Italian for "mouthful," bocconcini are small round balls of fresh mozzarella cheese, about 1 inch in diameter. They are generally packed in water or whey, and can be purchased at gourmet cheese shops. After the liquid has been drained, the cheese can be marinated in olive oil, fresh or dried herbs such as rosemary and thyme, and hot red pepper flakes.

**CAMEMBERT** This cheese originated in the Normandy region of France, but now it is made in many countries and is readily available. It is characterized by its white, bloomy rind and straw-colored, creamy interior. It has a hearty, mushroomy flavor and oozes when served at room temperature. Serve Camembert with a fruity, elegant red wine.

**CHEDDAR** This versatile, widely distributed cow's-milk cheese was first made in the village of Cheddar in the Somerset region of England. Cheddar should always be smooth and firm enough to slice, not dry and crumbly. It ranges in color from pale white to annatto-dyed orange. The flavor ranges from very mild to extra sharp, according to how long it is aged.

**COMTÉ** A wonderful melting cheese, Comté is a cow's-milk cheese made in France. It has a strong, fruity flavor, with hints of hazelnut. Firm yet supple, its interior is shot through with pea-size holes. The best Comté cheeses are marked with a symbol of a bell, and the word "Comté" is stamped in green on the rind. Serve Comté with strong red wines, such as Red Burgundy, or with fruity reds such as Beaujolais.

**EMMENTALER** Made in the mountains of Switzerland, Emmentaler is one of the most significant Swiss cheeses. In fact, it is what most people think of as "Swiss cheese." It has a beige rind and a golden, tender, somewhat oily interior spotted with olive-shaped holes. The flavors are mild, nutty, and buttery. It is produced in giant wheels weighing up to 220 pounds—a result, it is said, of having to make enough cheese to store over the long winter months in the Alpine regions. Because the flavor is so mild, this cheese is very versatile; when young, it is best used grated in soups and stews or in salads; the aged, or reserve, Emmentaler is wonderful as a table cheese; the cave-aged version makes a delicious after-dinner treat. It is also the main ingredient in traditional Swiss fondue (see page 405).

**FETA CHEESE** Greece's best-known cheese, feta is traditionally made from sheep's milk, although it may also be made from a combination of cow's, goat's, or sheep's milk. The short bricks of feta have a soft, crumbly texture and are packed in brine, which produces its characteristic salty flavor. Feta has a slightly sharp bite and is wonderful used in salads. With the addition of olives, crusty bread, and wine, feta cheese can be made into a meal. French feta, Bulgarian feta, and American-made feta are also widely available and vary in intensity and texture

**FONTINA** Fontina is currently made in many countries, but it originated in the Piedmont region of Italy. Supple and creamy, fontina is a cow's-milk cheese with a mild yet distinctive flavor, a golden-brown rind, and ivory-yellow interior that is dotted with holes. Because it melts very easily and smoothly, fontina is wonderful for dishes that require melted cheese. For the best flavor, look for fontinas with natural, rather than wax, rinds.

**GRUYÈRE** Originally produced only in Switzerland, this cow's-milk cheese is now made in both the United States and France. It is aged for 10 to 12 months and has a firm, pale yellow interior, spotted with pea-size holes. Gruyère is sweet, rich, nutty, and fruity, making it wonderful as a table cheese or as an ingredient in an array of dishes.

**JACK CHEESE** An American creation, Jack cheese was first produced by a Scotsman named David Jacks near Monterey, California, in the 1890s. Jack is now produced throughout the country, its surname reflecting its point of origin, such as Sonoma Jack and Wisconsin Jack. Allowed to ripen for only about 1 week, Jack cheese is soft, white, and mild with a semisoft texture. It is prized for its easy melting quality, and is often flavored with jalapeños, dill, or herbs. When Jack cheese is aged for 7 to 10 months it is known as aged or dry Jack, which has a firmer, drier texture and more tang. Dry Jack is suitable for grating into many dishes.

**LABNEH** A tart, refreshing fresh cheese made from cow's milk, labneh is very popular in Middle Eastern cuisine and is as versatile as cream cheese. Delicious spread on warm pita, then drizzled with olive oil and sprinkled with fresh oregano, it's also wonderful as an alternative dip for the Lima-Bean Falafel Fritters (page 299). Stir ½ cup labneh into Roasted Red Pepper and Eggplant Dip (page 390) for richer flavor and texture.

**MONTASIO** Made from partially skimmed cow's milk, Montasio is a mild, tangy, hard cheese. Hailing from Italy, it has a beige interior with very small holes throughout. The best Montasios are from Friuli, where the cheese originated. When young, Montasio cheese is wonderful to slice and serve with light and fruity red wines. When aged, the cheese can be grated into a variety of dishes and served alongside bolder and coarser red wines.

**MOZZARELLA** As popular in America as it is in Italy, mozzarella is made from milk of either the water buffalo or the cow. It is a sliceable curd cheese made by the pasta filata, or spun-curd, method, in which the curd is dipped into hot whey until it becomes elastic and can be wound into a ball. It has a mild, creamy texture and is very white. Buffalo mozzarella is made with a combination of cow's and buffalo's milk, and is sold packaged in its whey. It has a sweet, delicate flavor and texture. Mozzarella is the cheese that is most often used on pizza because it has excellent melting properties.

**PARMESAN** This hard, nutty, salty cheese is produced in a variety of countries, but none compares with its original producer, Italy. Properly known as Parmigiano-Reggiano, this cheese is made from partially skimmed cow's milk and has a rich, sharp flavor. The more mature the cheese is, the more intense the flavor becomes. A cheese marked "vecchio" has matured for 2 years, one marked "stravecchio" has matured for 3 years, and "stravecchione" for 4 years. Parmigiano-Reggiano is termed "grana" in Italy, which means "grain," and refers to its texture. It is a wonderful cheese for grating into Italian dishes, and is also great with wine and fruit for dessert.

**PECORINO** Like Parmigiano-Reggiano, aged pecorino cheese, which is made in Italy, is classified as grana, identifying its grainy texture. By definition, pecorino is any cheese made from sheep's milk, including Pecorino-Romano. Fresh pecorino, known as ricotta pecorino, is soft and mild. Aged pecorino has a somewhat lower fat content and is intensely flavorful. The rind of pecorino ranges from white to dark yellow, and the interior is yellowish-white and hard and becomes oily with age. Aged pecorino is best suited for grating into any number of dishes.

**ROBIOLA** Similar to mascarpone cheese, fresh Robiola is a soft, moist, creamy cheese that is sold in cubes, disks, or tubs. It is made from cow's, goat's, or sheep's milk, usually with cream added to it. It is slightly tart and mild, and is a wonderful cheese to serve at breakfast or brunch with fresh fruit. Aged Robiola is produced in limited quantity and has an assertive aroma and a luscious, creamy interior.

**VACHERIN FRIBOURGEOIS** Vacherin is a generic name that indicates a large group of cheeses from the alpine regions of France and Italy. This particular cow's-milk Vacherin is from Switzerland. It has a semifirm texture and has occasional holes throughout the interior. The flavor is big and nutty, and it pairs nicely with bold red wines.

( 9 )

# SIPS
# AND
# DRINKS

*Photographs for these recipes appear on
pages 202–217*

each served in an appropriate glass and set out on a bar, or ice-filled pitchers of sangria made from red, rosé, and white wines, with colorful fruit garnishes floating whimsically in them. Or they could even be samplings of soup, such as spicy gazpacho ladled in cups fashioned from cucumbers. The main criteria for a potable hor d'oeuvre is that it be flavorful and festive.

I frequently pass sips of soups on a tray at the beginning of a cocktail party. Inspired by the French chef's custom of serving dinner guests once they've been seated an enchanting hors d'oeuvre known as an *amuse bouche*, I find that this special gesture always sets a festive tone.

Part of the fun of serving sips is finding unusual containers for them. In addition to the tiny cucumber bowls of gazpacho (or whatever cold soup you like), consider serving savory soups such as butternut squash, mushroom, or beef consommé in small tea cups, sake cups, or demitasse cups. These diminutive vessels will allow your guests to appreciate each taste more fully—and will add to the convivial air of the party as well.

Over the past few years, cocktails have come into their own again. In this chapter you will find seventeen of these libations, which I call party cocktails. The tried and true are well represented, but usually with a little twist. Martinis, perhaps the most famous bar drink of all, are served here in three ways. In addition to the Classic Martini (garnished with caper berries in place of the olive), I

make a Reverse Martini for those who prefer a milder drink, along with a Pear Martini, in which Poire William, a French pear eau de vie, and a rather novel pear garnish enticingly enrich the taste, aroma, and appearance.

I have also included recipes for a number of slightly more exotic drinks from tropical lands. Some are classics, such as Brazil's national drink, the Caipirinha, or the Mai Tai, said to mean "out of the world" in Tahiti. Others, such as the kumquat, mango, and ginger cocktails, I devised myself. You will also find punches and sangrias for those occasions when you want to mix a big batch of drinks for a crowd.

Perhaps best of all are my five homemade cordials. These luscious, sweet drinks—made by slowly infusing flavoring ingredients such as fruits, herbs, and spices into a spirit base—are wonderful to drink neat, over ice, mixed into cocktails, or combined with soda. Set decanters filled with several of these concoctions out on a tray along with cordial glasses, and they will become the signature drinks of your gatherings. In fact, most of your guests will be surprised to find that they can be made at home at all.

Whether it's a glass of Pimm's Cup to celebrate the arrival of spring, Fresh Lime Daiquiris rimmed with colored sanding sugar to greet a summer sunset, or warming Beef Consommé Sip in an espresso cup on a winter night, there's a sip here to suit every occasion.

# BEEF CONSOMMÉ SIP

**MAKES 3 DOZEN ¼-CUP SERVINGS** | photograph on page 214

*Consommé is an elegant clarified broth. For this beef sip, have your butcher saw the veal bones into smaller pieces. The stock can be made ahead; it will keep in the refrigerator for 3 days and in the freezer for 3 months. To save time, you may buy the best-quality frozen beef stock and then clarify it.*

BEEF STOCK

8 sprigs fresh flat-leaf parsley

6 sprigs fresh thyme

4 sprigs fresh rosemary

2 bay leaves

1 tablespoon whole black peppercorns

1 pound beef stew meat, cubed

5 pounds veal bones, sawed into smaller pieces

1 large onion, peel on, quartered

2 large carrots, cut in half

2 celery stalks, cut in half

½ pound mixed mushrooms, whole, wiped clean

2 cups dry red wine

**1** Heat the oven to 450°F. Make a bouquet garni by wrapping the parsley, thyme, rosemary, bay leaves, and peppercorns in a piece of cheesecloth. Tie with kitchen twine and set aside. Arrange the meat, veal bones, onion, carrots, celery, and mushrooms in an even layer in a heavy roasting pan Roast, turning every 20 minutes, until the vegetables and the bones are deep brown, about 1 hour and 15 minutes. Transfer the meat, bones, and vegetables to a large stockpot and set aside. Pour the fat from the roasting pan and discard. Place the pan over high heat on the stove. Add the wine and use a wooden spoon to scrape up the brown bits; boil until the wine has reduced by half, 3 to 4 minutes. Pour all the liquid into the stockpot.

**2** Add 6 quarts of cold water to the stockpot, or enough to just cover the bones, and bring to a boil. Reduce to a simmer and cook, partially covered,

and skim off the foam that rises to the surface. After most of the foam has been skimmed, add the bouquet garni and simmer over the lowest possible heat for 3 hours, skimming frequently. Add water if at any time the level drops below the bones.

**3** Strain the stock through a fine sieve into a large bowl. Discard the solids. Let the stock cool to room temperature. Cover and refrigerate overnight.

**4** Remove the hardened layer of fat that has collected. You should have about 3 quarts of stock.

CONSOMMÉ

1 recipe Beef Stock (above)

6 large egg whites and shells

1 small carrot, cut into ⅛-inch cubes

2 ounces enoki mushrooms

1 black truffle (¼ ounce), very thinly shaved

6 haricots verts, cut crosswise into ⅛-inch pieces

Kosher salt and freshly ground black pepper

**1** In a large bowl, whisk together 2 cups of the stock with the egg whites. Stir in the eggshells. Return the remaining stock to a stockpot and bring to a boil. Slowly pour in the egg mixture, whisking constantly. Reduce the heat to low. As soon as the stock simmers, stop whisking and reduce the heat to the lowest possible setting. The egg whites and shells will rise to the top to form a foamy "raft." Let the stock simmer for 30 minutes; turn the heat off and let it sit for 15 minutes.

**2** Wet and wring out a thin kitchen towel. Line a fine sieve with it. Carefully place a ladle into the stock to make a hole in the "raft." Scoop out and discard the crust from the hole. Ladle the stock through the hole into the sieve, taking care to avoid picking up any of the crust. Return the stock to a clean medium pot and heat over low heat.

**3** Add the carrots, mushrooms, truffles, and haricots verts. Cover and let warm throughout. Season with salt and pepper to taste. Serve warm.

A bowl of soup is a wonderful way to begin a sit-down meal, so why miss the pleasure at a cocktail party? By using tiny containers instead of spoons, guests can enjoy a teaspoon or two of a soothing consommé, a few sips of a luxurious creamy soup, or a mouthful of refreshing gazpacho. What's more, you can prepare several different kinds of soup and invite guests to taste a little of each.

When choosing containers, whether crafted from vegetables and fruits or inspired by the contents of your kitchen cupboards and china cabinet, keep in mind that the same rule applies to sips as other hors d'oeuvres: Limit the number of sips in each serving to two. If you plan to serve them on a passed tray, circulate frequently with a tray for the empty containers. If you set the sips out on a table, provide a cloth-lined tray for the empty cups. Below are some of my favorite containers for serving tiny sips.

Sake cups
Juice glasses
Shot glasses
Ceramic or stainless-steel ramekins
Cordial glasses
Demitasse cups
Delicate miniature vases
Aperitif glasses
Espresso cups
Egg cups

# BUTTERNUT SQUASH SIP WITH SEASONED PEPITAS

**MAKES 4 DOZEN ¼-CUP SERVINGS** | photograph on page 215

*Pepitas, the Spanish word for pumpkin seeds, are often found, shelled, in health food stores. Adding a rind of Parmesan cheese to the liquid as the soup cooks is an old secret of Italian peasant cooks; it adds a rich, deep flavor.*

1 tablespoon canola oil
½ cup unsalted pepitas or shelled pumpkin seeds
1¼ teaspoons whole cumin seeds, toasted and ground (see page 386)
Kosher salt
3 tablespoons olive oil
2 medium leeks, white and light green parts only, roughly chopped, well washed (see page 271)
2 garlic cloves, smashed
2 baking potatoes, chopped into 1-inch pieces
4 pounds butternut squash, cut into ½-inch pieces
1½ quarts homemade chicken stock or low-sodium canned broth, skimmed of fat
1 3-inch rind of Parmigiano-Reggiano cheese (optional)
½ cup heavy cream
Freshly ground black pepper

**1** Heat the canola oil in a medium skillet over medium heat. Add the pumpkin seeds and cook, stirring the seeds for even browning, until they start to pop, 2 to 3 minutes. Transfer to a bowl and season while warm with 1¼ teaspoon of the ground cumin and salt to taste. Set aside for garnish.

**2** Heat the olive oil in a stockpot over medium heat. Add the leeks and the garlic and cook until soft, 3 to 5 minutes. Add the potatoes and the squash, and cook until softened, but not browned, about 3 minutes. Add 5½ cups of the stock and the

Parmesan rind. Simmer until the squash is tender, 12 to 15 minutes. Remove the Parmesan and discard. Working in batches, transfer the soup to a blender (do not fill more than halfway) and purée until very smooth. (Alternatively, a handheld immersion blender may be used to purée the soup in the stockpot.)

**3** Return the puréed soup to a clean pot over medium-low heat. Add the cream, remaining cumin, and salt and pepper to taste. Add the remaining stock to thin the soup as needed. Ladle the warm soup into small cups and garnish with the reserved toasted pumpkin seeds.

## MUSHROOM SIP WITH BARLEY WONTONS

**MAKES 4 DOZEN ¼-CUP SERVINGS** | photograph on page 216

*I love wontons and have made many variations over the years, whether as "purses" or as traditional dumplings served in soup. Here the wonton and soup are consumed in one bite or sip— there's no chasing the dumpling around the bowl.*

*The mushroom soup in step 1 may be made a day ahead. The wonton filling also may be made a day ahead and refrigerated. The dumplings may be shaped several hours ahead, covered and refrigerated, and then steamed just before serving. Or they may be made 1 week ahead and frozen.*

SIP

2½ tablespoons olive oil

1 large shallot, finely chopped

8 ounces shiitake mushrooms, caps and stems finely chopped

8 ounces white button mushrooms, caps and stems finely chopped

Kosher salt and freshly ground black pepper

4 quarts homemade beef stock or canned beef broth, skimmed of fat

FILLING

1 tablespoon unsalted butter

1 small onion, finely chopped to yield about ½ cup

2 garlic cloves, minced

1 carrot, cut into ¼-inch dice

½ cup barley, rinsed

¼ cup dry red wine

11½ ounces homemade vegetable stock or canned vegetable broth

2 teaspoons finely chopped fresh thyme

1 tablespoon finely chopped fresh flat-leaf parsley

Kosher salt and freshly ground black pepper

48 square wonton wrappers (2¾ × 3¼ inches)

Lettuce leaves to line the steamer

1 bunch of chives, cut into 2-inch lengths

**1** To make the sip, heat the olive oil in a large saucepan over medium heat. Add the shallots and cook until soft, 3 to 5 minutes. Increase the heat to medium-high and add the mushrooms. Cook until the mushrooms are dark golden, stirring occasionally, 6 to 10 minutes. Season the mushrooms generously with salt and pepper. Add the beef stock to the pan, scraping up any browned bits that may be on the bottom of the pan. Simmer the mixture, covered, over low heat, for 45 minutes. Keep warm.

**2** Meanwhile, make the filling. Melt the butter in a small saucepan over medium heat. Add the onions, garlic, and carrots, and cook until softened, 4 to 5 minutes. Add the barley and cook, stirring, about 5 minutes, until the barley starts to turn golden. Add the red wine and cook, stirring, until the liquid is absorbed. Pour in the vegetable stock and bring to a boil. Reduce the heat, cover, and simmer until the barley is tender, 20 to 30 minutes. Drain any excess liquid from the barley. Transfer

CONTINUED ON FOLLOWING PAGE

the barley to a bowl. Add the thyme, parsley, and salt and pepper to taste.

**3** Line a baking sheet with parchment paper. Work with one wonton at a time and keep the remaining wrappers covered with plastic wrap so they won't dry out. To make a wonton, moisten the edges of a wrapper with water. Place a generous teaspoon of the barley mixture on the center of the wrapper and pull up the edges, forming a purse. Moisten your fingers and cinch the neck of the purse tightly, sealing it closed. Repeat with the remaining wrappers until all the wrappers are filled. Place the dumplings on the baking sheet and cover with plastic wrap.

**4** Set a steamer basket in a wok or shallow saucepan and add water to just cover the bottom of the basket. Remove the steamer from the pan and let the water come to a simmer. Arrange the lettuce leaves to cover the bottom of the steamer basket. Working in batches if necessary, arrange the dumplings on the lettuce in the steamer, being careful that the dumplings do not touch as they might stick together. Place the whole steamer, covered, into the simmering water. Steam until the wrappers are cooked through and the filling is warm, for 7 to 10 minutes.

**5** Ladle the warm mushroom soup into small cups. Place a dumpling in each cup, garnish with a chive, and serve.

## GAZPACHO IN CUCUMBER CUPS

**MAKES 4 DOZEN** | photograph on page 217

*Small sips of gazpacho, the classic cool summer soup of Spain, are served here in cups fashioned from cucumbers. The soup may be made 1 or 2 days ahead and kept covered in the refrigerator.*

1 red bell pepper, seeds and ribs removed, cut into ¼-inch dice
1 medium jalapeño pepper, seeds and ribs removed, finely diced
1 small red onion, cut into ¼-inch dice
1 pound ripe tomatoes, cut into ¼-dice
1 seedless cucumber, peel on, cut into ¼-inch dice
3 tablespoons coarsely chopped fresh cilantro
½ cup tomato juice, or more if needed
2 tablespoons extra-virgin olive oil
1 tablespoon red wine vinegar
2 tablespoons fresh lime juice
1 teaspoon kosher salt
¼ teaspoon freshly ground black pepper
48 Cucumber Cups (page 229)

**1** In a medium bowl, place ⅓ cup of the bell pepper, 1 teaspoon of the jalapeño, ⅓ cup of the red onion, ⅓ cup of the tomatoes, ⅓ cup of the cucumber, and 1 tablespoon of the cilantro. Set aside. Place ½ cup of the cucumber in a small bowl and set aside for garnish.

**2** In the bowl of a food processor, combine the remaining bell pepper, jalapeño, red onion, tomatoes, cucumber, and cilantro. Add the tomato juice, olive oil, vinegar, lime juice, salt, and pepper. Process until smooth. Add the combined reserved ingredients from the medium bowl (not the ½ cup cucumber). Pulse just to combine, leaving the soup slightly chunky. Transfer the gazpacho to an airtight container.

**3** Chill the gazpacho for 4 to 6 hours, or overnight, to allow the flavors to blend. Taste for salt and pepper seasoning and thin if needed with more tomato juice. To serve, spoon about 1 tablespoon of the gazpacho into each Cucumber Cup. Top each cup with some of the reserved diced cucumber. The cups may be eaten after the gazpacho is sipped.

## PUNCHES

There are two theories for the origin of the word "punch." One is that it is derived from the word "puncheon," a huge cask that holds about 70 gallons of liquid. The other is that it comes from the Hindu or Persian word *panca,* which means "five," apparently because every true punch must be made from at least five ingredients. Wherever the name came from, punches are wonderfully cool and refreshing. Lightly alcoholic, flavored with a bit of sugar and a variety of fruits, they are perfect for a relaxed gathering.

## PIMM'S CUP

**MAKES TWELVE 6-OUNCE DRINKS** | photograph on page 210

*Served throughout the United Kingdom at the first blush of spring and summer, Pimm's is an integral part of any garden party. This rather unusual punch contains cucumbers in addition to the more traditional orange rounds and strawberries.*

1 cucumber (8 ounces), peel on, cut into sticks measuring ¼ inch thick and 2½ inches long

1 blood orange or navel orange (8 ounces), cut into ¼-inch rounds

7 strawberries, stems removed, cut in half

1 bottle (750 ml) Pimm's #1

1 bottle (750 ml) sparkling apple cider or ginger ale

Place all of the fruit into a 2-quart pitcher. Add the remaining ingredients and stir once to combine. Ladle the drink into 8-ounce glasses, dividing the fruit among all of the glasses. Fill each glass with ice and serve.

---

**NOTE** | Party Ice

As with any recipe, a good cocktail begins with the best ingredients, including the ice. When a drink calls for cubes, I make them crystal clear either by boiling tap water for 10 minutes before freezing or by using distilled water. Because boiling removes much of the air from the water, the cubes are denser and slower to melt than those made directly from tap water.

When a cocktail calls for crushed ice, avoid substituting cubes, as they change the nature and experience of the drink. Many supermarkets sell crushed ice in bags, but it's also very easy to make your own. One method is to fill a sturdy zipper-seal bag halfway with ice cubes. Seal the bag and place it on a stone or concrete surface between two dish towels. Using a mallet, hammer, or even a small, heavy frying pan, pound the ice firmly until the pieces are about the size of peas. This consistency of crushed ice can also be achieved by placing the ice in a food processor and pulsing.

## WHITE WINE PUNCH

**MAKES SIX 6-OUNCE DRINKS** | photograph on page 210

*Using a combination of different melons—cantaloupe, water-melon, or gala in addition to the honeydew—makes for a colorful punch.*

1 small honeydew melon

10 ounces blanc de blanc or dry white table wine

10 ounces sweet Riesling wine

16 ounces Moscato d'Asti wine

6 red grapes, sliced crosswise into ¼-inch pieces

**1** Using 3 different-sized melon ballers, measuring from ⅓ to ⅞ inch in diameter, scoop the melon into balls. Carefully place the melon balls onto a baking sheet, taking care to see that they don't touch one another. Freeze until solid, 2 to 3 hours or overnight.

**2** Mix the wines in a 3-quart pitcher. Add the grape slices and frozen melon balls to the pitcher and serve.

---

**NOTE** | Drinks Conversion Chart

The ingredients in traditional drink recipes are always written in ounces, but if you are making drinks in batches for a crowd, it is easier to use standard kitchen measures.

| | | |
|---|---|---|
| ½ ounce | = | 1 tablespoon |
| 1 ounce | = | 2 tablespoons |
| 2 ounces | = | ¼ cup |
| 4 ounces | = | ½ cup |
| 8 ounces | = | 1 cup |

---

## RED SANGRIA

**MAKES SIX 7-OUNCE DRINKS** | photograph on page 210

*The black currant juice adds a lovely color to this fruity version of sangria, but can be omitted if not available.*

24 ounces Rioja or medium-bodied red wine

6 ounces black currant juice

12 ounces fresh orange juice

2 tablespoons superfine sugar

½ ounce brandy

6 ounces club soda

1 medium black plum, thinly sliced into rounds

12 blackberries

1 navel orange, thinly sliced into rounds

Combine all of the ingredients in a large pitcher and fill with ice cubes. Serve.

## ROSÉ SANGRIA

**MAKES SIX 6-OUNCE DRINKS** | photograph on page 210

*Like all sangrias, this version should be served cold, over ice.*

6 ounces assorted grapes, such as moscato, black, red, or green

24 ounces rosé wine

3½ ounces grapefruit juice

¼ cup plus 3 tablespoons superfine sugar

3½ ounces tequila

3½ ounces cranberry juice

**1** Place all the grapes in a single layer on a large baking sheet so that they are not touching. Freeze overnight or until frozen solid.

**2** Combine the remaining ingredients in a 3-quart pitcher. Add the frozen grapes and serve.

## TOM COLLINS

**MAKES TWO 6-OUNCE DRINKS** | photograph on page 208

*By definition, a "collins" is a tall, iced cocktail made with liquor (gin, rum, vodka, whiskey, or brandy), lemon juice, sugar, and soda water, and garnished with a lemon slice. It is served in a 10- to 12-ounce "collins" glass. Gin is the liquor in the most popular version of this cocktail, the Tom Collins, the name of which most probably memorializes its inventor.*

¼ cup fresh lemon juice, strained

4 ounces gin or vodka

2½ teaspoons superfine sugar

3 ounces club soda

2 very thin orange slices, for garnish

1 kumquat, sliced into very thin rounds, for garnish

Shake the lemon juice, gin, and sugar together in a cocktail shaker filled with ice. Add the club soda and strain into ice-filled glasses. Garnish the rim of each glass with the oranges and kumquats.

## GINGER FEVER

**MAKES FOUR 4-OUNCE DRINKS** | photograph on page 208

*Bourbon is generally known as the king of American whiskeys. It is named for Bourbon County, Kentucky, and is distilled from fermented grain, such as corn. Here I've mixed it up with ginger, sugar, and soda for a sweet, refreshing cocktail with a little zing.*

1 5-inch piece of ginger, peeled and grated

½ cup sugar

6 ounces bourbon

6 ounces club soda

4 pieces (1 inch to 1½ inches) crystallized ginger, partially split down the middle, for garnish

**1** Simmer the fresh ginger, sugar, and ½ cup of water together for 15 minutes over medium-low heat to allow the flavors to infuse. Cool to room temperature. Strain out and discard the ginger.

**2** Place the ginger syrup, bourbon, and club soda in a pitcher and stir to combine. Fill four 6-ounce glasses with ice and divide the drink among the 4 glasses. Garnish the rim of each glass with a piece of the crystallized ginger.

## PLANTER'S PUNCH

**MAKES FOUR 6-OUNCE DRINKS** | photograph on page 204

*If you prefer your punch without alcohol, this one tastes just as wonderful if you substitute sparkling cider for the rum.*

3 tablespoons fresh lime juice

3 tablespoons fresh lemon juice

3 tablespoons superfine sugar

½ to 1 ounce grenadine

6 ounces fresh orange juice

6 ounces fresh or canned pineapple juice

4 ounces sparkling apple cider or grape juice

4 ounces dark rum

4 ounces light rum

Orange slices and cherries, for garnish

Combine all the ingredients except the orange slices and cherries in a large pitcher and stir well. Fill 4 tumblers with ice cubes. Divide the punch among the tumblers. Garnish with orange slices and cherries.

## BLUE MARGARITA

**MAKES TWO 6-OUNCE DRINKS** | photograph on
page 208

*Traditionally made with tequila, orange-flavored liqueur
(such as Triple Sec or Cointreau), and lime juice, this well-
loved cocktail can be served straight up, on the rocks, or as a
slush. The rim of the glass may be dipped in lime juice and
then in coarse salt. We add a splash of curaçao for color, then
use thinly sliced star fruit as an untraditional, but attractive,
garnish for this festive blue cocktail.*

  1 teaspoon kosher salt

  1 lime, cut into wedges

  4 ounces tequila

  1 ounce Triple Sec liqueur

  ¼ cup fresh lime juice

  2 ounces blue curaçao

  1 teaspoon superfine sugar

  2 ¼-inch slices of star fruit, for garnish

  **1** Pour the kosher salt into a shallow dish big
enough to incorporate the rim of the glass size you
are using. Using 1 lime wedge per glass, rub the
rim of each glass. Dip the rim of each glass in the
salt and rotate gently in order to cover the rim
evenly. Set the glasses aside.

  **2** Fill a cocktail shaker halfway with ice. Place the
tequila, Triple Sec, lime juice, blue curaçao, and
sugar in the shaker, and shake hard for 30 seconds.
Fill the prepared glasses with ice cubes. Strain the
margarita into the glasses. Garnish each with a slice
of star fruit or a lime wedge.

## POMEGRANATE MARGARITA

**MAKES TWO 6-OUNCE DRINKS** | photograph on
page 204

*Pomegranate juice is often sold in gourmet grocery stores in
the juice section or freezer section. Of course, you can also
juice your own; to do so, scoop out the ruby-red seeds from the
fruit, then push them through a fine-mesh sieve, saving the
juice and discarding the solids. Keep in mind that pomegranate
juice stains, so work carefully with it. The sugared rose petals
give these pretty drinks a very special look.*

  5 ounces tequila

  1½ ounces Triple Sec liqueur

  5 ounces fresh lime juice

  2 ounces pomegranate juice

  1 tablespoon superfine sugar

  Sugared Rose Petals (recipe follows), for garnish

  Fill a cocktail shaker halfway with ice. Place all of
the ingredients except the rose petals in the shaker
and shake hard for 30 seconds. Fill 2 glasses with
ice and strain the liquid into them. Garnish each
glass with the rose petals, if desired.

### SUGARED ROSE PETALS
**MAKES 2 TO 3 DOZEN**

*For best results, choose a dry, cool day to prepare these sugared
rose petals. In low-humidity locations, you can store the
petals in an airtight container for up to 1 year. Be sure to use
only unsprayed roses.*

  1 small bunch of pale pink edible 1-inch roses

  1 large egg white

  1 cup superfine sugar

  **1** Place the roses in a vase filled with cool water
while you work. Line a baking sheet with parchment paper. In a small bowl, whisk together the
egg white with 4 or 5 drops of water to thin the
consistency. Place the sugar in a second small bowl.
Place a pair of tweezers and a teaspoon nearby.

**2** Remove a few petals at a time 1 rose at a time; choose the petals that are smooth, and discard curled and wrinkled petals from the interior of the bud. Working 1 petal at a time, dip the petal into the egg mixture and use your fingers to coat it. Cover the entire petal, as the egg white will help preserve the rose petal. Wipe off any excess egg white so that the petal is lightly veiled in the egg white mixture.

**3** Hold the damp petal at the base with the tips of the tweezers. Using a teaspoon or a sifter, sprinkle the sugar onto one side of the petal. Quickly turn the petal over and tap the tweezers gently against the side of the bowl to shake the excess sugar from the front of the petal. Sugar the back of the petal in the same manner and set the petal to dry, right-side up without touching other petals, on the prepared baking sheet. Repeat with the remaining petals. Allow the petals to dry for at least 4 hours or until crisp and brittle.

**4** Store the petals in even layers, lightly packed between finely shredded wax paper.

## SUMMERTIME CHARTREUSE

**MAKES TWO 5-OUNCE DRINKS** | photograph on page 208

*The aromatic liqueur called "chartreuse" was originally made by the Carthusian monks in France's La Grande Chartreuse monastery. It comes in green and yellow varieties, is rather sweet, and is made with 130 herbs and spices.*

5 ounces gin
1 teaspoon strained lemon juice
2 teaspoons chartreuse

**1** Place 2 martini glasses in the freezer for at least 10 minutes until frosty.

**2** Shake all the ingredients together in a cocktail shaker filled with ice. Strain into the chilled glasses.

## COSMOPOLITAN

**MAKES TWO 5-OUNCE DRINKS** | photograph on page 204

*This pretty, pink crisp drink is among my favorite cocktails.*

3½ ounces lemon-scented vodka
2 tablespoons fresh lime juice
2 ounces Cointreau liqueur
1 tablespoon fresh cranberry juice
Zest of 1 lime

**1** Place 2 martini glasses in the freezer for at least 10 minutes.

**2** Fill a cocktail shaker halfway with ice. Add the vodka, lime juice, Cointreau, and cranberry juice to the shaker. Cover and shake hard for 30 seconds. Strain the liquid immediately into the chilled glasses and garnish with strips of lime zest.

> **NOTE** | Fruit Mixers and Garnishes
>
> Instead of using orange and grapefruit juices, I sometimes like to make cocktails with colorful fruit mixers such as pomegranate, blackberry, and fresh cranberry juice. When you make drinks that call for orange, grapefruit, lemon, or lime juices, always squeeze your own. Fresh juices are aromatic and tart without being acrid.
>
> Garnishes are another easy way to provide color and variety to cocktails. Search your local produce market for seasonal fruits to use, such as exotic blood oranges and kumquats, beautiful plump grapes, sweet honeydew melon, aromatic passion fruit, plums of all colors, spiky star fruit, and tart caper berries.

## CLASSIC MARTINI

**MAKES TWO 4-OUNCE MARTINIS** | photograph on page 202

*The name "martini" is derived from the company Martini & Rossi, which is known for its vermouth. Martinis may be made with either vodka or gin. I love to serve vodka martinis with classic hors d'oeuvres such as blini and caviar. Caper berries, the teardrop-shaped fruit of the caper bush, taste wonderful in this martini, but if you can't find them, a green brine-cured olive makes a fine substitute.*

½ ounce of vermouth

8 ounces vodka

2 large caper berries or brine-cured olives, for garnish

**1** Pour the vermouth into a martini glass. Swirl the vermouth around the glass to coat the inside, and pour it into a second glass. Swirl it around the second glass and discard the vermouth. Place the glasses in the freezer for at least 10 minutes.

**2** Fill a cocktail shaker with 3 cups of ice. Pour in the vodka and shake hard until the vodka is ice cold, about 45 seconds. Strain the vodka into the glasses and garnish each drink with a caper berry.

## PEAR MARTINI

**MAKES TWO 5-OUNCE DRINKS** | photograph on page 204

*Eau de vie is French for "water of life" and describes any potent, colorless brandy or spirit distilled from fermented fruit juice. Poire William, a colorless pear eau de vie made in Switzerland and France, adds a wonderful light pear fragrance to this unusual martini. This drink may be made up to 3 days ahead without the ice or the garnish, kept in the freezer, then served without shaking in ice.*

5½ ounces lemon-scented vodka

1½ ounces Poire William

1½ teaspoons Cointreau liqueur

Pear Chips (recipe follows), for garnish

**1** Place 2 martini glasses in the freezer for at least 10 minutes.

**2** Place the vodka, Poire William, and Cointreau in a cocktail shaker. Fill the shaker halfway with the ice. Close and shake hard for about 30 seconds. Strain the liquid into the chilled glasses. Garnish with a Pear Chip, if desired.

## PEAR CHIPS

**MAKES 24 TO 30**

*These chips may be made up to 5 days in advance and stored in an airtight container at room temperature until ready to use. The sugar syrup on the pear slices sticks too much to use parchment paper, so instead I use Silpat mats, which are specially coated nonstick mats (see Sources, page 486). They add no grease to the recipe and may be used over and over again.*

½ cup sugar

1 unripe pear, such as Seckel or Bosc

**1** Preheat the oven to 175° F. with 2 racks. Line 2 baking sheets with 2 Silpat mats and set aside. In a medium saucepan, combine the sugar with ½ cup water and bring to a boil over high heat. Cook, stirring occasionally, until the sugar has dissolved completely, about 3 to 6 minutes.

**2** Using a mandoline, slice the pear lengthwise as thin as possible, about 1/16 inch. Each slice should remain intact and be uniform in thickness. Working in batches, place 5 of the slices in the simmering syrup. Cook for 30 seconds. Use a slotted spoon to transfer the slices, ¼ inch apart, to the baking sheets. Continue with the remaining pear slices.

**3** Cook the pear slices in the oven, rotating the pans halfway through the cooking time, until they are dry and crisp, but not brown, about 3 hours; check them regularly. Transfer the slices from the baking sheets to cool on a wire rack. Store them in an airtight container, layered between plastic wrap.

## REVERSE MARTINI

**MAKES TWO 4-OUNCE MARTINIS** | photograph on page 208

*I call this a "Reverse Martini" because of the proportion of vermouth to gin. Traditionally, martinis are made with only a hint of vermouth. The less vermouth a martini contains, the drier it is, so you could also call this a "Wet Martini."*

6 ounces gin

2 ounces dry white vermouth

1 green oil-cured olive, pitted and cut into
    thin rings

1 black oil-cured olive, pitted and cut into
    thin rings

**1** Place 2 martini glasses in the freezer for at least 10 minutes.

**2** Shake gin and vermouth in a cocktail shaker filled with 3 cups of ice. Strain the drinks into chilled martini glasses. Garnish with 2 or 3 rings of olives in each glass.

---

**NOTE** | Basic Bar Equipment

When making party cocktails for a crowd, the following equipment is indispensable. Have everything set out before guests arrive, so that every item will be at hand.

| | |
|---|---|
| Ice bucket | Bottle opener |
| Blender | Ice cracker |
| Cocktail shaker | Sharp knife |
| Cocktail strainer | Lemon zester |
| Glass pitchers | Melon baller |
| Jigger measures | Cocktail napkins |
| Corkscrew | Cocktail stirrers |

---

## SAZERAC

**MAKES TWO 4-OUNCE DRINKS** | photograph on page 204

*It is said that this rather potent drink originated at the Sazerac Coffee House in New Orleans. Some Southerners even claim that it was the nation's first cocktail. Peychaud bitters, which originated in New Orleans, make the most authentic Sazerac, but Angostura bitters are also fine. This drink can be made 1 month ahead without the ice and kept tightly covered in the refrigerator.*

1 lemon

Crushed ice (see page 427)

10 ounces bourbon

¼ teaspoon Peychaud or Angostura bitters

1½ teaspoons Pernod

2 teaspoons superfine sugar

**1** Peel four 3-inch strips of lemon zest off the lemon using a vegetable peeler or a paring knife. Rub 2 pieces of the zest, yellow skin-side down, around the edge of each of two 8-ounce glasses. Discard the zest. Fill the glasses with crushed ice and place them in the freezer.

**2** Fill a cocktail shaker halfway with ice cubes. Add the bourbon, bitters, Pernod, and the sugar. Cover and shake for 30 seconds and strain into the prepared glasses. Top each drink with the 2 remaining pieces of lemon zest.

## MANGO COCKTAIL

**MAKES FOUR 6-OUNCE DRINKS** | photograph on
page 204

*Mangos are harvested in many warm climates throughout the
world, but are mainly available in the United States from May
through September. Look for mangos that have unblemished,
yellow skin blushed with red. This cocktail is more delicious
with fresh mango juice made in the blender with ripe mangos,
but you may also use canned or bottled mango nectar for a
satisfying treat.*

4½ ounces light rum

1 tablespoon superfine sugar

1½ cups mango purée (about 2 mangos)

¾ teaspoon Cointreau

¼ teaspoon pure vanilla extract

2 teaspoons fresh lime juice

6 ounces seltzer or sparkling water

**1** In a large pitcher, whisk together the rum and
the sugar until the sugar has dissolved. Add the
remaining ingredients. Whisk to combine.

**2** Fill 4 tumblers with ice. Divide the liquid
evenly among the tumblers.

## LIMÓN (LEMON DROP)

**MAKES TWO 6-OUNCE DRINKS** | photograph on
page 204

*This is a more civilized version of the popular lemon drop
shot, allowing you to savor the flavors of the lemon, mint, and
sugar. The fresh mint adds a very delicious aroma.*

1 cup crushed ice (see page 427), plus ice cubes
    for chilling

½ cup fresh lemon juice, strained

2 tablespoons superfine sugar

4 ounces vodka

3 sprigs of mint

**1** Fill the glasses with the crushed ice and place
them in the freezer. Pour the lemon juice, sugar,
and vodka into a shaker filled with ice and shake
hard for 30 seconds or until the sugar is melted.

**2** Pour the liquid over the crushed ice in the
glasses. Rub the lip of each glass hard with a mint
leaf just before serving, and garnish with a fresh
mint sprig.

## KUMQUAT COCKTAIL

**MAKES ABOUT TEN 6-OUNCE DRINKS** | photograph on
page 204

*Available from November to March, kumquats are small oval
or round citrus fruits. The rind is sweeter than the fruit inside
and can be eaten raw, candied, pickled, or in marmalades.
With this recipe, you can make your own delicious kumquat
vodka. It will keep indefinitely covered and refrigerated, and
can be used in whatever proportion you like with seltzer or
sparkling water. I like to serve it half and half.*

1 cup sugar

3 tablespoons grated kumquat zest (from about
    12 ounces kumquats)

1 tablespoon fresh lemon juice

24 ounces vodka

Seltzer or sparkling water

**1** Combine the sugar with 1 cup of water in a
small saucepan. Bring to a boil over medium-high
heat, stirring occasionally until the sugar has dissolved. Set aside to cool. Transfer the sugar syrup to
a glass jar. Add the zest, lemon juice, and vodka.
Refrigerate for 5 days. Strain the liquid through a
double layer of cheesecloth. Discard the solids.
Return the strained liquid to a clean glass jar. Keep
refrigerated until using.

**2** To make a cocktail, fill a glass halfway with
ice. Add the kumquat vodka and seltzer in equal
proportions.

## FRESH LIME DAIQUIRI

**MAKES SIX 6-OUNCE DRINKS** | photograph on
page 204

*Tinted sugars of various crystal sizes are an ideal decoration,
not only for baking, but also around the rim of a cocktail
glass. Select shades that contrast nicely with the drink you are
making. To order already colored sanding sugar, see Sources,
page 487. To make your own, add just the smallest toothpick-
ful of paste or gel color to superfine sugar, then blend until the
color is combined with the sugar and the desired shade has
been reached.*

> 2 tablespoons light green sanding sugar for the
>     rims of the glasses (optional)
> ¾ cup fresh lime juice (save halves)
> ¼ teaspoon grated lime zest
> 6 ounces light rum
> ⅓ cup plus 1 tablespoon superfine sugar

**1** Pour the sanding sugar into a saucer big
enough to encompass the rim of the glass you are
using. One at a time, rub the rim of each glass with
the reserved half of a lime, so that the lip is wet
about ⅛ inch deep into the glass. Immediately dip
the rim of the glass into the sugar and gently rotate
until the rim is covered with sugar. Gently tap the
glass to remove excess sugar. Set aside.

**2** Add the lime juice, zest, rum, and sugar to a
blender. Stir until the sugar has dissolved. Add ice
to fill half the blender. Blend on high until all
the ice is puréed and the mixture is slushy, about
1 minute. Pour immediately into the prepared
glasses and serve.

## MAI TAI

**MAKES TWO 7-OUNCE DRINKS** | photograph on
page 204

*Victor Bergeron, the original owner of Trader Vic's restaurant,
claims that he created this drink one day for some Tahitian
friends. When they tasted the drink they exclaimed, "Mai
tai!"—meaning "out of this world." You will find this cocktail
simply wonderful—a sophisticated and delicious mixture of
rum, liqueur, citrus, and spices.*

> 1 fresh passion fruit (optional) or 2 to
>     3 tablespoons passion fruit juice
> 6½ ounces fresh or canned pineapple juice
> ⅓ cup fresh orange juice
> 1 tablespoon fresh lime juice
> ½ teaspoon grated fresh ginger
> ⅛ teaspoon powdered cardamom
> 2 ounces light rum
> 1 ounce Triple Sec or Cointreau liqueur
> Crushed ice (see page 427)
> 2 ounces Myer's dark rum
> 1 orange or clementine, cut into wedges, for
>     garnish

**1** If using, halve the passion fruit crosswise.
Scoop out the flesh into a sieve over a small bowl.
Press the flesh through the sieve, discard the solids,
and set aside the juice.

**2** Combine the pineapple, orange, and lime
juices, the ginger, cardamom, light rum, Triple
Sec, and passion fruit juice, if using, in a cocktail
shaker. Shake well. Pour the drink among 2 highball glasses, each half filled with crushed ice. Pour
1 ounce of dark rum on top of each drink. It will
float. Garnish each glass with a wedge of orange or
clementine.

## CAIPIRINHA

MAKES TWO 6-OUNCE DRINKS | photograph on page 204

*The main ingredient in this cocktail, which is considered to be the national drink of Brazil, is cachaça, a potent sugarcane brandy. You can substitute light rum if you can't find cachaça. There are 2 methods for making this popular drink. I prefer the first, the way it is traditionally made in Brazil.*

4 limes, halved

2½ tablespoons superfine sugar

Coarsely crushed ice (see page 427)

4 ounces cachaça

**1** Place 2 lime halves in each of 2 tumblers. Sprinkle 2 teaspoons of the sugar into each tumbler. Using a wooden reamer, crush the flesh of the limes.

**2** Fill the glasses with the ice and add the cachaça. Stir well and serve.

### VARIATION

6 ounces fresh lime juice, plus 2 halves of lime reserved

2½ tablespoons superfine sugar

4 ounces cachaça

Coarsely crushed ice (see page 427)

**1** Place the lime juice, sugar, and the cachaça in a cocktail shaker filled halfway with the ice. Shake for 30 seconds to dissolve the sugar.

**2** Place 1 half lime in each of 2 tumblers. Fill each glass with ice. Pour the liquid from the shaker into the glasses.

## BLOODY MARY

MAKES FOUR 9-OUNCE DRINKS | photograph on page 204

*Buying the best-quality tomato purée you can find, rather than resorting to canned tomato juice, is an excellent way to make a delicious Bloody Mary. You may make the mix without the vodka 2 to 3 days ahead of time and keep it in the refrigerator. The cucumber tile garnishes are optional, of course; you may use cucumber spears instead.*

1 seedless cucumber

28 ounces tomato purée or best-quality tomato juice

8 ounces vodka

¼ cup plus 2 tablespoons fresh lime juice

1 tablespoon prepared horseradish

2 teaspoons Worcestershire sauce

¼ teaspoon freshly ground black pepper

1 teaspoon kosher salt

½ teaspoon Tabasco sauce

½ teaspoon celery seed

**1** To prepare the cucumber tiles for garnish, trim ½ inch off of each end of the cucumber. Stand the cucumber on one end and with a paring knife remove a lengthwise slice of the peel, about ¼ inch thick and ¼ to ¾ inches wide. Repeat until you have 4 long slices of peel. Trim the strips into square tiles of descending size. Skewer about 10 tiles onto each of 4 wooden skewers in descending order. Wrap each skewer in a piece of damp paper towel and refrigerate until ready to serve. Alternatively, cut the cucumber into 4 long seedless spears.

**2** In a pitcher, whisk together the remaining ingredients. Fill four 10- to 12-ounce glasses with ice. Pour the drink into each glass, and garnish with the reserved cucumber skewers.

## PUB DRINKS

The term "pub" is an abbreviation of "public house," a private home of a brewer opened to the public for drinking the beer made there. Cocktails referred to as pub drinks are those containing ale or beer, such as these four favorites.

## BLACK VELVET

**MAKES SIX 8-OUNCE DRINKS** | photograph on page 206

*Although this bubbly drink is said to have originated in the Brooks Club in London, it was quickly appropriated by the Irish.*

    1 bottle (750 ml) champagne, chilled
    2 bottles (12 ounces each) Guinness stout,
        chilled

Fill 6 pilsner glasses halfway with 4 ounces of champagne. Fill with 4 ounces of stout to the top of each glass. Serve chilled.

## SNAKEBITE

**MAKES SIX 8-OUNCE DRINKS** | photograph on page 206

*Despite its name, this drink is refreshing rather than overpowering.*

    24 ounces light-colored hard cider, chilled
    2 bottles (12 ounces each) amber beer, chilled

Fill 6 glasses each with 4 ounces of cider and 4 ounces of beer. Serve immediately.

## PANACHE

**MAKES FOUR 6-OUNCE DRINKS** | photograph on page 206

*This is a more refined version of a Shandy, a classic British pub drink made of beer and lemonade.*

    4 teaspoons superfine sugar
    ¼ cup plus 2 tablespoons fresh lemon juice,
        strained
    8 ounces club soda or sparkling water
    1 bottle (12 ounces) Bass ale or other amber
        beer, chilled
    1 lemon, cut in slices

Stir the sugar and lemon juice together in a small bowl until dissolved. Divide the mixture among 4 glasses and add 2 ounces of club soda to each glass. Fill to the top of each glass with the ale, garnish with a slice of lemon, and serve.

## SNAKEBITE AND BLACK

**MAKES SIX 9-OUNCE DRINKS** | photograph on page 206

*Black currant juice gives this drink a deep, rich color. If you can't find it, red grape juice is a good substitute.*

    2 bottles (12 ounces each) amber beer, chilled
    24 ounces light-colored hard cider, chilled
    6 ounces black currant juice or red grape juice

Combine all of the ingredients in a large pitcher and divide among 6 glasses. Serve immediately.

Many people refer to sparkling wine as champagne, but the two should not be confused. Whereas sparkling wines are made around the world, true champagne is made only in the Champagne region of northern France, which has superior grapes for making this exquisite drink. Other countries have different names for their sparkling wines, such as Italy's spumante and prosecco, Germany's sekt, and Spain's cava. Better sparkling wines are labeled "champagne process" or "methode champenoise," which indicates that they have been made using the same strict high standards as those employed to make the very best champagnes.

Although I believe French champagne is in a class by itself, many sparkling wines are also very good, and offer better value when you are having a large party. All are labeled according to their level of sweetness. Brut is the driest, followed by extra-sec or extra-dry (dry), sec or dry (slightly sweet), demi-sec (sweet), and doux (very sweet). Brut, extra-sec, and sec are traditionally served with hors d'oeuvres, while demi-sec and doux are reserved for dessert.

Sparkling wines should be served chilled, between 40 and 50°F. Never place a bottle in the freezer; it can burst within 15 minutes.

It is best to serve sparkling wines in tall and slender glasses, often called flutes, because they have a very small surface from which the bubbles can escape.

By definition, a cordial is a sweet alcoholic beverage made by infusing flavoring ingredients, such as fruits, herbs, and spices, into a spirit, such as rum or vodka. Time is an element because these cordials can take months to mature. But they are well worth the wait, since they have wonderful, unusual flavors and can be stored for months after they are ready to drink. They are delicious served straight up, over ice, or mixed into cocktails. Or, for a simple but festive drink, mix your favorite cordial with club soda or tonic water; it's like a grown-up version of soda pop.

If you use the cheesecloth method to strain the sediment from the liquid, use a wide-mouth jar, then decant the cordial into a pretty container for serving.

## RASPBERRY-THYME CORDIAL

**MAKES 36 OUNCES, EIGHTEEN 2-OUNCE SERVINGS** | photograph on page 212

1½ pounds fresh raspberries
1 cup sugar
2 bunches of fresh thyme
16 ounces sweet Riesling wine
8 ounces 80-proof vodka

**1** In a food processor, combine the raspberries with ½ cup sugar and blend until just puréed. Allow to stand for 30 minutes.

**2** Meanwhile, combine 1 cup water and the remaining sugar in a small saucepan over medium-high heat, stirring frequently to dissolve the sugar, about 5 minutes. Add the thyme and simmer for 15 minutes. Remove from the heat and allow to cool to room temperature. Strain the thyme out of the syrup and discard.

**3** In a large bowl, combine the thyme-sugar mixture, the raspberry mixture, the wine, and the vodka. Transfer to a very clean glass jar or bottle, using a funnel if the mouth is small, and cover tightly; allow to cure in the refrigerator or a cool dark place for 1 week.

**4** Strain through a fine-mesh sieve and allow to cure in the refrigerator or a cool dark place for 1 week. Strain again and let cure for 1 month in the refrigerator. It is important from this time until it is siphoned that the bottle remain upright and the sediment undisturbed. Siphon or strain through a fine mesh sieve lined with cheesecloth (see Note, right) before serving.

## PASSION FRUIT CORDIAL

**MAKES 32 OUNCES, SIXTEEN 2-OUNCE SERVINGS** | photograph on page 212

*Passion fruit juice is available in gourmet grocery stores and often in the beverage section of supermarkets.*

3 ounces light rum
9 ounces spiced rum
24 ounces passion fruit juice

**1** In a large bowl, combine all the ingredients. Transfer to a very clean glass jar or bottle, using a funnel if the mouth is small, and cover tightly; allow to cure in the refrigerator or a cool dark place for 2 to 3 weeks.

**2** Strain through a fine-mesh sieve lined with cheesecloth. Allow to cure 1 week more or until the sediment settles. Siphon or strain again (see Note, right) before serving.

---

**NOTE** | Crystal-Clear Cordials

After the cordials have cured and aged for their respective periods of time they must be siphoned or carefully strained out of their containers to achieve their jewel tone. All of these cordials, except the Vanilla Rum, need to be strained from the sediment to make the resulting liquid smooth-tasting, clear, and beautiful. As the cordials age, do not disturb the sediment in them or the drink will be cloudy.

To decant the cordial without disturbing the sediment, I recommend siphoning. Begin by placing the cordial container on a countertop next to the sink. Place an empty bottle of equal capacity in the sink. Place one end of a plastic tube, long enough to stretch between the two bottles, $\frac{1}{2}$ inch above the sediment in the liquid. Suck at the other end, keeping your head below the cordial-filled bottle. Then, just before the liquid comes through the tube, place it in the empty bottle in the sink; the liquid will flow into the empty container. When you reach the sediment, pull the tube from the cordial container in the sink. Discard the sediment.

To strain the liquid, line a fine strainer with a double layer of damp cheesecloth. Carefully pour or ladle out the liquid, taking care to not disturb the sediment at the bottom. Discard the sediment. Clean the container and return the strained liquid. After straining, any slight sediment that might remain will settle as the cordial is stored in the refrigerator.

## STRAWBERRY CORDIAL

**MAKES 20 OUNCES, TEN 2-OUNCE**
**SERVINGS** | photograph on page 212

*This is delicious mixed with equal parts seltzer or tonic.*

1 pound strawberries, washed, hulled, and
    quartered
1½ cups sugar
12 ounces 80-proof vodka
Zest of 2 lemons
Zest of 2 navel oranges
3 tablespoons fresh lemon juice

**1** In a food processor, combine the strawberries
with the sugar and blend until just puréed. Let
stand at room temperature for 1 hour.

**2** Combine the strawberry-sugar mixture with
the vodka, zests, and juice in a bowl. Transfer to a
very clean glass jar or bottle, using a funnel if the
mouth is small, and cover tightly; allow to cure in
the refrigerator or a cool dark place for 1 week.

**3** Strain through a fine-mesh sieve and allow to
cure in a cool dark place, or the refrigerator, for 1
month. Remove the sediment by siphoning (see
page 439), and cure for 1 week in the refrigerator.

## VANILLA RUM CORDIAL

**MAKES 16 OUNCES, EIGHT 2-OUNCE**
**SERVINGS** | photograph on page 212

*If you can't locate vanilla beans, substitute 3 teaspoons of
vanilla extract, though the drink's flavor won't be as rich.*

½ cup sugar
4 whole vanilla beans, split in half lengthwise
6 ounces dark rum
10 ounces light rum

**1** In a small saucepan, combine the sugar and
½ cup water and bring to a simmer over medium-
high heat, stirring frequently, until the sugar is dissolved, about 5 minutes. Add the vanilla beans and
simmer for 10 minutes over medium-low heat.
Allow the mixture to cool to room temperature.

**2** Combine the 2 rums with the vanilla syrup.
Transfer to a very clean glass jar or bottle, using a
funnel if the mouth is small, and cover tightly. Let
stand for 1 month in the refrigerator or a cool dark
place. The cordial need not be strained or siphoned.

## ORANGE-ROSEMARY CORDIAL

**MAKES 32 OUNCES, SIXTEEN 2-OUNCE**
**SERVINGS** | photograph on page 212

*Valencia oranges are the best for this cordial because their zest
is particularly fruity and hardly bitter. This drink tastes best
up to 2 weeks after curing.*

1 cup sugar
3 sprigs rosemary
3 tablespoons zest of Valencia oranges
1 tablespoon fresh lemon juice
24 ounces 80-proof vodka

**1** In a small saucepan, combine 1 cup of water
and the sugar and heat over medium-high heat,
stirring frequently to dissolve the sugar, about 1
minute. Add the rosemary and simmer for 10 minutes over medium-low heat. Remove from the heat
and allow to cool to room temperature. Strain the
rosemary out of the syrup and discard.

**2** Combine the rosemary syrup with the zest,
the lemon juice, and the vodka in a bowl. Transfer
to a very clean glass jar or bottle, using a funnel if
the mouth is small, and cover tightly; allow to cure
in the refrigerator or a cool dark place for 1 month.

**3** Siphon or strain through a fine-mesh sieve
lined with cheesecloth (see page 439) before
serving.

There are no rules about what a home bar has to consist of; it can be as complicated or as simple as you wish. If you are a frequent party giver and want to offer your guests virtually unlimited options, the list below will allow you to create just about any drink. On the other hand, your drink selection may be as simple as a huge tub filled with ice and stocked with beers, sodas, and splits of champagne. This creates a particularly bountiful feeling and is perfect for a casual gathering of friends.

If you are not going to have any extra helping hands, serve cocktails in big ice-filled glass pitchers set on a cloth covered table and surrounded by flowers. However, if you are hiring a catering service or can convince a friend or spouse to help out, it is always elegant to serve the drinks in individual glasses passed on trays. Make sure that the cocktail glasses are well chilled and that the cocktails themselves are very colorful.

**THE BASIC BAR**
Bourbon: 1 liter
Gin: 1 liter
Vodka: 2 liters (1 in the freezer)
Scotch: 1 liter
Single-malt whiskey: 1 fifth
Bourbon: 1 fifth
Light rum: 1 fifth
Dark rum: 1 fifth
Dry sherry: 1 fifth
Cream sherry: 1 fifth
Dry vermouth: 1 fifth
Sweet vermouth: 1 fifth
Cassis: 200 milliliter bottle
Lillet or Dubonnet: 1 fifth
Port: 1 fifth
Cognac: 1 fifth
Tequila: 1 fifth
Triple Sec: 1 fifth
Cointreau: 1 fifth
Bitters: 1 small bottle

**LIQUORS FOR SPECIAL DRINKS**
Flavored vodkas
Pimm's #1
Rosé wine
Sweet Riesling wine
Moscato d'Asti
Blue curaçao
Chartreuse
Poire William
Pernod
Cachaça
Hard cider
Grappa
Anejo 100% Blue Agave Tequila

**WINE**
Red wine: six 750-ml bottles
White table wine (blanc de blanc): six 750-ml bottles
Champagne or sparkling wine: one 750-ml bottle

**BEER**
Lager, dark, and light: 1 case each
Micro-brewed: 4 six-packs from different breweries

**ALCOHOL-FREE DRINKS AND MIXERS**
Sparkling and mineral water
Seltzer and tonic
Ginger ale
Cola and diet cola
Best-quality tomato juice
Fresh orange juice

**GARNISHES AND FLAVORINGS**
Lemons, limes, oranges
Oil-cured olives
Prepared horseradish
Worcestershire
Tabasco sauce
Celery seed
Kosher salt
Superfine sugar

$10$

## CLASSICS

Photographs for these recipes appear on
pages 218–223

IT'S WONDERFUL TO TRY OUT NEW CONCEPTS, TO WIDEN YOUR REACH AND TREAT YOUR GUESTS TO SOMETHING THEY HAVE NEVER TRIED BEFORE. BUT THERE IS ALWAYS ROOM IN ANY HORS D'OEUVRES SELECTION FOR A CLASSIC OR TWO, A LITTLE BITE

that has proved its worth over time. I have had many people tell me that, over the years, they have lost track of some of their favorites. "I've forgotten —exactly how do you make those little shrimp wrapped in snow peas?" is the kind of question I hear over and over again as I meet people around the country and all over the world.

With this in mind, I've compiled a chapter's worth of my favorite hors d'oeuvres from earlier works. Among the hundreds of ideas for hors d'oeuvres that I have presented over the years, these are the ones that people always mention, the ones that, once tried, will become a mainstay of your party food repertoire.

These recipes have become classics for a variety of reasons. Some, such as Snow Peas with St. André or the Roquefort Grapes, combine unusual and attractive presentation with an interesting juxtaposition of flavors. When you bite into the little balls of nut-garnished Roquefort cheese, for example, and are rewarded with a spritz of juice from the grape inside, it's a wonderful treat. Some of the recipes in this category require a little extra time to prepare, but the rewards are worth the effort.

Other recipes included here, on the other hand, have become popular precisely because they are model ways to serve a crowd with little effort but with no compromise in quality or flavor. Gravlax on Black Bread with Mustard-Fennel Sauce or Chicken Liver Pâté on Pear Slices are perfect examples of these type of hors d'oeuvres. So is the caramel-coated wheel of Brie, which requires only two or three ingredients to make, can be put out

without another thought just as your guests arrive, and will serve dozens. If you are throwing a party for a large crowd, an hors d'oeuvre such as turkey cut into slivers and served on orange-raisin muffins with quince jelly is especially satisfying.

Some of the recipes here primarily involve recognizing that high-quality ingredients need only the proper presentation to transform them into a fantastic hors d'oeuvre. Red Potatoes with Sour Cream and Caviar, for example, are simple to prepare yet luxurious to serve. Similarly, assembling a raw bar makes the most of fresh shellfish and seasonal vegetables, and though it will take some organization to create one, you are bound to have a memorable party if you do.

The recipes in this chapter have been organized in the same way as the chapters have been organized in the rest of the book, and the same principles outlined in those chapters apply here. When selecting produce to be used as cups for Chapter 3, for example, consider the filled snow pea recipes as well. Likewise, when making a batch of Puff Pastry for the straws in chapter 6, you might want to double the recipe to use for the Savory Palmiers. And when reviewing chapter 9 for drink ideas, be sure to consider the sips that are staples at my cocktail parties.

Whichever are your personal favorites among these recipes, I recommend that you treat them as I do: Just as your guest list should include old friends and some newcomers, so should your hors d'oeuvres selection. In my experience, it's an approach that is likely to please just about everybody.

## ORANGE-RAISIN MUFFINS WITH SMOKED TURKEY

**MAKES 2½ DOZEN** | photograph on page 222

*These may be assembled up to 2 hours before serving. Keep them covered with a damp kitchen towel to keep the bread and turkey from drying out.*

½ pound thinly sliced smoked turkey breast
30 Gayla's Orange-Raisin Muffins (recipe
    follows), split in half horizontally
¾ cup Quince Jelly (page 446) or prepared

Cut the turkey into small pieces, about 1½ inches long. Place a small amount on each muffin bottom. Top the turkey with ½ teaspoon quince jelly, cover with the muffin top, and serve.

## GAYLA'S ORANGE-RAISIN MUFFINS

**MAKES 2½ DOZEN** | photograph on page 222

*I fondly remember my friend Gayla sharing her recipe for these delicious muffins with me when I admired them at a wedding reception years ago.*

1½ cups sugar
4 tablespoons unsalted butter, at room
    temperature, plus 1 tablespoon
    for the pans
2 large eggs
1 teaspoon baking soda
1 cup nonfat buttermilk
2 cups all-purpose flour
½ teaspoon kosher salt

1 cup golden or dark raisins
Zest of 1 orange, grated
Juice of 1 orange

**1** Preheat the oven to 400°F. Lightly butter muffin tins with openings that measure 2 inches across the top. (Muffins may be made in batches if you do not have enough tins.) In the bowl of an electric mixer, cream 1 cup sugar with the butter on medium-low speed until smooth. Add the eggs one at a time, and beat until fluffy.

**2** In a small bowl, dissolve the baking soda in the buttermilk. Sift together the flour and salt. With the mixer on low speed and working in batches, gradually add the flour mixture to the butter mixture, alternating with the buttermilk. Start and end with the flour. Blend until just combined.

**3** In a food processor, process the raisins with the orange zest until well combined. Add to the batter and combine. Spoon the batter into the prepared muffin tins and bake until golden brown and firm to the touch, 16 to 18 minutes.

**4** Transfer the tins to a cooling rack and place close together. Brush the tops of the muffins with the orange juice and sprinkle with the remaining ½ cup sugar while the muffins are still warm. Cool before serving. The muffins may be made up to 1 day ahead and kept in an airtight container at room temperature.

## QUINCE JELLY

**MAKES 4 PINTS** | photograph on page 222

*This beautiful amber-colored jelly with its distinctive sweet-sour flavor is traditionally served with pork or made into a dessertlike paste. Homemade quince jelly tastes freshest, but if quinces are not available (in the fall), you can find quince jelly in the international section of the grocery store or shelved with other jams and jellies.*

12 large, very ripe quinces, peeled, cored,
    and thinly sliced
4½ cups sugar
Sprigs of fresh rosemary

**1** Place the quinces in a large pot, and add water to cover. Bring to a boil over high heat, then reduce the heat to medium-low, and simmer until the fruit is tender, about 45 minutes. Add more water as needed to keep up the level. Pour the quinces and the liquid into a jelly bag (see Sources, page 486), or pour the quinces and the liquid in batches through a fine strainer lined with a double layer of cheesecloth. Allow the juices to drip into a bowl.

**2** Measure 6 cups of juice into a large heavy-bottomed pot and bring to a boil over medium heat. Add the sugar, stir until it is dissolved, and increase the heat to high. Continue to stir while the mixture boils.

**3** Approximately 3 to 4 minutes after adding the sugar, begin to test the syrup. When drops form and hang from a spoon (the "sheeting" stage) the jelly is done.

**4** Remove the jelly from the heat and skim the foam. Pour into hot, sterilized ½-pint jars, add sprigs of rosemary, and seal. Let the jars cool to room temperature. Jelly may be kept at room temperature for 2 weeks or in the refrigerator for several months.

## EGGPLANT CAVIAR ON FRENCH BREAD TOAST

**MAKES 5 TO 6 DOZEN** | photograph on page 222

4 eggplants (about 4 pounds total)
¼ cup vegetable oil, plus more for the pan
½ cup low-sodium soy sauce
¼ cup rice wine vinegar
1 tablespoon sugar
¼ cup finely grated fresh ginger
2 tablespoons sesame oil
⅓ cup finely chopped fresh cilantro
4 scallions, green and white parts, finely
    chopped
Hot pepper sauce
French Bread Toasts (recipe follows)
Fresh cilantro, chives, or scallions, for garnish

**1** Preheat the oven to 350°F.

**2** Cut the eggplants in half lengthwise, brush all sides with the vegetable oil, and lay down in an oiled shallow pan. Roast until the eggplants collapse and are tender, about 45 minutes. Cool, saving the juices.

**3** In a medium, nonreactive saucepan, heat the soy sauce, vinegar, sugar, and 2 tablespoons of the ginger to boiling. Reduce the heat and add the sesame oil. Cook for 1 minute.

**4** Scrape the cooled eggplant from the skin and chop fine. In the bowl of a food processor, add the oil mixture to the eggplant, along with the remaining ginger, chopped cilantro, and scallions, and pulse until well combined but the mixture still has some texture. Season to taste with the hot sauce, and refrigerate overnight to let the flavors meld.

**5** To serve, spoon eggplant mixture on toasts and garnish each with a fresh cilantro leaf or a fine sliver of fresh chive or scallion.

## FRENCH BREAD TOASTS

**MAKES 5 DOZEN** | photograph on page 222

1 or 2 loaves (2-inch diameter) good-quality
    French bread
Light sesame oil

**1** Preheat the oven to 325°F.

**2** Slice the bread into ¼-inch-thick slices and
arrange on a baking sheet in one layer. Brush each
slice with the sesame oil and bake until dry but not
colored, about 10 minutes. Cool on wire racks.


## GRAVLAX ON BLACK BREAD WITH MUSTARD-FENNEL SAUCE

**MAKES 4 TO 5 DOZEN** | photograph on page 221

¼ cup Dijon mustard
1 teaspoon dry mustard
3 tablespoons sugar
2 tablespoons white vinegar
⅓ cup light vegetable oil
Tops of 1 small bunch of fennel, finely chopped,
    or 2 tablespoons fresh dill

Gravlax with Fennel (recipe follows)
2 large loaves (about 60 slices) thinly sliced
    black bread

**1** To make the sauce, combine the mustards,
sugar, and vinegar in the bowl of a food processor.
With the machine running, add the oil drop by
drop until the mixture is thick. Stir in the fennel.
Refrigerate until ready to use, up to 4 weeks.

**2** To serve, place slices of gravlax on half-slices of
black bread; top with the mustard-fennel sauce.


## GRAVLAX WITH FENNEL

**MAKES 4 TO 5 DOZEN** | photograph on page 221

*I like to use a center-cut portion of Norwegian salmon—it is
fine-grained, pale in color, and delicately flavored. Weighing
down the salmon while it cures compresses the flesh and
squeezes out any liquid, creating a finer-grained gravlax.*

1 cup plus 2 tablespoons sugar
1 cup plus 2 tablespoons kosher salt
1 tablespoon coarsely ground black pepper
1 3-pound boned fillet of Norwegian salmon,
    skin left on
1 cup coarsely chopped fresh fennel tops or
    fresh dill
½ cup light olive oil

**1** In a medium bowl, combine the sugar, salt, and
pepper and set aside.

**2** Line a 8½ × 12-inch nonreactive baking pan
with plastic wrap. Sprinkle ¾ cup of the salt mixture onto the plastic wrap. Cut the fillet in half
crosswise. Put half of the salmon skin-side down
onto the plastic wrap. Use your hands to pack
¾ cup of the salt mixture and the fennel onto the
flesh of the salmon. Place the remaining salmon
skin-side up, directly on top, sprinkle with the
remaining ¾ cup of salt mixture, and wrap tightly
with plastic wrap.

**3** Place another pan on top of the salmon and
weigh it down with any heavy object; several cans
work well. Refrigerate for at least 3 days, turning
the fish twice a day and draining off any juices.

**4** No more than 2 to 3 hours before serving, put
half of the fish on a cutting board. Scrape off the
fennel and salt mixture. Cut the fish into 2-inch
crosswise pieces, and with a very sharp, long knife,
cut each 2-inch piece into very thin slices. Arrange
them on sheets of plastic wrap, taking care to keep
each slice separate. Repeat with remaining half of
salmon. Refrigerate until ready to use.

## PHYLLO TRIANGLES WITH FETA AND SPINACH

**MAKES 6 DOZEN** | photograph on page 221

*You can substitute two 10-ounce packages of frozen chopped spinach for the fresh. Defrost it and squeeze it in a colander to press out the excess liquid.*

⅓ cup olive oil
1 bunch of scallions, white and green parts,
    finely chopped
3½ pounds spinach, well washed
1 bunch of fresh flat-leaf parsley, roughly
    chopped
1 bunch of dill, roughly chopped
¾ pound feta cheese, drained and crumbled
3 large eggs, slightly beaten
Kosher salt and freshly ground black pepper

1 pound phyllo pastry (see page 297)
1 pound (4 sticks) unsalted butter, melted

**1** Heat the oil in a large skillet over medium heat and cook the scallions until soft, 3 to 4 minutes. Add the spinach and cook until wilted, stirring frequently. Transfer the mixture to a colander placed over a bowl and press out the liquid. Transfer the liquid to a skillet and boil down the liquid until it measures 2 tablespoons. Roughly chop the pressed spinach. Mix the spinach, spinach liquid, parsley, dill, feta cheese, and eggs until well blended. Season with salt and pepper to taste. Allow the mixture to cool completely.

**2** To prepare the triangles, follow the instructions in the Note (right), using 2 teaspoons of the filling for each triangle.

**NOTE** | Making Phyllo Triangles

Learning to work with paper-thin leaves of phyllo pastry may be frustrating at first, but it is the only way to become adept at making quantities of phyllo triangles. (For more information on working with phyllo, see page 297.) Most brands of phyllo come in sheets measuring 15½ × 11 inches. I use this size in these phyllo triangle recipes. **PREPARING THE TRIANGLES** Trim the edges of the pile of phyllo dough so that it is easier to work with. To assemble, place 1 sheet of phyllo on a flat surface and brush with melted butter. Top with 2 more sheets, buttering each. Cut the combined sheets in half crosswise. Then cut each half lengthwise into 2½-inch-wide strips. Spoon the filling onto the center of the end of each strip and form a triangle by folding the lower right-hand corner to the opposite side, as you would a flag. Continue folding to the end of the strip. Repeat with the remaining phyllo and filling. **STORING THE TRIANGLES** If you want to prepare the filled triangles ahead of time, unbaked filled triangles can be refrigerated for up to 2 days, or frozen immediately; do not thaw the frozen triangles before baking.

**3** Preheat the oven to 375°F. with 2 racks. Line 2 baking sheets with parchment paper. Working in batches, place the phyllo triangles on the baking sheets. Brush them with melted butter and bake until golden brown, 7 to 10 minutes.

## PHYLLO TRIANGLES WITH CURRIED WALNUT CHICKEN

**MAKES 6 DOZEN** | photograph on page 221

2½ pounds whole chicken breasts

2 tablespoons unsalted butter

2½ tablespoons all-purpose flour

1½ teaspoons curry powder

1 cup milk

½ teaspoon kosher salt

½ cup chopped toasted walnuts (see page 361)

1 pound phyllo pastry (see page 297)

1 pound (4 sticks) unsalted butter, melted

**1** Heat the oven to 375°F. Arrange the chicken breasts in a roasting pan and cook until the juices run clear when pierced with a knife, about 45 minutes. Let cool. Remove the skin and bones, and discard. Cut the meat into small pieces. Set aside.

**2** Heat 2 tablespoons butter in a small pan. Add the flour and curry powder and cook over low heat, stirring occasionally, about 2 minutes. Whisk in the milk, and whisk until the mixture thickens. Add salt. Stir in the walnuts and the chicken. Set aside to cool completely.

**3** To prepare the triangles, follow the instructions in the Note on page 448, using 2 teaspoons of the filling for each triangle.

**4** Preheat the oven to 375°F. with 2 racks. Line 2 baking sheets with parchment paper. Working in batches, place the phyllo triangles on the baking sheets. Brush them with melted butter and bake until golden brown, 7 to 10 minutes.

### VARIATION

Add ½ teaspoon turmeric along with the curry powder, and add ¼ cup golden raisins, the grated zest of 1 orange, and 1 tablespoon chopped fresh dill when you add the nuts.

## PHYLLO TRIANGLES WITH WILD MUSHROOMS

**MAKES 6 DOZEN** | photograph on page 221

5 tablespoons unsalted butter

1½ pounds chanterelle or shiitake mushrooms, stems removed, caps coarsely chopped

½ cup Homemade Crème Fraîche (page 394) or prepared

1 large bunch of fresh flat-leaf parsley, roughly chopped to yield about ¾ cup

Kosher salt and freshly ground black pepper

Freshly grated nutmeg

1 pound phyllo pastry (see page 297)

1 pound (4 sticks) unsalted butter, melted

**1** Melt 5 tablespoons butter in a medium skillet over medium-high heat. Add the mushrooms and cook, stirring occasionally, until the water is released and evaporated and the mushrooms are soft, 6 to 8 minutes. Remove from heat allow the filling to cool slightly.

**2** Add the crème fraîche and parsley to the mushrooms. Stir in salt, pepper, and nutmeg to taste. Set aside to cool completely.

**3** To prepare the triangles, follow the instructions in the Note on page 448, using 2 teaspoons of the filling for each triangle.

**4** Preheat the oven to 375°F. with 2 racks. Line 2 baking sheets with parchment paper. Working in batches, place the phyllo triangles on the baking sheets. Brush them with melted butter and bake until golden brown, 7 to 10 minutes.

## PHYLLO TRIANGLES WITH LOBSTER FILLING

**MAKES 4 DOZEN** | photograph on page 221

*One 1½ pound lobster provides enough meat to make about 4 dozen of these phyllo triangles. The lobster can be cooked up to 4 hours ahead and kept refrigerated in an airtight container.*

1 1½ pound lobster
4 tablespoons unsalted butter
6 scallions, white and green parts, finely
    chopped
¼ cup white wine or vodka
1½ tablespoons all-purpose flour
¼ cup heavy cream
Pinch of cayenne pepper
Kosher salt and freshly ground black pepper

1 pound phyllo pastry (see page 297)
1 pound (4 sticks) unsalted butter, melted

**1** Bring a large pot of salted water to a rolling boil. Add the lobster and simmer, covered, 10 to 12 minutes. Remove the lobster from the water and submerge in a large bowl of ice water to stop the cooking. Remove the lobster from the water, drain, and keep refrigerated if not using right away. Remove all the meat from the lobster and chop finely. Set aside.

**2** Melt 2 tablespoons of the butter in a small skillet, and cook the scallions until soft for 2 to 4 minutes. Add the lobster meat and wine, and stir quickly to combine over high heat, about 1 minute. Drain the mixture through a fine sieve, reserving the liquid.

**3** Melt the remaining 2 tablespoons of butter in another skillet over medium-low heat. Add the flour and cook slowly, stirring without coloring

the flour, for 5 minutes. Add the reserved liquid and the cream, and stir constantly until the mixture begins to thicken, about 1 minute. Stir the lobster meat into the mixture, add the cayenne pepper, and add salt and pepper to taste. Cool the mixture completely before filling the triangles.

**4** To prepare the triangles, follow the instructions in the Note on page 448, using 1 teaspoon of the filling for each triangle.

**5** Preheat the oven to 375°F. with 2 racks. Line 2 baking sheets with parchment paper. Working in batches, place the phyllo triangles on the baking sheets. Brush them with melted butter and bake until golden brown, 7 to 10 minutes.

## CHINESE PEARL BALLS

**MAKES 3 DOZEN** | photograph on page 221

*Water chestnuts are available in cans in the international section of most grocery stores. These can be prepared ahead and steamed in the kitchen as guests arrive.*

¾ cup sushi rice
6 dried shiitake mushrooms
1 pound lean pork, finely ground
1 large egg, beaten
1 tablespoon low-sodium soy sauce
½ teaspoon sugar
2 teaspoons grated fresh ginger
24 slices water chestnuts, finely chopped to yield
    about ⅓ cup
2 scallions, white and green parts, finely
    chopped
Kosher salt and freshly ground black pepper
Lettuce leaves to line the steamer
Scallion-Soy Dipping Sauce (page 394)

**1** In a medium bowl, soak the rice with water to cover by several inches for 3 to 4 hours. Drain the rice, pat dry, and set aside.

**2** Soak the mushrooms in ½ cup hot water until soft, about 20 minutes. Drain. Discard the stems. Finely chop the caps.

**3** In a medium bowl, mix together the mushrooms, pork, egg, soy sauce, sugar, ginger, water chestnuts, scallions, and salt and pepper to taste (your hands are best for this job). Shape the mixture into 1-inch balls.

**4** Spread the rice on a baking sheet and roll the balls in it, one at a time, coating each completely. Set the balls on a baking sheet lined with parchment paper or wax paper. Cover with plastic wrap and refrigerate for up to 4 hours. (The pearl balls may also be frozen at this point; bring them to room temperature before proceeding.)

**5** Line a steamer with lettuce leaves. Set the steamer in a pan or wok and add enough water to come to within 1 inch of the bottom of the steamer. Bring the water to a boil. Remove the steamer and arrange the balls on a steamer rack. Return the steamer to the pan, cover tightly, and steam until the pork is cooked through, 30 to 35 minutes. Serve warm with the dipping sauce.

## ROQUEFORT GRAPES

**MAKES 4 DOZEN** | photograph on page 220

*These cheese-coated grapes can also be rolled in chopped unroasted pistachio or macadamia nuts. They may be made up to 2 days ahead and kept refrigerated in an airtight container. Any leftover cheese mixture can be frozen.*

10 ounces almonds, pecans, or walnuts

8 ounces cream cheese, at room temperature

4 ounces Roquefort cheese, at room temperature

2 tablespoons heavy cream

1 pound (about 48) red or green seedless grapes

**1** Heat the oven to 300° F. Spread the nuts evenly on a rimmed baking sheet and bake until lightly toasted and aromatic, 8 to 12 minutes. Cool slightly.

**2** Chop the toasted nuts coarsely in a food processor or by hand. Transfer to a platter and spread out evenly.

**3** In the bowl of an electric mixer, combine the cream cheese, Roquefort, and cream and beat on low speed until smooth, 2 to 3 minutes. Drop clean, dry grapes into the loose cheese mixture. Use a rubber spatula to stir the grapes in the mixture until each grape is coated. Working one at a time, transfer the grapes to the chopped nuts and roll the grapes in the nuts until they are well coated. Transfer the grapes to a rimmed baking sheet lined with parchment paper or wax paper. Cover with plastic wrap and refrigerate until serving.

## SNOW PEAS WITH CRABMEAT FILLING

**MAKES 4 DOZEN** | photograph on page 221

50 tender young snow peas

4 ounces cream cheese, at room temperature

4 ounces lump crabmeat, picked over for
cartilage

1 red bell pepper, seeds and ribs removed,
minced

2 tablespoons fresh lemon juice

Kosher salt and freshly ground black pepper

**1** Removed stem end from snow peas, string them, and blanch in a large pot of rapidly boiling water for 30 seconds. Plunge them immediately into cool water to stop the cooking and preserve their green color.

**2** Combine the remaining ingredients for the crabmeat filling in a mixing bowl.

**3** With the sharp point of a paring knife, slit open the snow peas on the curved side. Using a small spatula, stuff some of the filling in each split snow pea. Arrange on a serving platter and refrigerate to rechill the filling. Snow peas may be filled and refrigerated up to 1 hour before serving.

## SNOW PEAS WITH HERBED CHEESE

**MAKES 4 DOZEN** | photograph on page 221

*Snow peas can also be stuffed with Bleu de Bresse cheese.*

50 tender young snow peas

8 ounces cream cheese, at room temperature

¼ cup chopped fresh flat-leaf parsley or chervil

¼ cup chopped fresh dill

1 garlic clove, minced

Freshly ground black pepper

Sprouts or watercress leaves for garnish

**1** Remove the stem end from the snow peas, string them, and blanch in a large pot of rapidly boiling water for 30 seconds. Plunge them immediately into cold water to stop the cooking and preserve their green color. Set aside.

**2** Blend the cream cheese, parsley, dill, garlic, and pepper in a mixing bowl until smooth.

**3** With the sharp point of a paring knife, slit open the snow peas on the curved side. Using a small spatula or pastry bag fitted with a ¼-inch tip, stuff the herbed cheese into the peas. Garnish as desired and arrange on a serving platter. Snow peas may be filled and refrigerated for up to 1 hour before serving.

## SNOW PEAS WITH ST. ANDRÉ

**MAKES 4 DOZEN** | photograph on page 221

50 tender young snow peas

8 ounces St. André cheese or Boursin or
Boursault, at room temperature

Fresh mint (optional)

**1** Remove the stem end from the snow peas, string them, and blanch in a large pot of rapidly boiling water for 30 seconds. Plunge them immediately into cool water to stop the cooking and preserve their green color. Set aside.

**2** With the sharp point of a paring knife, slit open the straight seam of each snow pea. Pipe softened cheese into each one, using a small-tipped pastry tube, or spread with a small spatula. Garnish each pod with a small leaf of mint just poking out the top of the snow pea. Snow peas may be filled and refrigerated for up to 1 hour before serving.

## SNOW PEAS WITH PIMIENTO CHEESE

**MAKES 4 DOZEN** | photograph on page 221

50 tender young snow peas
8 ounces cream cheese, at room temperature
1 roasted red bell pepper (see page 266)
1 small fresh red chili pepper, ribs and ~~seeds~~
    removed, minced
Kosher salt and freshly ground black pepper

**1** Remove the stem end from the snow peas, string them, and blanch in a large pot of rapidly boiling water for 30 seconds. Plunge them immediately into cold water to stop the cooking and preserve their green color. Set aside.

**2** In the bowl of a food processor fitted with a metal blade, purée the roasted bell pepper and the chili pepper. Pour off any liquid. Pass the pepper purée through a fine sieve into a large bowl. Use a fork or the back of a spoon to combine the purée with the softened cream cheese. Stir until smooth and creamy. Season with salt and black pepper, and chill until ready to use.

**3** With the sharp point of a paring knife, slit open the straight seam of each snow pea. Pipe the softened pimiento cheese into each one, using a small-tipped pastry tube, or spread with a small spatula. Snow peas may be filled and refrigerated for up to 1 hour before serving.

## PÂTE À CHOUX WITH ONION JAM

**MAKES 7 DOZEN** | photograph on page 220

*This onion jam is also delicious as a pizza topping, with freshly grated Parmesan cheese and fresh thyme.*

6 tablespoons unsalted butter
5½ pounds onions, thinly sliced
1 bottle dry red wine
¼ cup plus 2 tablespoons crème de cassis
3 tablespoons sugar
Kosher salt and freshly ground black pepper
Seasoned Pâte à Choux Puffs (page 241)

**1** Melt the butter in a large saucepan over medium-low heat. Add the onions and stir to coat with the butter. Cook, covered, stirring occasionally, until the onions are wilted but not browned, 20 to 30 minutes. Add the red wine, increase the heat to medium-high, and simmer, uncovered, until there is no liquid (or very little) left, 40 to 50 minutes. Add the cassis (add just enough to turn the onions a deep burgundy color) and correct the tartness with as much sugar as necesssary (this will depend not only on your taste, but also on the onions used). Simmer the mixture until all liquid has been cooked away. Season with salt and pepper to taste.

**2** To assemble, cut the tops off the warm pâte à choux puffs (cold or frozen puffs should be recrisped in a 325°F. oven) and fill with a teaspoon of warm onion jam. Serve immediately.

## PÂTE À CHOUX WITH CRABMEAT

**MAKES 7 DOZEN**

*This crabmeat filling is also delicious stuffed into blanched snow peas or the cups and wrappers (pages 229–231).*

4 ounces cream cheese, at room temperature
4 ounces Montrachet or other soft goat cheese, at room temperature
1 red bell pepper, seeds and ribs removed, finely chopped
1 green bell pepper, seeds and ribs removed, finely chopped
6 scallions, white and green parts, finely chopped
8 ounces lump crabmeat, picked over for cartilage
⅛ teaspoon Tabasco sauce
Kosher salt and freshly ground black pepper
Seasoned Pâte à Choux Puffs (page 241)

**1** To make the filling, combine all the ingredients except the pâte à choux.

**2** To assemble, cut the tops off the warm pâte à choux puffs (cold or frozen puffs should be recrisped in a 325°F. oven) and fill with a teaspoon of the filling. Serve immediately.


## PÂTE À CHOUX WITH CURRIED ONIONS

**MAKES 7 DOZEN**

3 tablespoons unsalted butter
2 pounds onions, finely chopped
Kosher salt and freshly ground black pepper
½ tablespoon all-purpose flour
2 teaspoons curry powder, or to taste
¼ cup plus 2 tablespoons heavy cream
Seasoned Pâte à Choux Puffs (page 241)

**1** Heat 1½ tablespoons of butter in a skillet; sauté the onions until transluscent. Add salt and pepper.

**2** Melt the remaining butter in a saucepan over medium heat. Add the flour and cook for 3 to 4 minutes, stirring constantly. Add the curry powder and cream. Cook, stirring constantly, until smooth, about 5 minutes. Add the onion mixture. If the sauce is too thick, thin it with a little more cream.

**3** To assemble, cut the tops off the warm pâte à choux puffs (cold or frozen puffs should be recrisped in a 325°F. oven) and fill with a teaspoon of the filling. Serve immediately.


## TARTLETS FILLED WITH SCRAMBLED EGGS

**MAKES 2½ DOZEN**

*Soft, creamy scrambled eggs are delicious day or evening. The secret to restaurant-style eggs is to avoid overcooking them. Move them around the pan slowly with a spatula to prevent this. Parsley, chervil, or dill may be substituted for the chives. After adding the eggs to the tartlet shells, top with 1 teaspoon caviar or a dollop of Homemade Crème Fraîche (page 394).*

4 tablespoons unsalted butter
15 large eggs, beaten
Kosher salt and freshly ground black pepper
1 bunch of fresh snipped chives
30 baked Basic Pastry Dough Tartlet Shells (page 232)

**1** Melt the butter in a large heavy skillet over medium-high heat. Let the butter melt until it bubbles. Add the eggs all at once and move them around the pan, including the sides, with a spatula to scramble lightly, 6 to 8 minutes. Do not overcook. Season with salt and pepper generously.

**2** Spoon 1 heaping tablespoon of egg into the prepared tartlet shells. Sprinkle each tartlet with chives and serve.

## TARTLETS WITH MELTED BRIE AND HERBS

**MAKES 2½ DOZEN**

30 baked Basic Pastry Dough Tartlet Shells
    (page 232)
¾ pound Brie, chilled, finely chopped
8 sprigs of fresh flat-leaf parsley, roughly
    chopped

**1** Preheat the oven to 350°F.

**2** To assemble the tartlets, place 1 level tablespoon of chopped Brie into each tartlet shell.
Sprinkle each with parsley. Bake just until the
cheese melts, 5 to 6 minutes. Serve immediately.

## ORIENTAL CHICKEN SALAD TARTLETS

**MAKES 2½ DOZEN**

1¼ pounds boneless and skinless chicken breasts
1 tablespoon olive oil
3 tablespoons low-sodium soy sauce
Kosher salt and freshly ground black pepper
3 tablespoons rice wine vinegar
¼ cup vegetable oil
14 sprigs of flat-leaf parsley, chopped
4 scallions, green and white parts, thinly sliced
    crosswise
30 baked Basic Pastry Dough Tartlet Shells
    (page 232)

**1** Heat the oven to 350°F. Place the chicken
breasts on a lightly oiled baking sheet. Season with
salt and pepper and bake until the chicken is
cooked through, 15 to 20 minutes. Do not overcook. Let cool.

**2** Cut the chicken breasts into ¼-inch pieces.
Transfer the cubes to a medium bowl. Set aside.

**3** In a medium bowl, combine the soy sauce,
vinegar, and vegetable oil. Season with salt and
pepper to taste. Pour the soy mixture over the
chicken and stir to combine. Stir in the parsley and
scallions. Spoon 1 heaping tablespoon into the prepared tartlet shells and serve.

## TARTLETS WITH LEEK CHIFFONADE

**MAKES 2½ DOZEN** | photograph on page 221

*A French term for vegetables cut into strips or shredded and
then sautéed, chiffonade is also a word used to describe the cut
of garnishes. The leek mixture can be made ahead, refrigerated,
and reheated in a double boiler over simmering water.*

4 tablespoons unsalted butter
2 medium leeks, thinly sliced crosswise, well
    washed (see page 271)
1 tablespoon chopped fresh dill
⅓ cup Homemade Crème Fraîche (page 394)
    or prepared
Kosher salt and freshly ground black pepper
30 baked Basic Pastry Dough Tartlet Shells
    (page 232)

**1** Melt the butter in a small saucepan over
medium-low heat. Cook the leeks until softened
but some texture still remains, about ten minutes.
Do not brown the leeks.

**2** Add the dill, crème fraîche, and salt and pepper
to taste. Increase the heat to medium, and bring to
a simmer. Remove from the heat. Spoon 1 tablespoon into the prepared tartlet shells, and serve.

## PATTYPAN SQUASH FILLED WITH RED PEPPER CHEESE

**MAKES 2½ DOZEN** | photograph on page 222

*Look for small yellow or green pattypan squashes that are no larger than 1½ inches in diameter. If you cannot find these bite-size squashes, use ⅓-inch-thick slices of zucchini or summer squash and hollow out the centers with a melon-ball scoop.*

RED PEPPER CHEESE FILLING

    1 medium red bell pepper, seeds and ribs
        removed, minced
    3 ounces sharp Cheddar cheese, grated on the
        small holes of box grater to yield ½ cup
    1 large egg, beaten
    Pinch of cayenne pepper
    Kosher salt and freshly ground black pepper

    30 pattypan squashes, 1 inch to 1½ inches in
        diameter

**1** Preheat the oven to 375°F.

**2** Combine the bell pepper, cheese, egg, cayenne pepper, and salt and pepper to taste.

**3** With the point of a small, sharp knife or a melon-ball scoop, hollow out the top part of each squash. Do not overcook. Arrange the squashes in a steamer basket and place over 1 inch of boiling water in a medium saucepan. Cover tightly, and steam until the squash is just tender when pierced with the tip of a knife, 2 to 4 minutes.

**4** Spoon 1½ teaspoons of filling into each hollowed-out squash. Transfer the squashes to a rimmed baking sheet. Bake until the cheese is melted and the filling is hot, about 10 minutes. Serve warm.

## SKEWERED AND THREADED

## MARINATED SHRIMP WRAPPED IN SNOW PEAS

**MAKES 2½ DOZEN** | photograph on page 221

*This is one of my most popular hors d'oeuvres.*

    1 bay leaf
    1 pound medium shrimp, peeled and deveined
        (see page 340), tail on
    1 tablespoon champagne vinegar
    1 tablespoon rice wine vinegar
    ¼ cup olive oil
    1 large garlic clove, crushed
    15 to 20 tender, young snow peas

**1** Bring a large pot of salted water to a boil and add the bay leaf. Add the shrimp and cook just until the shrimp is pink and cooked through, 1½ to 3 minutes. Do not overcook. Drain the shrimp, immerse in ice water to stop the cooking, and drain again. Transfer to a shallow, nonreactive glass or stainless-steel dish.

**2** Combine the vinegars, oil, and garlic. Pour the mixture over the shrimp, and stir to coat well. Cover the dish with plastic wrap, and refrigerate for 1 to 2 days, tossing the shrimp every 12 hours.

**3** String the snow peas and blanch in boiling water for 30 seconds. Chill in ice water, drain, and dry thoroughly. Split the pods lengthwise, so that you have enough separate halves for each shrimp.

**4** Wrap a pea pod around each shrimp, and fasten by piercing with a round natural wood toothpick. Serve cold or at room temperature.

## SKEWERED TORTELLINI

**MAKES 3½ DOZEN** | photograph on page 220

PARMESAN-LEMON DIP

½ cup Homemade Crème Fraîche (page 394)
    or prepared
1 ounce Parmesan cheese, grated on the small
    holes of a box grater to yield ¼ cup
Grated zest of 1 lemon
1 tablespoon fresh lemon juice
3 cloves roasted garlic (see page 265)
Kosher salt and freshly ground black pepper

1½ pounds tortellini
Extra-virgin olive oil

**1** In a small mixing bowl, combine the crème fraîche, Parmesan cheese, lemon zest, lemon juice, garlic cloves, and salt and pepper to taste. Set the dip aside until ready to use.

**2** Bring a large pot of lightly salted water to a boil and cook the tortellini until just tender. Drain the pasta and sprinkle with some olive oil to prevent sticking.

**3** Put 2 warm tortellini on small, 6-inch skewers and serve immediately with the dip.

## CHEESE

## BRIE EN CROÛTE

**SERVES 36**

*This hors d'oeuvre can be baked several hours before serving; it is just as delicious at room temperature. The cheese can be enclosed in the dough the day before serving, then chilled until it is baked the next day. Any remaining puff pastry can be wrapped tightly in plastic wrap and frozen for up to 3 months.*

1 pound Puff Pastry (page 240)
1 wheel of ripe Brie (60 percent butterfat),
    2.4 to 2.8 pounds
1 large egg yolk
4 tablespoons heavy cream

**1** Roll out the puff pastry into a circle approximately 24 inches in diameter. Remove the label from the Brie if one is attached. Place the Brie in the center of the dough and gather up the edges, as evenly as possible, to encase the cheese completely. You should have a bundle of dough at the top. Tie this with a 12-inch strand of cotton twine to hold it together. Using scissors, trim off excess dough and chill the cheese and dough, well wrapped in plastic wrap, on a parchment-lined baking sheet for at least 1 hour.

**2** Preheat the oven to 400°F.

**3** Whisk together the egg yolk and the cream and brush the mixture on top of the pastry, covering as much as possible. Bake for 35 to 40 minutes, or until pastry is puffed and golden brown. (You may need to reduce the oven temperature during cooking to keep the pastry from browning too quickly.)

**4** Cool the Brie en croûte on a rack and serve warm at room temperature.

Note: You can also use store-bought puff pastry. Place two ½-pound sheets side by side, overlapping by about ⅛ inch, and press to seal the edge. Roll out to a 24-inch square and proceed with the recipe.

## RUTH LESERMAN'S CARAMEL BRIE

**SERVES 36** | photograph on page 219

*My friend Ruth Leserman, who entertains all of the time, served this at a party I attended many years ago. It remains one of my favorite hors d'oeuvres. Present the cheese with small cheese knives. The guests will have to crack through the caramel coating, but this is part of the fun of eating such an unusual treat.*

1 wheel of ripe Brie (60 percent butterfat), 2.4 to 2.8 pounds

2 cups sugar

12 to 16 walnut or pecan halves (optional)

**1** Put the Brie on a rack over a large sheet of parchment paper or aluminum foil.

**2** Combine the sugar and ½ cup water in a small, heavy saucepan and melt the sugar, swirling the pan from time to time, over high heat. Do not stir. When the mixture begins to boil, cover the pan to allow condensation to drip back down and melt the crystallized sugar on the side of the pan. Uncover the pan after 3 to 5 minutes and continue cooking over high heat until the sugar becomes a deep amber color.

**3** Immediately pour the caramel over the cheese to cover the top evenly, allowing the excess to drip down the sides. You may have to tilt the cheese a little to spread the caramel evenly. Be very careful not to touch the hot caramel. Press nuts around the perimeter, if desired. The caramel will harden quickly. Once cool enough to handle, transfer the wheel of brie to a serving platter. Serve within 1 hour.

## STEAMED MUSSELS AND TOMATO–RED ONION SAUCE

**SERVES 12 TO 16** | photograph on page 222

SAUCE

8 ripe red tomatoes, peeled, seeded, chopped

½ cup chopped fresh coriander

2 medium red onions, peeled, finely chopped

1 sweet red pepper, seeds and ribs removed, finely chopped

¼ cup balsamic vinegar

Kosher salt and freshly ground black pepper

4 tablespoons (½ stick) unsalted butter

4 shallots, minced

2 cups dry white wine

3 tablespoons finely chopped fresh flat-leaf parsley

3 to 4 mussels per person, debearded (page 353)

Allow 3 to 4 raw shellfish per person (a combination of clams and oysters)

Lemon wedges, for garnish

**1** Combine all ingredients for the tomato–red onion sauce and refrigerate until ready to use.

**2** Melt the butter in a deep, covered pot and sauté the shallots. Add the wine and parsley and bring to a boil. Add mussels, cover, and cook for 4 minutes, shaking the pot frequently. Uncover the pot to see if the mussels have opened; if not, cover again and continue to check every minute. As soon as most of the mussels have opened, remove them from the pot and let cool.

**3** Arrange each mussel on one shell and keep chilled until ready to serve with the clams and oysters, lemon wedges, and tomato sauce.

The components of a raw bar can include any or all of the following: clams on the half shell, oysters on the half shell, steamed mussels on the half shell, boiled crawfish, boiled shrimp (peeled or unpeeled), sea urchins, king crab claws, rock crab claws from Maine, stone crab claws from Florida, and crawfish from Louisiana. Allow 2 to 3 pieces of each shellfish variety per person. When determining how much seafood to buy, remember that:

1 bushel of littleneck clams holds approximately 225 to 250 clams

1 bushel of mussels (small to medium) holds approximately 500 mussels

1 bushel of oysters holds anywhere from 200 to 275 oysters

10 jumbo shrimp to the pound

18 large shrimp to the pound

35 small shrimp to the pound

King crab claws should be served chopped into pieces and cracked

Rock crab claws are purchased cooked and ready to eat

Stone crab claws, also purchased cooked, should be carefully cracked

To serve 24 guests, you will need:

6 dozen littleneck clams

6 pounds mussels

6 dozen oysters

4 dozen jumbo shrimp

10 dozen large shrimp

20 dozen small shrimp

4 dozen king crab claws (2 per person)

4 dozen rock crab claws (2 per person)

4 dozen stone crab claws (2 per person)

In addition, you will need the following to assemble the bar:

A large shallow tray, fitted with a rubber tube drain

Lots of ice cubes and crushed ice

Seaweed or decorative leaves and ferns for decoration

Lemon wedges or halves, preferably wrapped in cheesecloth

Bowls or shells to hold the sauces

Small spoons for serving the sauces

Baskets lined with leaves or ferns for discarded shells

For a large raw bar, hire two experienced workers to open the shellfish. Provide them with gloves, appropriate knives, wooden boards, and rinsing water. All the shellfish should be scrubbed clean and be kept very well iced until serving time.

The tray can be filled with ice, garnished, and filled with shellfish right before guests arrive. As the shellfish is eaten, it should be replenished with freshly opened and cleaned shellfish.

## OYSTERS WITH SEVRUGA CAVIAR

**MAKES 100**

*You can also use golden caviar or other black caviar, such as osetra or beluga. For added flavor and color, oysters can also be topped with a few black sesame seeds and a sprig of fresh dill.*

100 oysters (see page 354)
14 ounces sevruga caviar (see page 380)
Lemon halves wrapped in squares of cheesecloth

**1** No sooner than ½ hour before serving, open the oysters and loosen them from their shells.

**2** Arrange the oysters on the half shell on a bed of crushed ice and top with ½ teaspoon caviar. Serve immediately with lemon halves.

## OYSTERS WITH LEMON BUTTER

**MAKES 18**

*Fresh lime juice or ⅓ cup freshly squeezed ornage juice can be substituted for the lemon juice.*

Juice of 1 lemon
¼ cup white wine
1 teaspoon grated lemon zest
Kosher salt
8 tablespoons (1 stick) unsalted butter, at room
    temperature, cut into small pieces
18 oysters (see page 354)

**1** In a small, nonreactive saucepan, combine the lemon juice, wine, and zest, and add salt to taste. Bring to a boil and cook until the liquid has been reduced to about 2 tablespoons.

**2** Remove the pan from the heat and cool slightly. The liquid should be warm enough to incorporate the butter but not hot enough to liquefy it. Whisk in the butter, a bit at a time, until the mixture is well blended and creamy.

**3** No sooner than 30 minutes before serving, open the oysters and loosen them from their shells. Arrange the oysters on the half shell on a bed of crushed ice and drizzle with the warm butter.

## OYSTERS WITH MAGENTA BUTTER

**SERVES 18**

*To make this recipe with white wine butter, substitute white wine for the red, and tarragon vinegar for the balsamic.*

2 tablespoons minced shallots
½ cup red wine
½ teaspoon kosher salt
1 tablespoon balsamic vinegar
8 tablespoons (1 stick) unsalted butter, at room
    temperature, cut into small pieces
18 oysters (see page 354)

**1** In a small, nonreactive saucepan, combine the shallots, wine, salt, and vinegar. Bring to a boil and cook until the liquid has been reduced to about 2 tablespoons.

**2** Remove the pan from the heat and cool slightly. The liquid should be warm enough to incorporate the butter but not hot enough to liquefy it.

**3** Whisk the butter, a piece at a time, into the wine mixture until the mixture is well blended and creamy. If the mixture becomes too cool and the butter will not incorporate, return the pan to a low heat for a moment or two. Do not melt butter.

**4** No sooner than 30 minutes before serving, open the oysters and loosen them from their shells. Arrange the oysters on the half shell on a bed of crushed ice and drizzle with the warm butter.

## SHRIMP TOAST

**MAKES 3 DOZEN** | photograph on page 220

*Shrimp toast may be frozen, uncooked. Fry the frozen toast in hot oil, as directed below, right from the freezer.*

1 pound shrimp, peeled and deveined
   (see page 210)
1 medium onion, roughly chopped
1 ½-inch slice of fresh ginger, roughly chopped
½ teaspoon kosher salt
Large pinch of freshly ground black pepper
2 large egg whites
36 strips (1 × 3 inches) thin-sliced sandwich
   bread, crusts removed (from about
   13 slices)
½ cup fine fresh bread crumbs (made in a food
   processor from bread crusts or trimmings)
Light vegetable oil for frying

**1** In a food processor or blender, process the shrimp, onion, ginger, salt, and pepper until finely chopped. With the motor running, drop the egg whites through the feed tube, and process until the mixture is well combined.

**2** Spread the shrimp mixture (approximately ¼ inch thick) on the strips of bread and dip the mixture-coated side in bread crumbs, covering well. Chill until ready to cook, shrimp side up on baking sheets. Cover with plastic wrap.

**3** Heat oil 1½ to 2 inches deep in a large skillet. When hot (360° F.), fry toast on both sides until golden brown. Drain on paper towels and serve.

## MOCK DRUMSTICKS I

**MAKES 40** | photograph on page 222

1 cup plum wine
¼ cup low-sodium soy sauce
¼ cup molasses
2 tablespoons wine vinegar
2 scallions, white and green parts, minced
2 garlic cloves, minced
1 tablespoon grated fresh ginger
40 chicken wings (about 8 pounds)
Scallion-Soy Dipping Sauce (page 395)

**1** Combine the wine, soy sauce, molasses, vinegar, scallions, garlic, and ginger in a large mixing bowl. Set aside.

**2** Cut off the tips and middle portions of the wings. Use in stock, or grill separately. With a sharp knife, loosen the meat around the middle joint and push the meat down gently, scraping the bone, to about three-fourths of the length. Turn the meat inside out around the big joint to form a "drumstick."

**3** Transfer the chicken to a large nonreactive pan. Pour the marinade over the chicken and toss to combine. Cover with plastic wrap and marinate the chicken in the refrigerator for 4 or 5 hours, or overnight.

**4** Grill the "drumsticks" over hot coals for 8 to 10 minutes, until golden brown, or arrange the chicken wings in a large roasting pan and cook in a 400° F. oven until crispy and golden brown, 25 to 30 minutes. Serve with Scallion-Soy Dipping Sauce.

## MOCK DRUMSTICKS II
**MAKES 40**

40 chicken wings (about 8 pounds)

BATTER
1½ cups all-purpose flour
2 tablespoons cornstarch
2 tablespoons baking powder
1 teaspoon kosher salt
½ teaspoon freshly ground black pepper
1¾ cups ice water

APRICOT SAUCE
1 cup apricot preserves
½ cup cider vinegar
1 teaspoon paprika
Kosher salt to taste
Pinch of cayenne pepper

Light vegetable oil for frying
Scallion-Soy Dipping Sauce (page 395)

**1** Cut off the tips and middle portions of the wings. Use in stock, or grill separately. With a sharp knife, loosen the meat around the middle joint and push the meat down gently, scraping the bone, to about three-fourths of the length. Turn the meat inside out around the big joint to form a "drumstick."

**2** Prepare the batter 30 minutes before using. Mix all the batter ingredients, stirring until smooth.

**3** To make the sauce, heat all the sauce ingredients over low heat.

**4** In a deep skillet or an electric fryer, heat 2 inches of oil to 375° F. Dip the chicken in the batter; fry 4 or 5 pieces at a time until crispy, about 5 minutes. Drain on paper towels. Serve the "drumsticks" on a platter with Scallion-Soy Dipping Sauce.

## PÂTÉ ON PEAR SLICES
**MAKES 2 DOZEN** | photograph on page 221

*Slices of firm apples may also be used.*

Chicken Liver Pâté (page 464)
3 to 4 crisp pears (Anjou, Bartlett, or Bosc)
2 ounces cornichons (about 18), thinly sliced

No more than 20 minutes before serving, core the pears and cut in half lengthwise. Place each half cut-side down and slice crosswise ¼ inch thick (the slices will be crescent shaped). Spread pâté on the slices and decorate with two or three thin slices of cornichon.

## RED POTATOES WITH SOUR CREAM AND CAVIAR
**ALLOW 2 TO 3 PER PERSON** | photograph on page 220

*Sour cream and caviar is a classic topping, but any of the following are always popular: sautéed onion; crumbled crisp bacon; sour cream and fresh herbs; chopped ham; chopped scallions; grated cheese; chopped walnuts; alfalfa sprouts; or kosher salt, freshly ground black pepper, and melted butter.*

**1** Choose the smallest, most blemish-free red-skinned potatoes. Allow 2 or 3 potatoes per person. They should be washed, and either boiled gently until tender or baked in a 350° F. oven until tender, about 30 minutes.

**2** To serve, cut the potatoes in half and place cut-side down on trays. With a melon-ball scoop, spoon out some of the top to create a small cavity.

**3** Fill with a dollop of sour cream and top with red caviar (salmon or lumpfish), black caviar (sevruga or osetra), or golden caviar (whitefish) (see page 380).

## SAVORY PALMIERS

**MAKES 5 DOZEN** | photograph on page 222

*If you use store-bought puff pastry and it comes in 2 sheets, use half of the ingredients listed below on each sheet.*

2 tablespoons pine nuts

1 garlic clove

¼ teaspoon kosher salt

⅛ teaspoon freshly ground black pepper

1 cup fresh basil leaves, blanched for 30 seconds, drained, and dried

¼ cup freshly grated Parmesan cheese

¼ cup freshly grated Romano cheese

Approximately ½ cup extra-virgin olive oil

1 pound Puff Pastry (page 240)

1 cup freshly grated Parmesan cheese

**1** In the bowl of a food processor, combine the pine nuts, garlic, salt, pepper, basil, Parmesan and Romano cheeses, and 2 tablespoons olive oil, and process until finely ground. Add the remaining oil as needed in a steady stream and process until smooth and creamy.

**2** Roll out the pastry into a rectangle approximately 8 inches wide and no less than ⅛ inch thick; cut the edges so that they are even. Sprinkle the cheese evenly over the rectangle and press it into the pastry with a rolling pin. Spread the pesto filling evenly over the cheese and roll each long end of the pastry to the center of the rectangle, making sure the pastry is tight and even. Chill well.

**3** Cut the log crosswise into ⅜-inch slices, and place them 3 inches apart on parchment-lined baking sheets. Chill for at least 1 hour.

**4** Preheat the oven to 450° F.

**5** Bake the palmiers until puffed and lightly golden, 6 to 7 minutes. Remove from the oven, quickly turn them over, and return them to the oven and bake for another 4 to 5 minutes. Let cool completely on wire racks.

**6** Baked palmiers can be refrigerated for 2 to 3 days in an airtight container or frozen. To recrisp, place them, unthawed, in a preheated 350° F. oven for 5 minutes.

---

**NOTE** | Palmiers Fillings

Try any of the following fillings in the palmiers, or create your own combinations.

4 ounces Parmesan cheese, grated on the small holes of a box grater to yield about 1 cup

½ cup black olive tapenade or paste

4 ounces Parmesan cheese, grated on the small holes of a box grater to yield about 1 cup

½ cup anchovy paste

4 ounces Parmesan cheese, grated on the small holes of a box grater to yield about 1 cup

¼ cup plus 2 tablespoons chopped fresh rosemary

A sprinkling of cayenne

Soft goat cheese mixed with chopped fresh herbs

Puréed roasted garlic (page 265)

---

## SPICY ALMONDS

**MAKES 2 CUPS** | photograph on page 220

*Other nuts can be prepared this way, with excellent results.
Also try cooked chickpeas or pumpkin seeds.*

3 tablespoons peanut oil

2 cups whole blanched almonds

½ cup plus 1 tablespoon sugar

1½ teaspoons kosher salt

1½ teaspoons ground cumin

1 teaspoon red pepper flakes

**1** Heat the oil in a heavy-bottomed frying pan
over medium-high heat. Add the almonds and
sprinkle the ½ cup sugar over them. Sauté until the
almonds become golden brown and the sugar
caramelizes.

**2** Remove the almonds from the pan and toss in a
bowl with the salt, cumin, pepper flakes, and the
remaining sugar.

**3** Serve warm or at room temperature. Store in an
airtight container.


## SMOKED TROUT MOUSSE ON CUCUMBER SLICES

**MAKES 3½ DOZEN** | photograph on page 220

*Smoked whitefish or mackerel can be substituted for
the trout.*

1 4-ounce piece smoked trout

2 tablespoons heavy cream

Kosher salt and freshly ground black pepper

1 tablespoon fresh lemon juice

1 tablespoon fresh or prepared grated
   horseradish

8 ounces cream cheese, at room temperature

2 seedless cucumbers, cut into ¼-inch slices

**1** Remove the skin and bones from the trout. Put
the flesh into the bowl of a food processor and
chop until very fine. With the machine still running, add the cream in a steady stream. Add the salt
and pepper, lemon juice, and horseradish.

**2** Transfer the mixture to a bowl and add the
cream cheese. Blend until well combined and
smooth. Using a rubber spatula, press the mixture
through a fine sieve to remove any lumps. Refrigerate until ready to use.

**3** Using a pastry bag fitted with a decorative tip,
pipe 1 teaspoon mousse onto the center of each
cucumber slice.


### DIPS AND SPREADS

## CHICKEN LIVER PÂTÉ

**MAKES APPROXIMATELY 1 CUP** | photograph on
page 221

*The pullman loaf pan, 16 × 3½ × 3½ inches (see Sources,
page 486), works perfectly for making this pâté. Use it without the lid. A large earthenware bowl is also nice to use to
both prepare and serve the pâté.*

½ pound chicken livers, cleaned

¼ cup brandy

1 tablespoon minced shallots

2 tablespoons unsalted butter, at room
   temperature

½ teaspoon chopped fresh sage or ¼ teaspoon
   dried sage

Kosher salt and freshly ground black pepper

**1** Soak the chicken livers in the brandy for 3 to 4
hours in a cool place; do not refrigerate. Drain the
livers and reserve the liquid.

**2** Sauté the shallots in 1 tablespoon butter until
wilted. Add the chicken livers, sage, and salt and

pepper to taste. Sauté until the livers are no longer pink inside, approximately 5 minutes. Transfer the mixture to the bowl of a food processor, add the remaining butter, and process until smooth. Add the reserved brandy and process another 30 seconds. Transfer to a bowl, cover, and refrigerate for at least 24 hours before serving.

## SIPS AND DRINKS

## THE ORIGINAL EGGNOG

**SERVES 2 DOZEN** | photograph on page 223

12 large eggs, separated
1½ cups superfine sugar
1 quart milk
1½ quarts heavy cream
24 ounces bourbon
4 ounces dark rum
6 ounces cognac
Freshly grated nutmeg

**1** Beat the egg yolks until thick and pale yellow in a very large bowl. Gradually add the sugar to the yolks. Whisk in the milk and 1 quart of the cream. Add the bourbon, rum, and cognac, stirring constantly. The mixture may be made up to this point and kept refrigerated, covered with plastic wrap, for 4 hours.

**2** Just before serving, beat the egg whites until stiff. Fold into the mixture. Whip the remaining heavy cream until stiff. Fold into the eggnog and sprinkle with nutmeg. Serve the eggnog chilled in small cups or glasses.

*Note:* Because of the slight risk of bacterial poisoning, the USDA advises against the consumption of raw eggs by pregnant women, babies, young children, and anyone with a weakened immune system.

## PIÑA COLADA

**MAKES TWO 6-OUNCE DRINKS** | photograph on page 223

4 ounces unsweetened pineapple juice
2 ounces dark rum
2 tablespoons coconut cream
1 cup ice cubes
Spears of fresh pineapple, for garnish

Blend all ingredients except the pineapple spears in a blender at high speed until the mixture is frothy. Pour immediately into 2 iced goblets, garnish with pineapple, and serve.

## OCEAN SUNRISE

**MAKES TWO 4-OUNCE DRINKS** | photograph on page 223

¼ cup fresh lime juice
¼ cup plus 2 tablespoons cranberry juice
¼ cup plus 2 tablespoons tequila
Crushed ice

Put all ingredients in a cocktail shaker; shake well. Pour into 2 balloon goblets or wineglasses.

## CAMPARI AND FRESH ORANGE JUICE

**MAKES TWO 7-OUNCE DRINKS** | photograph on page 223

1 cup fresh orange juice
½ cup soda water
¼ cup Campari

Mix all of the ingredients and serve in tall glasses over ice cubes.

the
# GUIDE

As much as we might like to fantasize about spontaneously "just having a few friends over," I know from experience that advance planning is crucial to having a successful party where you can relax and enjoy spending time with your guests. Here are some issues to consider when planning your gathering.

**SELECTING THE SITE** Try to choose a setting that suits the occasion as closely as possible. For example, a room with a fireplace would be ideal for a midwinter gathering. One with views of a garden would make a great site for a spring party, and the garden itself would be wonderful for a midsummer event. A more formal gathering such as a New Year's Eve cocktail party might take place in both the living room and dining room.

Once you've chosen a site, make sure there is ample space to accommodate the number of intended guests. An overcrowded party not only irritates guests, but can also wreak havoc with whatever plans have been made for serving food and drink. To help estimate the ideal number of people a site can hold, visualize the floor space populated with just enough people to create a sense of movement and conviviality. Is there enough room to eat and drink without being jostled? Could you easily make your way across the room to mingle? If so, estimate the number of people in the space, and that's the maximum total you should invite.

**MAKING A GUEST LIST** Taking into account your space limitations and the amount of work you want to do, decide how many people you would like to invite and make a tentative guest list. Some events, such as showers or family gatherings, determine the guest list by their very nature. Others leave you a free hand to mix and match friends, acquaintances, and business associates as you please. When you have your list made up, check to be sure that you have a good mixture of interesting people who will enjoy being in the same room with each other.

**A GENERAL PLAN** The time of day and the nature of your party will help you decide what food to provide: Should it be a light afternoon snack? Tea? Hearty hors d'oeuvres in place of a meal? Will your guests expect a meal based on the hour? These are important considerations, since you don't want to leave your guests feeling either underfed or overindulged.

Next, think about whom you are inviting and what kind of food they might enjoy. Often, good friends or family members are to be included, so you probably will be familiar with their tastes and with any special dietary needs they might have.

Finally, determine how much of the preparation work you can do yourself. Do you want to make all the food yourself, or do you want to ask for a helping hand or two?

**PASSED OR STATIONARY HORS D'OEUVRES?** This question must be answered in the earliest planning stages, because having hors d'oeuvres passed requires extra help. Except on the most formal of occasions, I think it is best to have both.

Passed hors d'oeuvres are ideal at a party, since guests may keep conversing and enjoy your food without moving. Be aware, though, that this does require extra hands in order to keep the food flowing from the kitchen onto the trays and out to the guests. How much you enjoy your own party depends a great deal on how realistically this is organized. If you don't mind working at your own party, you can manage passing 2 or 3 different hors d'oeuvres for a group of 16 to 20 by yourself. Of course, if you decide to add help in the form of caterers, friends, or family, you may be more flexible in your serving choices and the number of foods you may serve.

If you are throwing a party without assistance, you will want to remain relaxed and in control. It will be difficult to keep everyone's glass full, so set up a free-standing bar table from which guests may serve themselves. Arrange a few food stations around the room; seasoned bread sticks, herbed olives, and spicy nut mixtures are easy and popular favorites. It is also important to have dishes of food you may put out just before your guests arrive that require no more thought than an occasional refill.

CREATING A BALANCED MENU Make a list of foods you would like to serve. I always include several personal favorites that I know will be a success, and then add a few new things to try for the first time. Once you have your list, go through it to make sure you have a balanced variety of foods in your selection: hearty and light, strong and mild, spicy and refreshing.

The main change I have seen in entertaining in the past years is that guests want the opportunity to indulge in something rich one minute and then eat something equally delicious but healthy the next. Most guests are happy to eat a few rich, decadent hors d'oeuvres, particularly if they are also offered crisp fresh vegetables and the pure, clean flavors of raw oysters or boiled shrimp.

Be sure to balance the selection of bread, meat, fish, and vegetables. Do not serve all meat and bread, or all vegetable dishes and tea sandwiches. Always include food for vegetarians, for those with shellfish allergies, and for anyone on low-cholesterol or low-fat diets.

Complement strong flavors with mild; caviar is assertive, for example, and should be served with something gentler, like salmon or crab. In the same way, it's important to offset spicy food with something cool, such as filled cherry tomatoes. You should also try to balance the selection of hot and cold hors d'oeuvres.

Finally, be sure that when planning your menu you consider the degree of difficulty and ease of pre-paration. Do not choose all hors d'oeuvres that require last-minute preparation or intensive work. Instead, balance those that involve multiple steps or need last-minute attention with some that are simple to prepare or can be made in advance, or require only arranging on platters or in bowls. For menu suggestions, see page 472.

CHOOSING THE FRESHEST SEASONAL INGREDIENTS In our increasingly global food market, we now see strawberries in the winter and winter squash in the summer. Still, the most delicious produce is grown in season locally. These fruits and vegetables, as well as fresh seafood, need much less fussing over because they can stand on their own flavors. An oyster party is ideal for the cooler months, when the flesh of oysters is sweet and firm. Conversely, lobster is at its best, and least expensive, in the summer. Salsas and tarts made with late-summer tomatoes just off the vine are imbued with the sun, and there is nothing like sautéed fresh morel mushrooms scooped up and served on crisp crostini in the spring. Also, remember that lighter foods taste better in the warmer months. Brandade and cassoulet, for example, tend to be soul-warming, cool-weather foods, perfect for a December gathering. Fruit salsas or gazpacho would be more appetizing at a July garden party.

There are plenty of nonseasonal fresh foods to choose from for excellent party fare, too. Artisanal cheeses, bakery-fresh breads, and richly textured smoked fish are always popular. Whenever possible, however, you should take advantage of the season to make your food its most delicious.

DETERMINING THE QUANTITY OF HORS D'OEUVRES Even if you think your guest list is made up of light eaters, do not underestimate the appetites of your guests. I am no longer surprised at the quantities of sausage and hot crab dip that even a small group can eat.

Keep in mind when planning your menu what purpose the hors d'oeuvres will serve. If a meal is to follow, they should not be too filling. Generally, if hors d'oeuvres are to precede a substantial meal, make 5 to 6 different ones, each yielding 1 to 2 per guest.

Often hors d'oeuvres will be used in a cocktail party context where guests are invited for only a few specific hours. In these instances, you will need fewer hors d'oeuvres per person. I find the informal selections in the "Bites and Pieces" chapter to be particularly useful in this context, since they can easily be replenished if your guests are a bit hungrier than you had anticipated.

On the other hand, hors d'oeuvres–only parties, where guests are invited at the cocktail hour and provided with enough food to make a meal, have become increasingly popular. In planning this type of party, select hors d'oeuvres that are most substantial: skewered meats and shrimp, cheese platters, fondues with bread dippers, and glazed ham with tender biscuits. Always include crisp accents such as filled lady apple cups and endive petals. Even for weddings, it is perfectly acceptable to have a reception with a large number of hors d'oeuvres rather than a seated dinner or buffet. Offer 8 to 10 choices, each yielding 2 or 3 servings per person.

**BUYING THE INGREDIENTS** Once you have selected the menu, review each recipe and make a master shopping list. For easier and more efficient shopping, I divide the list into sections according to the different stores and markets from which the food will come: seafood, meat, bread and baked goods, fresh produce, and so on. You might also want to divide your lists between items for hors d'oeuvres that will be made in advance, and items that need to be bought the day before the party so they will be fresh. For large quantities and special orders, be sure to place your orders in advance.

**PREPARING THE FOOD** This is where planning really pays off. It is far easier to do a little bit of the prep work every day for a week before your party than to do it all at the last minute. Once you have your shopping lists organized, make a list of what needs to be done to prepare each recipe. Once the prep work has been outlined, divide it into tasks that can be done well in advance, those that can be done the day before the party, those that must be done the day of the party, and last-minute details. I think that the easiest way to make these lists without forgetting anything is to work backward from the moment the guests are arriving.

Since most kitchens do not have a lot of space for cooking, prep work, or cold storage, there are certain things that are good to do in advance because they help get the large, bulky items out of the way. For example, bunches of vegetables take up a lot of room in the refrigerator, but once they are trimmed and cut and packed away in plastic containers with damp paper towels, they take up far less space. Prepare and freeze as many items ahead as you can, and remember that most sauces will keep for several days if tightly covered and refrigerated.

**PRESENTING THE HORS D'OEUVRES** When it comes to hors d'oeuvres, visual allure is as important as great flavors and enticing aromas. This does not mean that you have to spend a lot of money on "props"; your imagination is really all you need. A jar of pistachios from the store may not look very inviting, for example, but several jars' worth emptied into a pretty enameled bowl will tempt every guest.

As for selecting serving pieces, look around your house—you may be surprised by what you find outside of the kitchen and dining area. A selection of sturdy trays and platters is very useful, for example. Cutting boards, baskets, tall jars, glass and ceramic vases, and bowls of all kinds can also be pressed into service. The photographs in this book should give you plenty of ideas for presenting your hors d'oeuvres in the most attractive way possible.

To add color and visual interest, it is a nice touch to line trays of hors d'oeuvres with different materials. Look for things that will hold up well for the extent of the party. Use banana leaves, for instance, or large chunks of rock salt, a bed of fresh chives or other herbs, flowers, or large cinnamon sticks. Edible garnishes, of course, are a wonderful way of accessorizing hors d'oeuvres. A good source of inspiration in this regard is the recipe itself, since existing ingredients, such as herbs, fruit, and vegetables, often make beautiful garnishes in their natural state.

Today's hors d'oeuvres party can be an updated potluck, with each guest bringing a favorite dish. When asked to bring an hors d'oeuvre to a party, I like to contribute something unique.

Some hors d'oeuvres, no matter how delicious or visually stunning, simply are not suitable for this purpose. The best hors d'oeuvres for travel fall into three categories: those that need nothing more than to be plated when you arrive, those that need only to be rewarmed, and those that need some last-minute assembly.

**FOR PLATING ONLY** These hors d'oeuvres cause the least disruption for the host. Dips (pages 385–390) are extremely easy because they can be fully made at home, then placed in airtight containers or resealable plastic bags for travel. Salsas (pages 400–401) offer unusual flavor combinations that you can be quite sure will not be duplicated at the party you are attending; use 3-cup airtight containers for transporting them, because a plastic bag might cause them to get too mushy. Boiled and peeled shrimp (page 340) is a portable hors d'oeuvre if prepared in advance and placed in airtight containers; bring along one or two of the shrimp sauces (pages 397–398) packed in small airtight containers or in freezer-weight plastic bags. If you take chilled hors d'oeuvres or sauces to a party that requires more than a few minutes' travel, place them in a cooler with blue ice so they stay fresh.

Many of the Bites and Pieces are great for bringing along, too, such as the icebox crackers on pages 364–366 (except for the Blue Cheese-Pecan Crackers, which are too fragile), olives (pages 356–358), and Escabeche (page 379). Slice, bake, and cool the crackers at home, then place them in airtight containers lined with several layers of paper towel to prevent breakage. Store the olives in 3-cup airtight containers, and pack the Escabeche in large, upright, round airtight containers. Spiced Chickpeas (page 363), Crunchy Split Pea Bites (page 363), seasoned nuts (pages 360–362), and biscotti (pages 372–373) can be packed in plastic bags.

**TO BE REWARMED** Hors d'oeuvres in this category should need only to be reheated briefly, as you don't want to occupy your host's oven for very long. To travel, the Fontina Risotto Balls (page 303) should be closely packed in an airtight container so that they cannot move around and fall apart. Just before you are ready to serve, reheat them as directed in the recipe. Sweet Peppered Bacon Bites (page 349) carry well in flat airtight containers and can be rewarmed in the oven right before serving. Butternut Squash Sip (page 424) can be packed in 12-cup airtight containers and reheated.

**TO BE ASSEMBLED** I advise against taking anything to a party that actually needs further cooking. The following suggestions need some quick assembly once you arrive, but otherwise can be fully prepared ahead of time. Tartlets (pages 289–292) can be packed between wax paper in flat containers lined with paper towels. Lemon Chicken Salad (page 289) and Calamari Salad (page 292) can each be packed in a 3-cup airtight container for travel. The toasted Pita Cups (page 242) can be packed neatly in a flat, paper towel–lined airtight container or in an empty egg carton wrapped in plastic. Gazpacho (page 426) can be carried in a 12-cup container; place the Cucumber Cups (page 228) in a flat, airtight container lined with damp paper towels.

The hors d'oeuvres in this book can be mixed and matched to create entire parties around a theme, cuisine, or specific occasion. I have compiled the following menus in the hope that you will use them as a guide—tailor them to suit your specific needs.

## BRUNCH

*Unlike other meals, brunch is an informal, unstructured event. Your guests won't have set expectations about what they will be served, so you can surprise them with something a bit unusual. Most of the hors d'oeuvres in this group contain at least one component that can be prepared in advance.*

Savory French Toast **page 262**
Swiss Chard, Shallot, and Parmesan Tartlets **page 291**
Quail Eggs with Tarragon Mayonnaise **page 358**
Cherry Tomatoes with Grilled Shrimp and Corn **page 305**
Sweet Peppered Bacon Bites **page 349**
Blini with Caviar and Crème Fraîche **page 381**
Vegetable Crudités with Buttermilk Peppercorn Dip **page 389**
Roasted Red Pepper and Eggplant Dip **page 390** with assorted dippers **pages 247–248**
Bloody Mary **page 436**

## ASIAN DUMPLING PARTY

*These juicy and delicious little packages are the quintessential finger food of Asian cuisines, just perfect for a cocktail party. Best of all, dumplings and their dipping sauces are the ultimate make-ahead food.*

Crabmeat Soup Dumplings **page 283**
Potstickers **page 281**
Shrimp and Bean Sprout Shao Mai **page 284**
Jicama and Green Papaya Summer Rolls **page 286**
Scallop, Arugula, and Lemongrass Dumplings **page 282**
Adzuki Bean, Daikon, and Shiso Leaf Salsa **page 401** in Cucumber Cups **page 229**
Ice-cold beer such as Singha, Tsing Tao, and Asahi
Hot sake

## JAPANESE MENU

*Japanese-inspired hors d'oeuvres make a beautifully serene presentation. This menu features a range of flavors, with a delicacy not often found in finger foods. It is a bit labor-intensive, though, so in addition to preparing whatever you can in advance, you might want to ask a friend to help you bring it all together just before your guests arrive.*

Nori Stacks with Smoked Salmon **page 270**
Grilled Shiitake Mushrooms on Rosemary Skewers **page 337**
Wasabi Caviar and Daikon Canapés **page 326**
Edamame with Sea Salt **page 379**
Asian Meatballs on Snow Pea Picks **page 344** or Grilled Beef Rolls **page 342**
Plum Wine Flank Steak in Green Tea Crepes **page 298**
Spicy Tuna Rolls **page 285**
Grilled Swordfish on Ginger-Jalapeño Rice Cakes **page 274**
Adzuki Bean, Daikon, and Shiso Leaf Salsa **page 401**
Hot sake
Ice-cold beer such as Kirin or Sapporo

## TROPICAL MENU

*The strong flavors and bright colors of tropical cuisines give guests a feeling of being on vacation, so they tend to relax and enjoy themselves more. Many of these hors d'oeuvres can be prepared in advance, but try to find an extra set of hands to help you assemble them. To enhance the island feeling, arrange tropical flowers on the tables.*

Jerk Chicken Sandwiches with Mango Chutney **page 276**
Tropical Fruit Salsa **page 400** with assorted dippers **pages 247–248**
Scallop Ceviche with Avocado Purée in Toasted Corn Cups **page 287**
Mango Crab Stacks **page 273**
Coconut Curry Macadamia Nuts **page 361**
Tropical Chicken on Sugarcane Skewers **page 338**
Mango Cocktail **page 434**
Mai Tai **page 435**
Caipirinha **page 436**

## ITALIAN MENU

*No type of food is more popular among Americans today than the regional cuisines of Italy, and for good reason. As these hors d'oeuvres show, the food of Italy is imbued with freshness and deep flavors.*

Fava Bean and Pecorino Crostini **page 333**
Assorted Frico: Cheddar, Asiago, Parmesan Rosemary, Marjoram Gruyère **pages 408–409**
Potato Bacon Pizza **page 253**
Frico Tacos with Mâche **page 293**
Browned-Butter, Lemon, and Caper Biscotti **page 372**
Fontina Risotto Balls **page 303**
Prosciutto-Wrapped Shrimp **page 341**
Stuffed Mushrooms **pages 300–301**
Cherry Tomatoes with Panzanella **page 304**
Vegetable Crudités **page 374** with Bagna Cauda **page 390**
Italian white and red wines

## INDIAN MENU

*These slightly spicy, slightly exotic hors d'oeuvres are ideal for a small gathering and can be almost completely prepared in advance. To round out the selection, fill Cucumber or Cherry Tomato Cups (page 229) with labneh or whole-milk yogurt and top with toasted sesame seeds.*

## WEEKNIGHT COCKTAIL PARTY

*Hosting a party after a full day's work can be a challenge, so choose dishes that can be prepared in their entirety in advance, such as the recipes listed here. Simply pick up the ficelle on your way home from work, then reheat and assemble everything just before your guests arrive.*

## COCKTAILS FOR A CROWD

*When you are having a large evening gathering, it is important to have some dishes that can be prepared ahead of time and some that are simple to put together. This menu includes several of each.*

## MEZZE MENU

*Like the Middle Eastern appetizer banquets after which it is modeled, this menu features hors d'oeuvres substantial enough to make a meal. With the exception of the dolmades and the canapés, everything can be prepared and cooked in advance.*

## LATE SUNDAY AFTERNOON WITH FRIENDS

*A casual weekend gathering calls for comfortable, familiar food. This menu features subtle reinterpretations of some of my favorite classic hearty hors d'oeuvres.*

## FORMAL COCKTAIL PARTY

*This delicate assortment is perfect for a truly elegant gathering in which you want the food to be at once festive and refined. Most of these dishes should be made on the day of the party.*

## AFTERNOON TEA PARTY

For this menu I've included suggestions for a rather elaborate tea table; tailor it to suit your gathering. Be sure to offer some relatively substantial hors d'oeuvres such as Curried Egg Salad Tea Sandwiches along with lighter fare such as Piped Crudités.

Quail Eggs with Fines Herbes and Bacon and Thyme **page 359**
Simple Piped Crudités with Dill Cream Cheese **page 377**
Parmesan Puff Pastry Straws **pages 369–370**
Lemon Chicken Salad in Poppy Seed Tartlets **page 289**
Mango Crab Stacks **page 273**
Smoked Salmon Tea Sandwiches **page 318**
Tarragon Shrimp Salad Tea Sandwiches **page 314**
Curried Egg Salad Tea Sandwiches **page 319**
Goat Cheese and Chive Tea Sandwiches **page 319**
Honey-Roasted Almonds **page 362**
Parmesan-Rosemary Icebox Crackers **page 365**
White Wine Punch **page 428**
Orange-Rosemary Cordial **page 440**
Raspberry-Thyme Cordial **page 438**
Assorted teas

## DO-AHEAD PARTY MENU

Every hors d'oeuvre on this menu can be prepared in its entirety before guests arrive.

Boiled Shrimp with Fresh Cocktail Sauce **page 397** and Chili-Lime Aïoli **page 397**
Chèvre Grapes **page 302**
Vegetable Crudités **page 374**
Toasted Pepita Dip **page 388**
Crunchy Split Pea Bites **page 363**
Nori Stacks with Smoked Salmon **page 270**
Roasted Vegetable Terrine **page 264**
Spicy Paprika Cashews **page 362**
Assorted Quick Sticks **pages 368–369**
Tom Collins **page 429**
Panache **page 437**

## AN HORS D'OEUVRES TABLE

These hors d'oeuvres can be set out in advance of your guests' arrival. Serve the salsa and guacamole with dippers such as sourdough crostini and corn chips.

Mixed Tomato Salsa **page 400**
Guacamole **page 339**
Beef Empanaditas **page 295**
Cherry Tomatoes with White Bean Purée **page 304**
Shrimp Gumbo Skewers **page 341**
Pissaladière **page 256**
Orange-Honey Glazed Black Forest Ham and Biscuits **page 350**
Classic Swiss Fondue **page 405** with fondue dippers
Red Sangria **page 428**

## SUMMER-BY-THE-SEA PARTY

I particularly love this menu because it offers a wide variety of seafood flavors, each cooked in a different way.

Classic Crabcakes **page 352**
Baked Mussels **page 353**
Lobster and Mushroom Quesadillas **page 260**
Edamame with Sea Salt **page 379**
Calamari Salad in Pita Cups **page 292**
Toasted Goat Cheese and Shredded Beet Crostini **page 331**
Grilled Vegetable Salsa **page 401** with assorted dippers **pages 247–248**
Fresh Lime Daiquiri **page 435**
Bloody Mary **page 436**

## CHAMPAGNE PARTY

This particular menu is somewhat spare, yet the selection of hors d'oeuvres are perfectly suited to enjoying the champagne.

Endive with Goat Cheese, Fig, and Honey-Glazed Pecans **page 307**
Sea Scallops with Minted Pea Purée on Potato Chips **page 271**
Caviar **page 380**
Oysters **page 354** with Four Sauces **page 396**
Crumbled Parmigiano-Reggiano with Truffle Oil **page 410**

Beef Carpaccio Canapés **page 327**
Orange, Pistachio, and Black Olive Biscotti **page 373**
Champagne **page 438**

## BRIDAL/BABY SHOWER

Since these events are very often held between lunch and dinner, light, delicate flavors are appropriate.

Chèvre Grapes **page 302**
Quail Eggs with Caviar and Crème Fraîche **page 358**
Simple Piped Crudités with Wasabi Cream Cheese **page 377**
Classic Quick Sticks **page 368**
Gravlax, Crème Fraîche, and Caviar Napoleons **page 272**
Seared Tuna in Sesame-Orange Tartlets **page 289**
Asparagus and Shiitake Mushroom Terrine **page 267**
Tomato, Basil, and Olive Tartlets **page 292**
Sesame-Crusted Chicken Salad Tea Sandwiches **page 320**
Fresh Lime Daiquiri **page 435**
Cosmopolitan **page 431**
Pimm's Cup **page 427**

## FIRESIDE GATHERING

When the wind is blowing and the temperature dips below freezing, friends are particularly grateful to be invited over for a cozy cocktail party by the fire. For a special seasonal touch, serve hard cider in Lady Apple Cups (page 229).

Butternut Squash Sip with Seasoned Pepitas **page 424**
Golden Ravioli with Arrabbiata Sauce **page 302**
Roasted Root Vegetable Skewers **page 338**
Cassoulet Croustades **page 288**
Crispy Chorizo with Cabrales and Apples **page 352**
Blue Cheese–Pecan Icebox Crackers **page 365**
Mixed Provençal Olives with Preserved Lemon and Oregano **page 356**
Snakebite **page 437**
Black Velvet **page 437**

Most of the following equipment can be found in kitchenware stores and specialty baking-supply stores or by mail (see Sources, page 486).

**AIRTIGHT CONTAINERS** When preparing hors d'oeuvres in advance, airtight containers are essential, not only for keeping them fresh and protected from absorbing odors in the refrigerator, but also to help you keep an organized refrigerator. For airtight containers to be at all useful, they must have very tight fitting lids. Those with loose seals allow air to enter, causing food to harden and spoil quickly. Buy high-quality, rigid plastic containers that hold up well in the dishwasher and are microwave safe. I prefer transparent containers so I can see what is inside. If you use the opaque variety, be sure to clearly label them.

If you don't already own appropriate containers, start with the following assortment. The capacity of the containers is usually marked on the bottom.

Upright, round:
Four 2-cup containers; for dips, fillings, garnishes
Four 3-cup containers; for salsas, fillings, olives
Four 6-cup containers; for batters, prepped ingredients, nuts
Four 10-cup containers; for sips, crudités, dips

Flat, long (particularly good for layered items):
Three 7-cup containers
Three 12-cup containers
Three 17-cup containers
Three 33-cup containers

**ASIAN SOUP SPOONS** Traditionally served with soups in Chinese restaurants, these spoons have a short handle and a deep, flat bowl that makes them ideal for scooping dumplings out of soup. With their flat bottoms, they sit sturdily on a tray, making them an ideal serving vehicle for hors d'oeuvres, particularly those that release a bit of liquid once bitten into. They are usually made of porcelain and are available in a range of colors and patterns.

**BAKING SHEETS** For this book, I have used two types of baking sheets: a plain metal baking sheet that is professionally known as a cookie sheet (17 × 14 inches), and a rimmed baking sheet, which is known as a jelly roll pan (17 × 12 inches). Buy only heavy, even-surfaced baking sheets; they won't warp and buckle over time from repeated exposure to high heat. The weight is also important for even heat distribution, which helps prevent the food from burning on the bottom and ensures even cooking. I prefer those made from heavy-duty aluminum. A good test is to poke your finger in the middle of the sheet; if the pan ripples or moves, it is not heavy enough. Buy baking sheets that clear your oven, once they are inside on a shelf, by 2 inches on all sides. Some cookie sheets are manufactured in a double layer, with air filling the middle layer. If you use these, the cooking time may vary from the recipe due to this extra layer of insulation.

Use flat baking sheets to toast and bake hors d'oeuvres that will stay in place on the sheet. Use rimmed baking sheets for items that can easily slide off when coming in or out of the oven or for skewered hors d'oeuvres that release juices.

Have the following on hand:

Three 17 × 14-inch baking sheets
Three 17×12-inch rimmed baking sheets

**BAMBOO STEAMER** Because they stack one on top of another, usually in layers of three, bamboo steamers are terrific for steaming a large quantity of different types of food at one time. Stackable steamers are also available in metal, but they are quite expensive and produce the same results as the inexpensive bamboo version. The floppy metal steamer inserts that are sold everywhere work fine for steaming very small quantities of food such as broccoli or carrots, but for hors d'oeuvres I prefer a sturdier steamer. I like it to have a diameter of at least 10 inches so I can fit as much food as possible on each level.

The best way to use a bamboo steamer is to set it in a wok or a wide, shallow saucepan. Fill the wok or saucepan with water to a level just below where the food will sit in the steamer. Remove the steamer and arrange food in it while bringing the water to a boil. The woven, tightly fitted lid prevents steam from escaping and also prevents condensation. Soak a new bamboo steamer for at least 20 minutes in cool water before using to rid it of its bamboo odor.

**BLENDER** There are occasions when the short, strong blades of a blender are more efficient than a food processor at thoroughly combining small quantities of ingredients. A blender also incorporates more air into the mixture, which can make sauces and dips lighter. I prefer a blender with only two settings: low and high. The other options are unnecessary. Also useful are immersion blenders. These are hand-held wands with a rotating blade on one end and a motor and electric cord on the other. They are most useful for puréeing soups and for making emulsions such as salad dressings and mayonnaise.

**BOX GRATER** A box grater is indispensable for grating cheese, citrus zest, vegetables, nutmeg, and even bread. There are two shapes: rectangular, which is also called a four-sided grater, and trapezoidal, which I find to be sturdier. Each side has different-size holes, some small enough to produce a fine powder and others large enough to create ¼-inch-wide shreds.

**CHANNEL KNIFE** Also called a citrus stripper, this knife slices vegetables into pretty scalloped flowers. It has a bulging V-shaped tooth that cuts thin decorative strips from fruits and vegetables. One of my favorite uses for the channel knife is to cut strips lengthwise around an entire vegetable, such as a carrot, and then cut the remaining carrot crosswise, creating flower-shaped carrot pieces. I also like to use the channel knife to make citrus garnishes for drinks. Long, curling strips of lime, lemon, or orange zest transform a simple drink into an elegant and exotic one.

**CHEESECLOTH** Originally used for pressing cheese, this lightweight, woven cotton cloth can be used to hold foods together, strain liquids, and shape foods. I also use it paired with a sieve to act as a fine strainer (see Chinois, below). It is inexpensive and easy to find in most supermarkets, kitchenware stores, and gourmet food shops.

**CHINOIS** A conical stainless-steel sieve made of extremely fine wire mesh, a chinois is the ultimate tool for straining soups, stocks, and sauces. In fact, the mesh is so fine that I often use a ladle to press the liquid through the sieve. A chinois is rather expensive but there is no substitute if your goal is to make crystal-clear soups and the very smoothest sauces. (The best alternative, however, is a cheesecloth-lined strainer.) Look for a chinois with a lipped rim, which is meant for hanging on the bowl into which the liquid is being strained. This allows you to use your hands to push the food through the strainer.

**CITRUS ZESTER** This handheld kitchen tool is designed to remove only the flavorful peel from citrus fruit, leaving the bitter white pith behind. The five tiny holes that line the stainless-steel edge create decorative strands when dragged across the surface of the fruit. A vegetable peeler can do the job, too, but the strands will be uneven. I also use a citrus peeler to make colorful garnishes from vegetables, including carrots, daikon, radishes, cucumbers, and beets.

**COCKTAIL SHAKER** For mixing drinks with hard-to-combine ingredients, a cocktail shaker is an essential piece of bar equipment. It is available in two models: the three-piece standard shaker with a built-in strainer and lid, and the two-piece Boston Shaker, which consists of two tumblers, one stainless steel, the other glass, which fit into each other end to end. A strainer must be used when pouring the chilled drink from the Boston Shaker into a glass. Either shaker generally holds two to three 4-ounce drinks, depending on the amount of ice used.

**COOKIE CUTTERS** I prefer stainless-steel rather than plastic cookie cutters for making hors d'oeuvres. Not only are they sturdier, but the sharp edges make more precisely cut tea sandwiches and canapés. You can use a serrated knife to cut squares, triangles, and rectangles, but circles really require sharp-edged cutters.

If you plan to purchase cutters, a good starter set should include one box set each of graduated round and square cookie cutters.

**DEEP-FAT FRYING THERMOMETER** Unless you are particularly adept at frying, it is enormously helpful to use a thermometer to fry hors d'oeuvres successfully. It is the same thermometer you might use for candy, measuring temperatures from 100° F. to 400° F. A good deep-fat thermometer should have a stainless-steel brace, a plastic handle, and an adjustable hook or clip to attach to the side of the pan. Look for a thermometer that is easy to read; you don't want to be peering too closely at it over a pan of hot oil.

**DEMITASSE SPOONS** The tiny spoons traditionally used with demitasse cups are perfectly sized for filling small tartlet shells or placing a dollop of crème fraîche onto a potato wafer. Demitasse spoons are available in fine housewares stores.

**DOUBLE BOILER** Ingredients that are sensitive to direct heat are best cooked in a double boiler, which is essentially two pots shaped to fit one on top of the other. The bottom pot holds simmering water, which is the heat source for the top pot. (You can improvise by setting an appropriately sized heatproof mixing bowl over a pot of steaming water.) Do not allow the simmering water to touch the bottom of the top pot, or the mixture may scorch.

**ELECTRIC JUICER** Nothing can chop, shred, and spin the pulp of fruits and vegetables to extract every bit of juice the way an electric juicer can. It is a good investment if you want to make your own fruit juices and vegetable soups. If you don't own one, buy fresh juices from a local juice bar or health food store.

**FOOD MILL** Used for straining and puréeing, food mills come with three interchangeable disks perforated with small, medium, or large holes. A food mill is especially useful for making smooth sauces and dips.

**FRY DADDY** An electric fryer sized perfectly for home frying, a Fry Daddy is indispensable for making fried hors d'oeuvres without making a mess. Holding up to 4 cups of oil, it heats food to 365° F. and automatically controls the temperature. It has a snap-on storage lid that makes storing oil very easy. One word of caution: The heavy cast-aluminum body becomes very hot and should be kept out of reach of children.

**GRILL PAN** If you can't grill outdoors year-round or your oven doesn't have a stovetop grill, a grill pan is a must in your equipment pantry. There are single- and double-burner models, the double allowing you to grill more food at one time. The grill pan is most effective on a gas stove; it will work on an electric stove, but will take longer for the pan to adjust to heat fluctuations. The pan must be very hot in order to properly sear and mark foods, and it is designed to tilt slightly so fat drains to the side. As with all cast-iron pots and pans, grill pans must be properly seasoned before using and well dried after washing.

**KNIVES** Knives are among the most essential kitchen tools. When shopping for them, try them on for size; they should feel like an extension of your hand, the blade and the handle balanced. Buy knives made of high-carbon steel or stainless steel. If well cared for, good knives will last a lifetime. Store them in a drawer tray with slits that isolate each blade, or in a felt-lined drawer that is wide enough to accommodate the width of each knife. Always wash and dry knives by hand. Sharpen them with a whetstone every few months to redefine the blade's edge.

While it seems there is a knife for every task, a basic set of the following five knives is really all you need.

**PARING KNIFE** A 3-inch or shorter knife that provides enough flexibility for peeling, cutting, and shaping fruits or vegetables or thinly slicing cheese and vegetables.

**SLICING KNIFE** At least 10 inches long and 1 inch or less wide with either a pointed or round tip, it is used to very thinly slice fruits as well as raw and cooked pieces of fish and meat.

**SERRATED KNIFE** Also called a bread knife, this has a scalloped blade that saws easily and cleanly through hard crust and tender crumb. Because it is designed to be used in a sawing motion, a serrated knife is also very useful for making clean cuts through foods such as tomatoes that might otherwise fall apart under the pressure of a slicing knife. Buy a knife with at least an 8-inch-long blade.

**CHEF'S KNIFE** A broad, substantial blade with a curved bottom and a width of at least 2 inches, designed to steady the rocking motion when chopping firm vegetables, distinguishes a chef's knife from the others. Though an 8-inch blade is adequate for an all-purpose knife, a 10-inch one is best.

**BONING KNIFE** The narrow blade of a 5- or 6-inch boning knife wiggles between meat and bone, allowing you to trim off fat, tendons, or cartilage easily.

**MANDOLINE** A manually operated machine with an adjustable blade, a mandoline allows you to cut uniformly thick or thin slices of vegetables and fruit. The traditional French mandoline is made entirely of stainless steel and has adjustable blades, including ones for straight, coarse, and fine shredding, and a cutter for making waffle chips. The French mandoline is an investment, but there is no substitute for it. A less expensive alternative, however, is the Japanese mandoline, also called a Benriner. Made of plastic with a fixed straight stainless-steel blade, the Japanese mandoline is smaller and a little less sturdy than the French one.

**MEAT POUNDER** Also called a meat bat, tenderizer, and mallet, a meat pounder is ridged on one side and flat on the other. The ridged side is used for tenderizing meat, the flat side for pounding and thinning. Though the results may be uneven, a cast-iron skillet may be used to pound and thin meat.

**MELON BALLER** Also known as a Parisienne scoop, a melon baller is an indispensable tool for scooping out balls or ovals from vegetables and fruits. A good melon baller has a tiny hole in the center of the scoop to break suction, making it effortless to remove the ball of fruit from the flesh. The bowls of melon ballers range in size from about 3/8 to 1 1/4 inches in diameter.

**MOLCAJETE** A Mexican version of a mortar, a molcajete (mohl-kah-HEH-teh) is made from black basalt (porous, volcanic rock) and often comes with a tejolote (teh-hoh-LO-teh), a pestle. A molcajete has a very rough surface, which gives spices, herbs, and tomatoes a wonderful texture when ground in it. I use a molcajete not only to grind spices, but also as a serving vessel for guacamole, salsas, and dips.

**MUFFIN TINS** When purchasing muffin tins, buy the nonstick variety, since they eliminate the need for additional grease and fat and are easiest to clean. I recommend the following:

Two or three standard muffin tins—2-inch diameter at the base, fitted with 12 or 24 cups

Two or four mini muffin tins—1 1/2-inch diameter at the base, fitted with 6 cups

**OFFSET SPATULAS** The handle of this spatula is set at an angle so that your hand is raised up and away from the work surface, making for easier and more even spreading of batters and flipping crepes, blini, and frico. An offset spatula with a 4 1/4-inch blade is a good multipurpose size.

**PARCHMENT PAPER** A nonstick, grease-free, heavy paper, parchment is used for a host of culinary purposes. Baking sheets lined with it do not generally need extra grease or butter. Baked foods slide right off the paper, and cleanup is easy. One small piece rolled up into a cone, its end snipped, makes a simple piping bag. Parchment paper can also be used for decorative purposes as in the preparation of pommes Anna (see photograph, page 37).

**PASTRY BAG** This cone-shaped bag is used to squeeze fillings and doughs through a small decorative tip. Pastry bags are sold in nylon, polyester, plastic, plastic-lined cotton, or canvas and in disposable plastic. They range in size from 7 to 24 inches long. A 16-inch-long bag is a good multipurpose length. I like to use reusable vinyl-coated cotton bags. They don't absorb odors and are easy to clean.

Parchment paper rolled into a cone shape, the small end snipped, is a suitable alternative to a pastry bag when piping in very small quantities. For larger quantities, a plastic freezer bag may be used in the same way, with one corner snipped out. When working with very loose batters or fillings, secure the open end of the bag by folding it over and clipping it with a clothespin.

**PASTRY BRUSHES** Two basic pastry brushes, one with nylon bristles, the other with natural, are essential for performing different brushing tasks. Nylon bristles are very durable and are best for brushing glazes and sauces onto meats and vegetables. They are also great for brushing melted butter between layers of phyllo dough, into muffin tins, and onto baking sheets. Natural bristles are softer than nylon and are wonderful to use on fragile items, such as unbaked pâte à choux. Though not essential, a third brush, reserved and labeled as a "dry brush," is very helpful for brushing away excess flour from any pastry or puff pastry doughs when rolling them out.

**PASTRY TIPS** Pastry tips allow you to create limitless decorative toppings on everything from vegetable slices to quail eggs. Tips can be purchased individually or in sets. I use Ateco brand tips, which are numbered to help you identify them. Among my favorite tips for hors d'oeuvres include:

straight tip #45
curved basket tip #98
closed star tip #16
open leaf tip #352
basket weave tip #47
closed star tip #30
ruffle tube tip #100
plain round #4
plain round #2

**PIZZA PEEL** A shovel-like flat wooden board with tapered edges and a long handle, a pizza peel is used to effortlessly slip pizza in and out of a hot oven and onto a pizza stone. When the peel is lightly dusted with semolina or cornmeal, the pizza may be formed directly on it. Before setting out to purchase a peel, measure the width and depth of your oven to assure proper fit.

**PIZZA STONE** Also known as a baking stone, a pizza stone is a very heavy, porous, unglazed piece of ceramic tile. The substantial weight is important because it distributes the heat evenly while the porous texture helps absorb excess moisture, creating very crispy crusts. Pizza stones vary in size, so be sure to measure the width and depth of your oven rack before purchasing one.

**PULLMAN PAN** A pullman pan is used to make pain de mie, also called a pullman loaf. The distinguishing component of this long, rectangular metal loaf pan is the built-in lid that slides smoothly and snugly along the top of the pan. It is designed to keep the dough compressed while it rises and bakes, resulting in a near-perfect square slicing bread with a compact, fine texture and crumb. This bread is ideal for making tea sandwiches, canapés, and croustades. If you do not have a pullman pan, cover a rectangular bread loaf pan with a heavy weighted sheet pan while the bread bakes.

**REAMER** Using an old-fashioned wooden reamer is my favorite way to quickly juice lemons and limes. The ridged, teardrop-shaped head is about the size of an egg and has a pointed tip that penetrates the fruit. To extract the most juice possible, roll the fruit on a work surface to soften it before reaming. Slice the fruit through the waist and juice by twisting the reamer back and forth into the flesh. Strain the juice before using.

**TARTLET AND PETIT-FOUR MOLDS** Tartlet molds are simply miniature versions of larger tart pans, and measure between 2¼ inches and 2¾ inches in diameter. Whether fluted or straight-edged, nonstick molds are the best. Two different tartlet pans are used in this book: a deep, fluted brioche shape, measuring 2¼ inches in diameter and ¾ inch deep; and a shallow, fluted pan, measuring 2¾ inches in diameter and ⅜ inch deep.

Petit-four molds are tiny, tin-plated steel molds that, by definition, hold no more than 2 tablespoons of filling. They are available in many different shapes, the most common being square, triangular, rectangular, oval, and crescent. The specific sizes used for making tartlets in the petit-four molds are as follows: the boat-shaped mold is 3 inches long; the round mold is 2⅜ inches in diameter; and the square mold is 2¼ inches square.

**TERRINE MOLD** Like the pullman pan and the chinois, a terrine mold is designed for a very specific use. Terrine molds are available in several sizes, though standard ones are generally 14 or 16 inches long and 3 to 4¾ inches high. Smaller molds are available for the express purpose of making terrine hors d'oeuvres. Some models have hinged sides for easy unmolding while others have fixed seams. Both are available in nonstick varieties, but I always line the mold with plastic wrap to make removal of the terrine easier. To make the terrines in this book, you will need a 12 × 2¼ × 1¾-inch metal terrine.

**WHISKS** The most versatile whisk to have on hand measures from 3 to 3½ inches across at the widest point. A small whisk (about 1½ inches at its widest point ) is also handy for mixing together sauces and vinaigrettes before they go into their serving bowls.

**ADZUKI BEANS, DRIED** The adzuki bean is second only to the soybean in popularity in Japan. Available in most supermarkets, these small, dried, reddish beans are high in protein and vitamin B and impart a sweet flavor to my Asian-inspired rice (page 191), salads, and rice and vegetable dishes.

**ARBORIO RICE** A plump, short-grained, high-starch rice grown in Italy, Arborio rice is most commonly used in risotto. It absorbs considerable moisture without becoming soggy, giving risotto its characteristic creamy texture. If you can't find Arborio rice in your supermarket, look for Carnaroli or Vialone Nano, which have a similar starch content.

**BLACK ONION SEED** These tiny—they're about the size of poppy seeds—slightly crunchy, jet-black seeds impart a nutty, slightly peppery flavor to foods. The combination of their striking color, intense flavor, and diminutive size make them a perfect garnish for finger foods, and they are particularly delicious sprinkled over mild cheese.

**BUCKWHEAT FLOUR** Not a true grain but an herb, buckwheat flour is simply the ground seeds of the buckwheat plant, cultivated primarily in Russia. Because it is rather dense, buckwheat flour is generally combined with another flour in a ¼ cup to ¾ cup ratio to achieve an appealing texture without sacrificing its deep, pleasantly sour flavor. Perhaps the most familiar food made with buckwheat is blini.

**CAPERS** Capers are the unopened buds of the caper flower, which usually are sun-dried and then pickled in salted white vinegar. They range in size from as tiny as a peppercorn to as large as a blueberry. I rinse them under cool water to reduce their intense saltiness before using them. Capers make excellent garnishes, but they can also be used as an ingredient to give a dish a salty-sour bite.

**CAPER BERRIES** The teardrop-shaped fruit of the caper bush, caper berries are a specialty of the Andalusia region of Spain, where the arid conditions allow the bushes to thrive. The berries are picked with the stem intact and traditionally are pickled in a lightly salted brine. They are especially delicious eaten out of hand with dry sherry or as a garnish for a martini. Serve them with a small bowl for the discarded stems.

**CHILI PASTE** A pungent mixture of ground chilies, oil, salt, and sometimes garlic, chili paste can make a mundane dish mouthwatering. The heat level can range from mild to very hot, depending on the chili peppers used. Intensely flavored, a little chili paste goes a long way. I often stir a tiny bit into the Arrabbiata (page 394) for an extra-hot and spicy tomato sauce.

**CHILI PEPPERS, DRIED** Because they keep very well, I always have dried chilies on hand. They vary dramatically in size, which generally indicates their level of heat intensity. The larger the chili, the milder. Smaller chilies should be used sparingly and prepared with caution; handle the seeds especially carefully, since they harbor much of the heat. Larger chilies can be chopped and sprinkled into sauces for subtler heat. Dried chilies are hotter than fresh because the drying process concentrates the heat of the chili. They should be shiny, pliable, and evenly colored in rich earth tones that vary as much as their flavors.

**CHILI OIL** Used extensively in regional Chinese cooking, beautiful red-tinged chili oil is made by steeping dried red chilies in vegetable oil. It can be added to dishes to impart a fiery flavor, combined with milder oils and used to stir-fry, or served as a condiment for dumplings. As with all cooking oils, store chili oil in a dark, cool place to prevent it from going rancid. Chinese varieties tend to be milder than Thai and Malaysian, which can be quite hot.

**COCONUT MILK** Canned, unsweetened coconut milk is made by simmering fresh coconut pieces in water and straining the liquid to extract as much milk from the coconut as possible. It is often found in spicy Asian soups and rice dishes, and should not be confused with sweetened coconut milk, which is generally used to make mixed drinks. The best coconut milk is made in Thailand and Malaysia. Shake the can before opening in order to mix the liquid thoroughly. Opened coconut milk can be kept in a covered glass jar in the refrigerator up to 2 days.

**CORNMEAL** Cornmeal is made from dried corn kernels that are steel-ground, a process by which the hull and germ of the kernel are removed. Cornmeal typically is white, yellow, or blue, depending on the variety of corn used; the taste is virtually the same. It is sold three ways: fine (also known as corn flour), medium (the most commonly sold), and coarse. Fine and medium cornmeal are used frequently in baking, and coarse cornmeal is used to make polenta. Cornmeal can be stored almost indefinitely in an airtight container in a cool, dry place. Stone-ground cornmeal, a coarser relative of cornmeal, is water-ground; this process results in the meal retaining some of the hull and germ, giving foods a deeper flavor and rougher texture. Stone-ground cornmeal must be kept in the freezer and remains fresh for up to 4 months.

**COUSCOUS** A staple of North African cuisine, couscous is the pellet-size grain of hard durum wheat, or precooked semolina. It is traditionally steamed and served with vegetables, fish, or poultry; its versatility, delicate flavor, and tender texture are well suited to tossing with somewhat more aggressively flavored ingredients. I like to spoon a little couscous salad into a cherry tomato or onto a cucumber round for a quick, healthy hors d'oeuvre.

**CRYSTALLIZED GINGER** Also called candied ginger, this is fresh ginger that has been cooked in sugar syrup and then coated in coarse sugar. The flavor is simultaneously sugary and spicy, making it a delightful garnish for cocktails. For an unusual cold-weather sip, simmer crystallized ginger in water and serve it in Lady Apple Cups (page 229).

**DUMPLING WRAPPERS** The growing popularity of Asian cuisine in the past decade has given rise to a number of widely available dumpling wrappers. Most supermarkets carry at least two different frozen wrappers, usually wonton, spring roll, shao mai, or egg roll. Many are made by machine with rice or wheat flour. They vary greatly in thickness and can be steamed, fried, or boiled. If you have the opportunity to shop at an Asian market, buy an assortment of wrappers and store them, well wrapped, in the freezer. Dumpling wrappers defrost fully in about an hour.

**FIGS** Grown widely in California, Texas, and Louisiana, fresh figs are available commercially from June through October in at least three varieties. Figs are also sold canned, dried, and preserved in syrup year-round. Dried figs give a dish a very pronounced, sweet flavor. I soak them in liquid before adding them to recipes, which intensifies their flavor and softens them. Keep dried figs tightly wrapped to prevent them from drying out and becoming too tough to soften.

**FILÉ POWDER** Made from the dried leaves of the sassafras tree, filé powder is heavily used in Cajun and Creole cooking; its earthy flavor is perhaps best showcased in gumbo. Filé should be stirred into a dish toward the very end of the cooking; if cooked for too long, it will cause food to become thick and gelatinous.

**FIVE-SPICE POWDER** Composed of an equal mixture of cinnamon, cloves, fennel seed, star anise, and Szechwan peppercorns, five-spice powder imparts a fragrant, sweet, and spicy aroma to dishes. Because of the variety of its ingredients, it can be used in both sweet and savory dishes.

**GRAPE LEAVES** The large leaves of the grapevine are commercially available only packed in brine, not fresh. Used primarily in Middle Eastern cooking, they are particularly useful for wrapping foods, such as dolmades, but can also be used to line a platter or as a garnish.

**GREEN TEA POWDER** The ground dried leaves of the first picking of green tea leaves, green tea powder, also known as matcha, is traditionally used in Japanese tea ceremonies to make hot green tea. Its soft, delicate green color belies its strong, bitter flavor, which mellows when used in baking. While excellent for making a warm tea, green tea powder is also a beautiful colorant for crepes, cookies, and batters.

**HARISSA PASTE** Made from dried red chili peppers, garlic, oil, and salt, harissa is a spicy and fiery Middle Eastern relish that adds heat to stews, couscous, sauces, and marinades. Imported from Tunisia, harissa is sold in tubes in specialty food stores. For serious heat lovers, serve harissa on bread and butter accompanied by olives before a meal.

**HERBES DE PROVENCE** A mixture of dried herbs frequently used in southern French cooking—thyme, basil, fennel, savory, sage, rosemary, tarragon, and lavender—herbes de Provence can be found in the spice section of most supermarkets. I always have a crock on hand for seasoning sauces, soups, and a variety of dishes.

**LEMONGRASS** Indispensable in Thai cooking, lemongrass is a tough reedlike plant that resembles a very tall scallion. It is lovely added to soups, rice dishes, and sauces. Its aggressive lemon aroma is released when its greenish-white root end is smashed, bruised, or finely ground. For pure lemongrass flavor, smashed pieces of the stalk can be added during cooking and removed just before serving. If lemongrass is to be used as an ingredient, the stalk must be peeled and very finely chopped. Lemongrass is sold in stalks that can be up to 2 feet long, and is available fresh or dried. Fresh lemongrass has the strongest flavor. The root end contains the most flavor, so avoid the upper leaves of the stalk, which sometimes are packaged for sale.

**LENTILS** Lentils are tiny, round legumes that grow in about 1-inch long pods. When ripe, the pods are picked, dried, and beaten to release the seeds. The seeds are then dried further and left whole or split. They are available in grayish-brown, black, red, and yellow, the most common of which is brown.

**MIRIN** This slightly syrupy, sweet rice wine is a highly valued ingredient in Japanese cuisine. Frequently added to sushi rice, it adds a delicate sweetness to foods and imparts a depth of flavor. Made from fermented, glutinous rice, mirin is generally not meant to be drunk, although some finer varieties can be sipped straight up.

**NORI** A mainstay of Japanese cooking, nori are thin sheets of dried seaweed, most commonly used to make sushi. With a distinct, sweet and salty sea flavor, nori is very rich in protein, calcium, iron, minerals, and vitamins. It is well worth spending the extra money for high-quality nori. Look for sheets that are black and shiny, with a faint green-and-purple sheen. Nori can be sold pretoasted (called yakinori), or brushed with soy sauce (called ajijsuke-nori), or simply plain. As with nuts and seeds, toasting nori releases its deepest flavor. In addition to using nori to make sushi, thinly sliced nori makes a flavorful garnish.

**PANKO (JAPANESE BREAD CRUMBS)** Made from wheat flour and honey, these large and flaky bread crumbs are used to coat foods before deep-frying. They create a wonderful crispy texture and maintain it long after frying. Store panko in an airtight container to prevent the bread crumbs from becoming stale.

**PEPITA SEEDS** These hulled and roasted pumpkin seeds are very popular in Mexican cooking. They are dark green, a result of the white hull being removed. They can be eaten as a snack but are often used in cooking as a thickener. I love to roast pepita seeds and sprinkle them with coarse salt. They have a delightful nutty flavor and are superb when used as a garnish or ground into a paste.

**PEPPERCORNS** There are three basic types of peppercorns: black, white, and green. The black kind is picked when the berry is slightly underripe, and then dried until black and shriveled. The white type is a fully ripe berry that has had its skin removed and then been dried. The green variety is an underripe berry that is either preserved in brine or sold dried. All types are spicy and vary in intensity. The pink peppercorn is not a peppercorn at all, but a dried berry from the 'Baies' rose plant; it is mild and slightly sweet.

**PICKLED GINGER** Made from preserving fresh ginger in sweet vinegar, this condiment is most frequently used with sushi and sashimi. The color ranges from light golden to pink; higher-quality ginger is light golden. The pink color comes from added coloring. Don't hesitate to use pickled ginger with mildly flavored foods to add crunch and zing, or as a pretty garnish on delicate foods, such as quail eggs. Pickled ginger is now available in jars in the Asian food section of most grocery stores; keep it refrigerated once the jar has been opened.

**RICE PAPER WRAPPERS** These round or triangular wrappers are sold dried and must be quickly reconstituted in warm water before using. Made from a mixture of rice flour, water, and salt and rolled to paper thinness by machine, they are then dried in the sun on bamboo mats, giving them their unique texture and pattern. They can be used for cold, fresh summer rolls or can be rolled around a filling and fried. Available in packages of 50 to 100, they are very inexpensive. Look for brands from Thailand and Vietnam, which are especially good. Avoid wrappers that are yellowish in color; they may be old. Handle wrappers with care, as they tend to be brittle.

**SAKE** A popular beverage and an essential cooking ingredient in Japanese cuisine, sake is made from fermented rice. It can be sipped hot or cold and has a very strong and slightly sweet flavor. Often used to balance salty ingredients and in marinades to tenderize meats, it suppresses saltiness and eliminates fishy tastes.

**SEA SALT** Available fine or coarse-grained, sea salt is simply salt from evaporated sea water. It has a distinct, fresh flavor, but is more costly than other salt, so it should be used only for those most special dishes. Kosher salt makes a fine substitute.

**SESAME SEEDS** Sesame seeds are sold in many forms: black, red, shades of brown, and white. White seeds are sold both hulled (pure white) and unhulled (grayish-brown). I prefer to use unhulled because they have a much more distinct sesame flavor. All sesame seeds should be toasted lightly before using to release their fragrance and flavor. Sesame seeds have a high oil content and tend to turn rancid rather quickly; store them in the refrigerator in an airtight container for up to 6 months, or in the freezer for up to a year.

**SESAME OIL** There are two types of sesame oil on the market. Light-colored sesame oil is slightly nutty and very versatile; its high smoking point makes it excellent for frying. Dark sesame oil is made by pressing roasted sesame seeds and it has a very assertive, nutty flavor. It is used sparingly for marinades, dressings, and stir-frys. Look for oil that is sold in glass bottles. The oil in plastic bottles tends to turn rancid more quickly. I like to add a few drops of dark sesame oil to my Asian-inspired dishes just before serving to infuse them with fragrant sesame flavor.

**SUPERFINE SUGAR** Superfine sugar (sometimes referred to as castor sugar) is nothing more than finely granulated sugar. It is good to use in cold mixed drinks because it dissolves easily. To make your own superfine sugar, process regular granulated sugar in a food processor with a metal blade until it's powdery.

**SUSHI RICE** Japanese sushi rice is a short-grained glutinous white rice that becomes moist, firm, and sticky when cooked. It has a higher proportion of waxy starch molecules, known as amylopectin, than other rice, which gives cooked sushi rice its characteristic firm, sticky texture. If you can't find Japanese sushi rice in your area, substitute regular short-grained rice (also known as pearl rice), which is another starchy and glutinous rice.

**TAHINI** A thick oily paste made of ground sesame seeds, tahini is a staple in Middle Eastern cooking. Although it keeps well unrefrigerated, it tends to separate and needs to be vigorously stirred to recombine the oil and solids. It imparts a nutty, sesame-like flavor to dishes and can be used for both sweet and savory hors d'oeuvres.

**TRUFFLES** Prized for the exquisite aroma and earthy flavor they impart to foods, truffles are among the world's most expensive ingredient because cultivating them is a lengthy and labor-intensive task. Truffles are black (the more prized of the two) or white. They are grown in Italy, France, and England and are imported fresh, frozen, canned, or as a paste. I like to use truffle oil because it has the wonderful, earthy aroma of fresh truffles without the expense. A simple drop of truffle oil can transform a small hors d'oeuvre into a heavenly experience. Keep truffle oil refrigerated for a longer shelf life; it will solidify, but can be easily liquefied at room temperature in about 30 minutes.

**VANILLA BEANS** The thin, black fruit of the celadon-colored orchid, vanilla beans are actually pods, picked when green, then cured and fermented to become the aromatic bean that we know. Fresh vanilla will keep for up to 6 months tightly wrapped and refrigerated in an airtight container. If you can't find vanilla beans, use pure vanilla extract as a substitute. Steer clear of imitation vanilla, which provides a moderate amount of aroma but absolutely no flavor.

**WASABI** Similar to horseradish, wasabi is the root of a perennial Asian plant. It has a very spicy, sharp flavor and is used as a condiment, often with sushi. Wasabi is available fresh, as a paste, or in powdered form. I keep it in both its powdered and paste forms in my pantry. Powdered wasabi can be reconstituted with water or sake to make a paste. It is delicious spread lightly on raw vegetables, such as daikon and radishes, or mixed with mayonnaise for a spicy sandwich spread.

**ASIAN SOUP SPOON:** Katagiri

**BAKING DISH (1 1/2 QT.):** Bridge Kitchenware, Broadway Panhandler, N.Y. Cake & Baking

**BAMBOO STEAMERS:** Katagiri, Bridge Kitchenware, Broadway Panhandler, Williams-Sonoma

**BAR KIT:** Martha by Mail

**BARQUETTE MOLDS, SMALL:** Bridge Kitchenware, Broadway Panhandler, N.Y. Cake & Baking

**BENCH SCRAPER:** Bridge Kitchenware, Broadway Panhandler, N.Y. Cake & Baking

**CAVIAR SPOONS:** Martha by Mail

**CHANNEL KNIFE:** Bridge Kitchenware, Broadway Panhandler

**CITRUS ZESTER:** Bridge Kitchenware, Broadway Panhandler, N.Y. Cake & Baking

**COOKIE CUTTERS (FLORAL, ROUND, AND SQUARE SETS):** N.Y. Cake & Baking, Bridge Kitchenware

**COOKIE CUTTERS (2-INCH OVAL AND TEAR DROP):** N.Y. Cake & Baking

**CREPE PAN (8-INCH):** Bridge Kitchenware, Broadway Panhandler, N.Y. Cake & Baking

**ELECTRIC MIXER, PADDLE, DOUGH HOOK:** KitchenAid, N.Y. Cake & Baking

**FRENCH MANDOLINE:** Bridge Kitchenware, Broadway Panhandler, N.Y. Cake & Baking

**FOOD MILL & DISCS:** Bridge Kitchenware, Broadway Panhandler, N.Y. Cake & Baking

**FOOD PROCESSOR:** KitchenAid

**FRYING THERMOMETER:** King Arthur Flour, Bridge Kitchenware

**GARNISHING KIT:** Martha by Mail

**HORS D'OEUVRES KIT:** Martha by Mail

**HORS D'OEUVRES SERVING SET:** Martha by Mail

**JAPANESE MANDOLINE:** Katagiri, Broadway Panhandler

**JELLY BAG:** Bridge Kitchenware

**JUICER:** Bridge Kitchenware, Broadway Panhandler, Williams-Sonoma

**KNIVES:** Bridge Kitchenware, Williams-Sonoma

**MUFFIN TINS (2-INCH MINI):** Bridge Kitchenware, Broadway Panhandler, N.Y. Cake & Baking

**MUFFIN TINS (1 1/2-INCH PETITE):** Broadway Panhandler, N.Y. Cake & Baking

**NESTING COPPER TRAYS:** Martha by Mail

**PARCHMENT PAPER:** Bridge Kitchenware, Broadway Panhandler, N.Y. Cake & Baking

**PASTRY BAGS AND BRUSHES:** N.Y. Cake & Baking

**PASTRY TIPS, SET:** N.Y. Cake & Baking

**PETIT-FOUR MOLDS (SMALL):** Bridge Kitchenware, Broadway Panhandler, J. B. Prince, N.Y. Cake & Baking

**PIZZA STONE:** King Arthur Flour, Bridge Kitchenware, N.Y. Cake & Baking

**PIZZA PEEL:** King Arthur Flour, Bridge Kitchenware

**PULLMAN LOAF PANS (16 x 3 1/2 x 3 1/2-INCHES):** Bridge Kitchenware, Broadway Panhandler, N.Y. Cake & Baking

**ROASTING PAN (ALL-CLAD):** Williams-Sonoma, Broadway Panhandler, Bridge Kitchenware

**SANDING SUGAR SET:** Martha by Mail, N.Y. Cake & Baking

**SHEET PAN (12 x 17-INCH):** Bridge Kitchenware, N.Y. Cake & Baking

**SHEET PAN (12 x 17-INCH, RIMMED):** Bridge Kitchenware, Broadway Panhandler, N.Y. Cake & Baking

**SILPAT BAKING MAT:** Martha by Mail, Bridge Kitchenware, Broadway Panhandler, N.Y. Cake & Baking, King Arthur Flour, Williams-Sonoma

**SKEWERS:** Bridge Kitchenware, Broadway Panhandler

**SPOONS, CAVIAR:** Martha by Mail

**SPOONS, DEMITASSE:** Bridge Kitchenware, Broadway Panhandler, Williams-Sonoma

**TARTLET PANS (2 3/4 x 3/8-INCH, FLUTED, AND 2 1/4 x 3/4-INCH, FLUTED):** N.Y. Cake & Baking

**TERRINE MOLDS (16 x 2 x 1-INCH AND 12 x 2 x 1 3/4-INCH):** Bridge Kitchenware, Broadway Panhandler, J. B. Prince, Williams-Sonoma

**TOOTHPICKS:** Bridge Kitchenware, Broadway Panhandler, N.Y. Cake & Baking

**TOOTHPICKS, BAMBOO:** Katagiri

# FOOD SOURCES

**ADZUKI BEANS, DRIED:** Uwajimaya, Dean & Deluca

**ANCHO CHILIES, DRIED:** Kitchen Market

**BACON, THICK-SLAB PEPPERED:** New Braunfels Smokehouse

**BELUGA LENTILS:** Dean & Deluca

**BLACK ONION SEED:** Adriana's Caravan

**BOCCONCINI:** Murray's, Formaggio Kitchen

**CAPER BERRIES:** Zabar's

**CAVIAR:** Caviarteria, Petrossian, Dean & Deluca, Russ & Daughters

**CHEESE:** Murray's, Zingerman's, Formaggio Kitchen

**CHERRIES, DRIED:** American Spoon Foods

**CHILI PASTE, SUCH AS SAMBAL OELEK:** Kitchen Market, Uwajimaya

**CHORIZO:** Dean & Deluca

**COCONUT MILK, UNSWEETENED:** Katagiri, Kitchen Market, Dean & Deluca, Uwajimaya

**CRANBERRIES, DRIED:** American Spoon Foods

**CURRY LEAVES, FRESH:** Adriana's Caravan

**DRIED LAVENDER:** Balducci's

**DUCK LEG CONFIT:** D'Artagnan

**DUMPLING WRAPPERS:** Katagiri, Sunrise Mart, Uwajimaya

**DYES (GEL & PASTE):** N.Y. Cake and Baking

**EDAMAME:** Katagiri, Sunrise Mart, Uwajimaya

**FIGS, DRIED:** Dean & Deluca

**FLOUR, WHOLE BUCKWHEAT:** King Arthur Flour

**FOIE GRAS PÂTÉ:** D'Artagnan

**GINGER, PICKLED:** Katagiri, Sunrise Mart, Uwajimaya

**GRAPE LEAVES IN BRINE:** Dean & Deluca

**GREEN TEA POWDER:** Takashimaya, Katagiri, Sunrise Mart

**GYOZA SKINS, POTSTICKER WRAPPERS:** Katagiri, Sunrise Mart, Uwajimaya

**HAM, SERRANO:** Dean & Deluca

**HAM, 2–2½ LB., BLACK FOREST:** Karl Ehmer

**HARISSA PASTE:** Kitchen Market, Adriana's Caravan

**HOT CHILI OIL:** Kitchen Market, Uwajimaya

**KAFIR (SHEEP'S MILK):** Dean & Deluca

**LOTUS ROOT, BOILED:** Uwajimaya

**MASSUR DHAL:** Adriana's Caravan

**MIRIN:** Katagiri, Sunrise Mart, Uwajimaya

**MORELS, FRESH (APRIL–JULY) AND DRIED:** Marché aux Delices, Urbani

**MUSHROOMS, DRIED:** Melissa's

**NOODLES, RICE:** Katagiri, Uwajimaya

**NUTS:** A. L. Bazzini

**PANCETTA:** Dean & Deluca

**PANKO:** Katagiri, Sunrise Mart, Uwajimaya

**PEPITA SEEDS:** Kitchen Market

**PEPPERCORNS, GREEN IN BRINE:** Dean & Deluca, Zabar's

**PEPPERCORNS, TRICOLOR:** Zabar's

**PHYLLO DOUGH:** Dean & Deluca

**PLUM SAUCE:** Katagiri, Uwajimaya

**PRESERVED LEMONS:** Dean & Deluca

**PULLMAN BREAD:** E.A.T.

**QUAIL EGGS:** Dean & Deluca, Uwajimaya

**RED BELL PEPPERS, SUN-DRIED:** Arthur Avenue Caterers

**ROBIOLA CHEESE:** Murray's, Formaggio Kitchen

**SAFFRON:** Penzey's, Dean & Deluca

**SALT COD, DRIED:** Dean & Deluca

**SALT, PRETZEL:** King Arthur

**SALT, SEA:** Dean & Deluca, Uwajimaya

**SANDING SUGARS:** N.Y. Cake and Baking

**SAUSAGES:** D'Artagnan, Dean & Deluca, New Braunfels Smokehouse, Kurowycky

**SESAME SEEDS, BLACK:** Kitchen Market, Penzey's, Uwajimaya

**SESAME SEEDS, UNHULLED:** Kitchen Market

**SHISO LEAVES, FRESH:** Katagiri, Sunrise Mart, Uwajimaya

**SPICES:** Penzey's, Dean & Deluca

**SUGARCANE:** Frieda's

**TAHINI:** Dean & Deluca, Krinos

**TARAMASALATA:** Russ & Daughters

**TARO ROOT:** Uwajimaya

**TOMATILLOS:** Kitchen Market

**TOMOLIVES (PICKLED GREEN TOMATO):** Zabar's

**TORTILLAS, SPINACH AND TOMATO:** Maria and Ricardo's Tortilla Factory

**TRUFFLES:** Marché aux Delices, Urbani, Caviarteria

**VANILLA BEANS:** Penzey's

**WASABI CAVIAR:** Russ & Daughters

**WHEAT-CAKE WRAPPERS (GYOZA):** Sunrise Mart

**WHITE TRUFFLE OIL:** Dean & Deluca, Urbani

**ADRIANA'S CARAVAN**
409 Vanderbilt Street
Brooklyn, NY 11218
718-436-8565 or 800-316-0820
Adricara@aol.com
*Catalog available. Spices and ethnic ingredients, including black onion seed, fresh curry leaves, harissa paste, massur dhal*

**THE A.L. BAZZINI COMPANY**
200 Food Center Drive
Hunts Point Market
Bronx, NY 10474
718-842-8644 or 800-228-0172
*Catalog available. Roasted nuts and seeds, in-shell nuts, dried fruits, nut butters, chocolate-coated products, brittles*

**AMERICAN SPOON FOODS**
P.O. Box 566
Petoskey, MI 49770
616-347-9030 or 800-222-5886
(customer service)
888-735-6700 (catalog)
www.spoon.com
*Catalog available. Dried fruit, including cherries and cranberries, nuts, preserves, dried Michigan morel mushrooms*

**ARTHUR AVENUE CATERERS**
2344 Arthur Avenue
Bronx, NY 10458
718-295-5033
fax 718-933-5903
www.arthuravenue.com
*Italian specialty foods, including sun-dried red bell peppers, prosciutto, mortadella, sausages, cheeses, marinated vegetables*

**BALDUCCI'S**
424 Sixth Avenue
New York, NY 10011
212-673-2600 or 800-225-3822
www.balducci.com
*Catalog available. Specialty foods, pancetta, farmhouse cheeses, estate-bottled olive oils, varietal vinegars, smoked fish, caviar, coffee, tea, exotic foods, bake-house breads, fresh and dried fruits, vegetables, chorizo, dried lavender, green peppercorns*

**BRIDGE KITCHENWARE**
214 East 52nd Street
New York, NY 10022
212-838-6746 or 800-274-3435
www.bridgekitchenware.com
*Catalog $3 (applied to first purchase). Imported professional-quality copper and stainless-steel cookware, knives, parchment paper, sheet pans, mandolines, barquette and petit-four molds, muffin tins, grill pans, bamboo steamers, juicers, skewers, toothpicks, citrus zesters, channel knives, food mills and disks, pullman loaf pans, bench scrapers, crepe pans, baking dishes, wooden reamers, melon ballers, Pyrex measuring cups, whisks, box graters, pastry brushes, scales, kitchen twine, timers, blenders, rolling pins, cheesecloth, cocktail shakers, double boilers, demitasse spoons, fine strainers/chinois.*

**BROADWAY PANHANDLER**
447 Broome Street
New York, NY 10013
212-966-3434
www.broadwaypanhandler.com
*Specialty pots and pans, appliances, knives, parchment paper, sheet pans, mandolines, barquette and petit-four molds, muffin tins, grill pans, bamboo steamers, juicers, skewers, toothpicks, citrus zesters, channel knives, food mills and disks, pullman loaf*

pans, bench scrapers, crepe pans, baking dishes, wooden reamers, melon ballers, Pyrex measuring cups, whisks, box graters, pastry brushes, scales, kitchen twine, timers, blenders, rolling pins, cheesecloth, cocktail shakers, double boilers, demitasse spoons, fine strainers.*

**CAVIARTERIA**
Delmonico Hotel
502 Park Avenue
New York, NY 10022
212-759-7410 or 800-4-CAVIAR
www.caviarteria.com
*Catalog. Caviar and smoked fish, truffles*

**D'ARTAGNAN**
280 Wilson Avenue
Newark, NJ 07105
800-327-8246
www.dartagnan.com
*Catalog available. Fresh game, foie gras, poultry, duck leg confit, foie gras pâté, garlic sausage*

**DEAN & DELUCA**
560 Broadway
New York, NY 10012
212-431-1691 or 800-221-7714
www.dean-deluca.com
*Catalog available. Specialty foods, pancetta, farmhouse cheeses, estate-bottled olive oils, varietal vinegars, smoked fish, coffee, tea, exotic foods, bake-house breads, fresh and dried fruits, vegetables, caviar, kitchen equipment, cookbooks, adzuki beans, beluga lentils, caviar, unsweetened coconut milk, coffee with chicory, dried figs, Serrano ham, sheep's-milk yogurt, pancetta, preserved lemons, quail eggs, dried salt cod, sea salt, tahini, white truffle oil*

**E.A.T.**
1064 Madison Avenue
New York, NY 10028
212-772-0022
*Specialty prepared foods, including pullman
bread, freshly baked breads, pastries, seafood
salads, cured meats, and pâté*

**FORMAGGIO KITCHEN**
244 Huron Avenue
Cambridge, MA 02138
617-354-4750 or 888-212-3224
*Catalog available. Imported and domestic
cheese, including bocconcini and robiola
cheese, olive oils, vinegars, imported pasta,
rice and grains, chocolate, honey, international specialty foods*

**FRIEDA'S**
4465 Corporate Center Drive
Los Alamitos, CA 90720-2561
Mail-order address:
P.O. Box 58488
Los Angeles, CA 90058
714-826-6100 or 800-421-9477
www.friedas.com
*Catalog available. Exotic and specialty
produce, including sugarcane*

**J. B. PRINCE COMPANY, INC.**
36 East 31st Street
New York, NY 10016
212-683-3553
fax 212-683-4488
*A source for professional chefs; a minimum
order of $25.00 is necessary. Mini nonstick
pâté molds, rectangular pâté molds with
removable bottoms, petit-four molds.*

**KARL EHMER QUALITY
MEATS**
63-35 Fresh Pond Road
Ridgewood, NY 11385
800-ITS-KARL
fax 718-456-2270
www.karlehmer.com
*Brochure available. Smoked hams, minia-
ture Black Forest hams, salami, bologna,
sausages, turkey, bacon, bratwurst*

**KATAGIRI & COMPANY**
224 and 226 East 59th Street
New York, NY 10022
212-755-3566, 212-838-5453
www.katagiri.com
*Japanese specialty foods, including unsweet-
ened coconut milk, edamame, pickled ginger, green tea powder, gyoza skins, dumpling
wrappers, potsticker wrappers, mirin,
panko, shiso leaves, sake cups, chokos, Asian
soup spoons, Japanese mandolines and cooking utensils, bamboo steamers and picks*

**KING ARTHUR FLOUR
BAKER'S CATALOG**
P.O. Box 876
Norwich, VT 05055-0876
800-827-6836 or 800-777-4434
www.kingarthurflour.com
*Catalog available. Extensive selection of
supplies, including pretzel salt, King Arthur
Flour, baking stones, baker's peels, pans*

**KITCHEN MARKET**
218 Eighth Avenue
New York, NY 10011
212-243-4433 or 800-HOT-4433
*Catalog available. Dried herbs; dried, fresh,
and pickled peppers; dried fruits; nuts and
seeds; beans and grains; spices. Mexican and
Southwestern food, tortillas, harissa paste,
hot sauce, dried ancho chilies, hot chili oil,
pepita seeds, black sesame seeds, unhulled
sesame seeds, tomatillos, unsweetened
coconut milk*

**KITCHENAID HOME
APPLIANCES**
P.O. Box 218
St. Joseph, MI 49085
800-541-6390
www.kitchenaid.com
*Home appliances, food processors, blenders*

**KUROWYCKY MEAT
PRODUCTS**
124 First Avenue
New York, NY 10009
212-477-0344
*Homemade hams, sausages, wursts, kiel-
basa, special mustards. No mail order*

**MARCHÉ AUX DELICES**
120 Imlay Street
Brooklyn, NY 11231
888-547-5471
www.auxdelices.com
email: staff@auxdelices.com
*Catalog available. Exotic fresh and dried
mushrooms, caviar, truffles, truffle oil,
truffle butter, sea salt, smoked fish, saffron,
vanilla beans, nuts, dried and frozen berries,
grains, baking supplies*

**MARIA AND RICARDO'S
TORTILLA FACTORY**
30 Germania Street
Jamaica Plain, MA 02130
617-524-6107
*Assorted flour tortillas, including spinach,
tomato, whole wheat, white, chili, blue and
white corn tortillas*

**MARTHA BY MAIL**
800-950-7130
*Copper trays, Silpat baking mats, hors
d'oeuvres and garnishing kits, cookie cutters, serving sets, bar kits, caviar spoons*

**MELISSA'S WORLD VARIETY
PRODUCE, INC.**
5325 South Soto Street
Vernon, CA 90058
800-468-7111
www.melissas.com
*Catalog available. Extensive variety of pro-
duce, including Asian produce, mushrooms,
herbs, dried fruit*

**MURRAY'S CHEESE SHOP**
257 Bleecker Street
New York, NY 10014
212-243-3289 or 888-692-4339
murrays_cheese@msn.com
*Imported and domestic cheeses, including
bocconcini and robiola*

**NEW BRAUNFELS
SMOKEHOUSE**
P.O. Box 311159
New Braunfels, TX 78131-1159
800-537-6932
www.nbsmokehouse.com
*Catalog available. Assorted meats, includ-
ing thick-slab peppered bacon, smoked
turkey, ham, dried beef, pork, pastrami*

**NEW YORK CAKE AND
BAKING DISTRIBUTOR**
56 West 22nd Street
New York, NY 10010
212-675-CAKE or 800-942-2539
*Catalog $3. Baking and decorating sup-
plies, chocolate, gel and paste dyes, sanding
sugars, Silpat baking mats*

**PENZEY'S SPICES**
P.O. Box 933
Muskego, WI 53150
414-679-7207
www.penzeys.com
*Catalog available. Spices, saffron, chili
peppers, vanilla beans*

**PETROSSIAN PARIS**
419 West 13th Street
New York, NY 10014
212-337-0808 or 800-828-9241
*Catalog available. Caviar, foie gras, choco-
lates, smoked fish, gift baskets*

**RUSS & DAUGHTERS**
179 East Houston Street
New York, NY 10002
212-475-4880 or 800-787-7229
fax 212-475-0345
*Assorted caviar (including wasabi caviar),
smoked fish, herring, cheese, dried fruit,
glacé fruit, nuts*

**SUNRISE MART**
4 Stuyvesant Street
2nd Floor
New York, NY 10003
212-598-3040
*Japanese specialty foods, including
edamame, pickled ginger, green tea powder,
dumpling wrappers, wheat-cake wrappers
(Gyoza wrappers), potsticker wrappers,
boiled lotus root, dark sesame oil, mirin,
rice noodles, panko, plum sauce, shiso leaves*

**TAKASHIMAYA—
THE TEA BOX**
693 Fifth Avenue
New York, NY 10022
212-350-0100 or 800-753-2038
*Eastern and French herbal teas, tea-related
accessories, Japanese kitchen utensils, green
tea powder*

**URBANI TRUFFLES AND
CAVIAR**
29-24 40th Avenue
Long Island City, NY 11104
718-392-5050 or 800-281-2330
www.urbani.com
*Fresh and dried mushrooms, morels, black
and white truffle oils, truffles, caviar*

**UWAJIMAYA**
519 6th Avenue South
Seattle, WA 98104
800-889-1928
fax 206-624-6915
www.uwajimaya.com
*Asian foods, including unsweetened coconut
milk, chili paste, edamame, pickled ginger,
gyoza wrappers, dumpling wrappers, potsticker wrappers, mirin, rice noodles, panko,
plum sauce, quail eggs, sea salt, black
sesame seeds, fresh shiso leaves, taro root*

**WILLIAMS-SONOMA**
800-541-2233
www.williams-sonoma.com
*Call for nearest location of store. Catalog
available. Specialty pots and pans, appliances, cookbooks, knives, Japanese mandolines, baking equipment*

**ZABAR'S**
2245 Broadway
New York, NY 10024
212-787-2000 or 800-697-6301
Zabars@infohouse.com
*Catalog available. Specialty foods, includ-
ing caper berries, tomolives, tricolor peppercorns, cheeses, meats, smoked fish,
estate-bottled oils, varietal vinegars, mustards, crackers, dried fruit, pastries, caviar,
coffee, tea, dried herbs*

**ZINGERMAN'S**
422 Detroit Street
Ann Arbor, MI 48104
734-769-1625
*Catalog available. Specialty foods, farm-
house cheeses, estate-bottled olive oils, varietal vinegars, smoked fish, coffee, tea,
bake-house breads, fresh and dried fruits,
vegetables*

**Note:** Boldfaced page references indicate photographs.

American cooks use standard containers, the 8-ounce cup and a tablespoon that takes exactly 16 level fillings to fill that cup level. Measuring by cup makes it very difficult to give weight equivalents, as a cup of densely packed butter will weigh considerably more than a cup of flour. The easiest way therefore to deal with cup measurements in recipes is to take the amount by volume rather than by weight. Thus the equation reads: 1 cup = 240 ml = 8 fl. oz.; $\frac{1}{2}$ cup = 120 ml = 4 fl. oz. It is possible to buy a set of American cup measures in major stores around the world. In the States, butter is often measured in sticks. One stick is the equivalent of 8 tablespoons. One tablespoon of butter is therefore the equivalent to $\frac{1}{2}$ ounce/15 grams.

## LIQUID MEASURES

| Fluid ounces | U.S. | Imperial | Milliliters |
|---|---|---|---|
| | 1 teaspoon | 1 teaspoon | 5 |
| $\frac{1}{4}$ | 2 teaspoons | 1 dessertspoon | 7 |
| $\frac{1}{2}$ | 1 tablespoon | 1 tablespoon | 15 |
| 1 | 2 tablespoons | 2 tablespoons | 28 |
| 2 | $\frac{1}{4}$ cup | 4 tablespoons | 56 |
| 4 | $\frac{1}{2}$ cup or $\frac{1}{4}$ pint | | 110 |
| 5 | | $\frac{1}{4}$ pint or 1 gill | 140 |
| 6 | $\frac{3}{4}$ cup | | 170 |
| 8 | 1 cup or $\frac{1}{2}$ pint | | 225 |
| 9 | | | 250, $\frac{1}{4}$ liter |
| 10 | 1$\frac{1}{4}$ cups | $\frac{1}{2}$ pint | 280 |
| 12 | 1$\frac{1}{2}$ cups | $\frac{3}{4}$ pint | 340 |
| 15 | $\frac{3}{4}$ pint | | 420 |
| 16 | 2 cups or 1 pint | | 450 |
| 18 | 2$\frac{1}{4}$ cups | | 500, $\frac{1}{2}$ liter |
| 20 | 2$\frac{1}{2}$ cups | 1 pint | 560 |
| 24 | 3 cups or 1$\frac{1}{2}$ pints | | 675 |
| 25 | | 1$\frac{1}{4}$ pints | 700 |
| 27 | 3$\frac{1}{2}$ cups | | 750, $\frac{3}{4}$ liter |
| 30 | 3$\frac{3}{4}$ cups | 1$\frac{1}{2}$ pints | 840 |
| 32 | 4 cups or 2 pints or 1 quart | | 900 |

## SOLID MEASURES

| ounces | pounds | grams | kilos |
|---|---|---|---|
| 1 | | 28 | |
| 2 | | 56 | |
| 3$\frac{1}{2}$ | | 100 | |
| 4 | $\frac{1}{4}$ | 112 | |
| 5 | | 140 | |
| 6 | | 168 | |
| 8 | $\frac{1}{2}$ | 225 | |
| 9 | | 250 | $\frac{1}{4}$ |
| 12 | $\frac{3}{4}$ | 340 | |
| 16 | 1 | 450 | |
| 18 | | 500 | $\frac{1}{2}$ |
| 20 | 1$\frac{1}{4}$ | 560 | |
| 24 | 1$\frac{1}{2}$ | 675 | |
| 27 | | 750 | $\frac{3}{4}$ |
| 28 | 1$\frac{3}{4}$ | 780 | |
| 32 | 2 | 900 | |
| 36 | 2$\frac{1}{4}$ | 1000 | 1 |
| 40 | 2$\frac{1}{2}$ | 1100 | |
| 48 | 3 | 1350 | |
| 54 | | 1500 | 1$\frac{1}{2}$ |
| 64 | 4 | 1800 | |
| 72 | 4$\frac{1}{2}$ | 2000 | 2 |

U.S. and Imperial Measures / Metric Measures

## EQUIVALENTS FOR INGREDIENTS

all-purpose flour—plain flour
arugula—rocket
buttermilk—ordinary milk
confectioners' sugar—icing sugar
cornstarch—cornflour
eggplant—aubergine
granulated sugar—caster sugar
half-and-half—12% fat milk
heavy cream—double cream
light cream—single cream
lima beans—broad beans
scallion—spring onion
squash—courgettes or marrow
unbleached flour—strong, white flour
zest—rind
zucchini—courgettes

## OVEN TEMPERATURE EQUIVALENTS

| Fahrenheit | Celsius | Gas Mark | Description |
|---|---|---|---|
| 225 | 110 | $\frac{1}{4}$ | Cool |
| 250 | 130 | $\frac{1}{2}$ | |
| 275 | 140 | 1 | Very Slow |
| 300 | 150 | 2 | |
| 325 | 170 | 3 | Slow |
| 350 | 180 | 4 | Moderate |
| 375 | 190 | 5 | |
| 400 | 200 | 6 | Moderately Hot |
| 425 | 220 | 7 | Fairly Hot |
| 450 | 230 | 8 | Hot |
| 475 | 240 | 9 | Very Hot |
| 500 | 250 | 10 | Extremely Hot |

## LINEAR AND AREA MEASURES

1 inch    2.54 centimeters